Ireland Develops

Administration and Social Policy 1953-2003

Edited by
Bryan Fanning and Tony McNamara

INSTITUTE OF PUBLIC
ADMINISTRATION

First published in 2003
by the Institute of Public Administration
57-61 Lansdowne Road
Dublin 4
Ireland
www.ipa.ie

ISBN 1 902448 96 0

British Library Cataloguing in Publication Data
A catalogue record for this book is available from the British Library

Cover design by Butler Claffey Design, Dún Laoghaire
Typeset by the Institute of Public Administration
Printed by Johnswood Press, Dublin

Contents

Foreword

Administration is fifty years old. This compilation of articles and book reviews celebrates the success of the five decades.

The journal emanated from a discussion group on public policy formed in 1952 by the Association of Higher Civil Servants. It was subsidised by the association to the tune of £100 per year (about €3,000 in today's money terms). An informal trust, comprising Tom Barrington, Brendan Herlihy, Des Roche and Michael O'Connor was set up to publish papers read to the discussion group, as well as commissioned papers. Hence *Administration* in 1953.

The editorial in the first edition surely reflects the administrative culture of the day: 'We are aware that what we aim at may not be understood and for that reason this publication is not on sale and its subscribers are drawn from those personally concerned in administration. It is supplied on condition that no public reference to its existence is made'. Certainly no freedom of information here.

The nervousness of the initiators was also reflected in the fact that the editor, Tom Barrington, was not named. The names of later editors, Jim O'Donnell, Bill Smyth, Des Roche, Frank Litton and Tony McNamara did grace the imprint pages.

Over its fifty years the journal has developed into a forum where public servants, academics and students meet. It has never sought to promote particular viewpoints. Rather, it has sought to reflect the concerns of the day, from different perspectives, inside and outside the administrative system.

Administration has produced a number of special issues, some of which have become required reading – *Unequal Achievement* (30.2 and 30.3), published on the occasion of its twenty-fifth anniversary, *The Constitution of Ireland 1937-1987* (35.4), *Strategic Management in the Irish Civil Service* (43.2) and *Protecting Irish Children* (44.2), are some of the more significant ones.

On this occasion, the celebration of the fiftieth anniversary of *Administration*, we have chosen to let the pages of the fifty years speak for themselves. This has of course necessitated selection, with the built-in danger of omitting some significant material. Nonetheless, we believe that we have in our selection of theme – social development – and choice of articles provided an interesting and thought-provoking insight to Ireland as it developed over those years.

We have not sought to impose modern editorial conventions throughout this work but have reproduced each article here in its original editorial style.

This fiftieth anniversary marks one of the significant contributions of the Institute of Public Administration to Irish public life. We are grateful to our guest editor, Bryan Fanning, for his trojan work on the project. And, we salute all of those who have contributed to *Administration* over the years, editors and authors.

Tony McNamara
Editor – *Administration*

Introduction

Administration, vol. 51, nos. 1-2 (Spring/Summer 2003), 3–18

The Construction of Irish Social Policy (1953-2003)

BRYAN FANNING

Bryan Fanning is a lecturer in the Department of Social Policy and Social Work, University College, Dublin.

INTRODUCTION

Administration has served as a crucial public forum for debates about the direction of Irish social and economic policy over the last half-century. The selections in this reader reflected the mood of the times when they first appeared even when, as was often the case in later decades, they evaluated past achievements. The journal emerged alongside, and reflected, a distinct state technocratic project of modernisation. This was formally instigated by *The First Programme for Economic Expansion* in 1958 but had been honed by T.K. Whitaker's influential study *Economic Development*, published the same year and, as outlined by a number of contributors, by the earlier groundwork of a number of civil servants, politicians and others who advocated shifts in fiscal and social policy in the years after the Second World War. The articles reproduced here are fragments of an ongoing and shifting debate, over the last half-century, about social policy and social change in Ireland.[1]

This chapter examines economic, social, political, and organisational aspects of the Irish welfare settlement as this evolved during the last half-century. The idea of a welfare consensus in society, articulated through politics and shifting over time, has been a much-used device in explaining the historical changes that have emerged in social policy at international and national levels. For instance, the notion of a post-war consensus about the direction of British social policy has been employed in discussions of the emergence of the 'welfare state'. Some recent approaches to social policy have related such political and economic settlements to processes of societal change through an examination of the ways in which social policy is constructed and reconstructed through shifts in dominant ideas about the nature of social problems (what social policy should do) and dominant constructions of social membership (who social policy is for). Within such perspectives social settlements are seen as crucial to understanding political and economic settlements. To these three headings a fourth, the idea of an organisational settlement, is added. This is employed to discuss the ways in which social policy is delivered with particular emphasis upon relationships between users and providers of welfare (Hughes, 1998: 3-38)

OUTLINE OF THE READER

The reader consists of four overlapping strands. The first of these, *The Pursuit of Growth*, contains a number of selections that collectively offer an account of the relationship between economic development and social policy in Ireland from the early 1950s when the Irish economy was poorly served by isolationist policies to the era of the 'Celtic Tiger'. The selections reflect, and reflect upon, shifting economic orthodoxies over time and, in number of cases, offer critical analysis of past achievements or failures. They reveal, to an extent, the shifting preoccupations and concerns of policy makers over the last fifty years, as an era of isolationism was superseded by Keynesian economic orthodoxies and then by post-Keynesian globalisation.

The second strand is entitled *Health and the Mixed Economy of Welfare*. The role of the state in Ireland, as elsewhere, in securing the welfare of its citizens is one that has developed over time but it is not the case that all welfare is provided through the actions of the state. A mixed economy of welfare has persisted within contemporary society even if the balance of welfare has shifted towards a formal role for the state as provider or regulator (Fanning, 1999: 51). This is particularly the case with respect to health care in Ireland where many services were established by the religious voluntary sector and subsequently became subject to regulation by the state. Some selections in the reader examine the development of provision *(Robins, 1960, Duffy, 1993, Tormey, 1992-3*). Others emphasise inequalities within the mixed economy of Irish health care in terms of the distribution of the burden of care, on the basis of socio-economic status, or within relationships between users and providers of services (*Cousins, 1994, Tormey, 1992-3, O'Sullivan, 1998*). Some selections, here and elsewhere in the reader, examine political and ideological debates that impacted on the development and control of health services (*Barrington, 1987, Duffy, 1983, Kavanagh, 1978*).

The selections in the third strand, *Social Change and Social Citizenship*, examine some debates on and shifts in social policy relating to gender, the family and child protection. These reflect changes in dominant understandings of social citizenship over time. This term was coined by T.H. Marshall to describe how social rights became woven into the fabric of citizenship through the development of universal welfare entitlements (Hughes, 1998: 10). Critiques of this concept have emphasised how some citizens experience lesser or differential rights and access to welfare goods and services for example, on the basis of gender, race and ethnicity (Hughes, 1998: 29). The section begins with an account of gender inequalities in the civil service during the 1950s (*De Paor, 1955*). There is an examination of the work of the First Commission on the Status of Women which instigated reforms in the areas of employment, social welfare and taxation (*Beere, 1975*). The final article in this strand initially appeared in a special issue of *Administration* on child protection in the wake of mounting evidence of child abuse as a social problem in Ireland (*Ferguson, 1996*).

The fourth strand, *Conflicts and Debates*, reflects some of the shifting academic debates about and understandings of Irish social policy that have emerged over time. These included critiques of the relationships between church and state (*Kavanagh, 1978, Taylor, 1995*), a preoccupation with underdevelopment and the crisis of the welfare state during the 1980s (*Garvin, 1986, Lavan, 1990*), and an engagement with the impact of neo-liberalism on Irish social policy during the following decade (Taylor, 1995). The final selection in the reader offers a critical analysis of social partnership and political accountability against the backdrop of recent corruption and administrative scandals (*O Cinnéide, 1998*).

THE DEVELOPMENT OF IRISH SOCIAL POLICY

In Britain welfare possibilities and debates are constructed in relation to, or in opposition to, the idea of the welfare state. British welfare discourses remain clustered along a left-right ideological axis. Attempts to reshape welfare politics in recent years, such as the idea of a 'third way', speak to the notion that social policy was predominantly a matter of left or right and state or market. By comparison left-right distinctions remain less clear within Irish welfare debates. Many of the major preoccupations and cleavages of Irish social policy have historically been articulated along an ideological continuum of responses to social change. At one end of the spectrum might be placed a range of traditionalisms articulated within Catholic conservatism. At the other end might be placed individualism and secularisation. A number of key social policy events and debates are more easily placed along such a continuum than along a left-right continuum. These include the 'Mother and Child Scheme' (a universal health scheme for pregnant and nursing mothers and children under sixteen years) crisis in 1951, the referendum on abortion in 1983, the divorce referenda in 1986 and 1995 and the 1998 Education Act which reduced direct Church control in primary education.

The British welfare state, as established in the immediate post-war era, has been depicted as a 'growth and security' consensus where the political settlement reflected an economic settlement based upon economic growth and expansion of state provision through manipulation of the economy to retain full employment. However, other factors have to be taken into consideration (Hughes, 1998: 27). These include a consensus about 'how' and 'for whom' welfare should be provided. British welfare practices were characterised by forms of bureaucratic and professional organisation that emphasised a passive role for welfare subjects. This organisational settlement emerged within a mixed economy of welfare in which the state was the dominant provider of welfare. The post-war welfare settlement reflected and reinforced dominant social constructions of the 'normal' family, of gender distinctions between public and private domains, of the norm of permanent and secure male employment and of exclusionary conceptions of social membership with respect to race and ethnicity.

Ireland, by contrast, did not experience a 'big bang' welfare resettlement after the Second World War. Change was characterised by a gradual expansion of a state role in the provision of welfare in some areas. The 1958 *Programme for Economic Expansion* marked a turning point in Irish economic policy from an emphasis on protectionism and self-sufficiency to agricultural and economic development. It emphasised that any welfare expansion must be dependant upon economic growth (Kaim-Caudle, 1967:103). A belated Keynesian settlement emphasised growth rather than security. The pursuit of economic growth was prioritised over welfare and infrastructural growth notwithstanding the interrelationships between these. Collectivisation was problematic given the influence of Catholicism in areas such as health and education. Welfare rights within the Irish mixed economy of welfare fell short of the Marshallian ideal of social citizenship. There were no universal rights to voluntary provision. Yet there were many similarities between post-war Irish and British social settlements around welfare. Both were rooted in developments which pre-dated Irish independence from Britain. Welfare entitlements were socially constructed with reference to ideals of social membership rooted in nation-building ideologies. This was the case both where welfare rights were formally linked to citizenship and where, as in the Irish case, voluntary sector providers continued to be able to choose their own clients according to ethnic-religious criteria. In both cases the state institutionalised dominant constructions of the family and gender roles within the allocation of welfare.

Many present day Irish welfare institutions are derived from the Poor Law of 1838 and the new-liberal welfare legislation of 1909 and 1911 which supplemented poor law provision for paupers with social insurance linked to paid employment. Irish institutions at the time of independence had been shaped by a nineteenth-century colonialist liberal project of modernisation and reform. The institutional and ideological legacy of the nineteenth century within twentieth-century Irish modernity should not be discounted. Other aspects of present day provision are rooted in the parallel development of Catholic controlled educational and health provision. To a considerable extent, pre-independence demarcations within the mixed economy of welfare have persisted.

Liberal welfare entitlements based upon paid employment rarely came into conflict with the principle of subsidiarity which underpinned Catholic social teaching. Subsidiarity, as outlined in the 1931 Papal encyclical *Quadragesimo Anno*, was a strategy to ameliorate the worst features of capitalism while resisting state interference within the sphere of civil society. In simple terms, it held that the state should not usurp the relationship between Catholic institutions and the family. The resultant welfare settlement was characterised by demarcated roles for both the state and voluntary sector in the provision of welfare.

Conflicts between both spheres did not emerge until the state became seen as advancing collectivist principles during the early 1950s. These conflicts were characterised, to some extent, by a common cause between the principles of free enterprise and Catholic social teaching (Fanning: 1999: 29). The liberal welfare subject, a male breadwinner, embodied a similar conception of gender roles to those emphasised in Catholic social teaching. As put in what was perhaps the most complete statement of Catholic social policy in the decades after the Second World War:

> That the husband is the final authority in the family is clear on natural grounds; every community must have a head, and the father being the breadwinner and the primary provider of the family is that natural authority (Kavanagh, 1966: 40).

Liberalism as a moral welfare discourse had considerable affinity with Catholic principles of subsidiarity. Catholic social teaching held that the state should only act when the male breadwinner was proven to have failed to provide for his dependants. Both liberalism and Catholic social teaching as such contributed to an official ideology of the privatised family. Reforms to the National Insurance Act (1911) extended the entitlements of men and continued to give lesser entitlements to women in paid employment than those given to men until, in the case of single men and single women, the Social Welfare Act (1953). Women continued to be regarded as a distinct and residual category within the welfare system. As more and more men came under the umbrella of unemployment assistance, forms of welfare entitlement not linked to paid employment such as outdoor relief (reformed as home assistance in 1923) became increasingly feminised. The construction of women as dependants within welfare practices was compounded by overt discriminations that prevented married women from working in the civil service until this 'marriage bar' was lifted in 1973 (*Beere, 1975*).

The welfare economy of the Irish Republic was to some extent shaped by aspirations for a Gaelic-Catholic Ireland adopted by those influential in shaping the ideology of the new Irish state in 1922. The newly independent Irish state was characterised, for its first few decades, by a concern with economic and cultural sovereignty (Hardiman and Whelan, 1998: 67). A dominant Gaelic and Catholic construction of nation and citizenship precipitated the marginalisation of the Protestant minority in areas such as education and health. The laws of the new state were not directed 'against Protestants' but the state came to embody the dominant construction that Ireland was fundamentally a Catholic society in that the moral teaching of the Catholic Church became institutionalised within the civil code through legislation on censorship, divorce, adoption and contraception (Fanning, 2002: 37).

The Catholic Church possessed a 'non-decisional' form of power. It had the capacity to mobilise politically in defence of its interests but rarely had to do so because these interests could be anticipated and addressed in a 'non-political' manner. As good Catholics, legislators and voters were deeply committed to expressing their faith in the laws and institutions of the country. This was particularly evident in the area of health care where the principle of Catholic denominational control over health services for Catholics coincided with a Catholic ideological control over health care provision as a whole. At times, Catholic politicians supported discrimination in favour of Catholics in state positions to ensure that Catholic moral sensibilities were not endangered (Bowen, 1983: 36). Growth in state involvement in health funding was accompanied by the supremacy of a Catholic ethos in the system as a whole.

This ethos also informed economic policy processes. Economic expansion and welfare development since the 1950s has been, to some extent, managed by a compact between unionised labour, employers and the state. This 'social partnership' has allowed for corporatist negotiation of societal goals by the most powerful groups in society much along the consensual lines advocated by Catholic social thought (*O' Cinnéide, 1998*, *Pellion*, 1995b: 368-376). It has expressed a conservative pluralism that excluded marginal groups in society even if it purported to represent a societal consensus (*Allen, 1999*, *O'Cinnéide, 1998*).

A BELATED POST-WAR CONSENSUS

Irish welfare reform since independence has been characterised by gradual institutional development and reform and the gradual extension of welfare rights and entitlements. For some theorists underdevelopment itself has been the key factor in explaining such gradualism (Pellion, 1995a: 184). In the Irish case underdevelopment has been explained as the result of colonialism (Crotty 1986 cited in *Garvin*, 1986). Both shaped the very societal base from which welfare possibilities might be understood to emerge. A lack of resources inhibited the expansion of universal welfare rights and entitlements. Aspirations for welfare expansion emerged within a context of economic underdevelopment. Class politics were moribund, partly because of a lack of industrialisation. Other forms of welfare ideology, such as expressed within Catholic social theory, also fell on fallow ground. Fahey argues that the impact of Catholic social thought on social policy in Ireland was limited because it emerged to counter extremes of *laissez faire* capitalism and state socialism that were not to be found in Ireland:

> Outside the industrialised north-east of the Island, capitalism had failed to take off and the socialist movement scarcely developed beyond the embryonic stage. The main targets of attack for Catholic social teaching were thus either weak or absent in Ireland (Fahey, 1998: 418).

In the absence of real possibilities for rapid welfare expansion in the post-war era welfare did not become politicised to the same extent as in Britain. In this context major debates on the restructuring of the mixed economy did not occur. Catholic social thought was better at rejecting than at advocating change (Fahey, 1998: 418). The persistence of the Irish mixed economy as an organisational settlement was signalled by the paucity of demarcation disputes between the state and the voluntary sector since independence.

Efforts to expand the role of the state during the early 1950s were influenced by the Beveridge Report. A Health Act first proposed in 1949 was implemented, following considerable opposition from the Church, in 1953. Opposition to proposals for a mother and child scheme resembled opposition to proposals in the National Insurance Act (1911) to provide maternity insurance with the added argument that such proposals contravened Catholic social thinking. What was important perhaps was that this was the first time that such Catholic social ideology had to be marshalled against proposals by Irish politicians and civil servants to extend the role of the state in welfare provision. It was also the last time that such opposition was politically viable (Deeney, 1989: 176).

There was a number of reasons for this. Church interference prompted considerable resentment. Increased access to education undermined the power of the Church as intellectual and cultural arbitrator (Garvin, 1982: 23). Education and economic and social change precipitated processes of secularisation similar to those which had occurred in other western countries. Furthermore, an ideological shift occurred from the 1960s within the Church whereby the state was more likely to be criticised for doing too little rather than too much in areas such as income maintenance (Fanning, 1999: 57). In this context the 'Mother and Child controversy' could be interpreted as a last hurrah of Catholic hegemony within Irish welfare debates. The Catholic voices which were marshalled against welfare expansion in the early 1950s were to a considerable extent displaced by the social changes which occurred after that decade.

Secularisation precipitated gradual institutional reform as the numbers of lay workers in Catholic voluntary organisations and schools increased (McCashin, 1982: 204). Secularisation in itself had little impact upon the mixed economy of welfare or indeed upon predominant assumptions that service users were Catholics. The state took an increased role in funding voluntary welfare without acquiring control. That said, from the 1960s the voluntary sector was characterised by secular expansion, such as in the area of urban and rural community development (Rush, 1999: 167).

The emergence of a distinct post-war era could be dated from as early as 1958 when the *Programme for Economic Expansion* ushered in a technocratic role for the state. It could also be dated from the mid-1960s when political parties broke with the tradition of viewing all state intervention as an outsider's intrusion into the family and the voluntary sector (Conroy, 1999: 27). Certainly, the 1960s was an era of heady social change. As put by Garvin: 'economic take-off, cultural revolution and the ecclesiastical upheaval sometimes labelled as Vatican II all occurred together and had devastating effects' (Garvin, 1982: 23). At the same time welfare reforms were slow and piecemeal. By the 1960s there was still no national health service, secondary education was fee-paying and industrial training was unknown (Conroy, 1999: 37). Proposals emerged to reform the Poor Law health system of dispensary doctors by a means-tested right to obtain prescriptions from chemists and to choose doctors, and through slum clearance legislation. Free secondary education was introduced in 1967.

The resultant welfare settlement, notwithstanding the gradualism of actual reforms, resembled those of other western countries. Welfare expansion was founded upon Keynesian economic orthodoxies and developed through technocratic process of social planning. Public spending and taxation rapidly expanded (*Rottman and O'Connell, 1982:82-3*).

Figure 1: Post-war settlement circa 1958

Political Coexistence of liberal and Catholic ideologies within mixed economy of welfare.	**Economic** Limited Keynesian settlement; growth (without universal security) as a precondition for welfare expansion.
Organisational Bureau-professionalism, authoritarianism and subsidiarity within a mixed economy of welfare.	**Social** Social citizenship envisaged in terms of a male-breadwinner welfare subject. Emigration as implicit social policy.

GROWTH, SECURITY AND EXCLUSION

The Irish 'growth and security' consensus that accompanied social and economic modernisation was the outcome of a very different social and political settlement to that which emerged in Britain. Keynesism provided the basis for gradual welfare expansion. However, expectations of economic growth were coupled with selective security of employment. Growth and security were underpinned by emigration. As Lee puts it: 'Few people anywhere have been as prepared to scatter their children around the world in order to preserve their own living standard' (Lee, 1989: 522).

Emigration of surplus labour was constructed as a 'useful safety valve' and a panacea for unemployment in Ireland. Around the same time that de Valera's 'dream' speech in 1943 extolled an agrarian variant of the Irish-Ireland ideal officials discussed, behind the scene, the savings to the exchequer on welfare expenditure bought about by emigration (Lee, 1989: 227). Over half of school leavers in the 1950s had emigrated by 1961. Between 1951 and 1961 net emigration totalled 409,000. On average 4 percent of the labour force emigrated each year (Blackwell, 1982: 43). The net outflow of emigrants totalled 130,000 for the years 1983 to 1988. By 1994, some 650,000 people born in the Republic of Ireland lived in the United Kingdom. Of these 590,000 were still Irish citizens (Ardagh, 1994: 313). The safety valve of emigration was also a brake on social and political change.

Employment security and high wages for some without the necessity of economic growth became possible through an acceptance of emigration (*Rottman and O'Connell, 1982*). Between 1980 and 1982 United Kingdom wage rates were slightly less than 10 percent higher than Irish rates even though output per head of population was 76 percent higher in the UK. Crotty argues that such high wage rates were possible because of the effectiveness of Irish trade unions in securing the interests of their members.

> People made unemployed by trade unions forcing wage rates above the level at which people would be willing to work rather than remain unemployed, have not remained in Ireland. Neither have those made unemployed by the substitution of livestock for people. Emigration has given to Ireland, for over a century, conditions approximating to 'full employment' with no large pool of unemployed labour to form a source of competing non-unionised labour, working either as self-employed persons or for non-union firms. These virtually 'full employment' conditions, bought about by mass emigration, have been fundamentally different from the normal conditions of massive, growing labour surpluses in the former capitalist colonies (Crotty, 1986: 84).

The Irish 'Keynesian' settlement in effect linked citizenship as well as welfare entitlements to paid employment insofar as emigration was the lot of the many who were unable to access the socially insured workplace in the first instance. The differential experiences of citizenship which often precipitated emigration were accompanied by the social construction of emigrants as outsiders. The act of emigration was often associated with social constructions of moral transgression, as defined by the dominant social conservatism, through which emigrants could be defined as outsiders. After the Second World War, in an era when female migration rates exceeded those of men, emigration was constructed as a threat to the sexual morality of women. In 1959, James Dillon, the leader of Fine Gael called for restrictions to be imposed on female emigrants unless they could prove they were proceeding to relatives (Lee, 1989: 377). In subsequent decades efforts were made by the state and Catholic voluntary sector to prevent the migration of women seeking abortions in Britain through the courts, by means of various forms of social control and through the censorship of information and advice. Emigration served as a safety valve to exclude people who differed from the citizenship ideals of the nation on the basis of gender or sexuality. There is some evidence to suggest that emigrants included disproportionate numbers of lesbians and gay men (Smyth, 1995: 225). In this sense welfare entitlements were, to a degree, constructed on the basis of moral criteria rather than citizenship.

UNSETTLING IRISH WELFARE

From the 1970s globalisation undermined Keynesian economic policies. In Britain, a neo-liberal critique of the welfare state (Thatcherism) became institutionalised. Neo-liberal thinkers such as Von Hayek opposed the linking of social rights to welfare and as such offered an ideological basis for unravelling the welfare state (*Taylor, 1995*). An economic and political unsettlement was accompanied by social unsettlement in the face of increasingly visible patterns of social diversity and welfare need. These critiques found expression through the dominant ideological cleavages of left and right with their respective emphasis on the state and the market in debates about the relationships between users and providers of welfare (Hughes, Clarke, Lewis and Moroney, 1998: 162). Many of the changes that precipitated the reconstruction of the British welfare consensus have similarly impacted upon Ireland. In Ireland, as in a number of other western countries, the backdrop for this was a perceived need for financial rectitude and public expenditure cutbacks during the 1980s (*Fitzgerald, 1994*).

In Ireland, urbanisation and secularisation have to an extent unsettled the Catholic conservative consensus within which Irish welfare practices had been framed. Gradual reforms occurred to the (lesser) welfare entitlements of women. These extended rights to social assistance to some single parents (the Unmarried Mothers Allowance (1973)) and to other groups. In essence, women's welfare was extended within separate gendered categories which envisaged women remaining in the home. Following the Employment of Married Women Act (1973) married women could be employed in the civil service. After 1984 married women became entitled to the same rates and duration of unemployment benefits as men. However, women continued to experience differential social citizenship; for example with respect to pension entitlements linked to duration of paid employment,

The budgets of the Fianna Fáil led government from 1997 onwards were characterised by ideological assaults on past hegemonic conceptions of gender in Irish welfare debates as articulated in the 1937 Constitution, which defended differential welfare citizenship. As stated in Article 41:

> In particular, the State recognises that by her life within the home, woman gives to the State a support without which the common good cannot be achieved.
>
> The state shall, therefore, endeavour to ensure that mothers shall not be obliged by economic necessity to engage in labour to the neglect of their duties in the home.

The contestation of gender inequalities from the 1970s onwards had led to some welfare reforms as women entered paid employment in ever increasing numbers and, as such, the differential welfare citizenship they experienced became more prominent. Catholic welfare reformists, such as the Conference of Religious in Ireland (CORI), advocated the introduction of a basic income, which would not be based upon paid employment, as a means of valuing work in the home. Here, the emphasis was upon revitalising subsidiarity in the face of social change in gender roles and the increasing economic necessity of dual income families. This thinking contributed to family policy proposals that emerged during the late 1990s. For example, in the final report of the *Commission on the Family* (1998) the concern that women not be forced to take up paid employment and childcare provision was, to an extent, depicted as a minority need. The report depicted a societal consensus very compatible with provisions within the 1937 Constitution.

> Many submissions expressed concern about women in low paid employment who were only marginally better off after their childcare and going to work expenses had been taken into account. Most submissions on this issue took the view that many women, given a choice, would prefer to take time out of the workforce to be at home with their children. The dominant view was that parents should be assisted in that choice. In addition to the concerns about pressures on parents balancing work and family life, submissions looked for support for mothers in their important job and for rights to further education and opportunities to take on training (Commission on the Family, 1998: 62).

The Commission advocated the introduction of a basic income – a single payment to all citizens replacing all social welfare payments and financed largely by a flat rate income tax – or, at least, the 'individualisation' of social welfare entitlements so that the tax allowances for married couples would be twice the individual rate rather than approximately 1.6 times the individual rate as at the time (Commission on the Family, 1998: 60). There was also an emphasis on income support policies taking account of previously unacknowledged costs of rearing a child.

The report was sidelined within the tax reforms that were proposed in the 1998 and 1999 budgets and supported by the social partners. These challenged the presumption that tax allowances for a single-income married couple should exceed those of an individual taxpayer. A cleavage rather than new consensus emerged with some retrenchment from proposals in both budgets due to the opposition of the constituency, including women's groups, which had supported the recommendations put to the Commission on the Family (1998). All this indicated an unresolved tension between the family, or more specifically the Catholic single male breadwinner family, and the individual as welfare subjects within Irish social policy (Figure 2).

The role of the Catholic Church in welfare debates has shifted in recent decades. An ongoing disengagement by religious personnel from the mass production of welfare, if not always its control, has combined with a new emphasis upon social justice and activism directed at the state (Fahey, 1998: 422). This has led to a reconstitution of aspirations for subsidiarity often bound up with an emphasis on social rights and with bottom-up community development. The former has included an emphasis upon welfare rights that would support the choice of women to withdraw from

Figure 2: Gender and social policy

Catholic/Liberal settlement(s) *A woman's place is in the home*	Secular/Neo-liberal contestations *'Right to remain in the home' challenged*
• gendered distinctions between the welfare entitlements of women and men from the Poor Law onwards • benefits for women in paid employment less that those to men in comparable employment • benefits aimed at reinforcing the notion that a woman's place in Irish society was in the home • differential social citizenship	• broader welfare debate linked to needs of economy • participation of women in labour market • emergence of women as a reserve army of labour • loss of male breadwinner wage • welfare for women increasingly linked to paid employment • persistence of differential social citizenship

paid employment. It has also advocated extending constitutional rights to housing, health and education (Irish Commission for Justice and Peace, 1998, *Taylor, 1995*). The latter has included arguments by CORI on the potential role of welfare programmes to reconstitute voluntarism as a 'right to useful unemployment' (*Taylor*, *1995*).

These aspirations have since been displaced, to an extent, by the influence of neo-liberalism on Irish social policy debates. For example, in 1998 the Minister for Enterprise, Trade and Employment began to restrict eligibility to community employment schemes following the publication of a report which evaluated such programmes purely upon their ability to lead to employment in the market (Deloitte and Touche, 1998). As in Britain, social inclusion policies have increasingly focused upon 'welfare to work' measures within an essentially neo-liberal thesis (the individualisation of risk) that poverty can only be addressed by employment.

RECONSTRUCTING IRISH SOCIAL POLICY

At the beginning of the new century, a number of interrelated challenges to past welfare settlements resulting from social change might be identified. They include (1) the ever increasing non-viability of gendered social citizenship, (2) the potential unravelling of existing forms of welfare solidarity (3) increased social diversity and (4) a growing focus on accountability linked to a growing focus on social rights. These challenges are interrelated. They find expression within a specific Irish context where the role of the state but also that of other providers of welfare comes under scrutiny.

In the past, the pursuit of growth was partly underpinned by emigration. The exclusion of emigrants was justified within an ideological discourse that has subsequently contributed much to anti-immigrant discourses at the current time. These drew upon a narrow construction of social membership historically bound up with land ownership or employment that allowed emigrants to be constructed as outsiders. It was bound up with an acceptance of emigrant remittances and emigrant tourism but with a 'zero sum' anxiety that returning emigrants would take jobs from the 'Irish'. The aforementioned Keynesian settlement, in effect, linked citizenship as well as welfare entitlements to paid employment insofar as emigration was the lot of the many who were unable to access the socially insured workplace in the first instance.

The pursuit of growth is now underpinned by immigration. This has been factored into economic planning (Government of Ireland, 2000). Past 'zero sum' constructions of emigration have been supplanted by a neo-liberal ideology of growth within which large scale immigration has been constructed as unproblematic. However, pronounced welfare stratifications (different levels of rights and entitlements) and divisions of labour on the basis of ethnicity have become increasingly evident. Many immigrants from non-EU countries, as non-citizens, have lesser social and economic rights. The exclusion of non-citizens from social citizenship will have profound implications for Irish social policy as the percentage of immigrants within the composition of Irish society rises.

The last decade has also witnessed a cascade of scandals and controversies relating, in one way or another, to accountability within politics, the state, the market and the Catholic voluntary sector. For example, the Beef tribunal, the Flood Tribunal and the Moriarty Tribunal have documented forms of political and administrative corruption specifically related to economic development and growth. The Hepatitis C crisis and ongoing disclosures of child abuse have revealed institutional failures within both the statutory and voluntary sectors (*Ferguson, 1996, O' Cinnéide, 1998*). More positively, there has been a growing emphasis on rights-based approaches to social policy on a number of fronts. This has included policies such as The National Children's Strategy (2000) designed to meet Ireland's obligations under the UN Convention on the Rights of the Child (1991). It has also included a growing role for judicial activism in seeking to secure the constitutional rights of marginal groups who have not had their rights secured through the Oireachtas (*O' Cinnéide, 1998*, Whyte, 2002: 9-57). However, it must be emphasised that these rights-based approaches have emerged in the context of profound ongoing inequalities. One example (the Sinnott case) has been an unwillingness of the state to secure adequate rights to education for people with intellectual disabilities. Collectively, these issues suggest a legitimacy crisis in Irish public life with profound implications for social policy that necessitates a new organisation settlement and the reformulation of the relationships between users and providers of welfare goods and services. A number of these themes are addressed in the final selection of the reader (*O' Cinnéide, 1998*).

NOTES

1 Contributions cited from elsewhere in this reader are referenced in *italics* by author surname and by original year of publication.

BIBLIOGRAPHY

Ardagh, J. (1994), *Ireland and the Irish*, London, Hamish Hamilton.

Blackwell, J. (1982), 'Government, Economy and Society', in Litton, F. (ed), *Unequal Achievement: The Irish Experience 1957-1982*, Dublin, Institute of Public Administration.

Bowen, K. (1983), *Protestants in a Catholic State: Ireland's Privileged Minority*, Belfast, Queens University Press.

Commission on the Family (1998), *Strengthening Families for Life*, Dublin, Stationery Office.

Conroy, P. (1999), 'From the Fifties to the Nineties', in Keily, G., O'Donnell, A., Kennedy, P. and Quin, S. (eds), *Irish Social Policy in Context*, Dublin, University College Dublin Press.

Crotty, R. (1886), *Ireland in Crisis: A Study in Capitalist Colonial Underdevelopment*, Dingle, Brandon.

Deeney, J. (1989), *To Cure and to Care*, Dublin, Glendale Press.

Deloitte and Touche (1998), *Review of Community Employment Programme*, Dublin, Stationery Office.

Dooley, D. (1998), 'Gendered Citizenship in the Irish Constitution', in Murphy, T. and Twomey, P. (eds), *Ireland's Evolving Constitution,* Oxford, Hart.

Fahey, T. (1998), 'The Catholic Church and Social Policy', in Healy, S. and Reynolds, B. (eds), *Social Policy in Ireland*, Dublin, Oak Tree Press.

Fanning, B. (1999), 'The Mixed Economy of Welfare', in Keily, G., O'Donnell, A., Kennedy, P. and Quin, S. (eds), *Irish Social Policy in Context*, Dublin, University College Dublin Press.

Fanning, B. (2001), 'Reluctant Hosts: Refugee Policy in Twentieth Century Ireland, *Administration*, vol 48.4.

Fanning, B. (2002), *Racism and Social Change in the Republic of Ireland*, Manchester, Manchester University Press.

Garvin, T. (1982), 'Change and the Political System', in Litton, F. (ed), *Unequal Achievement: The Irish Experience 1957-1982*, Dublin, Institute of Public Administration.

Government of Ireland (2000), *The National Development Plan 2000-2006*, Dublin, Stationery Office.

Hardiman, N. and Whelan, C. (1998), 'Changing Values', in Crotty, W. and Schmitt, D.E. (eds), *Ireland and the Politics of Change*, London, Longman.

Hughes, G., Clarke, J., Lewis, G. and Mooney, G. (1998), 'Reinventing "the public"?', in Hughes, G. (ed), *Imagining Welfare Futures*, London, Routledge.

Hughes, G. (1998), 'Picking Over the Remains: The Welfare State Settlements of the Post-Second World War UK', in Hughes, G. and Lewis, G. (eds), *Unsettling Welfare: The Reconstruction of Social Policy*, London, Routledge.

Irish Commission for Justice and Peace (1998), *Re-Righting the Constitution: The Case for New Social and Economic Rights: Housing, Health, Nutrition, Adequate Standard of Living,* Dublin, Irish Commission for Justice and Peace.

Kavanagh, J. (1966), *Manual of Social Ethics*, Dublin, Gill and Sons.

Kaim-Caudle, P. (1967), Social Policy in the Irish Republic, London, Routledge.

Lee, J.J. (1989), *Ireland 1912-1985: Politics and Society*, Cambridge, Cambridge University Press.

McCashin, T. (1982), 'Social Policy', in Litton, F. (ed), *Unequal Achievement: The Irish Experience 1957-82*, Dublin, Institute of Public Administration.

O'Tuathaigh, G. (1991), 'The Irish-Ireland Idea: Rationale and Relevance', in Longley, E. (ed), *Culture in Ireland – Division or Diversity*, Belfast, Institute of Irish Studies.

Pellion, M (1995a), 'Interest Groups and the State', in Clancy, P., Drudy, S., Lynch, K., and O'Dowd, L. (eds), *Irish Society: Sociological Perspectives*, Dublin, Institute of Public Administration.

Pellion, M. (1995b), 'Placing Ireland in a Comparative Perspective', *The Economic and Social Review*, 25.2, pp.179-195.

Rush, M. (1999), 'Social Partnership in Ireland', in Keily, G., O'Donnell, A., Kennedy, P. and Quin, S. (eds), *Irish Social Policy in Context*, Dublin, University College Dublin Press.

Smyth, C. (1995), 'Keeping It Close: Experiencing Emigration in England', in O'Carroll, I. and Collins, E. (eds), *Lesbian and Gay Visions of Ireland,* London, Cassell.

Whyte, G. (2002), *Social Inclusion and the Legal System: Public Interest Law in Ireland*, Dublin, Institute of Public Administration.

Part One
The Pursuit of Growth

Administration, vol. 51, nos. 1-2 (Spring/Summer 2003), 21-31

Some Problems of Public Enterprise
Public Enterprise in a Free Economy

PATRICK LYNCH

Originally published in 1954, vol. 2, no. 1, 11-20. Patrick Lynch was then a lecturer in the Department of Political Economy in University College Dublin.

PUBLIC authorities in Ireland are responsible, directly or indirectly, for a very substantial share of the nation's capital assets; in 1950 their share represented 55 per cent of gross domestic capital formation and 65 *per cent* of net capital formation, and it has not changed significantly since. In the opinion of the authors of the IBEC Report,[1] the "central and local government authorities direct the flow of a larger proportion of the country's gross capital investment than similar agencies did in the United Kingdom, under an avowedly socialist government." It is unnecessary, however, to be unduly alarmed by the emotive content of the later part of this comment; in practically every country in western Europe the economic responsibilities of the state have increased since the end of the war; in Italy about 40 *per cent* of gross investment has been undertaken directly by public authorities, and the proportion is about 30 *per cent*, or somewhat less, in Britain, Belgium, France, Sweden, Norway and Switzerland.[2] These proportions leave out of account the effect on private investment of special government grants and subsidies and of transfers from E.C.A. counterpart funds. In most European countries, major investment decisions are now no longer virtually or even primarily taken by private persons or institutions; for one reason or another, private enterprise alone has been unable to undertake the volume of investment required. "By default rather than from ideological persuasion"[3] governments have assumed a substantial part of this function of risk-taking; and as a result, the state not merely provides funds for a large amount of investment, but also determines and regulates the industries in which it takes place.

In Ireland, as stated in a later article[4] in this issue [not printed in this Reader], ". . . there exist no fewer than four 'public corporations' . . .

and some two dozen state-owned or mixed ownership companies, not to speak of supervisory bodies of a non-trading nature which exist in great profusion in all spheres of economic and social activity. . ." A complete picture of the state's role in determining the volume of Irish capital formation would also refer, of course, to the direct activities in this field of government departments and of local authorities and to the effects of the policy of industrial protection on the investment decisions of private persons and institutions risking their own capital. The present article, however, is concerned primarily with state-sponsored organisations.

Such, therefore, is the extent to which public feeling has, through its agencies, determined or influenced the volume and direction of such investment that it is largely a matter of opinion whether the Irish economy may be too accurately described in Mr. Ryan's phrase[5] as a "tolerably free economic system" in which the price mechanism "encourages the production of those goods that consumers want in the quantities and proportions in which they are willing to pay for them." In its classic conception the process by which investment took place in a free economy was assumed to be the result of decisions by many private persons and institutions, each of whom acted in the expectation of a profit. "A free, flexible system is assumed, indicating relative current and expected future scarcities. A free private capital market is assumed nationally and internationally, from which the investor can draw and within which a range of interest rates reflect the availability of capital and the average status of hopes and fears for various future time periods under various types of risk."[6] But that picture of the traditional method of investment in conditions of competitive capitalism is somewhat remote from present circumstances in which a very large part of investment is undertaken by private or state-sponsored monopolies. "The environment and institutional arrangements for the successful existence of a classical system of private investment," writes Rostow, " no longer appear to exist."[7]

More to avoid controversy than to achieve strict accuracy the Irish economy may be regarded as, basically, a private enterprise one. Where state enterprise exists-and it is fairly extensive – it is in no case the result of the application of any socialist doctrine that advocates nationalisation as a matter of principle. Most Irish state-owned or state-sponsored enterprises exist, not because the state sought to create or operate them, but because, anxious that someone should do so, the state undertook the task itself in default of the initiative of others. Irish public corporations and other state-sponsored agencies are, in general, expedients whose existence owes little to political or economic theories, but which in each case, was determined by the practical needs of a situation. "In sum," wrote the authors of the IBEC Report,[8] "under Irish procedure there has been built up a system of practices that have limited and importantly displaced private initiative without the corresponding assumption of a vigorous government initiative and responsibility for promoting a direct expansion of domestic production and foreign trading activities that are characteristic of socialist countries." However much some Irish state-sponsored institutions may resemble those of socialist countries, the resemblance is apt to be deceptive and misleading. There has been a deliberate avoidance of the collectivist organisation adopted in many countries in which socialist thought consciously influences public policy. The Irish economy may be remote from the classic pattern of competitive private enterprise, but it is also far from being in any sense a "planned economy." Indeed, criticism has been heard less of undue supervision or excessively rigid direction of state-sponsored bodies than of failures to secure a greater measure of coordination in the field of state enterprise generally. But this criticism raises well-known and difficult problems. When the state interferes in the economic affairs of a reasonably free economy it becomes easier to extend the scope and scale of the state's economic responsibilities than to stop at some intermediate point – and stay there. In the classic form of private enterprise economy, investment was expected to look after itself; in the fully collectivised system it becomes a matter solely for the central planning authority.

In the curiously "mixed" form of economy, such as exists in Ireland, there is a risk that the understandable fear of central economic planning may prevent the creation of suitable machinery for coordinating the investment decisions of private persons and those decisions which are the result of state action. It may be quite impossible consciously to influence the level of national investment if the "Government is in the position of a chess-player, some of whose important pieces are not subject to his will, but are free to make moves of their own volition."[9] In Ireland, however, no direct means exist of coordinating private and public outlay, much less of guiding the course of private investment. Indeed, the Minister for Finance decisively rejected suggestions that any such means should be created. "Against our economic background," he has said, "in which the basic limitation on national development is the low level of current savings, it is surely a misplacing of emphasis to give pride of place to a proposal for controlling and disposing of the nation's savings when the true national need is to induce our people to save as much as possible." "From that point of view," the Minister continued, "indeed, the introduction of a formalised control of investment would be harmful; for interference with the investor's freedom of choice would discourage private saving."[10] In short, the aim is to induce private interests to place as many pieces as possible on the national chess-board, the Government may provide the remainder of the pieces assigning to each a particular task, but it will make no attempt to impose its own pattern on the game generally.

Official policy is, therefore, opposed to collectivist economic planning and the ends of economic activity presuppose a preference – as a matter of principle – for the institutions of private property, private enterprise and decentralised initiative as against any alternatives. It may be a paradox that a society anchored, in principle, to private enterprise, as Ireland is, should, in practice, have departed so far from its ideals, but principles can be preserved when even their partial application may seem impracticable. A society can claim, presumably, to respect the concepts of private property and ownership if it shows a preference for the forms of private enterprise; and if, when adopted, any necessary agencies of public enterprise are designed, operated and supervised with a view to supplementing the effects of private enterprise and not to the creation of conditions that may lead to the supplanting of that system. To preserve the essential features of the reasonably free economic society, it is not enough to avoid centralised collective planning; any state-sponsored bodies must be designed so that the methods chosen to remove the defects of private enterprise are compatible with and not destructive of the characteristics of that system generally. The proliferation of state sponsored bodies, without any obvious design, method or plan, cannot easily be insured against the risks of administrative and economic anarchy. A private enterprise system can be paralysed by ubiquitous public enterprise, and public enterprise itself may have difficulty in reaching its valid goals if conscious central direction is lacking.

There has been no uniform practice governing the establishment and organisation of Irish state-sponsored agencies. Coras Iompair Éireann and Aer Rianta Teoranta, for example, are transport organisations, but have little else in common, structurally, in administrative conception or in statutory foundation. The archetype of such agencies in Ireland, if there were one, would be modelled in its organisation as closely as possible on a commercial business; imitation, it is said, is the sincerest form of flattery. On questions of general policy the agency would be responsible to the Oireachtas through a member of the Government, but it would be free to pursue the day-to-day aims for which it was set up without risk of having to answer in public for every action of its personnel. By adopting such methods public enterprise in Ireland, as represented by public corporations and state-sponsored companies, has achieved considerable freedom of action and independence; it has been able to operate the public monopolies or quasi-monopolies which were designed to function on "business lines;" and the firmness of Ministers in the Dáil has enabled these concerns to remain "outside politics" in their routine activities. But while the advantages of operating any one state enterprise without undue parliamentary interference are admitted, it may be asked whether public enterprise as a whole might not benefit if critical public attention were directed to its ultimate economic functions. Public enterprise has developed so rapidly in a comparatively short time that there have been few opportunities of modifying or adapting constitutional practices, parliamentary procedures or the methods of public finance to meet the changes that the enlargement of the state sector has produced in the nation's economic structure. The public is quite uniformed about the activities of many public enterprises. Sometimes the published reports of these bodies are sketchy, and existing Parliamentary procedure gives the Dáil little chance of examining the trend of policy, or indeed, even the financial results.

The structure and size of government departments have been largely the creation of historical circumstances, but little is known of the nature of the determinants employed in the case of state-sponsored bodies, or, indeed, whether there are any *a priori* determinants applied at all. In size, location and administrative structure some state companies seem to resemble more closely the government departments that created them rather than the representative firms of the private business sector whose methods they were intended to imitate. There may, therefore, be a risk that the present somewhat undefined attitude to public enterprise may, unwittingly, lead to results altogether at variance with the intentions of those who advocate the system. A state-sponsored concern in search of freedom may well find it easier to prevent the Oireachtas from interfering in its routine affairs than to escape the detailed supervision of a Minister and of his officials in a government department. Although answerable to the Oireachtas for every departmental action, neither the Minister nor his officials are so answerable for any attempts they make to shape the policy of the state-sponsored body which is nominally independent of them, which was set up because civil servants were considered unable to perform the duties to be entrusted to it within the restrictions and limitations of a government department.

The size of many state enterprises is in striking contrast to that of the average private commercial firm. Of about 4,500 private industrial firms in Ireland about two-thirds employ less than twenty workers and only 400 employ one hundred workers or more.'[11] No doubt, a relatively small number of firms account for the bulk of Irish industrial output; nevertheless, the representative firms in private business are "small or medium-sized concerns whose capital requirements are modest."[12] In public enterprise, however, most of the industrial units are very big and a few are giants with which there is nothing to compare in privately-owned industry. Sometimes the size of the unit employed is fixed by reference to an optimum below which it would be uneconomic to operate: this occurs when the indivisibility of some factor of production sets limits below which size cannot be reduced. But is the size of the unit adopted by public enterprise always determined by economic considerations? Is it ever settled arbitrarily or influenced by vague and quite unscientific "administrative considerations?" It becomes particularly necessary to raise these questions when a particular state enterprise is established under the Companies Acts, and has only limited independence of a government department to which, in a sense, it is an adjunct and whose officers have some voice in shaping its policies. In structure and size it would seem desirable that a public enterprise should follow the patterns of private enterprise unless the function of the enterprise calls for the special qualifications of civil servants, in which case there seems little justification for a special body at all. If an aim of a state-sponsored public utility is to find a form and a structure in which the flexible methods of private enterprise can be employed it is, surely, to defeat the object in view to create a structure which reproduces, perhaps to a heightened degree, the rigidities of a big government department or, indeed, of the conventional large-scale unit of private monopoly with even less of the tendency of such a unit occasionally to yield to outside pressures. To what extent, one wonders, is it possible in such monolithic bodies as the Electricity Supply Board or Córas Iompair Éireann to respect Mr. Ryan's principle[13] that in every line of production price should be equated to marginal cost and that the imperfection of monopolistic production should be eliminated. One may also wonder, indeed, whether it is really practicable to apply the criteria of the free market when the free market in a particular field has been abolished. But unless definite criteria are applied to the results of public enterprise it may be difficult to avoid "the consolidation of quasi-syndicalist blocks, unwilling even to reveal their accounts to the public and suppressing competition between their constituent parts even more remorselessly than the predatory private moguls."

Size is rarely synonymous with efficiency, least of all, perhaps, in a state-sponsored public monopoly where various pressures may operate to push expansion beyond the economic optimum. Scepticism has greatly increased in recent decades concerning unproved assertions about the "economics of scale"[14] which sometimes masquerade as self-evident truths. Nevertheless, there are still adherents of the cult of bigness in industry, private and public, although there is ample evidence that very big concerns are not in fact always as efficient as smaller ones. The early history of Córas Iompair Éireann is testimony to the ability of some public enterprises to become excessively big for efficient functioning and to continue, with state assistance, to expand even when their market is contracting. The economic limits to which an enterprise can grow are normally set by the inherent limitation of management. It is a monstrous fiction, which big organisations tend easily to accept, that efficiency consists merely in doing a task thoroughly and competently, irrespective of the resources in terms of personnel and time employed. Undue importance should not be attached to the ability of a very big concern to employ the most expensive – and, presumably, the best brains. "The truth," Mr. Dennison has remarked, is rather that the large concern *needs* to employ the scarce resources, and the larger it becomes the more imperative it is that it should find the 'best men' if its operations are to be controlled with any approach to efficiency. But the 'best men' are very few and there may not be enough to go round."[15] Much of the elaborate organisation, checks and controls associated with bigness in industry and government far from providing guarantees of efficiency may, on the contrary, "be costly attempts to solve problems created by size which do not exist for the small concern."[16] It has been said that this century of the "common-man" calls for most uncommon men as administrators; it cannot be presumed that men of ability are easily obtainable; in any event, it is bad national economics to permit public enterprise unnecessarily to attract abilities that might more fruitfully be employed in other fields of endeavour.

It is obviously unsatisfactory in a country in which enterprise is charged with so many and such varied duties that no standards should be generally accepted by which its merits can be fairly gauged. The blunt truth is that, despite the elaborate apparatus of cost-accounting and a profusion of internal checks, there are no criteria at present by which the operations of, say, Comhlucht Siúchra Éireann, Bórd na Móna or the Electricity Supply Board can be scientifically judged from the viewpoint of economic theory. All these organisations are working successfully, no doubt, towards the ends for which they were established, but it is quite impossible to tell whether different methods might not in each case have given services as good as those provided at present but at less cost to the public as taxpayers or consumers. There is no room, therefore, for self-satisfaction about the achievements of public enterprises. On one occasion a public monopoly did reveal sufficient of the economic thinking that informed its policy-making to enable some conclusions to be reached about its outlook. Just two years ago Córas Iompair Éireann disclosed that it had proposed that the Government should introduce legislation to limit the operation of all vehicles of more than two tons unladen weight to a radius of twenty miles. Exceptions would be made for bread and milk deliveries (presumably, because the rigid organisation of the Company would not be able to adjust itself to deliveries which are made outside "normal" working hours!). It was further proposed that in future all government contracts should contain a clause to provide that any transport work carried out by the contractor would be undertaken by public transport. A similar clause would apply to local authority contracts wholly or partly financed from public funds. Public utilities such as the Electricity Supply Board or Comhlucht Siúchra Èireann and companies "enjoying a high tariff protection" would be under "an obligation not to operate transport on their own account but to have this done by the public undertaking." Finally, it was proposed that companies seeking trade loans or guarantees from the Government should be accommodated only on condition that none of the capital advanced should be used for the purchase of any transport equipment and that any transport required by them should be done on their behalf by "the public transport undertaking." The drastic nature and far-reaching implication of these proposals require little comment. Here was one of the foremost and largest of State-sponsored public utilities attempting to shore-up its own financial structure by attracting to itself business which the interests concerned are presently able to transact by cheaper methods. Full allowance must be made, of course, for the disadvantageous position in which CIE is placed: it is obliged by law to carry a good deal of comparatively unprofitable traffic of a heavy and unwieldy character, whereas traffic which might yield a reasonable profit is generally carried by private undertakers. Nevertheless, any attempt to secure for CIE transport work which the ESB and other organisations presently carry themselves might be expected to raise the transport costs of these other bodies. The result, in effect, would be to impose on efficiently operated firms a tax for the purpose, indirectly, of subsidizing an organisation which in its existing form is uneconomic. A still bigger CIE might mean even bigger losses on public transport, but the proposals made by the Company two years ago would enable the full extent of these losses to be hidden from public gaze. The annual subsidy for CIE as voted by the Dáil might become smaller, but the transport costs of many organisations other than C1E would undoubtedly increase.

The extent and scope of the public enterprise sector varies from country to country. Sometimes, as in Denmark, cooperative methods are used to achieve what state agencies directly undertake elsewhere. In some countries, public utilities remain privately-owned but are subject to state regulation. But where the economic system is based primarily on private property and private enterprise it seems particularly desirable that the agencies of public enterprise should be designed to operate in harmony with the institutional structure of the economy. When such agencies are created for tasks which would normally have been entrusted to private interests, if the requisite capital and initiative had been available, the instruments of public enterprise must bear more than a formal, superficial resemblance to the representative firms of private industry. Clear criteria must be evolved by which achievements in the public sector of the economy can be evaluated and compared with those of the private sector. That means that the state-sponsored bodies must publish more information about their activities and policies than is presently available. It is not enough for these bodies merely to be assigned special functions. Data must be secured to enable determinants of their size and structure to be established as well as of sheer efficiency, and the public is entitled to be satisfied that pricing policies are the result of more than arbitrary decisions. There is small consolation for the consumer in the knowledge that a public corporation is precluded by law from making "a profit." Until it is demonstrated to the contrary, a consumer might argue that a profit-making concern might be able to provide the same service at a lower cost. Unless these conditions are satisfied the public has no real guarantee that its public enterprises are exercising their functions with the minimum use of the community's economic resources.

It is quite fruitless to try to decide whether the public or private sector of the economy is the more important since in most countries to-day publicly-owned or controlled enterprise and private enterprise have complementary functions. But nothing would afford greater evidence of the reality of the claim that private enterprise is the basis of the Irish economy than some demonstration that the administrators of public enterprise are conscious of the need for aiming, when opportunity offers, at the enlargement of the private business sector of the economy. Is there any reason why alongside the development of public enterprise there should not be a gradual transfer to private ownership, through the medium of the Stock Exchange, of state-owned public utilities which have satisfied the private investor of their merits as really productive investment projects? The recent decision to allow the Electricity Supply Board to issue its own securities may, perhaps, be a step towards the transfer of the assets of the Board as a whole to private ownership, subject, of course, to necessary state regulation of its charges and profits. If this method were adopted by public enterprises generally, where not undesirable in the public interest, the state might be able to acquire a most potent means of creating the wide and active market in Irish securities which is so notably lacking at present. It might also provide at least one practical way of achieving in an Irish context what Professor Lionel Robbins had in mind when he wrote: "within the present framework of law and institutions, I see no guarantee of good results from the free play of private interest.... [However] rather than to proceed by destroying the market and enterprise system, it is better to proceed by trying to improve it ...... rather than stake all on the dubious prospects of over-all collectivism, it is better to retain existing mechanisms, but to erect around them, so to speak, a system of laws and institutions within which they may be made to work the right way. It implies, that is to say, a belief, not in a spontaneously harmonious free enterprise, but rather in a deliberately competitive order."[17]

The community is the loser when a monopoly wastes some parts of its resources; but there is little merit in using the machinery of the state to eliminate private monopoly and to replace it by a public monopoly that retains the vices of the old system but reveals them less openly. Public enterprise need not necessarily be unduly obsessed by the problem of relating prices and marginal costs, but it is well that the existence of the problem should be recognised unless the consumer is to suffer. Otherwise there is little hope that state-sponsored agencies will be able to secure by structural changes and decentralization reductions in costs and the introduction of innovations. The consumers' interests are threatened not because deliberate and predatory attempts are made by public enterprise to charge unnecessarily high prices, but because prices may have been fixed by criteria which by economic tests are arbitrary or because policy is unduly influenced by unproved administrative assumptions which have become accepted as scientific theories. In Britain it may be true as *The Times*[18] wrote on the Report of the Select Committee on Nationalised Industries that "efficiency will be got neither by nagging nor by exhortation. It will be got by the appropriate Minister appointing the best Boards, by those Boards appointing the best people they can, and by the organizations then being allowed to get on with the job. If things go badly wrong they will not stay hidden for long. Then accountability to Parliament, which is properly always there, will powerfully come into play."

There should be no interference with the day to day activities of state-sponsored enterprise in Ireland, but it is clear that adequate means of enabling legislature and government to be really conversant with the policies of such enterprise have yet to be found.

NOTES TO ARTICLE

1 *Industrial Potentials of Ireland; an appraisal*: prepared by IBEC Technical Services Corporation, New York, 1952. Published by the Stationery Office, Dublin. p. 14.

2 *Economic Survey of Europe*: UN Economic Commission for Europe. Geneva, 1950.

3 W. W. Rostow: *The Process of Economic Growth*, p. 239.

4 B. Chubb: *Public Control of Public Enterprise*, in *Administration,* Vol. 2, No. 1, p. 21.

5 L. Ryan: *The Pricing Policy of Public Enterprise*, in *Administration*, Vol. 2, No. 1, p. 43.

6 W. W. Rostow: *The Process of Economic Growth*, p. 238.

7 Ibid p. 242.

8 Op. cit, p. 85.

9 A. C. Pigou: *Economica*, p. 21, February, 1948.

10 The Budget Statement, *Dáil Debates*, 7 May, 1953.

11 J. P. Beddy: *Capital for Industry*, Paper to Irish Management Institute, January, 1954.

12 Ibid.

13 L. Ryan: *The Pricing Policy of the Public Enterprise*, in *Administration*, Vol. 2, No. 1, p. 51.

14 L. Robbins: *The Economic Problem in Peace and War*, p. 78.

15 S. R. Dennison: *The Problem of Bigness.* Cambridge Journal, October, 1947.

16 Ibid.

17 Lionel Robbins: *The Economic Problem in Peace and War*, p. 83.

18 *The Times*, August 13, 1953.

Administration, vol. 51, nos. 1-2 (Spring/Summer 2003), 32–35

Economic Development and Planning

P.W. RYAN
Book Review

Economic Development and Planning, edited by Basil Chubb and Patrick Lynch. Dublin, Institute of Public Administration, 1969. Ryl. 8vo., viii + 369pp., 75s.

Originally published in 1970, vol. 18, no. 2, 190-192.

Planning, as Dr Whitaker wrote in an article reprinted in this volume [not included in this reader], is not a vitally exciting and warm-sounding word to the average human being; but it is a challenge to the intellect. It must be said that this collection of twenty-four articles, speeches and extracts from official documents forms a record of an intellectual as well as an economic revolution. The recurrent theme of many of the early pieces reproduced here is the absence of a national spirit of self confidence, making economic development impossible. The emergence of a sense of control over our economic destiny, achieved by conscious planning, is amply shown by the changing attitudes of the same authors in articles written some years apart. This shift in attitudes is equally apparent in the administrative sphere: contrast, for example, the view of the public service adopted by Dr Whitaker in his 1953 article on "The Finance Attitude" and that taken by him a decade later. The most hardened sceptic must recognise that institutions do change when men of eminence like Lemass or Whitaker decide that change is needed.

The range of this collection is very wide indeed. While political scientists and politicians might consider it to be economic history, economists might equally regard it as political and administrative history. In both cases they would be well satisfied with the coverage their own subject obtains as part of the single theme of social progress. Beginning with what might be called the prehistory of the subject, Patrick Lynch's 1953 article on "The Economist and Public Policy" sets the theme of the emergence of the state as a serious factor in economic activity, exercising not merely a regulative but a developmental function. Four comments published with the article express with varying degrees of vehemence the view of one of them that state activity is ‘a necessary evil’. By 1961 Mr Lemass could write that ‘in Irish economic development, the role of the Government is predominant’ – a view much more extreme than that expressed by any other contributor to the volume, or for that matter than that adopted by our economic programmes. The movement of informed opinion in the intervening years is apparent to the most casual reader; the part played by Mr Lemass in this remoulding of opinion should lay to rest the commonly expressed opinion that Ireland is ruled by the civil service over the heads of the politicians.

There was, of course, an element of desperation in Ireland’s conversion to planning following the economic collapse of the 1950s. Planning – the euphemistic ‘programming’ was by now almost abandoned – began to show its growing pains by the mid-1960s. In the early years there is some ground for suggesting that available resources surpassed the fund of developmental schemes available. By 1965 the reverse was true, and the NIEC’s Report on Economic Planning reprinted here pointed to the serious problem of co-ordination that had arisen. In particular, it stressed the need for the state’s own agencies to co-ordinate their activities and limit their demand on resources – a curious echo of Gunnar Myrdal’s assertion years before that “Planning is often the more ‘liberal’ alternative to the chaos caused by unco-ordinated state intervention.” Cynics may see in this a tendency for state intervention to justify itself in terms of its own mistakes; it may be suggested that this circularity, however regrettable, is tolerable if it yields economic growth.

The selection of readings is not limited to the role of the state as manifested in planning as such: the place of the state-sponsored bodies is analysed in a well-known article, again by Mr Lemass. This attitude to their operation must come as a surprise to some readers, and is worthy of the product of a North American business school: in order to encourage efficient achievement of their goals “. . . the relations between the Minister and the Board should never be too cordial”. State-sponsored bodies are, however, a limited device: as Dr Whitaker points out in another contribution, they can only operate where they have a clearly defined function and a stable policy to guide them.

The theory of state-sponsored bodies is to close gaps in the economic structure-to fulfil the original view of the ‘subsidiary function’ of the state where private enterprise has failed to operate. The wider view of the state’s role implied in economic planning requires that the administration of government itself must be recast. For an individual, character reform is difficult; for an organisation of thirty thousand, it is a task which risks multiple schizophrenia as the possible price of failure and the likely cost of transition. No less than six extracts deal mainly with the reform of the public service; almost all others emphasise its paramount importance in economic development.

T. J. Barrington writes that "the crucial factor in development is the quality and effectiveness of the administrative machine", and he is echoed by many others. The renowned passivity of "The Finance Attitude" possessed, perhaps, no more reality than the *laissez-faire* utopia of the nineteenth century economists; even if it did not, it affected the prevailing climate of opinion to an unconscionable extent. The articles here document the fundamental change in the view the public service took of itself, as other articles document the change in the externals of economic policy. The impression of the reviewer is that the authors regard the administrative as the more important of the two revolutions: it is too soon to foresee the outcome of the Devlin Committee's proposals – their chapter on the strengths and weaknesses of the public service is the last extract in the volume – but it is already evident that the developmental character of the public service is much stronger than it was.

A book of this type is not normally intended to be read as a connected whole and it probably will not be so read by most readers. This is a pity, even though inevitable for most readers because of the bulk of the collection. The function of a book of readings is documentation, not analysis, and hindsight should not be too obtrusive except in the selection of material; but, in a collection as large and diverse as this, it is perhaps unfortunate that a stronger analytical section has not been included. The authors provide a brief introduction to each piece, together with a general introduction and epilogue; but it is possible, for example, to come away from this book with the impression that the emphasis which was validly placed in the early days on 'productive' versus 'social' investment is still accepted now. This is so because the extracts run commendably up to date (1969) and there is not as yet a fund of published articles analysing the experience of the most recent years; a gap which might usefully have been filled by a more extended commentary, perhaps incorporating also a general profile of the Irish economy in 1958 and 1968 describing the level of income per head, population movement, and the alteration in the sectoral balance of the economy during Ireland's planning era.

The bias of the volume is necessarily retrospective: long-term issues confronting us at present are difficult to present from published material, and are chiefly represented here by the extract from Devlin. It is easy to think of issues equally pressing on the economic front: a reprint from Buchanan would be useful at this point. It is also possible to regret the near absence of criticism of either the theory or the practice of planning. It is true that planning, to an extraordinary extent, has been a consensus movement in Ireland, but a fairminded observer might wish for a fuller representation of the critical point of view, even if a lower standard of debate obtained in the piece than in the other contributions.

In other respects the authors have been remarkably thorough. Given that the purpose of a volume of readings is to gather material otherwise relatively inaccessible, it is perhaps surprising that they have decided to reprint so much directly from the three programmes, but the gain in completeness justifies the extra bulk. In economics, administration, and even in social theory, this is one of those books which inevitably attract the adjective 'essential'. It is not often that a silent revolution is so completely successful, and still rarer that it can be seen between the covers of one book. Such is the case here.

Administration, vol. 51, nos. 1-2 (Spring/Summer 2003), 36–59

The Changing Social Structure*

DAVID B. ROTTMAN and
PHILIP J. O'CONNELL

Originally published in 1982, vol. 30, no. 2, 63-88.
David B. Rothman was then a research officer in the ESRI and Philip J. O'Connell was a research assistant in the ESRI.

This is an interpretation of the transformation Ireland has experienced since the mid-1950s. It sets out the essential features, as we see them, of a rapidly industrialising society. The specific items of change have been well chronicled: new forms of work force participation, altered family relationships, an emphasis on education, and a higher level of material well-being, among many others. As sociologists, however, our interest is in the basic pattern which allows a multitude of people and groups to operate as a totality in these changed circumstances. That pattern is not adequately captured by simply describing Ireland as an industrial society. Though Ireland exhibits many characteristics of such a society, its development has differed in some important respects from that which is associated with other western countries, because it took place in the context of disengagement from unilateral dependence on the British economy and a simultaneous integration with the international economy. It is a difference that is too rarely acknowledged.

The structures of Irish society in the 1950s were viable only insofar as they linked with those of the United Kingdom; they were appropriate to one of the peripheral regions of the British Isles. British capital was the most substantial foreign investor in Ireland, the migration of Irish labour to Britain was increasing, and two-thirds of total exports was destined for the British market. By the late 1960s state induced economic growth, through the expansion of the industrial and service

* We gratefully acknowledge the critical comments made on an earlier draft of this chapter by Frank Litton, Ciaran McCullagh, James Raftery and Joseph Ruane.

sectors of production, had industrialised an economy formerly dominated by agriculture, and appeared to promise full employment. If so, for the first time, the massive redundancies created by the century-long restructuring of agricultural production could be absorbed.

It was a transformation set in motion as an act of will. Through state policy the outflow of labour in the 1950s has been replaced by the inflow of foreign capital. Policies adopted by successive governments re-oriented Ireland away from Britain and toward the world economy and made it possible for the national economy to capture most of each generation as it entered the workforce. Those policies released new forces in Irish society and accelerated processes, like farm mechanisation, which had been gathering momentum since the late 1940s. But by intervening so significantly the state had introduced changes whose logic would be worked out within the social structure, and over which no individual or government could retain control.

Structural change alters the ways in which the life chances of individuals are allocated – that is why it is so important a topic for study. By life chances we refer to inequalities in the opportunity people have of sharing 'in the socially created economic or cultural "goods" which typically exist in any given society'.[1] A transformation has taken place since 1957 in the allocation of life chances. What we offer is an explanation that treats social class as the most important indicator of a person's life chances, and we put emphasis on the specific life chances involved in migration flows and demographic patterns, which were dramatic reflections of class inequalities during the 1950s. Our basic theme is how the determination of life chances has over the past twenty-five years become for the most part self-contained within Ireland: the workforce no longer spans the Irish Sea, emigration has virtually ceased, and demography has been shaped by natural increase and immigration.

Because the change in social structure was so closely linked to policy choices, however unintended their consequences may have been, we begin our examination with an assessment of the development strategies adopted and the economic problems which they were designed to solve. The policies adopted had two crucial effects on the class structure: (1) the availability of various types of positions for economic participation and (2) the rules governing competition for vacancies in those positions.

THE CONTEXT OF STRUCTURAL CHANGE

The search for economic independence that dominated policy-making since the state's foundation had obviously failed by the late 1950s. Agriculture, then the dominant form of economic activity, especially as a source of foreign exchange, was dependent on exports of dairy products and cattle to Britain. Agricultural production had expanded only slightly, and the long-standing process by which agricultural labourers and small farmers were forced off the land, and into the British labour market, continued unabated, even becoming more vigorous in the 1950s. The industrial growth fostered to serve the domestic market during the protectionist 1930s had been exhausted decades earlier. Insulated by high tariffs, one of the legacies of the 1930s, from competition with foreign manufacturers, domestic industry was inefficient and produced for the restricted home market. A generally low level of linkages among firms, a further consequence of protection, and a distinct reluctance by private investors to provide capital offered little potential for any expansion of industry without effective state intervention.

By the late 1950s Ireland's ability to continue as a viable economic and social entity was in question. The 1950s had seen economic stagnation, continual balance of payments crises, rising unemployment and 400,000 emigrants. Gross national product (GNP) had increased by 8 per cent between 1949 and 1956, in contrast to the 21 per cent increase recorded in Britain and the 42 per cent recorded by the combined countries of the Organisation for European Economic Cooperation.[2] Left on that course, Ireland's future could only be grim. The value of gross agricultural output was rising by one-third the rate characteristic of the combined OEEC countries and the volume of industrial production grew at one-half the rate experienced in those countries.

The publication of the first *Programme for Economic Expansion* in November 1958 was a direct response to that critical situation, and marked a turning point in Irish economic policy. It followed closely the recommendations of the Department of Finance's major study of the national development problems and opportunities, *Economic Development*. These and subsequent planning documents marked the abandonment of the pursuit of self-sufficiency and turned the economy outwards with two inter-related strategies. First, agriculture, retaining its pre-eminence as the likely vehicle to prosperity, could increase production by integrating with the European market and its higher food prices. But increased agricultural production demanded the consolidation of small farms into larger, commercially viable units and more mechanisation – success in agriculture would yield less, not more, employment. Development strategy thus required a second focus: the attraction of foreign capital to invest in export-oriented manufacturing, an expansion of industry to be massively underwritten by state intervention. The main direct beneficiaries of development strategy therefore would be large farmers and overseas investors. An improved structure of living for all was promised for the not too distant future.

The pursuit of this dual strategy in 1958 was indeed a turning point. While certain of the institutions central to the success of the industrial development strategy had already been established – the Industrial Development Authority in 1949, An Foras Tionscal in 1952, and the Industrial Credit Company in 1933 – it was not until 1958 that the Irish economy was opened to the international market; protectionism was abandoned, and formal economic planning was initiated. This radical departure from former policies coincided with a major increase in the internationalisation of trade and investment.[3]

Such international developments ensured that foreign investment became the linchpin of Irish development strategies, although the invitation to foreign capital made in the first Programme was perhaps but one of several options at the initial stages of policy formation. Nevertheless, the influx of foreign capital was sufficient to provide 80 per cent of new private investment in the first six years of planning, contributing much to the success of the first Programme.[4] The second and third Programmes were far more optimistic, anticipating that the inflow of capital from overseas would make a major contribution, not simply in the form of direct investment but also in subscriptions to national loans and in loans to semi-state companies.

It was a bold development strategy. The growth in new industrial investment had to take place in tandem with a general shift to integration with the European economy, a move likely to result in a sharp contraction of the traditional domestic industries as protective tariffs were gradually removed. Adaptation grants were provided in order to improve the competitiveness of domestic industries, and their decline was compensated for, at least during the 1960s and early 1970s, by firms attracted from abroad. The strategy also incurred certain costs. Industrialisation through foreign capital required the state to provide a wide range of incentives and services to industry: direct aid in the form of investment grants, the provision and upgrading of infrastructural facilities, transport and communications, financing of research and development, as well as subsidising the education and training for an industrial work force. A range of tax incentives, including export profits tax relief, accelerated depreciation allowances and investment allowances for certain areas, enhanced Ireland's attractiveness as a location for both foreign and native investment.

These strategies enacted in pursuit of economic independence and stability generated an accelerated rate of growth during the 1960s and early 1970s. The resulting restructuring of the economy can be gauged in the changing shares which the main economic sectors contribute to gross domestic product (GDP). Between 1960 and 1979, the share of agriculture in GDP dropped from 22 per cent to 15 per cent of the total, while industry's share grew from 28 per cent to 38 per cent, and that of services dropped slightly, from 49 per cent to 48 per cent.[5] Changes in employment were also significant. Total employment in industry fell from 282,000 in 1951 to 257,000 in 1961 and increased thereafter to 319,000 in 1978, an increase since 1961 of 24 per cent. Employment in agriculture fell from 496,000 in 1951 to 379,500 in 1961 and 229,000 in 1978, a drop of 40 per cent between 1961 and 1978. Total employment in services grew by 20 per cent from 416,000 in 1961 to 500,000 in 1978, when it represented the largest employment sector. Public service employment expanded by 62 per cent between 1960 and 1980, from 182,000 to 295,000.[6] Over the same period, the Irish economy was successfully disengaged from its heavy reliance on Britain. British-owned companies, which in the period from 1960 to 1970 represented 22 per cent of new industry investment, accounted for less than 2 per cent in 1980, and the proportion of total exports destined for the British market fell from two-thirds of the total in 1956 to one-third in 1981.[7]

While the transformation since 1958 can hardly be regarded as a 'social revolution', the period did mark a watershed for the structure of Irish society. Nevertheless, Ireland remains a society with problems embedded in that structure, some of which had motivated the economic planners of the late 1950s. Though oriented toward the world economy as a coherent economic unit, the problem of dependence may in fact have been diffused rather than removed. And now that Ireland has largely withdrawn from participation in the British labour market, rising unemployment rather than increasing emigration threatens the society's viability.

Formal economic planning in the late 1950s emerged through the conviction held by a relatively small number of higher civil servants and academics that through the intelligent utilisation of fiscal policy and selective state interventions, the destiny of a society could be directed and controlled. Such assumptions underlay not only the publication of *Economic Development* and the subsequent *Programme for Economic Expansion*, but also the establishment of a number of organisations oriented toward the application of expertise, particularly of the economic variety, to the pursuit of national progress. Notable among these organisations were: the Institute of Public Administration, founded in 1957 to promote the study and improve the standard of public administration; the Economic Research Institute (later the Economic and Social Research Institute), founded in 1960 to conduct research and advance the knowledge of economics and other social sciences with particular reference to Ireland; An Foras Taluntais, founded in 1958 to undertake and assist agricultural research; and the National Industrial and Economic Council, the forerunner of the National Economic and Social Council, established in 1963 to report on the requirements for economic development and full employment.

These agents of economic development, like the planning documents, were the instruments of a decisive break with the past. Such significant interventions to a society release social forces which subsequently become independent of their immediate authors. The emergence of a wide range of organised interests during the next two decades, itself a consequence of economic restructuring, has involved the state in a complex network of relationships, often with conflicting interests, and considerably reduced the room for manoeuvre in any further state interventions. The success of the initial planning exercises both transformed the social structure and severely restricted the prospect that the same group of planners or another could intervene so decisively again in Irish society.

THE TRANSFORMATION OF THE CLASS STRUCTURE

By the mid-1960s, industrial expansion and economic growth generally were forging dramatic changes to the Irish class structure. A class consists of families that have a similar set of economic resources which they use to generate income. The life chances of individuals depend, by and large, on the quality of such resources, whether in the form of property, as in farmland, or in qualifications for wage employment. Thus, a changing class structure alters the relative advantage of possessing different forms of economic resources. In Ireland, as in other industrialising countries, this took the form of continuous contraction of employment possibilities for semi- or unskilled manual work and declining viability for small farm enterprises and work thereon; the converse was growth in employment prospects for those with credentials required for white collar and service occupations, and the still more rapid expansion of opportunities for those trained in skilled industrial work. Yet the change in class structure was to be less complete in Ireland than in most European countries, and the implications for equality of opportunity less substantial than is often believed.

Still, a contrast of the class structure of the early 1950s, as portrayed in the 1951 census, with that of today, as revealed in the 1979 Labour Force Survey, denotes the passing of an era and the emergence of a new order. Table 1, which traces the changing class composition of the male labour force in 1951, 1961, 1971 and 1979,[8] includes both the number of workers in each class category and the percentage of the total male workforce it represents. It is a total workforce that has been steadily declining in size since the mid-nineteenth century. Such was the devastation sustained through emigration during the 1950s that the 1979 labour force of 883,000 men was 50,000 fewer than that in 1951. So it is possible for a category to have increased its percentage share since 1951 though remaining unchanged in the number of workers it contains. Simple stability in numbers reflected economic viability for a class.

Slightly less than one-half of the early 1950s workforce fell within class categories which derived income from property-ownership: 38 per cent of the workforce were either employers or self-employed in agriculture with an additional 8 per cent so engaged in non-agricultural pursuits. Professionals, managers and senior administrative workers, 48,000 in number, represented only 5 per cent of the 1951 workforce. A further 11 per cent were skilled manual workers. One fourth of the workforce was involved in semi-skilled or unskilled manual work – typically as labourers; there were 125,000 agricultural labourers in 1951, nearly one worker out of seven. For the children of these individuals life chances centred on the prospects for inheriting the family business and the accompanying house and household goods. Realistically, education or training could secure a livelihood within Ireland for only a minority of those aspiring to the workforce. Of those born between 1936 and 1941, by 1961 only 59 per cent remained in Ireland, and of those remaining, one in four were at work in some form of family employment.[9]

For the 1951-61 period, the spectre of emigration overshadowed all trends by reducing the size of the male labour force by one seventh. Lower middle class and skilled manual categories retained constant levels of employment but became more considerable proportions of the total workforce. Where an actual increase in numbers was recorded, as for senior white collar employees, the effects of emigration accentuated the importance of the change for class structure. Perhaps the most basic of life chances in the 1950s was expressed as pressure to emigrate, and the viability of the class to which one belonged or could aspire to was of great relevance.

By the mid-1970s, wage bargaining in a class system sharply differentiated by skills and credentials became the dominant factor in determining one's life chances. Employers and the self-employed represented less than one-third of the 1979 total workforce, with proprietors in agriculture outnumbering those in other pursuits by 2 to 1. The declining size of proprietorial categories, however, is attributable to depletion of those engaged in agricultural production, with a proportionately greater decline for employers than for the self-employed. In contrast, non-agricultural proprietors have increased their share of the workforce over the past thirty years, and that growth in numbers was concentrated among employers (20,000 in 1951 and 28,000 in 1979). By 1979, Ireland had clearly ceased to be characterised as petit bourgeois: the predominant categories were of large scale employers and of well-qualified employees.

The distribution of employees among class categories in 1979 and the contrast with earlier years are shown clearly in Table 1. Employed professionals formed some 13 per cent of the workforce, more than doubling their representation since 1951; skilled manual employees also

Table 1: Distribution of males at work by class categories, 1951 to 1979

	1951		1961		1971		1979	
	No.	%	No.	%	No.	%	No.	%
Agriculture:								
(i) Employers	27,832	3.1	14,000	1.8	212,950[1]	27.4	8,700	1.0
(ii) Self-employed and relatives assisting	314,422	35.0	265,436	34.3			166,800	20.1
Non-agricultural activities								
(i) employers	19,701	2.2	12,583	1.6			27,900	3.4
(ii) Self-employed and relatives assisting	52,898	5.9	47,985	6.2	64,656[1]	8.3	53,800	6.5
Employers and Self-employed	414,853	46.2	340,004	43.9	279,606	35.6	257,200	31.1
(i) upper middle class (higher and lower professions managers and salaried employees)	47,780	5.3	58,934	7.6	84,512	10.9	110,200	13.3
(ii) lower middle class (intermediate and other non-manual)	123,011	13.7	121,159	15.6	139,991	18.0	169,300	20.5
(iii) skilled manual	95,308	10.6	96,050	12.4	130,625	16.8	167,400	20.2
(iv) semi and unskilled manual								
(a) Agricultural	90,049	10.0	61,335	7.9	37,676	4.9	24,700	3.0
(b) non-agricultural	124,789	13.9	96,731	12.5	105,384	13.6	98,300	11.9
Employees:	480,937	53.6	434,209	56.1	498,188	64.2	569,900	68.8
Total at work[2]	897,465	100.0	774,540	100.0	775,507	100.0	827,800	100.0
Total out of work	36,115		46,989		55,157		55,600	
Total out of work as % of gainfully occupied		3.9		5.7		6.6		6.3

Sources: 1951, 1961, and 1971: *Census of Population,* Various Volumes; 1979: derived from data specially provided to the ERSI by the Central Statistics Office from unpublished *Labour Force Survey* statistics.

1. Number of employers and self-employed were not disaggregated in the 1971 Census.
2. Total at work includes other and undefined workers, which are not separately given in the table above.

The total excludes "theological students", "professional students" and " articled clerks" and in 1951, those in hospitals.

grew markedly over that period, from 11 per cent to 20 per cent of the workforce, rising in numbers from 95,000 in 1951 to 167,000 in 1979. The number of 'lower' middle class workers – commercial travellers and junior clerks - also increased, but less dramatically, from 14 per cent to 21 per cent. Semi-skilled and unskilled manual workers represented nearly one quarter of the workforce in 1951 and 14 per cent in 1979, representing in particular a massive decline (from 90,000 to 25,000) in the number of agricultural labourers.

The 1979 employee workforce, 570,000 strong, was one-half middle class (though this covers a diverse range of occupations) and 29 per cent skilled manual; professionals, managers and senior salaried employees alone represented nearly one-fifth of the total employed, whereas in 1951 they represented one-tenth. The weight of family inheritance as a factor in life chance allocation had diminished. Only 15 per cent of young men aged 20-24 in 1971 relied on family employment; one third had been so employed in 1951.

We can observe two overarching trends: (1) the dwindling away of the viability of self-employment and the growing salience of wage employment and (2) the shift in the balance in the employed workforce from semi-skilled and unskilled labour toward white collar and skilled manual work. By 1971 the new hierarchy of class positions was apparent. The value of various forms of economic resources had shifted, changing the balance of advantage or disadvantage associated with particular skills, qualifications, land, and businesses. Inequalities of income, opportunity, and wealth were distributed in accordance with the new pattern. The contraction of the agricultural labour force and the expansion of senior white collar work were continuous processes. Most changes were not. The real growth in skilled manual and junior white collar work only commenced in the 1960s and continued unabated through the 1970s, as far as can be judged from census-type data.

The changes in the class composition of the Irish workforce emerged from industrial development that was later, more rapid and more state-inspired than in most western societies. So intense were the changes that it is easy to overlook their incompleteness. Even in 1979, a substantial share of the workforce was in residual classes stranded in the course of industrial development, especially farmers on marginal holdings and labourers without skills. The only European parallels for such a presence are in Greece, Portugal and Spain.[10] People in these marginal categories have little opportunity to transfer to the more favourably placed categories; their children's chances are little better, perpetuating marginality within families. So today's class structure contains a substantial number of positions that are viable only insofar as they are underwritten by state social welfare programmes and from which, especially given present economic circumstances, there appears to be no exit. In the mid-1970s, such positions accounted for more than one twelfth of the workforce.

ALLOCATING AND NEGOTIATING ECONOMIC REWARDS

A strategy to industrialise generally comprises the upgrading of the labour force as well as of infrastructure and machinery. Education was elevated to particular prominence in the *Second Programme*, published in 1963. Development and education were to have reciprocal links: the heightened levels of economic performance achieved under the programme could finance improvements in education and training, to be proposed by the 'Investment in Education' study commissioned in that year, and those improvements would '... support and stimulate continued economic expansion. Even the economic returns from investment in education and training are likely to be as high in the long-run as those from investment in physical capital'.[11] Decisions on revitalising Irish education, made and implemented over the next two decades, helped to set the definitive cast to the class structure. Irish society became more meritocratic. Entry to the positions opened up by the new order now depends on evidence of success in second and third level educational institutions.

It should not be assumed that a clear relationship exists between the attributes to which such credentials attest and the nature of the work to be done in the position that requires them. All hierarchies require objective criteria for evaluation and industrial hierarchies require criteria that are based on achievement and can be applied universally. The credentials of scholarly and technical accomplishment have become the general resource by which aspirants to the labour force are differentiated – the currency of social evaluation.

If educational credentials give a general sense of the quality of a workforce, then Ireland by the mid-1970s was on the road to having one of the finest in Europe. By then, Irish participation rates in second-level education exceeded those in Great Britain. The rise was dramatic. In 1964, one-quarter of 17 year olds remained in full-time education, a participation rate that grew to one-half in 1979. A two-thirds growth in participation rates had occurred over that period in third-level education, with some 20 per cent of each cohort of young people entering a third-level institution.[12]

The consequences of this education explosion were equally dramatic. The importance of educational institutions within the society was greatly enhanced, the population better or at least more extensively educated, and the content of that education greatly altered.[13] But the expansion of education, and particularly the opening of opportunities through 'free education' in the 1960s and 1970s, did more to consolidate the advantages of propertied and professional middle class families than to facilitate social mobility: the strong encouragement to educational accomplishment was disproportionately taken up by children from middle class backgrounds. The qualifications so obtained were used to secure for those families the bulk of opportunities becoming available in white collar and skilled industrial employment and self-employment. Participation in second and third-level education was and remained severely restricted along social class lines, with children from substantial proprietorial and upper-middle class professional families forming a share of the student population at higher levels which vastly exceeded their share of the student-aged population. Middle class dominance is strongly evident at the Leaving Certificate standard and in the late 1970s nearly three-quarters of the children of members of the major professions entered a third-level institution, in contrast to less than four per cent of the children of unskilled workers.[14]

The result is a virtual upper middle class monopoly of the advantages that depend on education. If, as in Table 2, we treat the major professions employers and managers as constituting the upper middle class, we find 38 per cent of university entrants in 1979 came from such a background. Working class children, who represented 52 per cent of those of university age, formed only 14 per cent of the university entrants. Certainly a Leaving Certificate or even a third-level degree no longer guarantees privileged employment. But the expected

Table 2: Social class selectivities among university entrants

Social Class	1971 Population Aged 0-13 %	1979 University Entrants %
Farmers	19.6	16.6
Upper middle class	9.8	37.9
Lower middle class	15.3	26.9
Working class	51.9	14.3
Unknown	3.5	3.5
Total	100.0	100.0

Source: Population percentages are from Census of Population of Ireland 1971 Volume IV *Occupations* (Dublin: Stationery Office 1975)] p. 146. University entrants are as stated in The Higher Education Authority *Accounts 1979 and Student Statistics 1979/80* (Dublin: The HEA 1981), p. 64. Upper middle class includes higher professionals and employers and managers; lower middle class includes lower professionals, salaried employees, and intermediate non-manual workers; the working class includes other agricultural occupations, other non-manual, and all three manual categories of the CSO socio-economic groups.

standard of preparation for candidates for a range of opportunities, such as recruitment grades in the civil service or even apprenticeships, has risen, sharpening the divide based on education and thus on class.

So class transformation, which fundamentally altered the hierarchy of positions within the class structure, coincided with processes that acted to ensure an essential stability in the distribution of privileges. The same families, by and large, occupied the most advantaged positions in the old and the new class structures. This is not to deny the gains recorded in working class and small farm families over recent years in educational participation - but so minute was their participation until recently and so extensive the middle class dominance of higher education, that the educational system today is a barrier to social mobility. Similarly, improvements in standards of living have been almost universally experienced, but the differentials between the top and the bottom of the class structure remain. Large scale property-holdings or professional qualifications in the 1950s were able to secure a comparable level of advantage for the children born to such families in the 1960s and 1970s, either through inheritance or through disproportionate shares in the educational credentials that had the greatest labour market value. Those without such resources emigrated or remained in marginal positions within Ireland. Economic growth did not secure the promised social progress.

A new hierarchy also implies a greatly altered set of organisations established or sponsored by class interests to preserve their relative positions. A transformed class hierarchy is thus reflected in the distribution of power within the society. The shift towards wage employment generally and skilled and white collar work particularly is reflected in greater numerical strength of trade union membership and its changing composition. From 328,000 trade union members in 1961, 51 per cent of all employees, membership expanded by 1979 to 499,000 – 65 per cent of all employees. That expansion was more marked – at more than twice the rate – in the 1970s than in the 1960s, with the bulk of the growth occurring in white collar unions. By the 1970s, Ireland had one of the highest levels of trade union membership in the EEC and the highest rate of union growth of any EEC country.[15]

Changes in trade union strength were complemented by extensive consolidation and expansion in the numerical and organisational strength of employer representative bodies over those years, and in the services they provided. The Federated Union of Employers had 1,497 firms as members in 1965; 3,000 firms were on its membership rolls by the end of 1980, together employing more than 50% of all non-agricultural/non-public service employers. Other specialised employer representative organisations, such as the Construction Industry Federation, represented the bulk of the relevant industries by the late 1970s.[16] Similar endeavours by organised agricultural interests have met with less success of late, a reflection of the reduced significance of that economic sector.

THE CHANGING POPULATION STRUCTURE

Economic prosperity and changed opportunities affect more than the way people earn their livelihoods. The frameworks within which people reach decisions – on whether to emigrate, on when to marry, or on the ideal family size – will be affected by the new forces governing life chances. For example, the declining significance of inheritance to life chances and the desire to ensure a full education for children, a costly and lengthy enterprise, cannot but influence the strategies people adopt – influence, not determine. Ultimately, the consequences of such altered perspectives become evident in the population structure.

The demographic consequences of Irish economic expansion were soon evident. The first sustained population growth since the Famine was recorded after 1961, and the ages at marriage and family size began to approximate the European norm. The total population of the twenty-six counties had declined steadily from 6.5 million in 1841 to 3.2 million in 1901, and stood at 2.8 million in 1961. That long decline had coincided with a population explosion in the rest of Europe. In the 1960s and 1970s, as the population elsewhere in Europe stabilised, that of Ireland grew, to nearly 3 million in 1971 and 3.4 million in 1981.

The post-1961 reversal reflects the virtual cessation of emigration and an accelerated rate of natural increase. The annual rate of net emigration fell to less than 0.6 per cent of the population between 1961 and 1966, from the 2 per cent experienced in some years during the 1950s, and in the 1971-79 period there was an annual net inflow of 0.4 per cent. The average annual rate of natural increase (the excess of births over deaths) rose from 0.9 per cent in the 1950s to 1 per cent in the 1960s and 1.1 per cent in the 1970s, a significant actual growth in population.[17]

The natural increase component of the growth in population was established by two offsetting trends; a rising marriage rate and a declining marriage fertility rate. Ireland in the early part of this century was characterised by high levels of celibacy and extremely late average age at marriage: 'in the generation born between 1896 and 1905 almost 30 per cent of the males and 25 per cent of the females remaining in Ireland never married, while for those who did marry the mean age of marriage was about 33 years for men and 27 years for women'. Infrequent and late marriages persisted through the economic depression of the 1930s, the Second World War, and agricultural restructuring. But by 1966 the median age at marriage had dropped to 24 for women and 27 for men, and subsequently levelled off in the 1970s at 23 for women and 25 for men. The number of marriages per

1,000 of population peaked at 7.4 in 1973 (as compared with a rate of 8.1 in England and Wales) and declined thereafter to 6.1 in 1977 in Ireland. The impact of economic recession and rising unemployment is in part responsible, but the Irish trend follows the general decline in the popularity of early marriage in the western world. [18]

If the rate of marriage earlier in the century was very low, the fertility of marriage was exceptionally high by European standards. By the middle of the century, Irish families were, on average, twice as large as those in other European countries. This pattern persisted until 'the sharp decline in fertility that occurred in the mid-1960s halted temporarily at the end of the decade, and accelerated during the 1970s'.[19] The falling number of families with four or more children is the most marked change. That decline seems likely to persist: the temporary halt in fertility decline between 1969 and 1971 may have been a response to the Roman Catholic Church's opposition to 'artificial' birth control, but there is no evidence that the 1968 Encyclical *Humanae Vitae* effected a more permanent halt to the declining prevalence of large families. The number of legitimate births per 1,000 married women between the ages of 15 and 44 dropped from 269 in 1946 to 245 in both 1951 and 1961. By 1971 this rate had fallen to 240, and in 1979 stood at 189 per 1,000 married women of child bearing age. As the effects of an increasing rate of marriage and a declining marriage fertility counterbalance, only minor fluctuations in the overall birth rate have occurred.[20]

Emigration, however, had the most decisive impact on Irish demography. Its consequences are manifest today as distortions in the population's age distribution. Approximately one person out of every five born since the foundation of the state and resident in 1951 had emigrated by the end of that decade. The ranks of the young were particularly diminished: of the 502,000 persons aged 10 to 19 in 1951, only 303,000 remained in the country by 1961. While some emigrants were to return during the post-1960 period of sustained employment growth, a large proportion of the generation, now in early middle age, was lost. That disproportion in the age distribution was accentuated by natural increase so that by 1979, 31 per cent of the population was less than 15 years old and 11 per cent was over 65 years of age (see Figure 1). The result is a dependency ratio far higher than that of any other EEC country and a rapidly expanding labour force.[21]

Because emigration was so selective in the social origins of those who left, it was a major force in shaping the post-1960 class structure. Equally, the selectivities as to which emigrants returned in the 1970s – and at least 100,000 did in the decade – proved important.

First, who emigrated? A full portrait is impossible but the broad answer is clear. The *Investment in Education* report noted that some 82 per cent of Irish-born British residents in 1961 had left school at the age

Figure 1: Population Distribution by age, 1951-1979

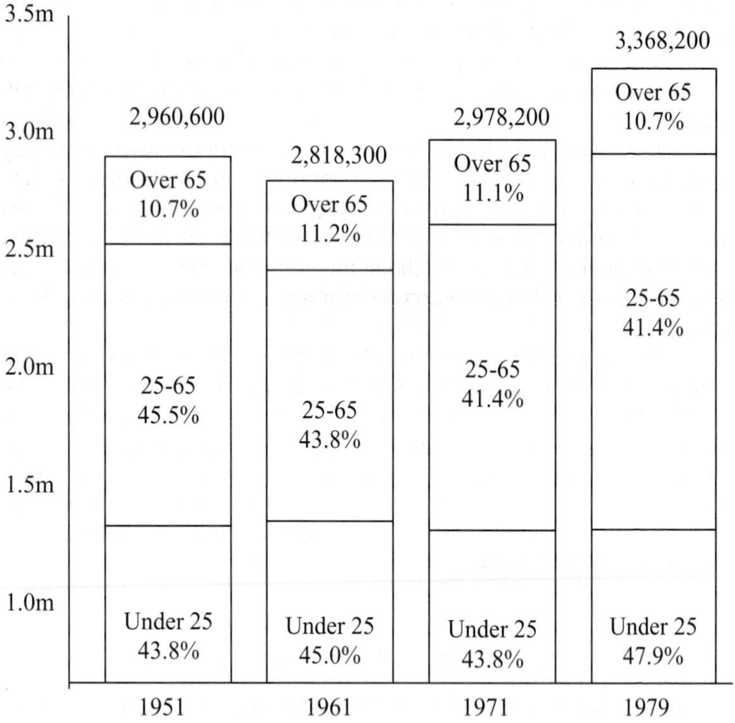

of 15 or earlier. Those leaving in the 1950s and early 1960s were predominantly young, and drawn from agriculture – farm labourers, children of small farmers, and owners of small farms – and from unskilled or semi-skilled manual labouring families. Many were unemployed or never employed before emigrating. Even in the mid 1960s, over two-thirds of recent male emigrants to Britain became manual workers, with another 14 per cent in occupations that paid little better. Female emigrants tended to work in slightly more advantageous occupations, 71 per cent in non-manual work, generally of a routine nature.[22]

The strongest break with the past came in the 1970s with a flow of former emigrants returning to take advantage of opportunities in Ireland. Most were aged 30 to 44 when returning and many reported having improved their occupational skills while in Britain. The limited evidence available suggests that while nearly one-half of the men had left Ireland as unskilled manual workers, only 28% returned as such; 16 per cent left with skills and 27 per cent were working in skilled manual work on their return. One in five returned to farms though only one in eight had been engaged in farming before emigrating.[23] Like their counterparts who had remained in Ireland throughout, those with some minimal level of skill or educational credential were able to improve their life chances and those without were consequently severely restricted.

A less heartening flow of migrants was taking the reverse journey throughout the 1970s. Smaller in number than those returning, the new emigrants were young, mainly in the 20 to 24 age group; some 13,000 individuals emigrated to Britain between 1971 and 1977. But the weight of the relationship between labour markets had clearly shifted, with aspiring emigrants in most years far outnumbering those returning from Britain.[24]

Increasing marriage rates, decreasing age at marriage, and returning emigrants were not evenly experienced by all class categories. Small farmers and unskilled manual workers in the 1970s were demographically as well as economically marginal. Heads of households in such categories were on average far older, fewer were married, and very few households in the categories were at the childrearing stages of the family cycle. Their situation still reflected the life chances of the 1950s.

THE REGIONAL PATTERN

The geographic as well as the class distribution of opportunities shifted in the course of economic development. Industrial location decisions and agricultural support policies established the strength of forces pushing individuals and families away from some areas and pulling them toward others. The results were to be found in the amount of rural depopulation and the influx to urban centres after 1958, as well as in the life chances of individuals and the balance of power between regions and between urban and rural in Irish society. The most basic consequence is that Ireland, unlike other European countries, did not experience a mass inflow of migrants into its largest cities, emigration to Britain was not replaced by migration to Dublin.

The late 1950s marked an important shift in regional development policy. Decentralisation of industrial employment was favoured earlier in the decade as a way of countering the severe regional inequalities in opportunities. The first planning exercise questioned that approach, and thereafter state investment was concentrated in special growth centres, though the desired number of centres remained controversial. The 1968 Buchanan Report expressed a preference for a small number of centres, but was never implemented; consistent policy on whether to seek dispersed or centralised industrial development did not emerge until the early 1970s.

State policy showed greater consistency after 1972, with the IDA's Regional Industrial Plans forming the centrepiece. New employment would be distributed so as to moderate the rate of growth in the Dublin region, encourage substantial industrial development in the other main urban centres, and make lesser population centres the nucleus for small industry concentrations. Development in the West was emphasised.[25] Since the vast bulk of net industrial employment gains during the 1960s and 1970s was through IDA subsidised schemes, the distribution of new employment opportunities closely followed the IDA's regional objectives. Regional shares of total manufacturing employment in 1961 and 1977 index the effect: the Dublin region accounted for 52 per cent in 1961 and 44 per cent in 1977; the combined share of the three most undeveloped planning regions – Donegal, North West, and West – grew from 7 per cent to 10 per cent of the national total. Concern over the rate of unemployment in the Dublin region, however, led to an IDA policy reversal in 1978; 19,000 jobs were targeted for the Eastern Region for 1978-82, to compensate for the net loss in employment the region had previously experienced.[26]

Manufacturing represents, even today, one-fifth of total national employment. A failure to challenge the concentration of administrative and service employment in Dublin, for example, maintained overall employment levels there. That concentration became even more marked in the 1970s. In rural areas, the continuing outflow from agriculture was only partially counterbalanced by the combined employment growth generated from manufacturing, other industry, services and the public sector. So, attention to the imbalance in manufacturing, though successful in dispersing new industrial growth to a degree which has few international precedents, left other imbalances unchanged. Over the 1960s, the Dublin area experienced a net employment gain of 44,000 jobs, while the South-East and the Midland/West lost, respectively, 8,000 and 33,000 net jobs.[27] And this occurred despite an apparent slowing of the decline in agricultural employment. Thus, even in the 1960s, the exodus from farming was shaping the class structure of individual regions.

Though economic trends and demographic patterns shifted the population to a more urban, Eastern, profile, suburbanisation is perhaps the most significant change of the recent past. The proportion of the population dwelling in urban areas stood at 42 per cent in 1951, 46 per cent in 1961, and became the majority in 1971 at 52 per cent. That growth reflects more the demographic realities of rural and urban areas as expressed in natural increases than internal migration, which is exceptionally low by international standards. But within the Dublin area there was a decisive transfer of population to suburbs. Over the 1970s the Dublin county borough actually declined in population; yet so dynamic were the trends of natural increase and net migration in the remaining areas of the county that its total population grew by 18 per cent over 1971-81 to stand at 1,002,000.[28]

But the Dublin area is populated overwhelmingly by the Dublin-born, an insularity rare among capital cities. If migrants to Dublin are more conspicuous than their numbers would lead one to expect, it is perhaps because they are better educated and of higher socio-economic status than their Dublin-born contempories.[29] Migration to Dublin was highly selective; the poorly educated rural-born with restricted life chances emigrated, and settling in Dublin indicated favoured life chances.

THE ROLE OF THE STATE

The principle that economic expansion was to draw primarily on private enterprise was inscribed at the onset of economic planning.[30] Despite that commitment, the state sector has grown at an accelerated rate over the last two decades. State expenditure on economic services, with the exception of agriculture and fisheries, expanded at a rate faster than GNP during the 1960s and 1970s.[31] State involvement in the provision of social services grew still more rapidly, increasing from the equivalent of 14 per cent of GNP in 1961 to 29 per cent in 1980. Social welfare payments formed the largest component of social expenditure (6 per cent of GNP in 1961 and 11 per cent in 1980), although total expenditure on health services increased more rapidly over that period, rising from 3 per cent to 8 per cent of GNP.[32]

In distributing these vast sums and in levelling taxation to obtain the revenue for doing so, the state increasingly impinged on the life chances of individuals and of families. The state has become a major source of income through its various cash transfer programmes such as unemployment assistance, pensions, and occupational injuries compensation. In 1973, nearly one household in four relied on state transfer payments for more than 30 per cent of its gross income. One half of marginal farmers and 41 per cent of unskilled manual workers were dependent on the state to that extent or greater. The state's responsibilities for income support increased during the 1970s: for urban families, by 1978 state transfers averaged £9.67 weekly, equivalent to nearly ten per cent of average gross income; in 1973, state support amounted to 8.2 per cent of average gross income.[33]

Through the provision of services in health, education, and housing, the state can redistribute income, mitigating inequalities between classes and across the life cycle. Expenditure on health and housing was progressive in 1973, benefiting lower income families more than higher income families. State support for education, on the other hand, was of greatest benefit to higher income families, enhancing the life chances of those already advantaged.[34]

The taxation burden imposed by expanding state responsibilities has been unevenly distributed. Taxation policy has shifted the tax burden on to families. The contribution from taxes on goods and services has been maintained at an exceptionally high level, falling slightly from 53 per cent of total tax revenue in 1965 to 47 per cent in 1978 when the average contribution in EEC countries was 30 per cent.[35] At the same time income taxation has risen rapidly, increasing its contribution to total tax revenue from 17 per cent in 1965 to 29 per cent in 1978. On the other hand, the state has been highly sensitive to the interests of the corporate sector and property owners, both of whose shares in total tax revenue dropped significantly between 1965 and 1978.

The most significant increase in taxation has occurred in income tax. As incomes rose steadily with inflation during the last two decades, personal tax allowances and the starting points of tax bands were left virtually undisturbed, yielding increasing amounts of tax, and capturing a larger proportion of income earners. As a result the average direct taxation taken from urban households grew from 8 per cent of direct income in 1965 to 14 per cent in 1973 and to 18 per cent in 1978. Increases in income taxation have seen certain class categories lose more than others. The effective rate of direct tax levied on semi- and unskilled manual households grew from 14 per cent to 18 per cent between 1973 and 1978, and the rates increased from 17 per cent to 20 per cent in the case of professionals and managers. Households headed by employers and proprietors fared rather better; direct taxes rose from 9 per cent of direct incomes to only 11 per cent between 1973 and 1978. Despite this important anomaly, income taxation is in general progressive, taking a greater proportion from higher incomes than from lower incomes. All other forms of taxation, however, were found to be regressive in 1973, taking a greater proportion from lower than from higher incomes. [36]

State expenditure and taxation as experienced over the 1960s and 1970s raise questions of equity. Working class households assume a substantially greater share of the tax burden. Yet what they receive from the state basically compensates for their disadvantages in the market place. Proprietors and employers, in contrast, are taxed at a far lower rate – facilitating private investment that will enhance their own life chances. Middle class employees, although they are more heavily taxed than proprietors and employers, are not taxed at a rate which would be expected in a rigorously progressive tax system, while they receive a major subsidy in the form of education, significantly improving the prospects of their children in the labour market.

The state also increasingly performs a mediating role in the market between organised interests. Conflicts between employers and employees have led to the creation of institutions for centralised collective bargaining over National Wage Agreements, and these dominated industrial relations from 1970 until 1981. That policy involves the state as a facilitator, but also as the underwriter, through the use of fiscal policy, of peaceful relations both between capital and labour and between the state and its own employees. State induced economic growth, by changing the balance between economic sectors, has allowed the interests of those in the more dynamic non-agricultural sectors to come to the fore. This has had the unintended consequence of displacing the formerly dominant agricultural interests, as evidenced, for instance, by the decline in farm incomes in recent years, the declining proportion of state expenditure on agriculture, and the attempted taxation of farm incomes.

PROSPECTS FOR THE 1980s: STABILITY AND CHANGE

Ireland entered the 1980s vastly changed from two decades of industrial development. Ironically, that transformation culminated in a narrowing of the possibilities for future development. Constrained by a newly consolidated class structure, a demographic pattern that ensures high levels of dependency within the population for the foreseeable future and a safety valve of emigration that is all but closed, as well as by regional and urban/rural imbalances, the structure of Irish society seems fixed for the 1980s. Moreover, the state has come ever-increasingly to underwrite the status quo through its expenditure commitments. Relativities cannot be altered.

Changes in class structure have altered the bases for the distribution of resources and rewards, but this has not meant that the high level of inequality prevalent in Irish society has been substantially reduced. Income and wealth continue to be highly concentrated, in spite of official promises that social progress would follow economic progress. Perhaps the major change has been the extent of state social intervention to counteract disadvantages thrown up by the market.

Class differences at present are self-perpetuating. The kinds of skills and credentials that offer the possibility of upward mobility are remaining within those families already possessing substantial resources. Even a dramatic expansion in economic growth would not guarantee substantial improvement in equality of opportunity.

The demographic vitality of the 1960s and 1970s was more universally experienced and made natural increase, rather than emigration, the main influence on the population structure. But it imposed major responsibilities: subsidies to ease the burden of dependency within families, a massive investment in education, and, above all, a need to improve employment prospects within Ireland. The concentration of natural increase within urban areas accentuated the imbalance in population between regions and between urban and rural areas. The resources to compensate regions for the outflow from the agricultural workforce through alternative employment are not available. The less developed an area, the greater the resources required to redress the imbalance. But given competition for resources, all in the form of plausible assertions of need, the demands from the urban centres are likely to carry the greatest weight.

The transformation we have described was shaped by economic development that had to redress the kind of distortions usually found in the social structure of post-colonial societies. Dispersed economic dependence has replaced dependence on a single country and many of the problems of an industrialised society have come to replace those of a predominantly agricultural one. It is unlikely, however, that the 1980s will be a period of stagnation or even of stability. One effect of the transformation is to create a highly complex society that is more vulnerable to international events and beyond the effective intervention of any single group. It is striking that today, in contrast to the late 1950s, there is no confidence in Ireland's ability to control its future. No new organisations are being proposed to assist in the task of national development and the experts can only warn of the limits to what state policy can achieve.

NOTES TO ARTICLE

1 Anthony Giddens, *The Class Structure of the Advanced Societies* (London: Hutchinson 1973) pp. 130-131.

2 *Economic Development* Dublin: Stationery Office 1958 p. 11.

3 The argument for importance of the international economic environment is developed in J. Wickham, 'The politics of dependent capitalism: international capital and the nation state' in A. Morgan and B. Purdie (eds.) *Ireland: Divided Nation, Divided Class* London: Ink Links 1980.

4 See Loraine Donaldson, *Development Planning in Ireland* (New York: Praeger 1965) p. 39.

5 Gross Domestic Product, is derived from Eoin O'Malley, *Industrial Policy and Development: A Survey of the Literature from the Early 1960s* (NESC Report No. 56) Dublin: Stationery Office 1980 p. 21 Table 3.

6 Employment statistics are obtained from *Trend in Employment and Unemployment* (Dublin: Stationery Office various years); public service figures are working estimates from a project on public

sector employment being carried out by Miceal Ross at the Economic and Social Research Institute.

7 Investment statistics are from industrial Development Authority *Annual Report* (Dublin: IDA Ireland various years), exports to Britain are derived from *Trade Statistics of Ireland* (Dublin: Stationery Office various years).

8 The Census of Population provides far more detailed information on occupations of men than it does for women. As a result, it is not possible to re-classify the female labour force statistics into adequate class categories.

9 Cohort emigration and family employment rates are calculated from Census of Population of Ireland volumes as follows: 1946: Vol V (Parts I and II) 1951: Vol III, Part II 1961: Volumes II and V 1971: Volumes II and V.

10 The comparable statistics are published in Eurostat *Basic Statistics of the Community* (Luxembourg, Statistical Office of the European Communities 1980) p. 17 and p. 19.

11 *Second Programme for Economic Expansion Part I.* Dublin, Stationery Office, 1963, p. 13.

12 The participation rate for 17 year olds is from *Investment in Education* (Dublin: Stationery Office 1966) p. 4; the 1979 rate is from Department of Education *Statistical Report* 1979/80 (Dublin: Stationery Office 1981, p. 2. Third level participation rate is estimated for 1964 in *Investment in Education* p. 4 at 5.9%; a 1979 rate of 10.1% for 18-24 year olds, the same base as the 1964 estimate, is calculated from Department of Education, *Statistical Report 1979/80* and Census of Population of Ireland 1979 *Volume II* p. 16. The estimate of a 20% entrance rate to third level institutions is from David Rottman, Damian Hannan, Niamh Hardiman, and Miriam Wiley, *The Distribution of Income in the Republic of Ireland: A Study of Social Class and Family Cycle Inequalities* (Dublin: The Economic and Social Research Institute 1982) p. 61.

13 A. Dale Tussing, *Irish Educational Expenditures – Past, Present and Future* (Dublin: The Economic and Social Research Institute 1978) p. 58. Tussing notes that in the 1950s and before, Irish first and second level education was concentrated on an 'arts' curriculum, with little scientific technical content: 'until fairly recently the schools have not been viewed principally in terms of their role in preparing youth for employment; rather, their role has been more moral, intellectual and religious.'

14 Rottman et al. pp. 50-66.

15 Statistics on trade union membership are derived from three sources: James F. O'Brien, *A Study of National Wage Agreements in Ireland* (Dublin: The Economic and Social Research Institute Paper No. 104 1981) p. 21; Commission of Inquiry on Industrial

Relations Report (Dublin) 1981 pp. 21-24; Christopher T. Whelan *Worker Priorities, Trust in Management and Prospects for Workers' Participation* (Dublin: Economic and Social Research Institute, draft report 1982) pp. 5.7-5.8.

16 The Federated Union of Employers *Annual Report for 1966* (Dublin: FUE 1967; The Federated Union of Employers *Annual Report for 1980* (Dublin, FUE, 1981); Commission of Inquiry on Industrial Relations Report pp. 41-45.

17 Central Statistics Office *Census of Population of Ireland 1981: Preliminary Report* (Dublin, Stationery Office 1981) p. xi.

18 Quote from Brendan Walsh 'Recent demographic trends in the Republic of Ireland', *Population Trends* (Autumn, 1980) p. 5; median ages at marriage are from Walsh 1980 p. 7. Marriages per 1,000 population are from Central Statistics Office, *Report on Vital Statistics 1977* (Dublin: Stationery Office, 1981) with England and Wales comparisons from Central Statistical Office, *Annual Abstract of Statistics 1982* (London: HMSO 1982).

19 Historical material and quote from Walsh 1980 pp. 6-7.

20 Information on births was derived from the following sources *Statistical Abstract of Ireland 1946; Report on Vital Statistics* 1966, 1977; *Quarterly Report on Births, Deaths and Marriages* December 1980. The number of men and women aged 15-44 is from the Census of Population of Ireland 1979 *Volume II* Table 1C. More generally, see Walsh 1980.

21 Central Statistics Office, Census of Population of Ireland 1979; Volume II, *Ages and Marital Status Classified by Areas* (Dublin: Stationery Office 1981). Comparative dependency ratios are given in Laraine Joyce and A. McCashin, *Poverty and Social Policy* (Dublin: The Institute of Public Administration 1982) p. 7.

22 Economist Intelligence Unit, *Studies on Immigration from the Commonwealth* (London, Economist Intelligence Unit, 1963); reproduced in *Investment in Education*, 1963, p. 180 and J. G. Hughes and B. M. Walsh, 'Migration flows between Ireland, the United Kingdom and the Rest of the world, 1966-71', *European Demographic Information Bulletin 7*, No. 4 (1976), pp. 125-149.

23 Age 30-44 is from F. X. Kirwan 'Recent Anglo Irish migration – the evidence of the British Labour Force Surveys' *Economic and Social Review* Vol. 13 No. 3 (1982) p. 202. Other data are from an EEC funded Study of Housing Conditions of Migrant Workers, sponsored by the Directorate for Social Affairs in 1974; the data cited are produced in B. J. Whelan and J. G. Hughes *A Survey of Returned and Intending Emigrants in Ireland* (Dublin, The Economic and Social Research Institute, draft report 1976) Tables 3A.4 and 3B.10.

24 Kirwan 'Recent Anglo-Irish migration' p. 203.

25 Miceal Ross, 'Comprehensiveness in regional policy', in B. Dowling and J. Durkan (eds.) *Irish Economic Policy: A Review of Major Issues* (Dublin: The Economic and Social Research Institute 1978) pp. 306-317.

26 Employment data for the 1961-71 period are from Patrick N. O'Farrell, *Regional Industrial Development Trends in Ireland 1960-1973* (Dublin, The Industrial Development Authority 1975) p. 15, data from 1971-77 are taken from M. Ross and B. Walsh *Regional Policy and the Full-Employment Target* (Dublin, The Economic and Social Research Institute, Policy Paper No.1 1979) p. 24. IDA targets are stated in IDA *Industrial Plan 1978-82* Dublin; IDA Ireland 1979.

27 Miceal Ross, 'Comprehensiveness in regional policy' 1979 p. 313.

28 1951 to 1971 urbanisation trends are from P. N. O'Farrell *Urbanisation and Regional Development in Ireland* The National Economic and Social Council Report No. 45 (Dublin, Stationery Office 1979) p. 30, and the changes between 1971-81 in County Dublin are from *Census of Population of Ireland 1981 Preliminary Results* 1981.

29 Bertram Hutchinson *Social Status and Inter-Generational Social Mobility in Dublin* (Dublin: The Economic and Social Research Institute 1969) pp. 7-9.

30 *Programme for Economic Expansion* (Dublin, Stationery Office 1958) p. 8.

31 F. Gould 'The growth of Irish public expenditure 1947-77' *Administration* Vol. 29 No. 2 (1981) p. 128.

32 Kieran A. Kennedy, 'Poverty and changes in the socio-economic environment in Ireland 1971-81', Paper read to the Council for Social Welfare Conference, Kilkenny, 6-8 November 1981 p. 15.

33 Rottman et al. p. 84; D. Rottman and D. Hannan, 'Fiscal welfare and inflation: winners and losers' in *The Irish Economy and Society in the 1980s: Proceedings of the 21st Anniversary Conference* (Dublin: The Economic and Social Research Institute 1981) p. 97.

34 Philip O'Connell, 'The distribution and redistribution of income in the Republic of Ireland' *Economic and Social Review* Vol. 13 No. 4 (1982) p. 268.

35 Organisation for Economic Co-operation and Development *Revenue Statistics of OECD Member Countries 1965-1980* (Paris: OECD 1981).

36 Central Statistics Office, Household Budget Inquiry/Survey 1966; 1973; Vol. 3 1978. Rottman and Hannan p. 97; O'Connell p. 276.

Administration, vol. 51, nos. 1-2 (Spring/Summer 2003), 60–72

Economic Planning: Lessons of the Past and Future Prospects

JOHN BRADLEY

Originally published in 1988, vol. 36, no. 1, 51-66.
John Bradley was then a senior research officer in the Economic and Social Research Institute in Dublin.

From the publication of the *First Programme for Economic Expansion* in 1958 to the Programme for National Recovery in 1987, Irish economic policy-making has, with few gaps, been formulated within the published guidelines of medium-term macroeconomic planning or programming frameworks. There is no unique definition of a 'plan' or a 'programme'. Dr Kenneth Whitaker, author of *Economic Development* (a background document to the *First Programme*), described a 'plan' and the part government plays in bringing it about as follows:

> A plan is a coherent and comprehensive set of policies for economic and social development over a period of four to five years ahead. The plan must be consistent with the availability of resources and its various parts must be well integrated. Since…a plan is the supreme policy document of the government, it should be settled early in the life of a government. Several projections ... the assumptions underlying them and the conditions for realising them, should be published and used as the basis for consultation with the major economic and social interests. (Whitaker 1983)

In the more formal economic language of planning (Tinbergen 1958), a plan must have at least four components. Firstly, clear analysis of the constraints facing the economy, both in terms of the external and internal economic environments and in terms of knowledge about the structure and characteristics of the economy. Typical constraints would include the public sector borrowing requirement and the balance of payments deficit. In more recent times, the availability of economic research allows this knowledge to be partially analytic and quantified in formal models of the economy and its sectors. Secondly, a choice of targets ranked in order of priority. The range of targets would typically include the unemployment rate, the inflation rate, and the growth and level of real incomes. Thirdly, the availability and selection of suitable policy instruments. Typical policy instruments would be public sector employment, direct and indirect tax rates, PRSI rates for employers and employees, public sector direct investment, and transfers and subsidies to persons and companies. Finally, the proper evaluation of the consequences of policy actions on the targets and constraints. If any one of these four aspects is ignored, there is a risk of committing serious policy errors.

Attitudes to these plans in Ireland have varied over time. Responsibility for drawing them up and monitoring them has also varied, ranging over origination directly from within the Department of Finance, from a special department with responsibility for planning functions and, at least partially, from outside the civil service in a special planning board. The somewhat ambivalent attitudes to these plans has tended to conceal the important role they have played within the economy. In particular, their relationship to the annual budgetary process has always been a little unclear. There is a sense in which the 'plan' represents what we would ideally like to do, or what would be 'good' for us in some normative sense, but that the budget is what we actually do when buffeted by world economic conditions outside our control, or when political exigencies become too important to ignore.

In this article, I would like to look at how the planning or programming process came to Ireland, the form it took, and its relationship to prevailing views on economic theory and economic policy. It is curious that no comprehensive evaluation of the Irish experience with economic planning has been published, although some excellent accounts of the origins and early stages are available (Chubb and Lynch 1969; FitzGerald 1968; Fanning 1978; Katsiaouni 1977). The next section covers the actual record of planning, and the final section draws some general lessons from the experience of the past and makes some 'modest proposals' for the future.

THE HISTORICAL PLANNING RECORD: 1958-1987

Life before Keynesian economics

Economic planning in its modern form was ushered in by *Economic Development* and the *First Programme*. The period 1922 to 1932 had been characterised by Irish adherence to the modified form of laissez faire and free trade which prevailed in the UK at the same time. Orthodoxy in economic and financial matters prevailed as the new state established itself. The period 1932 to the mid-1950s was marked by a drive to construct an Irish industrial base behind high tariff barriers. In relation to economic planning, political economists writing as late as the 1950s felt the need to justify state intervention in the economy (Lynch 1953) against prevailing views hostile to such intervention (King 1952). However, the economy from 1922 to 1958 was not 'unplanned'. Anybody who has read accounts written by contemporary observers (e.g. C. S. Andrews) will be aware of the state's role in creating the ESB, Bord na Móna, Aer Lingus, etc. However, what was missing from that earlier period was the Keynesian or macroeconomic language which characterised post-war economic policy in the UK and the US, and the ability to take a broad overview of the supply potential of the economy.

The revolution in economic thinking, when it came, was swift and comprehensive. As early as October 1955, Sean Lemass, in an address on financial aspects of full employment, set out the tasks of a future Fianna Fáil administration in an explicit Keynesian framework:

> The total amount spent every year by private persons and public authorities on both consumption and investment is not sufficient to bring total demand for goods and services to a level at which the labour resources of the country will be fully employed in meeting it.

The perceived failure of the policies of protection in bringing European-type growth to Ireland, and the failure of indigenous industries to reorient towards export markets from behind tariff barriers, led directly to fundamental policy changes, some of which were articulated and codified in the *First Programme*.

Economic Development and the First Programme

The *First Programme* grew out of the crisis of the late 1950s and, although a spirit of pragmatism motivates it, it represented the arrival of Keynesian macroeconomic thinking and policies in Ireland. Of crucial importance was the role staked out for the public authorities in the planning process. Speaking in 1961, Sean Lemass asserted:

> In Irish economic development, the role of the Government is predominant. Nobody believes that, in the circumstances of this country, economic progress on the scale which is needed is likely to be realised otherwise than through the medium of a strong and sound Government policy directed to that result ... The vast dynamic of growth which is inherent in free private enterprise cannot be fully availed of without Government drive and leadership.

However, there were clear differences between the explicit and unbridled Keynesianism of Lemass and the 'minimalist and, at least in the short-term, restrictionist' views of Whitaker (Bew and Patterson 1982, pp. 99-100). In this respect, Whitaker's critique of Keynesian policy prescriptions, and his insistence on the primacy of what we would today call 'supply-side' policies, was prophetic. Of particular interest is the section of his 1956 paper for the Statistical and Social Inquiry Society which deals with the Keynesian multiplier and its policy relevance for a small and open economy.

Certain aspects of the *First Programme* are of interest from the point of view of the development of planning in Ireland. It was almost unique in that it was the brainchild of one individual, the head of the civil service. Also, we have become so used to the language of later plans that the literary innovations and clarity of these first documents tends to be obscured. Indeed the *First Programme* defined, not just the form but also the language and rhetoric of planning for the next twenty-five years.

Some aspects of the *First Programme* can be highlighted. The 'psychological' aspect was emphasised, although the real meaning of this tends to be obscure. Clearly, the plan was merely the vehicle of decisive political action, not a substitute for it, and from Lemass's leadership, this political action was forthcoming. In the light of present-day sensitivities to the nuances of every interest group, a certain political naivety characterised the references to 'the virtual satisfaction of needs' in housing and other forms of social investment. This was an attitude which would be carefully excised from all future plans. A justification for the duration of the plan (1959-1963) was that the traditional budgetary year was too short a time frame for policy making in the presence of long lags. A much broader framework was needed. However, the limitations of the longer-term approach were not fully understood. For example, the expectation that the agricultural sector would provide the 'engine' of growth proved to be wrong, and that role was played by the industrial sector. Much attention was paid to the domestic sources of capital financing. In the event, the large inflows of private capital eased the domestic capital financing constraint. In part these capital flows were the result of the process of dismantling trade barriers, which was well under way even before the publication of the *First Programme*. Even the projections for the Public Capital Programme were exceeded, so the plan did not even serve well as a guide to the evolution of a key set of policy instruments. GNP growth of 23 per cent over the duration of the programme (1959-1963) exceeded the 'target' of 11 per cent. Understandably, this was not the subject of criticism. Quite the reverse! However, it opened up a gap between the planner's projections and the outturn which, being ill understood, would return to haunt the policy makers in later programmes.

The decline of planning: The Second and Third Programmes 1964-72

The loose framework of the *First Programme* contrasts sharply with the complex methodological structures of the *Second* and *Third*.

Developments in national accounting statistics, partially initiated as a result of the *First Programme*, provided a comprehensive national macroeconomic accounting framework which imposed a discipline and consistency which was lacking in the earlier work. The objective of both later programmes was to obtain a profile of the Irish economy at a specified terminal date (1970 for the *Second*, 1973 for the *Third*), which reflected the highest growth rate which could be achieved in the light of 'policy possibilities, the probable development of the external environment and resource availability'. In both programmes, a growth rate of approximately 4 per cent for GNP was broken down into internally consistent targets for the macroeconomic components. The 4 per cent growth rate chosen was never justified satisfactorily, but was broadly in line with projected OECD growth rates. An innovation in these programmes was the use of formal techniques, including an input-output (I/O) model of the Irish economy, to perform economic computations and consistency checks.

It may seem paradoxical to describe this period as representing the decline of planning. However, the very ambition of the planners to quantify at a high level of disaggregation contained the seeds of its own destruction. With hindsight, the methodological underpinnings of the plans were flawed, the I/O type approach being inadequate to capture the macroeconomic market dynamics of a rapidly developing, small and open economy. A pool of applicable empirical research was developing, in the then newly founded ESRI and elsewhere. However, it is worth remembering that the Economic and Social Review which, together with the *Journal of the Statistical & Social Inquiry Society*, is the main vehicle of economic publication in Ireland, was not founded until 1969. The first full-scale Keynesian macroeconomic model for Ireland was not constructed until 1966 (Walsh 1966), and was not available for operational use by policy makers.

As unfolding international and domestic developments rendered the projections of the *Third Programme* increasingly unrealistic, the programming process was gradually abandoned. Paradoxically, during the most turbulent period of the post-war world economy in the lead into, and immediate aftermath of, the first OPEC oil price crisis, there was no plan or programme formally in place. The extent of planning's fall from grace is captured by the remarks of the Minister for Finance, Richie Ryan, in the 1975 budget speech:

> Of all the tasks which could engage my attention, the least realistic would be the publication of a medium or long-term economic plan based on irrelevancies in the past, hunches as to the present and clairvoyance as to the future.

Such an approach 'would not be meaningful in the context of the unsettled world situation'. As a result, a policy change of major future consequence, i.e. the financing of budgetary deficits on current account by borrowing, went through without a comprehensive economic analysis of its macroeconomic consequences.

In summary, the first phase of economic planning in Ireland covered the period 1958 to the end of the 1960s. The extent to which the obvious increased growth of the Irish economy, towards rates prevailing in mainland Europe, was a result of these programmes remains an open issue. Neary (1984) concluded rather pessimistically that 'the programmes were not really the cause of the economic progress which occurred in the 1960s and the early 1970s. They accompanied it and charted its course'. He surmises that it was the new outward-looking policies towards foreign trade and investment, rather than the programmes, which caused the economy to take off.

Planning revived: National Development 1977-1980

The 1970s were characterised by fluctuations in the world economy of a kind which had not been experienced in peacetime since the 1930s. Even with the wisest and most prudent fiscal and monetary policies it would have been impossible to protect the Irish economy fully from the worldwide recession. This period also marked the onset of an extensive disenchantment with the Keynesian policies of demand management which had been widely used in the 1950s and 1960s in most Western economies. On the theoretical front, the rise of the New Classical macroeconomics, the progressively more sophisticated treatment of expectations formation and the Lucas critique of the use of econometric models for the evaluation of policy effects, revolutionised the economics profession. It was in this context that economic planning was revived in Ireland.

Whereas the *First Programme* originated from within the civil service in a relatively non-political way, the origins of a revival of economic planning over the period of 1977 to the end of the decade came from a party political manifesto. On entering into office in June 1977, the new administration set up a Department of Economic Planning and Development, a decision which was opposed strongly by the author of *Economic Development* in his role as Senator (reprinted in Whitaker 1983). Two publications in particular serve to characterise this period: National Development 1977-1980, and *Development for Full Employment*. What is of interest here is to decide whether these documents had all the necessary attributes of a 'plan'. In the introduction we isolated four characteristics of a 'plan': a choice of targets, selection of policy instruments, analysis of constraints and evaluation of consequences. Items one and two were clearly present: indeed the explicitness and ambition of the growth and unemployment targets, and the extent of expenditure increases and tax cuts, were much commented on. On the analysis of the constraints facing the economy the planners could not use the excuse available to earlier planners, that of a dearth of quantitative knowledge about the functioning and properties of the Irish economy. Even within the calculus of Keynesian macromodels, the low fiscal multipliers characteristic of small open economies were well known. A wide range of Irish models was available, if not for operational use then at least for examination (Bradley and Fanning 1983 give a comprehensive survey). On the evaluation of the policy consequences, the standard of the work reported in the published documents was less than adequate, and singularly failed to make use of the pool of economic expertise then available in the country. Consequently, the planning process, which had started out in 1958 commanding wide professional and popular consensus, became the subject of much public controversy.

Planning with binding constraints: 1981-1987

The second OPEC oil price crisis of 1979 spelled the end of the period of 'optimistic' planning which had started in 1977. It also ushered in a period of political instability, there being three general elections between June 1981 and December 1982. *The Way Forward,* published in October 1982, marked the start of a transition to a more realistic appraisal of the nature of the constraints facing policy makers in Ireland. It emphasised the economic problems besetting most developed countries: slower growth, high inflation, high unemployment and balance of payments deficits. However, in order to solve the Irish problems, it proceeded to make very optimistic assumptions about the future international environment and within these assumptions it proposed to eliminate the burgeoning current deficit completely by 1986, by a combination of expenditure cuts (mainly through public sector employment cuts combined with wage moderation) and charges for state services. Offsetting employment growth was to come from manufacturing and services through a process of wage moderation. Although targets and instruments were clearly isolated in the plan, its analysis of the constraints facing the achievement of these targets (particularly in relation to incomes policy) and the evaluation of policy consequences failed to carry conviction. In the event, the general election immediately after the publication of *The Way Forward* returned a new administration and the plan was never put into operation.

The plan, which covered the term of the following administration, came in four stages: the *Report of the Committee on Costs and Competitiveness* in 1983, the *Proposals for Plan 1984-87* in April 1984; the White Paper on Industrial Policy in July 1984; and *Building on Reality* in the Autumn of 1984. The study on costs and competitiveness focused on the severe decline in international competitiveness which occurred over the period 1977-82. The object of the report was to measure and evaluate this loss, and to recommend a 'norm' for domestic cost increases in 1982 which would prevent any further deterioration.

The study, by three professional economists, had the advantage of being narrowly focused and provided a clear exposition of the methodology of quantifying competitiveness. However, one disturbing aspect was that it highlighted the rather weak econometric evidence which could be adduced to support the behavioural implications of competitiveness loss as distinct from its measurement. Even if one accepts that 'excessive' wage inflation over the period 1977-82 had indeed resulted in a loss of international competitiveness (and the trade unions broadly did not), it remains to demonstrate convincingly that this loss in competitiveness caused lower growth and higher unemployment. To do this, a comprehensive view of the functioning of the economy must be taken, including the determination of investment (or capacity) in the exposed and sheltered sectors, the resulting determination of employment or staffing levels, the process of wage bargaining, the influence of taxation on the bargaining process, and the determination of production and retail cost prices. Clearly, the scope for disagreement at any or all these stages, even among professional economists, is very great. Nevertheless, a partial analysis runs the risk of being rejected on account of what it leaves out, thus causing neglect of what it includes.

The National Planning Board was established in March 1983 with the task of drafting a medium-term programme for the economy within which short-term economic planning could proceed. The Board consisted of seven members, all from outside the civil service, two of whom were professional economists, and had a director and a secretariat of professional economists. Their report, a comprehensive document containing 241 recommendations, was used as an input into the production of the actual government plan, *Building on Reality*, which was drawn up within the Departments of Finance and of the Taoiseach.

This document, beneath its optimistic rhetoric, was probably the most sober planning document of all published in the period since 1958. Essentially it is a manifesto on how to deal with the large fiscal imbalance without deflating the economy excessively. It was seen as a political document and, in the absence of political consensus on economic policy, was the subject of much controversy over its period of operation. In addition, the political will to tackle the legacy of Lemass, i.e. large-scale state involvement in the economy and a level of state indebtedness which has reached crisis proportions, seemed to have been lacking.

After a change of government in February 1987, the plan in operation at present, the *Programme for National Recovery*, was published in October 1987, and included a detailed pay agreement for both public and private sectors for the period to 1990. By this time, the size of the fiscal imbalance and of the debt-GNP ratio was perceived to be so large that major and immediate surgery was needed. The overriding objective had become the stabilisation of the debt-GNP ratio so as to break out of a vicious circle of ever-rising debt, an increasingly intolerable tax burden on wage income, loss of international competitiveness and spiralling unemployment and emigration. However, the fundamental ambivalence that characterises Irish plans remained: the *Programme* was relatively silent on the decisions being taken on expenditure cuts, the details of which were published afterwards in late October 1987 in the *Estimates* for the year 1988.

LESSONS FROM THE PAST

The economics of planning

David Henderson, in his recent series of Reith Lectures (Henderson 1986), coined the phrase 'do-it-yourself economics' (DIYE). In attempting to evaluate Irish economic plans, one is drawn to this concept. What are the characteristics of DIYE? Firstly, it is embued with ideas of manifest economic destiny, in which features or component parts of an economic system are cast in historic roles (e.g., 'The Irish nation faces a grave and historic test', *The Way Forward*, p. 7). Secondly, there is structure snobbery, or the widespread belief that winners and losers can be identified within a country's economy by well informed observers, politicians, civil servants, economists, etc. Thirdly, there is essentialism, according to which the outputs and activities of an economy can usefully be divided into two broad categories; essential and inessential. The final feature is unreflecting centralism, or a readiness to assume that decisions have to be taken by governments, and outcomes have to be planned and decided by governments.

To some extent these features of Irish economic plans are the necessary adjunct of their Keynesian intellectual underpinnings. One of the results of the Keynesian revolution was to play down the significance of resource allocation issues, and to stress the limitations, rather than the uses, of markets. To some extent at least, the underpinnings of the most recent plans have ceased to be Keynesian and have taken on aspects of the New Classical economics. Hence, the main economic issue in the planning debate today is not simply the choice of particular instruments or measures to achieve particular targets, but the properties and behaviour of the economic system that are assumed. If recent developments in macroeconomic theory have taught us anything, it has made us realise that the ability of state intervention to achieve policy goals is extremely circumscribed. This is the case whether one holds a Keynesian view of the economy (i.e. one which augments the simple demand side model with a neoclassical supply side) or a New Classical view. The role of the economics profession should not be to determine policy, nor to administer it. Rather, it should be to articulate clearly differing views of the functioning of the economy, to formulate them quantitatively and to attempt to interpret economic outcomes in terms of these theories.

Depoliticising planning

In attempting to look ahead to where the planning debate may lead, this uncertainty about the underlying functioning of the economy poses certain difficulties. We must now accept, as a fact of life, that economic planning no longer holds the 'high ground' of national consensus since more recent developments have broken with this tradition. Economic plans emanate from the political system and, to some extent, planning has taken on the attributes of a power game. If stable economic growth is to resume in Ireland, the conditions for the success of economic planning must be carefully reconsidered.

One way to go would be to formalise the evaluation of party political programmes. Such a service is offered to Dutch political parties by the Central Planning Bureau (CPB). The parties are free to approach the CPB, meetings are held during which the programmes are studied and policy implications evaluated with the analytical tools available to the CPB (including, but not exclusively, macroeconomic models). The CPB reserve the right to publish their evaluation independently if, in their opinion, what has been published by the parties is unbalanced. Inconsistencies in the programme are pointed out and the service is in every way similar to that provided to the government party. Essentially, the CPB attempts to help the parties cost their programmes, and the final assessment is an agreed document. This is particularly important in times of cutbacks when parties are forced to quantify their policies better. Both the parties and the media have come to attach some considerable importance to the CPB evaluation.

The difficulties in such a scheme in the Irish context are obvious, but the alternative may be less desirable, i.e. that of misleading political manifestos or the deliberate concealing of proposed policy measures prior to taking office. Firstly, there is probably less applied research done on the Irish economy than on any other European economy, not withstanding the claim one often hears that we are 'drowning' in studies of our problems. Secondly, Irish economic research has tended to be dissipated between universities, research institutes, government departments and private organisations. Hence, rather than being gradually accumulated over time, economic research findings tend to be lost. As an example of this process, I carried out a comprehensive survey of macro models of the Irish economy in 1983. In all, over the period 1958 to 1983 I found 24 models, most of which had never been published in complete form. Although they potentially provided an overall framework for bringing together wide-ranging and specialised studies of the economy and were useful instruments for interpreting the structure of the economy and exploring the effects of alternative policies, in themselves they provided very little empirical or conceptual knowledge of the Irish economy. Ireland must be unique today in that not one of the university economics departments have available for use a formal macroeconometric model. Hence, the strictures of academics on the government to 'plan' more efficiently must lose much of their force.

The prisoner's dilemma and the evolution of cooperation

A constant theme in all the plans and programmes has been the necessity for the social partners to cooperate in the achievement of national growth goals. It may be relevant to consider some recent research findings on the issue of cooperation and the development of successful cooperative strategies. The prisoner's dilemma concerns the highly stylised situation where two prisoners are being questioned as suspects for a crime. They are held in separate cells and have no way of communicating. The following deal is offered to each: if prisoner A testifies against B, A will go free and B will get five years; if neither testifies, circumstantial evidence will ensure two years each; if both testify, both will get four years. At issue in the prisoner's dilemma is whether logical analysis of possible outcomes prevents cooperation, the logic that if A refuses to testify but B does, A will go to prison for five years but B will go free. It is obvious that in a collective sense it would be best for both prisoners to cooperate together and refuse to testify. However, suppose that neither prisoner has any regard for the other, that there is no collective 'good' that both seek to achieve, that both are egoists?

Consider now a world populated by many beings playing prisoner's dilemma over and over with each other. The question arises as to whether totally selfish beings, living in a common environment, can come to evolve reliable cooperative strategies. Can cooperation emerge in a world of pure egoists? Can cooperation emerge out of non-cooperation? Three separate issues arise:

1. how can cooperation get started at all?
2. can cooperative strategies survive better than their non-cooperative rivals?
3. which cooperative strategies will do best?

Some light has been shed on these issues in recent research by Robert Axelrod of the Department of Political Science of the University of Michigan (Axelrod 1984). Axelrod held a computer tournament for prisoner's dilemma algorithms, and found that the winning algorithm was also the shortest: TIT FOR TAT, i.e.

1. cooperate on move 1
2. thereafter, do whatever the other player did in the previous move.

The analysis of the tournament results indicates a lot about how to cope in an environment of mutual power. Expert strategists made the systematic errors of being too competitive for their own good, not forgiving enough, and too pessimistic about the responsiveness of the other side. It turned out to be very costly to try to use non-cooperation to 'flush out' the other player's weak spots, and was more profitable to have a policy of cooperation as often as possible, together with a willingness to retaliate swiftly against any attempted noncooperation. There was no point in being envious of the other player's success, since in an iterated prisoner's dilemma of long duration the other's success is virtually a prerequisite of doing well yourself.

Axelrod summarised the four properties which characterised successful strategies as 'nice' (i.e. cooperate until faced with non-cooperation), 'provocable' (i.e. be firm with noncooperation), 'forgiving' and 'clear' (i.e. do not run the risk of having your complexity mistaken for lack of cooperation). Strategies possessing these four properties proved to be robust in all environments, and mutual cooperation can emerge in a world of egoists without central control.

CONCLUSION

In looking forward to future Irish plans, both our experience of the past and that of other small European states is relevant. Almost without exception, the small European states have carved a path between liberalism and statism, and have evolved towards indirect forms of economic control. What unites the political experience of the small European states and sets them apart from the large industrial countries is the premise of their planning efforts, adaptation to external market forces. They have generally found comprehensive or sectoral planning efforts increasingly inapplicable, simply because of their economic openness. They needed, in Raymond Vernon's words, 'to remain upright and watertight in a heaving international sea'. For them, therefore, the problem is one of selecting the devices of stabilisation that are in harmony with their social objectives. The strategy of the small European state must be flexible, reactive and incremental. It cannot counter adverse change by shifting its costs to others abroad. It should not attempt to preempt change by ambitiously reordering the economy at home. Instead, the small European state must continually improvise in living with change. The success or otherwise of this continual process of improvisation will depend in large part on the available detailed quantitative knowledge on how the economy functions and how it is integrated into the wider world economy. This is why public discussion of past economic plans is so important since if we do not learn from the past, we are condemned to repeat it.

REFERENCES

Robert Axelrod *The evolution of cooperation* New York: Basic Books, 1984.

P. Bew and H. Patterson *Sean Lemass and the making of modern Ireland* 1945-66 Dublin: Gill and Macmillan 1982.

J. Bradley and C. Fanning, 'A survey of Irish macromodels: 1958-1981', *Memorandum Series* No 155, Economic and Social Research Institute, 1983.

J. Bradley et al *Medium-term analysis of fiscal policy in Ireland: a macroeconometric study of the period 1967-1980*, Research Paper No 122, Economic and Social Research Institute, 1985.

B. Chubb and Patrick Lynch *Economic development and Planning* Dublin: Institute of Public Administration, 1969.

Ronan Fanning *The Irish Department of Finance*, 1922-88 Dublin: Institute of Public Administration, 1978.

Garret FitzGerald *Planning in Ireland* Dublin: Institute of Public Administration, 1968.

David Henderson *Innocence and design: the influence of economic ideas on policy* Oxford: Basil Blackwell, 1985.

Olympos Katsiaouni, 'Planning in a small economy: The Republic of Ireland', *Journal of the Statistical and Social Enquiry Society of Ireland* 23/5(1977).

F. C. King, 'Drifting to absolutism', *Journal of the Statistical and Social Inquiry Society* 1952.

Patrick Lynch 'The economist and public policy', *Studies* Autumn, 1953.

P. Neary, 'The failure of Irish nationalism', in *Ireland: dependence and independence* (The Crane Bag 8/1), 1984.

J. Tinbergen *Economic policy: principles and designs* Amsterdam: North-Holland, 1967.

B. M. Walsh, 'An econometric model of Ireland 1944-1962', PhD thesis, Graduate School, Boston College, Massachusetts.

T. K. Whitaker *Interests* Dublin: Institute of Public Administration, 1983.

Administration, vol. 51, nos. 1-2 (Spring/Summer 2003), 73–88

Life after Debt

JOHN D. FITZGERALD

Originally published in 1994, vol. 42, no. 2, 123-142.
John D. FitzGerald was then a research professor in The Economic and Social Research Institute.

INTRODUCTION

Over the last twenty years our understanding of how the economy works has undergone fundamental change. At the same time the process of integrating Ireland into the wider western European economy has been under way and this has itself changed the way the economy works. These changes have affected the Irish political system in many different ways. The expectations of the electorate and the resulting problems the political system has to deal with have, as a result, become much more complex. It has affected both the rhetoric and the substance of political life. This interaction between politics and the economy continues with the changing structure of the economy necessitating significant changes in the nature of political debate.

It is popular to decry the response of the political system to our economic problems in the last twenty years as inadequate. While much of this criticism may be justified it is nonetheless important to recognise the constraints which politicians and policy-makers in general faced over the period and the limited information available to them when making their decisions. With the benefit of hindsight many of the mistakes may seem glaringly obvious. However, when viewed in the light of the knowledge and advice then available to governments (and oppositions), the mistakes may be more easily understood. The sections *Fools Paradise and The Seven Labours* below examine how economic policy pursued by successive governments was affected by the limited nature of the available information.

While ignorance may provide a partial explanation for the travails of the Irish economy in the 1980s, it cannot absolve the Irish political system from its share of responsibility. In the section *They do it better Elsewhere?* below, I briefly compare the response of other developed democracies to fiscal crises since the early 1980s. The shortcomings of successive Irish governments are not unique.

In the section *Life after Debt* I examine how the changing economic structure will affect political debate in the 1990s. The limited scope for independent fiscal and monetary policy is now widely recognised. The Irish political system also faces serious constraints because of the openness of the Irish labour market and the degree to which the Irish electorate's expectations are driven by conditions elsewhere in Europe, especially in the UK. In spite of these restrictions Irish governments still have significant power to influence future economic developments through a wide range of supply-side interventions ranging from education to energy policy. The very disparate nature of the restrictions poses problems for politicians and the electorate alike as they grapple with issues which cannot be summarised in simple political slogans.

FOOLS PARADISE

Looking back, with the benefit of hindsight, the development of economic policy in the 1970s shows many serious errors of judgement by successive governments and by the electorates that put them into office.[1] These mistakes came to haunt the Irish economy and the political system in the 1980s and the consequences still live on in the 1990s. However, before passing judgement on the errors of the 1970s it is important to recognise the problems which faced politicians and policy-makers in that decade. The understanding of how the Irish economy worked was much more limited then than it is today and expectations of what the political system could achieve were also different.

In the early 1970s there was a widespread view that an active fiscal policy could contribute to growth by offsetting temporary deficiencies in demand and promoting stability. It was also felt that the Irish inflation rate, while influenced by outside events, was to a considerable extent under domestic control. As the decade progressed our understanding of how the economy operated developed, and these simplistic views were superseded for economists by a new understanding of the significance of the small size and the openness of the Irish economy. Not surprisingly, the new understanding of the limitations of domestic economic policy took time to feed through to the electorate and politicians. This gap in understanding resulted in very serious mistakes in economic policy in the late 1970s and early 1980s.

Here I take two case studies of how economists' perceptions of the way the economy worked influenced (or failed to influence) the political system: the process of inflation and the limitations on domestic fiscal policy. I illustrate the development of economists' thoughts by citing the Economic and Social Research Institute's *Quarterly Economic Commentary* (QEC), not necessarily because it was at the forefront of economic thinking, but rather because it was one of a limited number of sources of independent advice available to politicians.

The inflationary process

At the beginning of the 1970s the widely held view was that the domestic rate of inflation was largely a matter of domestic choice, crucially involving decisions by trade unions and employers. However, over the course of the 1970s our understanding changed.

In 1972 the ESRI QEC was still able to say that 'the basic dynamic of inflation appears to be internal'. However, by 1975 there had been a clear change in the way economists viewed the inflationary process. A series of articles, which were finally published in 1976,[2] were already influencing economists' thinking in samizdat form. They showed that the Irish rate of inflation was essentially externally determined and that the only way Irish governments could substantially change it was through changing the exchange rate.

The impact on policy-makers and the understanding of politicians was in this case only slightly delayed. The white paper *A National Partnership*, published in 1974, showed a clear belief that domestic inflation was subject to domestic control. However, by 1976 this view had changed sufficiently in the Department of Finance and among leading politicians that the government contemplated revaluing against sterling to control inflation. This change in understanding laid the foundations for Ireland's decision in late 1979 to join the EMS. In this case change in understanding of how the economy worked was transmitted to politicians and policy-makers very rapidly and they acted on the new *wisdom* in formulating policy in the latter part of the decade.

Fiscal policy

The situation was rather different in the case of fiscal policy. In the first half of the 1970s bad economics contributed to bad policy making. However, economists learned from their failures and from the developing literature outside Ireland. Politicians and the electorate were much slower to respond to the changing advice of economists than in the case of the inflationary process.

At the beginning of the 1970s most Irish economists still believed that an active fiscal policy could promote growth by ensuring that there was no *deficiency* of demand. Among other things this view ignored the fact that the Irish economy had opened up to the outside world over the 1960s. Even without joining the EC an increasing share of all the goods we consumed was imported. Thus any demand stimulus would inevitably leak out in the balance of payments doing very little for domestic demand. Many other important mechanisms (e.g. the effects on wage rates) were ignored or ill understood. Over the 1970s the implications of Ireland's openness and its small size began to influence economic thinking.

With the benefit of hindsight one can say that, beginning in 1972, fiscal policy was unduly stimulatory at a time when the economy was growing rapidly anyway. However, the advice given in the Winter ESRI *QEC* in 1971/2 was that emergency measures were needed to stimulate demand in the 1972 budget. Again in January 1973 the QEC talked of the 'encouragement of a high level of domestic demand by selective expansionary policies'. To some extent this advice reflected errors in forecasting the level of economic activity. However, it also reflected a failure to appreciate how the economy actually worked, a failure shared by many economists at the time.

The advice that successive governments received from the Department of Finance was probably along similar lines. Thus while with hindsight we realise that it was unwise for the government in 1972 or 1973 to run budget deficits, they were probably following not only their political inclinations, but also the best *objective* advice available to them. A similar situation prevailed in 1974 when the government in the budget speech stated that fiscal policy should not add to the deflationary consequences of the oil price shock but should allow a slow adjustment process. This course of action was in line with the advice they received in the QEC.

However, with the passage of the 1970s the understanding by economists of how the economy worked began to change. By the end of 1976 the *QEC* was questioning the efficacy of some capital expenditure. Suggestions that there was a need to stimulate the economy disappeared from the *QEC* to be replaced in 1977 by talk of impending supply bottle-necks. By 1978 there was widespread disquiet among economists.

While the outgoing coalition government talked in the 1977 budget about the problem of debt service, showing some concern for the level of indebtedness, this concern was replaced in the 1978 and 1979 budgets of the new Fianna Fáil regime by assertions of the need for stimulatory budgetary policy. By 1979, in spite of the fact that most economists could see the danger and futility of such policies, the budget speech could still say that the needs of the situation were for a budget which would be stimulatory.

Unlike the change in understanding of the inflationary process, the developing awareness among economists of the ineffectiveness of fiscal policy in promoting growth failed to communicate itself to the electorate or most politicians. The Fianna Fáil manifesto clearly caught the imagination of the electorate in 1977 and bleating by economists was ineffective.

The lessons of the 1970s

While considerable attention was devoted to economic issues in political debate in the 1970s much of it centred on short-term problems and essentially short-term palliatives. There was a desire to solve all problems immediately. Politicians half believed this was possible and the full complexity of the process of economic development was not appreciated; the potential role of education and training in contributing to economic development was little discussed; all expenditure classified as being for capital purposes was viewed as contributing to growth; little interest was shown in understanding the mechanisms through which this growth could occur.

Though what now appears as a population bulge (and then appeared as an explosion) was readily apparent in the late 1970s, no attempt was made to plan for its consequences in the 1980s. The need for a qualitatively higher rate of growth in employment in the second half of the 1980s was not recognised. The very short-term focus of public policy and of the policy-making process generally was confirmed. Whereas some other countries, such as France, had institutionalised the need for such a long-term view (in the Bureau du Plan) only fitful attention was devoted to issues stretching beyond the immediate electoral cycle (Kennedy 1992).

One further factor which underlay many of the developments of the 1970s was the change in expectations of the public. The increased openness of the economy, of which EC membership was one manifestation, meant that much more attention was given to what was happening elsewhere. As is discussed later, this raised the electorate's expectations concerning the possible achievements of domestic economic policy.

Raised expectations also affected the wage bargaining process where the decade saw a significant narrowing between labour costs in Ireland and in the UK. The electorate voted for increased living standards in the ballot box and on the shop floor. Governments continually talked of the need to control labour costs to preserve employment[3] while such statements were continually ignored as the wage bargaining process continued independently of all imprecations.

The central message I want to draw from the experience of the 1970s is that bad economic decisions were not merely due to foolhardy politicians or a foolhardy electorate. Ignorance of how the economy actually worked laid some of the ground-work for the many mistakes made in that decade. However, when faced with sound economic advice which conflicted with the electoral imperative in the late 1970s, politicians and electorate proved weak.

THE SEVEN LABOURS

In the 1980s the language and outcome of the political process came to be dominated by the problem of the burgeoning national debt. The imperative of resolving the debt crisis became the accepted wisdom of the electorate. While economists would say that the policies of the 1970s inevitably led to such an outcome, there was no certainty throughout much of the 1980s that the political system would be able to resolve the crisis. It was frequently suggested that a *deus ex machina,* such as the IMF, would be required to knock heads together. The fact that Ireland managed to jump through the necessary hoops remains a matter of considerable curiosity to outsiders (Dornbusch 1990).

While many of the problems which faced successive governments in the 1980s were home-made, they also faced a serious international recession in the early years of the decade and, more crucially, a major shock to the world monetary system which resulted in exceptionally high real interest rates throughout the decade. However, even allowing for these shocks, at least half the rise in unemployment which occurred in the 1980s was due to our own efforts, chiefly in the late 1970s.[4]

Interest rates

While the 1977-80 period saw the then government flying in the face of the advice of most economists with their new-found understanding of the ineffectiveness of fiscal policy, the government was unfortunate because these same economists failed to foresee the rapid change in the stance of monetary policy throughout the world in the early 1980s. The debts run up in the late 1970s in Ireland would not have proved so serious or intractable were it not for the huge rise in real interest rates (the difference between the nominal interest rate and the rate of inflation) in the early 1980s. Commenting on these problems Honohan, 1992, says:

> Growing interest costs to meet an ever-expanding debt, combined with the impact of retrenchment on the welfare bill, made fiscal correction a nightmare in the early stages.

If real interest rates had remained at their 1970s level or even risen to the moderate positive real rates experienced in the 1960s the consequences would not have been nearly as severe. However, no economists predicted this chain of events and, in the advice offered in the 1970s, there was little or no reference to the possibility of such an outturn. Thus the politicians of the late 1970s, in particular the then government, can complain that some of the information on which they based their decisions was faulty. However, this remains a rather weak excuse in the face of the other advice they received.

The effect of the rise in interest rates was simultaneously to aggravate the general economic situation and to seriously weaken the budgetary position. While taxes were increased rapidly after 1982, in the initial years all the increase went to meet the rapidly rising interest bill. This meant that, in spite of serious (and unpopular) deflationary action, the government was seen to be running and not even keeping still. The demoralisation which this caused to electorate and government alike is emphasised by Honohan, 1992.

Expectations

The expectations of the electorate affected the political process in the 1980s through two channels:

1. the aspirations of the electorate in terms of their standard of living. While the economic problems of the early 1980s played a large part in political debate there was still a demand for increased real incomes.
2. consumers' and industrialists' forecasts of future events. Recent economic research indicates that economic events can be greatly affected by changes in such expectations[5] with consequences for the political process.

The awesome nature of the economic problems faced by the country was effectively communicated through the political process in the period 1981 to 1983. The effect of this was to depress people's expectations or forecasts for the future of the economy. They reacted by cutting consumption and investment and saving more. In the short-run, in the period 1983-6, this reduced the level of economic activity, raised unemployment, and hence reduced government revenue, further aggravating the government's problems. This represented a particularly vicious circle.

While the figure for the debt continued to rise, the underlying situation showed a significant improvement (Bacon 1986). The albeit limited progress was not apparent to the electorate (or maybe even the government). The consequence can be seen in the election result in 1987. However, when serious cuts were made in expenditure in 1987 and 1988, which themselves deflated the economy, they were just enough to push the debt into reverse. Once this turning point was reached consumer and investor expectations reversed, consumption and investment picked up, interest rates fell, government revenue rose rapidly and the economy entered a virtuous circle of growth.

What is interesting about this process is that a necessary part of the adjustment process appears to have been the way consumers' (and the electorate's) expectations turned down and they lost faith for a period in economic growth (and in successive governments). It was only after a number of years of effort that the corner was turned, at which stage expectations reversed. This pattern makes it difficult for governments to implement such an adjustment process. The more severe the adjustment the longer the period of anger and depression among consumers (and voters) and the more likely the government is to fall before it can reap the fruits of the adjustment. This situation currently faces many European governments whose economies have experienced prolonged recession together with a serious deterioration in their public finances (Cantillon, Curtis, and FitzGerald 1993).

In the case of Ireland in the 1980s the understanding by Irish economists of how the economy worked came too late to inform political choice. If the coalition government had fully understood in 1983 the way expectations would magnify the impact of the adjustment process, would they have tried to speed up the process by a more rapid initial shock rather than postponing the evil day?

Tackling the problem

From a starting point at the beginning of the decade when there was little consensus on the need to tackle the problem of the debt the political situation evolved so that by 1987 all parties agreed on the central issue of controlling the debt, whatever about the means whereby this was to be achieved.

Because the debt problem was the central issue in four elections the electorate were unable to escape the realisation that change was needed, though this did not prevent the electorate from wriggling to get off the hook by changing government at each election. Irish politics of the period was possibly unusual in the concentration of attention on this issue.

By contrast with the 1970s, part of the process of education and understanding in the 1980s was a series of reports prepared under a range of different guises on the nation's economic problems: *The Way Forward*, the report of the National Planning Board, *Building on Reality*, and reports by the National Economic and Social Council (NESC). These reports may be criticised on a number of counts, but the main problem was that they were not implemented in full. However, they all concentrated on solutions to the country's pressing debt problem. They helped focus attention on the issue and, as a result, contributed to the eventual resolution of the problem.

The changing understanding of how the economy worked and the limitations on government affected not only the civil service and successive governments but also a wide range of interest groups. The developing thinking of the trade union movement over the decade is interesting. It reflects an extension of external links, traditionally with the UK, to take in the trade union movement elsewhere in Europe. The meetings of the EC Economic and Social Committee, by serving as a talking shop, helped further this development. By the late 1980s this change in outlook was reflected in the publications of NESC, in the acceptance by the parties of the left of the need to tackle the debt problem, and in the assent given to the *Programme For National Recovery*. It helped build a national consensus.

The 1980s saw an unusual concentration on a single economic issue throughout public life. This was reflected in the course of political debate over the decade. The problem of the debt had the advantage over other more complex issues, such as unemployment or even tax reform, that it could be explained to the electorate without recourse to complex economic theories or models. It provided a simple context within which parties' programmes could be assessed. The succession of weighty reports and plans for dealing with the problem, while not making solutions any more palatable, helped concentrate minds. The debt/GNP ratio which had never been heard of before, even by many economists, became an essential element of the political rhetoric of the 1980s.

THEY DO IT BETTER ELSEWHERE?

It is often suggested that in Ireland we are particularly inefficient or slow to recognise our problems (Lee 1989). The political process has come in for much criticism over the last ten years as economic growth has fallen well below the electorate's expectations. However, it is interesting to consider in a very cursory way how other countries have dealt with the same problem, a crisis in their public finances.

The most successful case in the 1980s was France. The new Mitterand government, at the beginning of the decade, at first provided a significant fiscal stimulus to the domestic economy. This policy had much in common with the approach of the Fianna Fáil government in the 1977-81 period. However, in the case of the French socialist government realisation of the folly of their policies dawned within two years and in 1983 the government reversed engines. This reversal involved some particularly unpleasant measures for a socialist government, including substantial closures of subsidised industry. While the government did not survive the next election, the President did and the French economy recovered very rapidly from its excursion into fiscal expansionism avoiding the trauma which Ireland faced in the 1980s.

In the case of the United States the political system has been much slower to tackle the problem of the federal budget. The difficulty in getting agreement between the President and an antagonistic Congress slowed budgetary reform. This partly reflects the fact that the US budget overrun was much smaller as a percentage of GNP and, while on an explosive path, the explosion could still be decades away. As a result, the budgetary problem never managed to dominate the political arena in the way that it did in Ireland in the 1980s.

The two countries in the EU which now have higher debt/GNP ratios than Ireland are Belgium and Italy. Their budgetary problems have built up over a long period through economic inertia by successive governments. There is still little sign that these problems will be dealt with. In both countries other issues prevent the debt problem from dominating the political agenda. In the case of Belgium the chronic split between the two linguistic communities makes the issue of who pays for the adjustment process a highly contentious issue. Similar regional pressures combined with the problem of corruption have provided ample distraction in Italy.

While their political systems have so far shown themselves less adept at handling the budgetary crisis than the Irish they have one advantage over the Irish case. As the bulk of the debt is denominated in domestic currency and held by domestic agents they still have the option to inflate away the debt. (Ireland was in a position much closer to a third world country because so much of the debt was denominated in foreign currencies and held abroad.) The movement towards EMU may put pressure on the economies of Belgium and Italy for financial reform.

The German economy also faces a budgetary crisis as a result of unification. So far there has been no consensus on how to resolve the problem. The German electorate is restive in the face of this uncertainty and there are signs that this threat may promote more vigorous action. It is too early yet to judge what the eventual outcome will be.

It is clear that Ireland's experience of a public finance crisis in the 1980s was not unique. As in Ireland, in many cases in Europe the process of adjustment has been combined with frequent political upheavals as the electorate express their unhappiness by changing governments at every opportunity. This is especially true of the new democracies of central Europe.

LIFE AFTER DEBT

While the imperative of reducing the debt drove economic policy in the 1980s, necessitating deflationary economic policies, the latest forecast for the 1990s indicates that, with a neutral budgetary policy, the debt/GDP ratio could fall to 60 per cent by the end of the decade (Cantillon, Curtis and FitzGerald 1994). Unlike the 1980s adjustment, this could be combined with limited cuts in real tax rates and limited increases in public services (and numbers employed).

With the imperative of the debt lifted the country faces a range of economic choices which were not available in the 1980s. It remains to be seen what economic issues attract the electorate's attention. One might hope that unemployment might provide the kind of focus of attention that the debt provided in the 1980s. However, it seems more likely that other distractions, such as the search for higher living standards for those at work, will compete for governments' attention.

What freedom for action does an Irish government still have to influence events?

As outlined below, the levels of economic policy around which political debate has traditionally centred are likely to be ineffective. The freedom to develop an independent policy to deal with the unemployment problems is further constrained by the expectations of the electorate, deriving from the openness of the labour market. The area where Irish governments retain freedom of manoeuvre is the field of supply-side policies – policies designed to change the efficiency of the productive sector through investment, education etc. These have not traditionally been a focus for political debate.

Traditional economic policy

The lessons of the last twenty years have highlighted the very limited scope for influencing the future development of the Irish economy through exercising an independent stance on fiscal or monetary policy. In the context of continuing very high real interest rates world-wide it will remain prudent to continue to slowly reduce our debt burden over the 1990s, no matter what the constraints of EMU.

The government has also lost some room for manoeuvre over the last twenty years in the field of taxation. The freedom of movement of individuals and of capital is forcing some convergence in tax rates throughout the EU. It remains to be seen whether there will be sufficient freedom of action provided by direct taxes and property taxes to allow governments to determine independently their levels of expenditure.

This gradual loss of power to operate an independent fiscal or monetary policy is not a recent event. As outlined above it has been a feature since at least the 1970s. The difference today is that we now understand how that power is limited. While monetary and fiscal policy may be ineffective, the key to changing the future development of the economy lies with detailed intervention to improve the output potential of the economy.

Expectations

A major complicating factor in the case of the Irish economy and a significant factor in explaining our high level of unemployment is the openness of the labour market. The traditional free flow of migrants between Ireland and the UK, while relieving temporary pressures on the Irish labour market, has also served to raise expectations among all those living in Ireland. For decades Irish people have compared their standard of living with the standard enjoyed by their friends or relatives in the UK.

The econometric evidence suggests that migration flows have been affected both by unemployment and by potential earnings in the UK (Sexton, Walsh, Hannan, and McMahon 1991). In the late 1980s the fall in the tax burden on middle to higher incomes in the UK created an immediate demand for a similar reduction in Ireland. It was argued that there was a need to stem the flow of highly-educated migrants by offering them comparable after-tax incomes in Ireland to what they could potentially enjoy in the UK.

This desire to emulate the standard of living of our nearest neighbour has also affected government expenditure. An important part of the standard of living is the quality of public services. Comparisons with the UK have also raised expectations in this area so that pressures to cut the burden of taxation could not be easily met by cutting the quality of public services. In the 1950s the absence of a developed social welfare system meant that people had to emigrate to survive. In the 1980s and the 1990s this is no longer acceptable.

Another aspect of the openness of the labour market has been the tendency for Irish labour costs to converge on UK rates. While they were roughly two thirds of the UK level in 1960, by 1988 labour costs in Ireland were in many cases the same as the UK. The Irish workforce had come to expect a similar standard of living to that enjoyed by comparable workers in the UK (Curtis and FitzGerald 1994). The effects of this pressure on labour costs has been aggravated by the increased tax burden required to pay for a higher level of public services. The net result has been very much lower employment and higher emigration than would otherwise have been the case.

This contrasts significantly with the experience of countries with much more closed labour markets such as Portugal. To date labour costs in Portugal have not adjusted to EU levels, leaving them far below levels in Ireland or Spain. This has contributed to a low level of unemployment in Portugal.

However, both through the political system and through bargaining in the labour market, the electorate have voted with their feet for comparability with the UK. These expectations are unlikely to change over the coming decade and this places a further constraint on the scope for economic policy to promote economic development to produce increased employment.

Over the last thirty years there has been frequent reference by governments to the need for a strict incomes policy. However, temporary gains achieved by government efforts to halt wage inflation have generally proved ephemeral. In a democratic society such as ours the levers of power are not available to government to control wage rates. If there is to be a change it will have to come through the development of a consensus involving the trade union movement.

Economic policy in the 1990s

The major area where Irish governments retain power to influence events is the supply side of the economy. There is a wide range of possible detailed interventions which governments can make which might improve the competitiveness and efficiency of the productive sector (FitzGerald and Keegan 1993). The emphasis on the supply side recognises that the Irish economy is competing in a world market and it is only through increasing efficiency and productivity that the growth rate can be raised. This contrasts with the emphasis in the 1970s on increasing demand for goods and services.

The problem for the electorate and for politicians with this approach to policy is that it cannot be summarised in simple terms as it involves a wide range of different kinds of intervention or reform. I refer here to only a sample of the topics which may be of importance.

The recent debate on education, opened up by the Culliton report and the white paper, is a sign of the changing times. While the issue of education and training was treated as important to economic development in the 1960s with the publication of *Investment In Education*, it fell from prominence in the late 1960s with the introduction of free secondary education. Since then there has been surprisingly little debate, in spite of a huge increase in participation in education and the creation of a new training empire from the end of the 1970s. The disadvantage of education as a development tool is that, if it is to produce a pay back, it will not be within the normal electoral cycle.

A range of complex issues will determine the course of energy policy over the decade: the need to promote competition to put pressure on costs; the need to ensure security of supply; the need to reduce pollution. The results of this process will affect economic growth and well-being in the medium to long term. Once again the effects of policy changes will take a considerable time to manifest themselves.

Similar changes are occurring in political debate on economic issues elsewhere in the EU:

> Regulation is becoming a major area of economics because in a world which has given up the debates between socialism and capitalism, it is going to be the major battleground of the opposition between more or less governmental interference in economies, very much like at the end of the eighteenth century when Turgot and Quesnay were debating with Galiani and Diderot the trade regulation of corn. This is quite apparent in Europe where the political debates of the seventies have been replaced by policy debates such as: which part of the telecommunication industry should remain regulated, can generation of electricity be privatised, how should environmental problems be dealt with, how should banks be regulated? (Laffont 1994)

The fields of industrial policy and tax reform are well tilled. They share some of the characteristics of the topics already referred to; changes in policy will not produce instant results while they could prove important to the long-term growth in living standards. They also depend on fairly detailed changes in tax codes or support schemes, details of which are not easy to encapsulate in a simple slogan.

Economics and political debate

The area of economic policy in the 1990s is thus much more complex than in the 1980s. The simple imperative of eliminating the debt has not been replaced with an alternative simple unifying goal for economic policy. In the 1970s economic policy and the interests of the electorate were firmly focused on today and tomorrow. The process of controlling the debt lifted their vision unwillingly to a somewhat longer time frame in the 1980s. However, in the 1990s what is needed is a debate about where the economy is going over the rest of the decade. However, there are major obstacles to such a debate.

The electoral cycle means that in many cases the benefits of the reforms will not be apparent till after the next election. While politicians may be prepared to act in the national interest, will the electorate have the same patience and foresight? The pressures for short-term palliatives, which could prove damaging to employment in the long term, remain serious (Baker, Scott and Wrenn 1992).

As outlined above, explaining the issues which are important for economic policy to a bored electorate is difficult, as evidenced in the low turn-out in the recent European Parliament elections. The complexity of the issues dealt with in the European Parliament (as in the Maastricht Treaty) is a foretaste of things to come. It is difficult for politicians or journalists to capture the essence of important policies in a few simple words. There is always the temptation, as in the recent campaign in Ireland for the European Parliament, to reduce the issues to simple terms such as: how much are we getting from the Structural Funds? However, debate on what the funds are to be invested in is almost absent because, for example, no one wants to discuss the merits of different ways of handling sewerage effluent, even if a significant proportion of the Structural Funds will be spent on this important task! Last year in the debate in the Dáil on the *National Plan* little or no attention was given to the details of the planned investments.

In the debate on the long-term development of the Irish economy the issues are likely to prove more complex still. The traditional political set piece of the budget is rapidly losing economic significance to be replaced in importance by the estimates process and the finance bill, neither of which attracts significant political or media attention.

If we are to do more than react to outside events over the rest of the decade, the political process will have to come to grips with the issues of planning for the long term (Kennedy 1992). If this is to happen it will require some change in the political system, to provide a necessary framework for debate.

NOTES TO ARTICLE

1 See Bradley, Fanning *et al.* 1985, and Barry and Bradley 1991, for an analysis of the effects of fiscal policy in the 1970s and the 1980s.

2 Geary and McCarthy 1976, Geary 1976 and Bradley 1977.

3 This was a central part of the Fianna Fáil programme in 1977, though it was not implemented.

4 See Barry and Bradley 1991. Newell and Symons 1990 using a less sophisticated and less satisfactory approach attribute more of the rise to external forces.

5 See Bradley, Whelan and Wright 1993,Giavazzi and Pagano 1991, and McAleese 1990.

REFERENCES

Bacon, P. (1986), *Medium-Term Outlook: 1986-1900*, Dublin: The Economic and Social Research Institute

Baker, T.S., S. Scott and A. Wrenn. (1992), Dublin: *Quarterly Economic Commentary*, The Economic and Social Research Institute, Spring

Barry, F. and J. Bradley. (1991), Dublin: 'On the Causes of Ireland's Unemployment', *The Economic and Social Review*, vol. 22, no. 4, July

Bradley, J. (1977), Dublin: 'Lags in the Transmission of Inflation', *The Economic and Social Review*, vol. 8

Bradley, J., C. Fanning, C. Prendergast, and M. Wynne. (1985), Dublin: *Medium-Term Analysis of Fiscal Policy in Ireland: A Macroeconometric Study of the Period 1967-1980*, The Economic and Social Research Institute, General Research Series no. 122

Bradley, J., K. Whelan, and J. Wright. (1993), *Stabilization and Growth in the EC Periphery*, Avebury

Cantillon S., J. Curtis and J. FitzGerald. (1994), Dublin: *Medium-Term Review: 1994 -2000*, The Economic and Social Research Institute

Curtis, J. and J. FitzGerald. (1994), 'Convergence in an Open Labour Market', *The Economic and Social Research Institute Working Paper No. 45*

Dornbusch, R. (1990), Dublin: *Ireland and Europe's New Money*, The Economic and Social Research Institute, Geary Lecture

FitzGerald, J. and O. Keegan (Eds.) (1993), *The Community Support Framework 1989-93: Evaluation and Recommendations for the 1994-1997 Framework*, The Stationery Office, Dublin

Geary, P. (1976), Dublin: 'World Prices and the Inflationary Process in a Small Open Economy', *The Economic and Social Review*, vol. 7

Geary, P. and C. McCarthy. (1976), 'Wage and Price Determination in a Labour Exporting Economy – The Case of Ireland', *European Economic Review*, vol. 8, no. 3

Giavazzi, F. and M. Pagano. (1990), 'Can Severe Fiscal Contractions Be Expansionary? A Tale of Two Small European Countries', Cambridge, Mass.: *National Bureau for Economic Research Macroeconomics Annual*, NBER

Honohan, P. (1992), Dublin: 'Fiscal Adjustment in Ireland in the 1980s', *The Economic and Social Review*, vol. 23, no. 3

Kennedy, K. (1992), 'Real Convergence, The European Community and Ireland', *Journal of the Statistical and Social Inquiry Society of Ireland*

Laffont, J.J. (1994), 'The New Economics of Regulation Ten Years After', *Econometrica*, vol. 62, no. 3, May

Lee, J. (1989), Cambridge: *Ireland 1912-1985. Politics and Society*, Cambridge University Press

McAleese, D. (1990), 'Ireland's Economic Recovery', *Irish Banking Review*, pp. 18-32

Newell, A. and J. Symons. (1990), 'The Causes of Ireland's Unemployment', Dublin: *The Economic and Social Review*, vol. 21, no. 5

Sexton, J., B. Walsh, D. Hannan and D. McMahon, Dublin: *The Economic and Social Implications of Emigration*, The National Economic and Social Council, Report no. 90.

Administration, vol. 51, nos. 1-2 (Spring/Summer 2003), 89–104

Planning and the Civil Service 1945-1970

STEPHEN LALOR

Originally published in 1996, vol. 43, no. 4, 57-75. Stephen Lalor was then a higher executive officer in the Department of the Taoiseach.

ECONOMIC BACKGROUND

More or less from the end of the Second World War onwards, but particularly from the end of the Korean War, Ireland was faced with the failure of its economy to compete successfully with the economies of the developed western democracies. The economic progress of western countries, associated with various forms of Keynesianism, was matched by economic and social decay in Ireland.

Some civil servants (such as Joseph Brennan and H.P. Boland) were attracted to the notion of civil service intervention, but their training and experience led them to see such intervention as a largely negative operation, preventing expenditure rather than producing a particular social or economic goal. Younger civil servants, however, including T.K. Whitaker and Patrick Lynch, were beginning to see that goal-directed state intervention in the economy was successful in other countries such as France, where Jean Monnet had been appointed the first General Planning Commissioner in 1945, and that it could produce beneficial results in Ireland if the right conditions arose which would allow state intervention to be initiated.

The economic crisis of the 1950s almost demanded the intervention of the state in the economy. During some economically very bad years, a number of civil servants had been working to create a climate of opinion favourable to a more activist civil service. They did this through papers to learned societies and through the suasion open to them in the course of their official duties. There were politicians and interested members of the public also who were sympathetic to their view, but it is significant that the civil servants never admitted that their enterprise might require administrators to make economic policy. Perhaps they were unaware of it, for both politicians and civil servants explicitly denied that they were doing what they were, in fact, doing. In any event, by the end of the 1950s everything was in place for the creation by the civil service of the most significant public policy of post-war years, the policy of state economic planning.

The plans were called 'Programmes', a word used by James Dillon, leader of the Fine Gael party, as a counterterm to 'plans', but as an OECD paper later pointedly implied, this was a distinction without a difference (OECD 1987, p. 37). The creation of the new policy was carried on by the civil service in what was, by its standards, a blaze of publicity, and with at least the acquiescence of the government of the day. It might be said that the civil service was doing no more than its government-directed duty, but that would be hard to square with what actually took place. To see how this can be so, we must return to the 1940s.

GROUNDWORK

On the 27 April 1945, Patrick Lynch and T.K. Whitaker took part in a debate on full employment at the Statistical and Social Inquiry Society of Ireland. Both were junior officers in the Department of Finance at the time. This, according to Whitaker, was the start of the new approach to national economics, the introduction of the concept of demand management (Whitaker 1983, p. 82). There was in fact an expansionary thrust to public expenditure during the years 1948 to 1951, the period of the first Inter-Party government, which can be attributed not only to post-war catching up with maintenance, development arrears and satisfying of pent-up demand, but also to ideological influences on government (Gould 1981, p. 128). Although the ideological influences to which Gould refers were government ministers, Whitaker implies that his and Patrick Lynch's championing of Keynesian concepts of demand management through fiscal policy inspired the budget speech of 1950 (Whitaker 1983, p. 165), of which speech he himself was the principal draughtsman (Whitaker 1983, p. 83).

The budget speech of 1950 had grown out of an important speech on economic and financial policy made on 19 November 1949 by the Taoiseach, John A. Costello, in which he declared that:

> Indeed, in view of their separate but equal importance, it is desirable to consider carefully whether the advantages of bringing the capital budget and the revenue budget separately to the attention of the Dáil and the public would justify a departure from the traditional practice (*The Irish Times* 21 November 1949).

As Ronan Fanning, the historian of the Department of Finance, pointed out, this speech represents an important intervention in policy-making by a non-politician.

> For Patrick Lynch, who, in consultation with Alexis Fitzgerald, drafted the speech ... it was an unrivalled opportunity firmly to install Keynesian principles at the centre of the government's economic policy. His efforts, embodied in the speech, were strongly if ineffectually resisted by his former colleagues in the Department of Finance (he had moved to the Department of the Taoiseach), with the exception of Whitaker and one or two others. Yet again, the reason why that resistance was ineffective was that their own minister was out of step with them, for McGilligan had been shown the Taoiseach's ... speech in advance and, after going through it word for word with Lynch, did not propose a single alteration of substance (Fanning 1978, p. 458).

The quotation raises the interesting constitutional position of a minister, in this case McGilligan, the then Minister for Finance, being out of step with his officials (while simultaneously demonstrating that civil servants are powerless without politicians). It also points to an interesting difference between developments in Ireland and the United Kingdom. After the 1945 general election in the United Kingdom, the new Labour government committed itself to various economic and social objectives, to be reached through an economic policy called 'democratic planning'. This new policy has been described by Plowden as:

> a mixture of physical controls, nationalisation and exhortation, laced with a dash of Keynesianism and a liberal dose of wishful thinking (Plowden 1989, p. 4).

In Ireland no government with a similar commitment to economic planning, democratic or otherwise, came to power. Any push there may have been to introduce an economic planning policy came from the civil service. The continuing influence of civil servants on the government's economic policy can be seen in the edition of *The Statist* of 3 February 1951, which carried a supplement on the Irish economy, with a number of articles of which one was by McGilligan as Minister for Finance (drafted by Whitaker), and another by Whitaker but published anonymously (Fanning 1978, p. 461). In 1951, however, there was a change of government and at least an apparent retreat from Keynesianism (Bew and Patterson 1982, p. 100). Whitaker would, to some extent, agree.

> In 1951, however, there was not only a change of government but a deterioration in the economic scene ... The new Fianna Fáil government took severely corrective budgetary action in 1952. Mr MacEntee, as Minister for Finance, had strong reservations about

> voted Capital Services because of their political background and the doubtful quality, in his view, of some of the components. Within the Department (of Finance) unease had grown on economic grounds about the automatic equation of 'Capital Service' and 'proper to be met from Borrowing'. The result of all this was that the Estimates Volume for 1952-53 dropped the classification altogether (Whitaker 1983, p. 86).

What this quotation shows, however, is not that the influence of the civil service was waning but that the influence of the younger 'turks' had waned, to the benefit of the older 'turks'. Neither questioned the right of the Department of Finance to have the largest say in economic policy. They disagreed only on its direction.

It is this assumption of the right of the Department of Finance to influence government economic policy which makes two speeches by Dáil Deputies from opposing parties, juxtaposed by Fanning for their remarkable similarity, all the more interesting to students of public administration. Both speeches were made in 1951 in Dáil Éireann, one by John A. Costello and the other by de Valera. Speaking of the officials in the Department of Finance, Costello, for the opposition, said in Dáil Éireann on 7 November 1951:

> They have, I emphasise this, a very distinct, a very valuable function to fulfil in the machinery of government of this State. They are the watchdogs of public finance. It is their duty to point out certain dangers but it is not their function to create economic policy. It is their function to work within the framework of a policy, economic and financial, devised by a government (quoted in Fanning 1978, p. 466).

De Valera replied for the government on 21 November 1951 and defended the Department of Finance against the abuse of TDs. While he admitted that he had his own differences with the Department of Finance, he outlined the duty of the Department as follows:

> It is the duty of the Department of Finance to point out to the Minister for Finance, if he does not see it himself, and through him, to point out to the government, the direction in which they are going. It is for the government then, knowing all the facts which have been brought out by the Department of Finance, to take their line and to choose their policy in their wisdom, even though it may not be in accord with the views of the Department of Finance (quoted in Fanning 1978, p. 467).

In practice the civil service was rather more interventionist than this implies. For example, during the sterling crisis of 1952 the Department of Finance made two submissions to government, both of which the government accepted.

> .... McElligott having taken the precaution of sending confidential and personal notes by hand to the secretaries of the three other major departments the previous evening, urging them to advise their ministers that the "line of action proposed by the memorandum, as deemed necessary by the Minister for Finance, is the right one to follow" (Fanning 1978, p. 480).

It is hardly surprising, therefore, that Costello, probably without knowledge of the events mentioned above and despite his previous praise for the officials of the Department of Finance in 1951, could declare that the economic development plans of the Inter-Party government's Minister for Finance '... have been set aside in favour of the Victorian concepts of economy and ... the officials of the Department of Finance have triumphed over progress' (Fanning 1978, p.481). Surely Costello would have known from his own time in government just how the Department of Finance acts towards its ministers. As with other ministers of various parties, while in government he appears to have been quite satisfied with the Department of Finance; his dissatisfaction appears only when he returns to the opposition benches.

It would be wrong to give the impression that there was singleness of purpose within the Department of Finance at all times, or indeed, ever. While Costello was speaking and at a time when the Department of Finance had removed expenditure to be considered 'proper for Borrowing', as a separate category, from the Estimates, Whitaker was affirming the necessity for exchequer borrowing to finance a state capital programme.

The privacy of the Department of Finance makes it difficult to say with certainty that any particular view which has become public as government policy is, or is not, in accordance with the advice of its officials. Patrick Lynch, who had left the civil service in 1951, wrote in 1953:

> Public confidence in the administrative machinery of the state and in the capacity and judgement of its personnel would be immeasurably strengthened if the facts and considerations on which policy decisions are based were frankly and fully disclosed to the public by means of an extended system of Departmental White Papers or otherwise (Lynch 1953, p. 22).

Difficult as it is to discern the thought process of the Department of Finance without such White Papers, Whitaker has suggested that such publications would not be able to convey the full force of Departmental thinking.

> Incidentally it is from the minutes and oral discussions in which these views are expressed, rather than from White Papers or other means of commending policy decisions to the public, that a

> judgement could best be formed of the "quality of the thought that informs public policy" (Whitaker 1954, p. 64).

The conflict between Lynch and Whitaker on this issue is, however, more apparent than real, if only because there was no question of information relating to the advice given by departmental advisers to government ministers or parliamentary secretaries ever being made public. Fortunately, as we shall see, with the passage of time we have been given some insight into the recesses of the Department of Finance.

If we have lost the oral discussions of the civil servants within the department we still have the minutes, however restricted of access, and there can be no doubt about the ability of the Department of Finance to put its arguments across, to whatever party happened to be in power.

> Early June of 1954 saw yet another change of government and the appointment of a new Minister for Finance, Gerard Sweetman, who, a fortnight after his appointment, submitted a harsh memorandum to the government which, both in form and content, bore a striking similarity to MacEntee's memorandum of the previous autumn ... The government might have changed – although the abstract reference to "a fundamental principle of government policy" did not denote even that; the message emanating from the corridors of Finance clearly had not (Fanning 1978, pp. 500-1).

Not only was the message the same, it was as compelling to the new government as it had been to the previous one. So powerful was the Department of Finance voice at that time that the only bane imaginable was the collapse of the economy and something like that almost happened in the 1950s when panic very nearly turned a crisis into a catastrophe. What gave the civil servants in the Department of Finance their right to persuade ministers was their concern for the national economy, a matter of extreme public interest, and it was that concern which led the Department to face the task of rescuing the economy.

A POLICY IS MADE

In the mid-1950s the economy, which was falling far behind those of its competitors in any event, went into deep crisis. In 1955 there was a marked deterioration in the balance of payments resulting in a deficit of £35m and a fall of the same amount in the net external assets of the banks, that is, about a quarter of the total assets. This was followed by severe corrective measures, special import levies, heavy increases in taxation, and reductions in government spending. These were followed by a collapse in economic activity and massive increases in unemployment and emigration. In the worst year, emigration reached 54,000 while unemployment stood at 74,000. Clearly the economy had gone desperately wrong and needed to be put right. With traditional policies failing, it became clear that new policies were necessary. In the end they came from the Department of Finance.

Although the depth of the crisis exceeded the fears of the Department of Finance, alternative policies to meet that crisis did not spring immediately into existence fully developed. Traditional policies still held sway, while the crisis gave those with alternative views greater credibility with decision-makers. Thus, on 25 May 1956, Whitaker read a paper to the Statistical and Social Inquiry Society of Ireland entitled 'Capital Formation, Saving and Economic Progress' in which his principal conclusions were that:

> (1) ... our national product needs to be enlarged and a greater proportion of it devoted to capital formation.
> (2) The raising of output in agriculture and industry should have a higher priority in the allocation of savings.
> (3) ... To the extent that our limited supply of savings is applied to objects other than to permanent increase in production, a drag is imposed on material progress, and opportunities for self-sustaining employment are restricted.
> (4) Saving and production should be encouraged and excessive consumption discouraged.

Whitaker told the Society that the views he expressed were purely personal, but his appointment as Secretary of the Department of Finance a few days later gives them official weight.

So much importance has been attached to these views expressed by Whitaker, that some commentators have seen in them a policy conflict between Whitaker and Sean Lemass. Paul Bew and Henry Patterson argue that both Lemass and Whitaker were agreed on the need to improve the level of capital formation, but while Lemass sought to finance the programme through the repatriation of assets held abroad, Whitaker followed the more deflationary path of increasing savings. This 'major division' between the two men, according to this view, put at issue

> two different forms of capitalist development. One, embodied in Whitaker's document was liberal, hostile to all impediments to the free working-out of market forces. The other, the 'Lemass line' was concerned, in Mao's words, to 'put politics in command', to pursue those economic policies suitable for the construction of a hegemonic relationship to the working class (Bew and Patterson 1982, p. 194).

Given that, in the event, it was foreign investment which paid for the growth in the economy, it is difficult to pinpoint the precise relevance of Bew's and Patterson's point. Given also that, while the 'major division' was supposed to be separating the Secretary of the Department of Finance from the Minister for Industry and Commerce, the Minister for Finance was appointing one of Whitaker's close colleagues, the Secretary of the Department of Industry and Commerce, John Leydon, to the very important Capital Investment Advisory Committee which had been set up in late 1956, it is difficult to believe that the 'major division' represented an important conflict.

Of greater importance is the fact that the Capital Investment Advisory Committee had, in John Leydon as its chairman, someone who was most unlikely to underestimate his own powers. Another civil servant in 1956 concerned to overcome the country's economic difficulties was Charles Murray, then Assistant Secretary at the Department of the Taoiseach, who, through the Department of External Affairs, was investigating the British Economic Planning Board (Fanning 1978, p. 515).

Within a year of his becoming Secretary of the Department of Finance, Whitaker had begun to take concrete steps to translate the desiderata of his 1956 paper into settled government policy. In May 1957 he held a meeting of his Assistant Secretaries and spoke of the need for the Department of Finance itself to do some thinking about the future economic development of the country.

> ...it is also desirable that this Department (of Finance) should do some independent thinking and not simply wait for Industry and Commerce or the IDA to produce ideas. One of the biggest problems is how to reshape and redirect the public capital programme so that, in association with developments in agriculture, industry, etc., it will provide *productive* and *self-sustaining* employment (quoted in Fanning 1978, p. 509).

The meeting also set up a departmental committee of Assistant Principals to pursue the issues raised at the meeting and to study the 'probable' decline in social investment and the possibilities for productive investments wholly or partly financed by the state. Although much work had to be devoted to other issues, such as negotiations with the World Bank, and the departmental committee had not completed its report, Whitaker felt in a position to approach Ryan, the Minister for Finance, with a proposal for a programme of national development at the end of 1957. The decision was reached at break-neck speed. The relevant documents, published as Appendix I to *Economic Development*, tell the story.

Oifig an Aire Airgeadais
16 Nollaig, 1957.

MEMORANDUM FOR THE INFORMATION OF THE GOVERNMENT

Economic Development

The Minister for Finance circulates, herewith, for the information of the Government, a copy of a minute dated 12th December, 1957, from the Secretary of his Department.

Minister,

1. This note records what I have said to you orally about the desirability of attempting to work out an integrated programme of national development for the next five or ten years, which I believe will be critical years for the country's survival as an economic entity.

. . . . . .

6. With all this in mind and feeling that the central position of the Department of Finance gives us a special responsibility for studying how economic progress can be promoted, I began some time ago the task of bringing together in an accessible form the information which seems most relevant to the determination of future policy in the economic sphere. I append the heads of the scheme on which, with the help of the Central Statistics Office, Mr C.H. Murray and others, I have been working.

7. This, I believe, is work that can best be done, as regards force, consistency and reasonableness, under one person's direction, provided that person has free access for information, advice and assistance to officers of the other Departments and State organisations concerned

8. I would willingly – and as quickly as possible – complete the work in hands, on the basis outlined above, if it is felt that it serves a need and would be of assistance to the Government…

T.K. Whitaker
12th December, 1957

The government considered the memorandum at its meeting on 16 December, and on 18 December, Whitaker got his decision.

Roinn an Taoisigh,
Baile Atha Cliath,
18 Nollaig, 1957

An Rúnaí Príobháideach,

An tAire Airgeadais,

I am to refer to the memorandum (quoted above) ... and to inform you that ... it was arranged:

(1) that the Minister would approve the proposals, submitted to him in the minute, for the preparation of a study embracing:

(a) as groundwork, a brief outline of the present state of the economy, concentrating on the main deficiencies and opportunities,

(b) a statement of the principles to be followed in order most effectively to correct the defects and realise the opportunities and

(c) that, for the purposes of the study, the Secretary of the Department of Finance would have free access, for information, advice and assistance, to officers of the other Departments and State organisations concerned.

M. O Muimhneacháin,
Rúnaí an Rialtais

Whitaker had submitted his minute to his minister on Thursday 12 December, the government considered the memorandum on Monday 16, and the decision reached Whitaker on Wednesday 18 December 1957. The same day he wrote to the heads of the other departments seeking their co-operation, which he received wholeheartedly throughout the preparation of the study (Fanning 1978, p. 515). On Thursday 19 December 1957, Whitaker wrote to the departmental committee arranging for talks on their recently completed report. The officials of the Department of Finance (S. Ó Ciosáin, M. Horgan, D. Ó Loinsigh, J. Dolan, and T. Ó Cofaigh, Dr B. Menton, and M.F. Doyle) who had prepared the departmental report went on to play an important part in the preparation of *Economic Development*, as the study came to be called. Others who played a significant part, or who were consulted in the preparation of the study were Charles Murray of the Department of the Taoiseach, J.J. McElligott at the Central Bank, M.D. McCarthy, the head of the Central Statistics Office; and C.F. Carter, P. Lynch and L. Ryan, the three economists serving on the Capital Investment Advisory Committee.

The urgency with which the decision was made carried into the work on the study itself which was completed and a printed copy circulated to the government on 29 May 1958. The tenor of the report was that we must plan our economic and financial policies with a view to maximising economic progress through devoting more resources to productive purposes. That position was considerably strengthened by the similar conclusions reached in the third report of the Capital Investment Advisory Committee of June 1958, and became impregnable when endorsed by the World Bank. The government, on 22 July, set up a cabinet committee paralleled by an inter-departmental committee to draw up such a plan. It was duly drawn up and the document which was to become popularly known as the 'First Programme' was published as a White Paper, under the title *Programme for Economic Expansion*, on 12 November 1958. On Saturday 22 November 1958, the study from which the *First Programme* had grown was published under the title *Economic Development*.

The *First Programme* outlined the direction which the government felt that various sectors of the economy should take. The policies to which it committed the government itself are set out in paragraph 10 of the introduction.

> The capital we need for productive development must come mainly from our current savings, supplemented by voluntary repatriation of past savings, by foreign investment here and, within due limits, by borrowing from international lending agencies. The facilities provided by the banks, financial institutions and the stock exchanges are of great importance in securing that capital is placed at the disposal of productive enterprise ... It will be the concern of the Government to make sure that capital for productive development is available as cheaply as possible. Saving will be encouraged and any tendency for consumer spending to cause an external payments deficit, and thus reduce the availability of capital for development need, will be checked. Subject to this, financial policy will favour the application of all available resources to productive home purposes, not to the accumulation of future external reserves or investments ... (Ireland *Programme for Economic Expansion* 1958).

The *First Programme* also contained more general statements on such matters as the need to encourage production and saving, holding the cost of services rigidly in check and striving to reduce the effective burden of taxation. Although it was not, and was not intended to be, a detailed statement of tactics, it was, and was seen to be, a crucial strategic policy initiative.

Writing in the autumn 1958 edition of the journal *Administration* Garrett FitzGerald, the future Taoiseach, described the arrival of the new policy as follows:

> The initial reactions, somewhat muted because of the dampening of the *Economic Development* squib in the public press, appeared to

> be remarkably favourable to the policies put forward in these documents. The first reactions of some of the vested interests affected were less violent than might have been expected and as knowledge of the many fundamental changes in policies has gradually spread through the community they have been received in many cases with genuine enthusiasm. The break with the past, implied in all these documents, is in tune with a widespread public mood (FitzGerald 1958, p. 198).

Writing a quarter of a century later, Whitaker was still able to describe the result of his efforts as '... a substantial change in the direction of policy' (Whitaker 1983, p. 90). Thus was a government policy created by civil servants from ideas expressed by a civil servant speaking in a personal capacity to a learned society, the Statistical and Social Inquiry Society of Ireland, in May 1956.

In his 1958 article, FitzGerald gives three possible reasons why the government had *Economic Development* published: first, the desire to provoke intelligent public debate on economic matters; secondly, the desire to use this means to try out the policies on the public; and thirdly,

> … a desire to secure the most widespread acceptance of these new policies by making it as clear as possible that they are not party political policies, but national policies, which, the Government might hope, could in large measure be kept out of the arena of party politics by thus revealing their impeccably non-political origin; ... (FitzGerald 1958, p. 198).

In almost an offhand way FitzGerald is here claiming what ought to be remarkable, that the government of the day not only allowed, but encouraged, the civil service to create government policy, and published that fact to help market that policy to the public.

Given the principles which are supposed to underpin our public administration, it was to be expected that the popular identification of the *First Programme* with the civil service would come under criticism. Reasonably enough, politicians are sensitive to anything that would even seem to diminish their status or power in relation to their civil servants. One forceful critic of the publication of *Economic Development* was Mr James Dillon, leader of the opposition Fine Gael party from 1959 to 1965 (FitzGerald 1968, p. 27). Even Sean Lemass, who knew as much about what was going on as anyone, felt constrained to say, in 1958, that 'In all cases the initiation and shaping of policy in the broadest sense is the prerogative of Government' (Lemass 1958, p. 227). It was said by commentators that civil servants as such 'had no business proposing policy, and certainly not policies of economic planning and development', and yet, in the revolution in public economic policy, civil servants 'aided and goaded by academic economists, played the key role' (Chubb and Lynch 1969, p. 2).

A consequence of the new economic policy and its success was its effect on the civil service itself.

> The first *Programme for Economic Expansion* and Dr Whitaker's publication, *Economic Development* (1958), were an implicit recognition that there was a need for the public service to undertake a new and constructive role in the formation of policy objectives and in devising the means of attaining them (Chubb and Lynch 1969, p. 358).

During the 1960s, with the *First Programme* being followed by the *Second* and *Third Programmes,* it might have been thought that the civil service was doing precisely that, undertaking its new role as policy maker and implementer. When the *Second Programme for Economic Expansion* was launched in August 1963, civil service involvement in the creation of the policy had been so far institutionalised that an Economic Development Division now existed in the Department of Finance. The creation of the Department of Economic Planning and Development in the late 1970s might seem to reinforce that view. Ireland's economic successes led to quite a paradoxical situation, however.

Although Ireland was becoming economically more successful, the civil service was now attacked for not doing better what, in strict theory perhaps, it ought not to have been doing at all (Chubb and Lynch 1969, p. 206). Some even argued that the civil service lacked the structures necessary to carry out those very activities. (It is all a little like those scientists who are said to have proved, aerodynamically, that the bumble bee cannot fly.) The report of the Public Service Organisation Review Group (*the Devlin Report*) contains a distillation of this position.

> Secretaries and Assistant Secretaries, ... are so involved in the stress of daily business that they have little time to participate in the formulation of overall policy for the Departments' functional areas. ... The Minister is forced to concern himself with the details of executive action and the Secretary of his Department must, therefore, be equally involved to the detriment of his role as policy adviser and director and controller of the organisation (Devlin Report 1969, §11.3.2).

Or again,

> If, as we believe, the Secretary's main roles are concerned with policy advice and overall direction and control, organisationally he is not well served. In planning, finance, organisation and personnel he lacks staff support and these important functions are either absent from the formal organisations of Departments or discharged by personnel who often have little or no training in these functions (*Devlin Report* 1969, 11.3.3).

According to the *Devlin Report* 'The new dynamic role expected from the state has everywhere produced demands for a renewal of the public service' (*Devlin Report* 1969, 11.3.11). One is left to wonder where the expectation came from.

If Chubb and Lynch are correct, many were conscious of a national malaise in the middle fifties, but did not know what to do about it, or what its causes were.

> If ever there was a generation enmeshed in its past, it was this one, the slaves not only, as Keynes said, of 'some defunct economist', but other expounders of equally anachronistic social and political principles and constitutional formulae (Chubb and Lynch 1969, p. 2).

While it would be wrong to suggest that the civil service was the only institution in the state to reflect constructively on the country's difficulties, it must be admitted that, despite being apparently administratively, structurally, constitutionally and educationally incapable of taking independent action, it nevertheless played a key role in the efforts to reverse the process of economic collapse, and it did that through the creation of national economic planning.

WHO MAKES POLICY?

Even lifelong members of the civil service seem unable to give a clearcut answer to the question: do civil servants make public policy? We have chronicled, above, the part played by Whitaker and his colleagues in the creation of the policy of national economic planning, yet consider what he said in his 1978 review of Ronan Fanning's history The *Irish Department of Finance 1922-58*:

> A classic definition of the function of an administrative official is given in a [Department of] Finance memorandum quoted on p. 255 of the book: 'it is the duty of civil servants to think all round a subject and give Ministers their unbiased opinions on matters referred to them when policy is being considered, and then when policy has been decided on, to carry out that policy to the best of their ability, regardless of their own personal views'. By and large this prescription has, I believe, been faithfully observed. There are instances in the book of both successful and unsuccessful attempts to have government decisions changed before they solidified. But these were prompted by departmental, rather than personal, motives. There are also, happily, instances of initiatives by public servants which helped rescue Ministers from remaining prisoners of outmoded policies (Whitaker 1983, p. 162).

Not only does Whitaker's career as the most honoured civil servant of his generation conflict with the 'classic' administrative official, but he also undermines the definition in the very paragraph in which he lauds its exemplars. He tries to excuse attempts to have government decisions changed 'before they solidified' on the grounds that they were prompted by 'departmental' motives. And as for the 'rescue of Ministers from remaining prisoners of outmoded policies', which means no more than successful attempts to have government decisions changed *after* they have solidified, he provides no excuse whatsoever.

We have seen that when Whitaker was creating the *First Programme* he believed that the economy was in such a crisis that the country's survival as an economic entity depended upon a fully worked out integrated programme of national development, and that the 'central position' of the Department of Finance gave it a special responsibility to study how economic progress could be promoted. In this belief he was assuming a responsibility which had not been formally devolved to the Department of Finance or its officials. He was also recognising that the nature of the crisis was such that it threatened the wellbeing of everyone who chose to remain a member of Irish society. The health of the economy was a public good, and with no individual, or institution, formally assigned responsibility for its maintenance, it was left to the Department of Finance to intervene to safeguard it in the public interest. Whitaker's response was, characteristically, to meet the challenge with all the resources available to him. It probably never struck him to ask where, in the regulations, it said that he should do so.

REFERENCES

Bew, Paul; Patterson, Henry (1982), *Sean Lemass and the Making of Modern Ireland 1945-66*, Dublin, Gill and Macmillan

Chubb, Basil and Lynch, Patrick (eds. and intro.) (1969), *Economic Development and Planning,* Dublin, IPA

Devlin, Liam St John (1969), 'The Devlin Report: an overview', *Administration*, vol. 17, no. 4, pp. 340-51

Fanning, Ronan (1978), *The Irish Department of Finance 1922-58*, Dublin, IPA

FitzGerald, G. (1958), 'Grey, White and Blue: A review of three recent economic publications', *Administration*, vol. 6, no. 3, pp. 193-203

FitzGerald, G. (1968), *Planning in Ireland: a PEP Study*, Dublin, IPA and London, PEP

Gould, Frank (1981), 'The Growth of Public Expenditure in Ireland; 1947-77', *Administration*, vol. 29, no. 2, pp. 115-35

Lemass, Sean (1958-9), 'The Role of State-sponsored Bodies', *Administration*, vol. 6, no. 4, pp. 277-95

Lynch, P. (1953), 'The Economist and Public Policy', *Studies*, Autumn, reprinted in Chubb and Lynch (1969)

OECD (1987), *Administration as Service: The Public as Client*, Paris

Plowden, William (ed.), *Advising the Rulers*, Oxford, Basil Blackwell (1987) tcd ARTS 351 M. Plowden, *Edwin An Industrialist in the Treasury: The post-war years*, London, Andre Deutsch (1989)

Report of the Public Services Organisation Review Group (1969), Dublin, The Stationery Office

The Irish Times, 21 November 1949

Whitaker, T.K. (1954), 'The Finance Attitude', *Administration*, vol. 2, no. 3, pp. 61-6

Whitaker, T.K. (1983), *Interests*, Dublin, IPA

Administration, vol. 51, nos. 1-2 (Spring/Summer 2003), 105–118

Towards a Corporate State? Sean Lemass and the Realignment of Interest Groups in the Policy Process 1948-1964

GARY MURPHY

Originally published in 1999, vol. 47, no. 1, 86-102.
Gary Murphy was then a lecturer in Government at the Dublin City University Business School.

INTRODUCTION

The decision of the Fianna Fáil government to seek membership of the European Economic Community (EEC) in 1961 marked the climax of a transformation in Irish economic policy formulation. From 1948 when the first inter-party government took office, successive governments were plagued by a series of balance of payment's crises and a general economic malaise, which by the time Fianna Fáil regained office in 1957 had reached epidemic proportions. It had become painfully obvious within the policy-making arena that protectionism, in place since 1932, and the country's over-reliance on the British market offered no real future for Irish agriculture or industry.

Yet this view was not unanimous within or outside the government. Some policy makers were reluctant to accept any form of multilateral trading arrangements which would weaken protected industry and the country's privileged access to British markets. By the end of the 1950s, however, this had become very much a minority view associated mainly with the Department of Industry and Commerce and sections of a number of interest groups, most notably parts of the trade union movement and segments of the protected industrial sector.

The process by which Ireland moved from a protected economy to one where interdependence with other economies was assumed was one in which interest groups participated fully. By the time of the failure of the first application to join the EEC in 1963, economic actors, whether state, political or interest group, realised that Ireland's economic future could not prosper in economic isolation. They were active partners with government in pursuing an aggressive agenda for economic growth. Fundamentally it was the government not the market which brought these actors into the process and it was the government in both its political and administrative forms which gave the lead in promoting new economic strategies. By pointing out these new approaches explicitly to the various economic actors in the Irish body politic, the government was able to set out a concrete agenda for the development of the economy by the early 1960s. Export-led industrialisation and economic co-operation with Europe were at the heart of these new methods.

A CHANGE IN POLICY FORMULATION

How and why did Lemass bring these interest groups with him in this journey towards free trade? The course of Irish economic policy formulation between 1948 and 1964 was determined largely by the political instability which plagued successive governments throughout the period. This instability can be put down to voter disenchantment with the economy. The elections of 1951, 1954 and 1957 were fought principally on economic issues. While there were differing viewpoints within both Fianna Fáil and Fine Gael on the course economic policy should take, voters inevitably blamed the party in government for the stagnation in the economy.

De Valera, although not a firm supporter in any sense of the new financial thinking which had taken root in the Department of Finance with the appointment of T. K. Whitaker as secretary in 1956, nevertheless realised that old remedies had not helped Fianna Fáil politically. By the time Fianna Fáil had lost power for the second time in six years in 1954, de Valera was remote from much of the debate raging within the party and the country at large. He was, however, politically astute enough to know that economic retrenchment, as associated with Fianna Fáil when they went to the country in 1948 and 1954, had been rejected by the electorate. Fine Gael, for their part, were equally as divided. In such circumstances the original dynamic for change in the Irish economy came from two sources: factions within the main political parties and within the civil service. Within this governmental arena, financial ideology reared its head. Supporters of both an activist approach and of the traditional retrenchment approach to economic policy existed in both camps and the story of the development of economic policy in this era was one of a struggle fought out between these two groups at a number of levels.

The introduction of Keynesian economic policies by the first inter-party government in 1948 was the first concrete change in economic policy for a generation (Fanning, 1978; Lynch, 1969). It had its dynamic within both administrative and political frameworks. The driving force behind the introduction of this policy lay in the political field. Patrick McGilligan, James Dillon and Sean MacBride all propagated a change in the prevailing financial ideology within which Irish governments pursued policy.[1] On the opposite side of the political fence Sean Lemass, who was involved in a long running battle with Sean MacEntee as to the course Fianna Fáil should take in economic policy, can be said in theory to have supported this departure; though in the tribal nature of Irish political discourse he opposed most of that government's economic and industrial policy, the creation of the Industrial Development Authority being a notable example.

The first inter-party government saw some intrinsic opposition to this about-turn in economic policy from within the civil service. Both the Central Bank and the Department of Finance took the view that such Keynesian policies would bankrupt the nation. Yet within the civil service, some key individuals, most notably the young Patrick Lynch, who had been seconded from the Department of Finance to act as John A. Costello's personal economic advisor, were avid enthusiasts of a Keynesian agenda. A new generation of civil servants was advancing up the administrative ladder and looked farther afield in the quest to develop the Irish economy. Men like Patrick Lynch, T. K. Whitaker, J. C. Nagle, Charles Murray, Tom Barrington and Tadhg O'Cearbhaill interested themselves in the economic workings of other states and took on wider tasks than those traditionally associated with the Irish civil service.[2] Whitaker, for instance, though a staunch defender of traditional Finance thinking during the first inter-party government, actively studied economic policy formulation in other countries and used this wider experience when he eventually became secretary in 1956.

The first inter-party government can be seen as a prime example of the primacy of politics over economics within a government framework, as the hegemony of Finance and the Central Bank was to some extent dissipated by the active political leadership of some government departments.

DIFFERENCES WITHIN FIANNA FÁIL

The administrative side of government regained control once Fianna Fáil resumed office in 1951. The appointment of MacEntee to Finance was the signal for the department to reassert itself in the wake of McGilligan's path-breaking stewardship. This reassertion must be viewed, however, in terms of Finance stressing the age-old solutions for economic problems that were associated with that department since the early 1920s. MacEntee was a classic deflationist. He was a firm believer in fiscal rectitude and abhorred the Keynesian policies of his predecessor. With J. J. McElligott, who had been secretary of the department since 1927, MacEntee set about placing financial policy back on the straight and narrow path of deflationary virtue (Lee, 1989, p. 324). Fine Gael, back in opposition, lost their collective nerve, leaving it to the Lemass wing of Fianna Fáil to provide the active opposition to such traditional thinking. The minutes of the Fianna Fáil parliamentary party show quite clearly how wide this dispute was. Lemass could not afford to leave MacEntee with a clear run and control of economic policy. There was no guarantee that he would automatically replace de Valera once 'the chief' retired.

Lemass could not let the economic assert itself over the political within the administrative framework of government at this time. Thus his disputes with MacEntee over the whole thrust of economic policy can be seen in these terms. One such dispute erupted in late 1952 when Deputy Michael Moran urged that 'a special meeting be held in the near future for a full discussion of government policy'.[3] A meeting of the full Fianna Fáil parliamentary party in January 1953 was consequently devoted entirely to economic policy. During the course of the discussion de Valera explained that the policy of the party was 'to pay its way and that any additional services called for by the people could only be paid for by taxation' and stressed that 'increased production – principally from the land – was the remedy for most of our problems'.[4] While this was traditional Fianna Fáil policy, it did not satisfy all within the party, and within six months a motion sponsored by twenty deputies was put before the parliamentary party declaring:

> The party is of the opinion that in present circumstances a policy of financial austerity is no longer justified and requests the government to frame a progressive policy suited to the altered situation, with a view especially to putting an end to the undue restriction of credit by the banks, and making low interest loans available for farmers and house purchasers.[5]

The debate which followed this motion lasted through July and, when no decision was reached, was then postponed until after the summer recess. The topic, however, was not discussed again until January 1954. The minutes of this particular meeting are brief, simply declaring that:

> …after a number of teachtai had contributed to the debate, the acting Minister for Finance, Prionsias MacAogain [Frank Aiken], replied and An Taoiseach made a comprehensive statement on the party's financial and economic policy, Deputy Carter withdrew the motion on behalf of the teachtai who signed it.[6]

There is no further record in the Fianna Fáil parliamentary party minutes dealing with economic policy until January 1957, by which time the second inter-party government had almost run its course. The attempts by some deputies to place government economic policy on an expansive footing did not succeed, as financial policy continued to be restrictive notwithstanding the launch of a national development fund for capital projects in 1953. Despite this scheme, Fianna Fáil would go to the country in 1954 defending a strictly conservative economic record. The result was to be a second spell in opposition within three years as they lost four seats in the general election and saw John A. Costello form a new administration. When Fianna Fáil regained office in 1957, de Valera, crucially, relegated MacEntee from Finance. In essence this left Lemass with the scope to reshape economic relations in the way he wanted. This was principally due to the electoral fortunes of Fianna Fáil, and not to any great shift in financial ideology. De Valera, although he can have had little stomach for it himself, undoubtedly realised that in the electorally fluid 1950s, economic expansion could well mean political success.

TOWARDS THE CORPORATE STATE

It is within these parameters that one can see Lemass's courtship of the various economic interest groups in the period. He instinctively knew that the development of the country in economic terms necessarily revolved around a corporatist-style arrangement with the government leading these groups in a new economic partnership. For that to happen, Lemass realised that government in its political form would have to be the hegemonic player in the administrative system. Of even more importance was that he be at the head of such a system, and for that to happen he would have to devise a long-term economic strategy that would return Fianna Fáil to government. While he bemoaned the fact that civil servants did not do enough independent thinking, he was firmly of the belief that it was political government which should lead.

It is in these terms that one can see the evolution in the process of the formulation of public policy towards a more conscious and overtly corporatist set of arrangements. Within these parameters, the political interests, particularly in the form of Lemass, would lead, but it was intrinsic that individual interest groups play a full and active role. Thus the formalisation of the identities of the major interest groups – farmers, business, and trade unions – began (Murphy, 1996). Moreover, aspects of the civil service became more active as the 1950s continued. Ultimately Whitaker's *Economic Development* (1958) was the culmination of a major strand of activism within parts of the higher echelons of the civil service. A decade earlier there had not been anyone saying that civil servants had a long-term policy-planning role in economic and social affairs. While it is true that many decision makers in the civil service were happy to take a back seat and perform their tasks as they had always done, there was a vigorous band within administrative circles who believed that it was not just the job of the senior civil servant to advise, but it was also imperative that they do some independent thinking which could then be presented to their political masters. Although the period of the second inter-party government was a time when traditional economy was in the ascendant, as the policies pursued by that government mirrored the previous administration, once Fianna Fáil regained power in 1957 the civil service, or more correctly some sections of it, should be seen as an acknowledged part of any tripartite arrangement between Lemass and the various economic partners (Lalor, 1996).

There was a gradual maturation of relations between the emerging interest groups and the government in the policy realm during this period. Relations between both the second inter-party government and the Fianna Fáil government which succeeded it, and the National Farmers Association (NFA), had been fraught with difficulty since the NFA' s foundation in 1955. This relationship, stormy at the best of times, took on an even more acrimonious tone once the abrasive Paddy Smith became Minister for Agriculture in 1957. By 1964 the government were in the process of redefining their relations with the agricultural lobby. After some nine years of vigorous lobbying the NFA were to receive formal recognition, as the government declared that in future they would welcome regular and full discussions and consultations with them in the formulation of government policy, both broad and specific. For Paddy Smith the government's difficulty had been in finding a 'basis for fruitful co-operation while the NFA reserve the right to be destructively critical of every move made by me to help farmers, and to use meetings with me and my officials as the basis of biased attacks on us and on government policy'.[7]

He thus considered that the government might as well be dealing with the NFA on a formal footing in the future. He was of the opinion that a well-organised farmers' organisation had a really valuable job to do and that it was in his own interests to work with them and give a fair hearing to any proposal of a constructive nature that they might put before him. Thus in the Dáil on 16 February 1964 Lemass gave official recognition to the NFA:

> We recognise that the NFA has a special status among farmers' organisations insofar as it is interested in all branches of agriculture and we made it clear to them that we welcome the prospect of regular comprehensive consultations and discussions with them in connection with the formulation of agricultural policies in the broad sense as well as their practical co-operation in respect of the different aspects of agriculture. This special status will be taken

> into account by us in appointing farmers' representatives on boards and so on.[8]

While the NFA received formal government recognition, Smith was disturbed at the whole thrust of Lemass's economic policies. After Lemass took over as Taoiseach in 1959, Smith found it increasingly difficult to accommodate himself to Lemass's economic and social viewpoints (Robins, 1993, p. 151). Lemass's co-opting of the farmers into a formal negotiating relationship with the government was mirrored in his attitude to the unions. Smith, however, saw the courting of the unions as sacrificing rural to urban interests. One can see both Lemass's courting of the unions and his formalising of relations with the NFA as the beginnings of a corporatist-style approach to government in the early 1960s, in that a formal political structure was put in place which integrated the NFA and Congress as socio-economic groups through a system of representation with the government. The farmers' organisations and the farming community in general, however, were extremely wary of Lemass.

The farming lobby's disappointment at losing out on the enlarged market of the EEC made them only more determined to advance their cause by any means possible. The government, notwithstanding the fact that the relationship had been formalised, continued to find it difficult to maintain harmonious relations with the farming bodies. An increase in government subventions in 1963, such that the cost of these agricultural supports to the taxpayer for the first time exceeded £40 million, did not satisfy the NFA. Moreover they proclaimed that the increase was entirely due to them. Lemass echoed the frustrations of the government:

> Notwithstanding the dimensions of this support to agriculture, notwithstanding the substantial increase in the volume of this support in recent years, the Government were getting very little thanks from the professional spokesmen of farmers' organisations. I want to make it clear that we are not looking for thanks. …But I want to say that I, and all members of the Government party, are becoming increasingly fed up with the constant propaganda which is being circulated amongst farmers that these provisions were made, this assistance given, and these new schemes of agriculture devised not because we wanted to do so but because we were forced into giving them by reason of pressure and agitation. This is not true; it was never true and it never will be.[9]

He also claimed that ordinary farmers in the community had a very lively appreciation of what the government had done and was striving to do to improve the situation for them. His quarrel was with the NFA, not ordinary farmers.

Yet there can be little doubt that ordinary farmers looked to their respective organisations for leadership and indeed blamed the government for what they saw as their increasing difficulties. The NFA was mobilised from the bottom upwards (Collins, 1993, p. 111). Any improvement in the general position of agriculture would be credited to their leadership, not to the government. In essence it was in an atmosphere of mistrust and suspicion that state-farmer relations were conducted in this period; a time when the government was trying to broaden Ireland's industrial base and in which the farming community feared that they would be left behind as industry boomed in a rising tide of prosperity. Yet this period also saw the formal recognition of the role of farmers' organisations in the formulation of policy. It was perhaps naive of Lemass to expect that, having invited the farmers to sit at the policy table, they should abandon the confrontational style that had in their eyes won them that approach. By the early 1960s, for all their blueshirt antecedents (Manning, 1986), the NFA had come to be seen by Fianna Fáil ministers as a troublesome but essentially apolitical grouping: ten years earlier they would have regarded them simply as 'Fine Gaelers' on tractors (Murphy, 1996, p. 198). The depoliticisation of interest group politics, as seen in the formalisation of relations between the Fianna Fáil government and the NFA, can be viewed as an example of how far Lemass had gone in his attempts to create new political relationships and structures in the Ireland of the early 1960s.

While clearly the farmers remained the most overtly selfish and sectional group, even they came to take some heed of the national, as distinct from the purely agricultural, interest. Moreover the vision articulated by the Irish Congress of Trade Unions (ICTU) is really quite striking, in that they were able to take a dispassionate and long-term view of the country's economic prospects in addition to attempting to advance the long-term sectional interests of their members. The reunification of the trade union movement in 1959 gave Lemass the opportunity to knit the unions and employers together into a new framework, that he hoped would achieve industrial progress (Horgan, 1997, p. 228). The crucial moment in the development of union/business/government relations in the period was the establishment of the Committee on Industrial Organisation (CIO) in 1961 in which Congress and the Federation of Irish Industries (FII) were directly represented. Originally Congress was left out and had to demand to be included. Garret FitzGerald, who at this stage was an advisor to the FII, argued that it had to work with the government in a general review of economic policy and approached Whitaker as to the feasibility of the study. This was truly a radical step for business to take. Whitaker readily agreed and FitzGerald maintained that it was simply due to an oversight that the unions were omitted, noting that they proved to be very constructive partners. Ultimately the tensions that existed within the CIO were between the Department of Industry and Commerce on the one hand and the Department of Finance, the FII and ICTU on the other, with the latter endeavouring to persuade Industry and Commerce into a psychological acceptance of free trade (FitzGerald, 1991, p. 59).

When the CIO reports began to appear in the autumn of 1962, they showed the weakness of Irish industry, especially when it came to export potential. Not all industrialists were in favour of entry to the EEC. One was Aodogan O'Rahilly, a successful businessman who was involved in the production of roofing tiles and became chairman of Bord na Móna in 1959. Although a close associate of Lemass, he was deeply worried:

> While I welcomed foreign investment, I believed that if we were going to enter the EEC then our sovereignty would be lost and in a free trade environment we would quickly go under. I drew comparisons between entry to the EEC and the passing of the Act of Union as I foresaw Irish industry dying, just as what happened in the early 1800s due to the operation of economic laws. In many ways I suppose I was an old-style Fianna Fáil nationalist.[10]

More typical, however, was the response of Jack Fitzpatrick of the FII who told *Hibernia* that Ireland would join the EEC and the result would be the 'blossoming of our economy'.[11] Officially the FII had become a supporter of Whitaker's policy of economic planning. It noted in its official journal that 'in the midst of the activities in preparing for entry into the EEC it is good to see that the Government have not lost sight of their economic planning programme which will have an important bearing on our preparedness to face the challenge of the common market'.[12]

The CIO was part of a continuing corporatist-style initiative by Lemass to involve the unions and industry in the policy of economic development in that it saw the development of a political structure which organised the socio-economic groups through a system of representation and co-operative mutual interaction at the leadership level and social control at the mass level. Moreover Lemass's desire to incorporate the unions found an echo in the dominant trend of corporatist thinking within the trade union movement itself (Hutton, 1991, p. 63). The Employer Labour Conference came into existence in 1962 and the National Industrial and Economic Council (NIEC) was established a year later. These new agencies paralleled the state's commitment to economic planning, although if Ireland had succeeded in gaining entry to the EEC in 1963 it is doubtful what impact they would have subsequently had in policy formulation (Girvin, 1994, p. 127). The unions did play a positive role in bodies such as the CIO and the NIEC, with both Donal Nevin and John Carroll, former general secretaries of ICTU and the Irish Transport and General Workers Union (ITGWU) respectively, arguing that they could have taken the attitude that 'it is none of our business, but instead played a positive role'.[13]

Although Congress only gave lukewarm support to the original EEC application they offered no dissension to Lemass's strategy when they met him in January 1962. Lemass urged them to accept that changes were underway in Ireland's relationship with the wider world and that existing preferential arrangements with Britain were already weakened. He reiterated his intention to seek membership under the best terms possible, but said that they would have to operate on the assumption that tariffs would have to be removed by the beginning of 1970. He stressed that it was his view that:

> State aids to industry designed to promote efficiency should be regarded as desirable ... though the form of aid in some cases would be modified... In general it appeared likely that the question of adjustment to common market conditions would be a problem of the position of individual firms rather than industrial groups.[14]

This implied that even in the absence of EEC membership considerable changes in the Irish economy would be necessary.

DEVELOPING A FREE TRADE ETHOS

In essence by the early 1960s the government had decided that the future direction of the Irish economy lay in it being associated with the EEC. The trade union movement were initially lukewarm in their endorsement of this approach but were co-opted by Lemass and subsequently involved in discussions on the future development of economic policy. Wage negotiations overlapped throughout this period with the evolution of an external economic stance and the union movement recognised that higher wages and higher productivity depended on the expansion of the Irish economy. The government, industrial groups and the trade unions recognised that industry would have to develop rapidly to meet the rigours of free trade competition. As John Conroy, General President of the ITGWU, pointed out at the time: 'freer trade is coming and unless we all realise this and prepare we will find that every workshop and factory not fully and efficiently equipped will cease to produce to economic requirements and all the employees will find themselves unemployed'.[15]

The CIO had pointed out the inadequacies of industry to cope with the transition from a protective framework to an interdependent economy. All parties involved recognised that there could be no return to a protectionist position and they resolved to adopt a trilateral approach in their attempt to revolutionise the Irish economy in the light of new free trade conditions. For instance the FII, although they urged hesitation before proceeding with a unilateral course of tariff reductions (Bew and Patterson, 1982, p. 142), had come to the realisation that their best hope of retaining influence on government policy lay in following Lemass's agenda: an agenda whose only variable was the pace of liberalisation. A consensus had emerged that it was better to face an unpredictable world as a member of an economic alliance rather than as an isolated economy, and an export-led growth initiative was to be adopted. Ireland's economic interests had taken on a wider agenda, one which required the input of the farming community, industry and the trade unions. Thus, as the debates about entry into Europe gathered pace in the late 1950s and early 1960s, in many ways the position of the business leadership was quite similar to that of the unions. While there were two distinct views, about any proposed entry of a trading bloc, within the business community as well as the unions, it is clear that they realised that the country's economic fortunes and those of their members were interlinked.

CONCLUSION

In essence, Lemass, from 1957 the undisputed prime economic player in government, embarked on a programme to haul the Irish economy out of the dark ages of financial austerity, mass emigration and inadequate employment. He did this by setting out to establish a broadly European style proto-corporatist social democracy, involving all the key players collectively in responsible decision-making.

By the early 1960s most states in Western Europe were actively intervening in the economy in order to achieve the economic expansion that their citizens were demanding. This was particularly true of the Scandinavian states, although most other countries also pursued a consensual approach to economic management in this period (Katzenstein, 1985). Lemass wanted Ireland to share in the rapid economic growth that had been a feature of most European states after the Second World War. He had a long-range vision for the Irish economy and realised that age-old methods had not worked in the past and were most unlikely to do so in the future.

His relations with ICTU and the NFA are clear examples of his attempts to build such a social democracy. The emergence of both players as recognised elements in national policy-making is the crucial sign in Lemass's attempts to build what we might call the broad-based church of economic interest groups. It was essential that both farmers and unions be involved as well as business. While Lemass's views did not please everyone in Fianna Fáil, as witnessed particularly by the resignation of Paddy Smith as Minister for Agriculture in 1964, the Fianna Fáil of the early 1960s was a distinctly different party to that which had lost power in 1948. A new generation of politicians, influenced greatly by Lemass, were comfortable with the innovative direction of economic policy that had Europe as its ultimate goal and left behind outmoded theories of self sufficiency.

By the early 1960s Europe was in fact the goal of the majority of politicians and interest groups, with even the Catholic Church voicing no overt protest.[16] By the time of the application to the EEC in 1961 all the interest groups which Lemass had co-opted in his quest to make Ireland a more competitive economy were advocates of entry. Policy was to be formulated with these interest groups in mind. Thus Lemass resolved that the state would have to show the way. His opportunity presented itself out of a national economic malaise and he was determined not to waste it. The government, of which he was all but nominally in charge from 1957 on, would pursue policies of economic expansion and would engage with the economic interests to see its aims succeed. Ultimately it was politics which had reasserted itself.

Yet Lemass still faced opposition from his old stomping ground of Industry and Commerce. While it was Whitaker who convinced Lemass that free trade had to be taken on board, it was Lemass who had to ensure that Industry and Commerce left their protectionist mentality behind.[17] He did this to such an extent that by 1963 Industry and Commerce were maintaining that they 'wholeheartedly' supported a phased cut in tariffs.[18] While European economic integration was not an explicit feature of either *Economic Development* or the *First Programme for Economic Expansion* (1958), developments within the economic superstructure had shown policy makers that they could not exist independently of the free trading blocs that had emerged in Europe from the 1950s onwards. This was particularly true once Britain decided that she could no longer ignore these developments. Whitaker was the main instigator in Ireland's move towards economic interdependence with Western Europe. Lemass took some convincing, but once persuaded, he became the most enthusiastic advocate of membership to such a bloc – in Ireland's case the EEC – since Britain had applied to join that body, and used his political power to ensure that some of the more reluctant civil service departments supported him. Ireland's economic needs had taken on a new agenda. An activist Taoiseach, Lemass had brought his party with him, and in the process had fundamentally changed their economic philosophy. Assisted by dynamic elements within the civil service, he had embarked on a route that assumed interdependence with other economies. To secure a consensus on this he engaged in meaningful and normal dialogue with economic interest groups. By 1964 the primacy of the political process was fully recognised. Civil servants and the economic interests had a vital role to play, but it was Lemass who was in charge of economic development.

NOTES TO ARTICLE

1 McGilligan was Minister for Finance, Dillon was Minister for Agriculture and MacBride was Minister for External Affairs in the first inter-party government.

2 Whitaker and Murray became secretaries of the Department of Finance, Nagle became secretary of the Department of Agriculture, O'Cearbhaill became secretary of the Department of Labour and Barrington became the first director of the Institute of Public Administration.

3 Fianna Fáil, Parliamentary Party Minutes, 441/A, 26 November 1952.

4 ibid., 14 January 1953.

5 ibid., 22 July 1953.

6 ibid., 27 January 1954.

7 National Archives, Department of the Taoiseach, S. 17543A/63, Smith to Lemass, 20 November 1963.

8 Dáil Debates, vol. 206, col. 1794, 16 February 1964.

9 Dáil Debates, vol. 206, col. 1218, 12 December 1963.

10 Author's interview with Aodogan O'Rahilly, 14 May 1994.

11 Fitzpatrick is quoted in *Hibernia*, March 1962.

12 *Industrial Review*, the Journal of the Federation of Irish Industries, vol. 18, no. 5, September/October 1961.

13 Author's interviews with Donal Nevin, 19 October 1995 and John Carroll, 29 August 1996.

14 National Archives, Department of the Taoiseach, S.17120A/62, meeting between the Taoiseach, the Minister for Industry and Commerce and the Irish Congress of Trade Unions, 11 January 1962.

15 Conroy is quoted in the *Irish Press*, 10 July 1963.

16 Author's interview with Archbishop Joseph Cassidy, 7 April 1996.

17 Author's interview with T. K. Whitaker, 16 May 1994.

18 Department of Finance, F.121/36/63, Department of Industry and Commerce, memorandum for the government, unilateral 10 per cent tariff cut, November 1962.

REFERENCES

Bew, P. and Patterson, H. (1982), *Sean Lemass and the Making of Modern Ireland*, 1945-1966, Dublin: Gill and Macmillan.

Collins, N. (1993), 'Still Recognisably Pluralist? State-Farmer Relations in Ireland', in R. Hill and M. Marsh (eds.), *Modern Irish Democracy: Essays in Honour of Basil Chubb*, Dublin: Irish Academic Press.

Fanning, R. (1978), *The Irish Department of Finance 1922-1958*, Dublin: Gill and Macmillan

FitzGerald, G. (1991), *All in a Life: An Autobiography*, Dublin: Gill and Macmillan.

Girvin, B. (1994), 'Trade Unions and Economic Development', in D. Nevin (ed.), *Trade Union Century*, Dublin: Mercier.

Horgan, J. (1997), *Sean Lemass: The Enigmatic Patriot*, Dublin: Gill and Macmillan.

Hutton, S. (1991), 'Labour in the post-independence Irish State: An overview', in S. Hutton and P. Stewart (eds.), *Ireland's Histories: Aspects of State, Society and Ideology*, London: Routledge.

Katzenstein, P. (1985), *Small States in World Markets*, New York: Cornell University Press.

Lalor, S. (1996), 'Planning and the Civil Service 1945-1970', *Administration*, vol. 43, no. 4, pp. 57-75, Dublin: Institute of Public Administration.

Lee, J. J. (1989), Ireland 1912-1985: *Politics and Society*, Cambridge: Cambridge University Press.

Lynch, P. (1969), 'The Irish Economy since the War, 1946-1951', in K. B. Nowlan and T. D. Williams (eds.), *Ireland in the War Years and After 1939-1951*, Dublin: Gill and Macmillan.

Manning, M. (1986), *The Blueshirts,* 2nd edn, Dublin: Gill and Macmillan.

Murphy, G. (1996), 'The Politics of Economic Realignment: Ireland, 1948-1964', unpublished PhD thesis, Dublin City University Business School.

Robins, J. (1993), *Custom House People*, Dublin: Institute of Public Administration.

Official Publications:

Programme for Economic Expansion (1958), Dublin: Pr 4696.

Economic Development (1958), Pr 4808.

Administration, vol. 51, nos. 1-2 (Spring/Summer 2003), 119–139

The Celtic Tiger, Inequality and Social Partnership

KIERAN ALLEN

Originally published in 1999, vol. 47, no. 2, 31-55.
Kieran Allen was then a lecturer in the Department of Sociology, University College Dublin.

The Irish economy is booming. In the five years to 1998 growth has averaged 7.58 per cent making Ireland the fastest growing economy in the OECD (Sweeney, 1998, p. 14). Of course, there are some difficulties with the bald claims for growth. Transfer pricing by multinationals has exaggerated the figures for production. Paul Sweeney, one of the more enthusiastic writers about the Celtic Tiger, cited the example of the Coca Cola factory in Drogheda, which employed 200 workers but claimed it made $400 million in profit (Sweeney, 1998, p. 47). These enormous profits seem to result from a policy of artificial pricing within the firm to take advantage of Ireland's low tax regime.

Nevertheless, the existence of transfer pricing does not quite justify the argument of one commentator, who noted that Irish economic figures had 'about the same empirical status as moving statues, flying saucers and the statues of Elvis-found-on-Mars stories' (Ó Gráda, 1997, p. 33). Evidence of Ireland's boom is everywhere. Dublin's skyline is now marked by scores of construction cranes. More women have joined the workforce in the five years between 1991 and 1996 than in the twenty previous years. A burgeoning restaurant culture has emerged as leisure habits change. It might even be argued that the new-found pride in Irish ethnicity is related to the tales of an economic boom.

Yet the boom has also produced considerable unease. Many complain that only the wealthy have gained. A greater sense of relative deprivation seems to have emerged in response to the more conspicuous consumption of wealth in some quarters. In the traditionally working-class area of Ringsend in Dublin, for example, local discontent at the building of 'gated communities' was heightened by the fact that there is no longer affordable housing for the offspring of those who normally resided in the area.

This discontent has rarely found adequate public expression in research institutes, colleges, or even lobby networks. There certainly have been criticisms, but they tend to be muted and restrained by a desire to celebrate Ireland's success story (see O'Hearn, 1998). One of the reasons for this is that few have questioned the social partnership ideology that has established a hegemonic position among the institutions. Where discontent is recognised among PAYE employees, for example, it is often conceived as a form of consumerism. Against the pressure for sectional demands, many advocate a form of social partnership which purports to give a voice to the excluded. From this perspective, Ireland seems to have escaped the rigours of neo-liberalism and has even pioneered a more caring approach to the market place.

I wish to challenge this ideology of social partnership. It is the contention of this chapter that the institutions and networks which have developed over the ten-year period of social partnership have masked a process whereby resources are being transferred back to the wealthier sections of society. The term ideology is used advisedly. An ideology may be defined as a set of ideas, shared by a large number of people, which forms some kind of coherent related system and is connected to the maintenance of power and economic privilege. Dominant ideologies typically work by masking conflicts of interest and by presenting their outlook as the most practical, rational and feasible. As Eagleton (1991) has pointed out, 'dominant ideologies help to unify a social formation in ways convenient for its rulers... it is not simply a matter of imposing ideas from above but of securing the complicity of the subordinated classes' (p. 30).

Such complicity is often secured through the ideological co-option of intellectuals associated with movements of subordinate groups or through exercising hegemony over official leaderships – so that they see no alternative but to work through a social partnership framework. My particular focus in this chapter is on how inequality is being ideologically articulated within the framework of social partnership at present.

MARGINALISATION AND SOCIAL EXCLUSION

The dominant concepts used to conceptualise inequality within the Celtic Tiger are 'marginalisation' and 'social exclusion'. Within particular limits these terms often convey an important meaning. The long-term unemployed are excluded from various forms of social activity. The children of unskilled manual workers experience forms of social exclusion when it comes to entry to a college education. Cities are increasingly structured so that ghettos of poverty are created on the suburbs. And the concerns of poor people are marginalised through a form of consensus politics that rhetorically expresses a concern about social exclusion while still ensuring that elite structures are maintained.

Nevertheless, there are also difficulties with the use of these terms. For one thing, the poor are conceived as objects of a most general process. They are described as 'marginalised' and 'socially excluded' but there is little discussion on who is excluding or marginalising them. It seems to be a process with no active subjects. If references are made to groups who are excluding others, they are usually made in the most general form possible. So one writer who argued that the socially excluded tend to be concentrated in particular social groups, explained that ' "insiders" may exploit cultural solidarities or the costs of their replacement, transforming boundaries that exclude outsiders into inequalities' (Silver, 1995). But who these insiders are or how they are structured in class terms is never explained. It would seem that no defined group has a direct interest in the maintenance of poverty or exclusion.

More importantly, the interests of the poor are conceived to be in opposition to the majority of society. Here for example is how one writer characterises the threefold division of the labour force:

> The first of these are 'tenured employees' who have job security, form the back bone of the trade union movement and are concerned to protect their own jobs. Secondly, there is a large body of 'temporary employees' who have jobs without the traditional life time security associated with these jobs. This group is growing in number and is engaged in contract, temporary, part time and casual employment. The third group are the permanently unemployed. This group finds it very difficult to get any form of paid employment and becomes trapped in a vicious cycle of poverty and idleness (Healy and Reynolds, 1990, p. 66).

What is interesting here is not so much the relative proportions of each category that is implied to exist – but how the interests of the 'tenured employees' are presented as opposed to those of the rest. The 'tenured employees' only look after their own sectional interests and therefore presumably need to be harnessed within the framework of social partnership so that lobby groups on behalf of the poor get a hearing.

The opposition between the 'deserving poor' and organised employees bent on class struggle is a familiar one in catholic social teaching. It has also played an important role historically in the populist policies associated with Fianna Fáil. This party has often presented itself as a 'compassionate' defender of the under-privileged while working actively to expand indigenous Irish capital (see Allen, 1997).

This separation and indeed opposition of the interests of the poor and the wider working population can draw on a substantial intellectual legacy. One is a notion that the working class has declined, only to be replaced by a privileged middle class who espouse sectional outlooks. This argument often draws heavily on the tradition of Weberian sociology, which has until recently achieved an almost unquestioned dominance within Irish sociology. The book *Understanding Contemporary Ireland* may serve as an example. Written by researchers who worked in the ESRI, it draws on the Weberian tradition of sociology to acknowledge the existence of inequality but to conceptualise it in terms of a privileged 'middle class' dominating state structures. The class system is seen in terms of a series of empty places which are filled by three basic market capacities – capital, educational skills, and labour skills. These are the attributes with which individuals 'can bargain in the markets of capitalist society in exchange for an income' (Breen et al., 1990, p. 11). Added to this traditional Weberian notion of the class structure is an 'underclass', who rely on social welfare income maintenance. Because of the growth of 'credentialism' Breen et al. argued that over one-half of the work force was 'middle class' in 1985 (p. 59).

> The class position of most families had already been established in the 1960s and 1970s. This depended by and large on the ability to take advantage of the opportunities for education opened up in those decades and consequently to secure access to a favoured niche in the class system (Breen et al., 1990, p. 68).

The notion that the Irish class structure is dominated by a 'middle class' who have secured a favourable niche, allows Breen et al. to both express a concern about inequalities but nevertheless adapt to the traditional ESRI demand for more public sector cuts.

Another less subtle and more direct source of the polarity between the marginalised and the majority of employees is John K. Galbraith's 1992 book *The Culture of Contentment*. Although it pointed to the growing inequalities in American society, it argued that the majority were not merely complicit but had a vested interest in these inequalities. According to Galbraith the fundamental division in society was now between a 'contented majority' and a 'functional underclass'. The contented majority believe that they are receiving their just deserts and are 'very articulate about what seems to invade their state of self satisfaction'. This majority, which includes 'a certain if diminishing number who were once called proletarians' will employ highly convenient social and economic doctrines that were once used by a handful of aristocrats or capitalists to justify their position (pp. 19-20). The underclass are excluded from the modern political structures and pose an ever-present hazard of inner-city violence and drug use which threaten to embrace the whole of society.

The debt which modern Catholic social teaching owes to Galbraith is openly acknowledged in the reports of the Conference of Religious of Ireland. Galbraith's notion of a selfish majority helps to transmute class conflict into a conflict over moral values. Thus one recent CORI report noted that the demands for social change are blocked because of:

> the present shroud over our western world where the majority of the people live in comfort and affluence. In the past the 'contented' class (the well off and privileged) were a small minority of the population. Now, however, they constitute a majority of most voting populations and consequently are in a position to ensure societies are run in their interests (Conference of Major Religious Superiors of Ireland, 1993, p. 17).

WHERE IS THE CONTENTED MAJORITY?

Many objections can be made about this polarity of a contented or middle-class majority and an excluded or underclass minority.

The first relates to the vagueness of the general category used to define a major section of society. In what sense, for example, is a routine clerical employee and a chief executive assigned to the same class grouping? The term middle class simply disguises the differences of interest that exist, even within occupations labelled 'white collar'. And as Stanley Aronowitz has pointed out, ' "white collar" is a label that presupposes an essential difference between the structure of labour in the factory and the office. It is a category of social ideology rather than of social science' (Aronowitz, 1973, p. 292).

Secondly, the Weberian model of stratification takes little cognisance of class conflict. It acknowledges only a form of social gradation – akin to a social ladder rather than any fundamental conflict of interest. Conflict of interest is reduced to a form of competitive closure that is practised by a wide variety of social groups.

Thirdly, both Galbraith's and the Weberian model look on social class as a form of consumption in the market place. By failing to acknowledge the role of production and the relations different groups possess to the means of production, it ignores the possible levels of exploitation and dominance that structure the conflict between classes.

Lastly, the term underclass possesses a similar vagueness. The groups that constitute the underclass vary greatly. In Galbraith's case it seems to refer to a working poor who take on jobs others find distasteful (Galbraith, 1992, p. 33). Other writers use the term to refer to the poor in general, minority ethnic groups or even, occasionally, women (Gallie, 1990). On the political right, the term underclass is associated with a form of moral decay. Thus Charles Murray (1990) argues, rather bizarrely, that illegitimate births are a leading indicator of the underclass and that violent crime also provides a proximate measure of its development!

However, aside from many conceptual objections, a more forceful refutation of this approach comes from a literature that focuses on the deprivations suffered by the majority sections of the working population (for example, Adonis and Pollard, 1997; Elliot and Atkinson, 1998). This literature provides considerable evidence to show that many workers have a dramatically different experience of the economic boom of the 1990s than their equivalents had of the long post-war boom of the 1950s and 1960s that characterised the golden age of capitalism (Hobsbawn, 1994). The example of the US miracle economy may serve to illustrate this point.

As difficulties in the Japanese economy have grown steadily worse, the 'Goldilocks economy' of the US is often seen as a successful model of capitalism. Yet the notion that a 'contented majority' can be empirically demonstrated seems to be highly implausible. Lester Thurow, for example, has noted that:

> The rapid and widespread increase in inequality in the United States in the last two decades has traditionally been the province of countries experiencing a revolution or a military defeat followed by occupation. Indeed this is the first time since the collection of income data began that the median real wages have consistently fallen over a twenty-year period. And never before have a majority of American workers suffered real wage reductions while the real per capita gross domestic product (GDP) was increasing (Thurow, 1996, p. 383).

All indicators point to a growing gap between the majority of workers and the corporate rich. Corporate profits which totalled $330 billion in 1989, the last business cycle peak, had grown to $631 million in 1996 (*Economic Report of the President*, 1997, p. 401). This 90 per cent increase in profits in the seven-year period was not reflected in a greater willingness to pay taxes in order to finance the infrastructure which made expansion possible. A 1993 study by the Government Accounting Office found that more than 40 per cent of corporations doing business in the US with assets of $259 million paid income tax of less than $100,000 (Danagher, 1996, p. 40).

By contrast, conditions for the majority of workers have deteriorated on a variety of fronts. CORI themselves have pointed out that 'four out of five people are worse off today than they were in 1980' but unfortunately this did not lead them to question the notion of a contented majority (Conference of Major Religious Superiors of Ireland, 1993, p. 17). Real hourly wages in the US peaked in 1973 and have been declining since then with every major wage settlement in the 1990s less than in the preceding year. American workers are also working longer. Today the average working week for US workers is higher than it was in 1967 (Bluestone and Harrisson, 1997, p. 67). Workers are more insecure and concerned about their long-term job prospects. Young workers are increasingly placed on low-income entry grades. The flexible, and disposable, employee with no benefits is becoming an increasing reality. So while the Fortune 500 companies reduced their workforce by more than 30 per cent between 1993 and 1998, the number of temporary workers grew by nearly 19 per cent in the period from 1995 to 1998 alone (Weber, 1997, p. 72).

This latter point also indicates another difficulty with the popular notion of the underclass as a group permanently dependent on welfare. The US economy has reduced unemployment to under 5 per cent of the workforce. It has done so through vigorous cuts in welfare programmes and pressurising social welfare recipients to take the many low-paid, 'flexible' jobs. Instead of an underclass permanently dependent on welfare, there is an impoverished section of the workforce who move in and out of temporary jobs. And as the recent UPS strike showed, there is no reason to assume that temporary workers automatically adopt a different approach to that of the more 'tenured' full-time employees.

Growing insecurity, reduced real wages and a longer working week would hardly seem to constitute the ingredients that make for a contented majority. No wonder Newsweek produced a marvellous parody of John F. Kennedy's famous promise that the American Dream would bring 'a rising tide raising all boats' when it ran a headline in May 1993, 'A Rising Tide Lifts the Yachts'.

LATE CAPITALISM AND CLASS POLARISATION

If the duality of a contented majority versus a socially excluded minority presents difficulties at both a theoretical and an empirical level then other approaches are required. It is my contention that the Marxist concepts of late capitalism and class polarisation present a far more useful framework from which to analyse recent trends in Ireland and abroad.

The term 'late capitalism' indicates that while there is a continuity in the economic dynamic of society in recent decades – as opposed to the rupture postulated by those who claim we are living in an 'information or post industrial age' (Bell, 1976) – there are nevertheless differences in how the wider system is functioning compared to its golden age.

Late capitalism is characterised, firstly, by slower rates of growth. From the early nineteenth century to the 1970s, the US economy grew by an average of 3.8 per cent a year. That meant that real economic output doubled roughly every nineteen years. After the early 1970s, however, growth rates showed a general tendency to decline. During the

1980s growth fell to just 2.7 per cent per annum, then after 1989 to 2 per cent. At that rate it would take nearly thirty-six years to double output again (Bluestone and Harrisson, 1997, p. 63).

Secondly, generalised recessions have occurred at more regular intervals. The notion that these recessions may be explained away by conjectural factors, such as oil prices, is less and less plausible. The recession in the mid 1970s, was followed by one in the early 1980s, again in the late 1980s and now the global economy seems to be tottering on the brink of yet another recession. Parts of the world which escaped previous recessions, such as Asian Tigers, have been pulled into subsequent recessions.

Thirdly, as industrial production has become more precarious, there has been an explosion in financial and share speculation – despite the rather sluggish growth of the US economy – for example, the paper value of equities has risen from 0.7 times annualised income to 2.1 times since 1988 because of rising stock prices (Financial Times, 1998). Wall Street has experienced an unprecedented bull run with share prices standing at a 125-year high – that is, until recently (Henwood, 1998, p. 3).

Fourthly, the internationalisation of capital has meant that states can no longer exercise the same degree of control as in the past. This is not necessarily to imply that large blocks of capital do not seek the protection of a nation state or that 'globalisation' implies that capital can simply rove the world at will (see Hirst and Thompson, 1996). It does, however, suggest that individual states or even groups of states are in a weaker position to adopt reflationary or protectionist measures to impose stability.

This is by no means an exhaustive list of the characteristics of late capitalism. However it may be sufficient to imply that there are important changes occurring in the relationship between the contending classes. A social class may be defined as:

> A group of persons in a community identified by their position in the whole system of production, defined above all by their relationship (primarily in terms of degree of ownership and control) to the conditions of production (that is to say, the means and labour of production) and to other classes (de Ste Croix, 1981, p. 43).

It should be noted that this definition of class makes no reference to forms of lifestyle, consumption patterns or status gradations but focuses on objective relations. And as Callinicos has noted, the term working class does not necessarily imply manual workers. If the sale of labour is qualified by the absence of control or autonomy over the conditions of work, then the majority of those currently classified as 'white collar' may be assumed to be part of an expanding working class. This still leaves a minority in 'contradictory class locations', who may formally exist as salaried employees but who possess rights such as to hire and fire and autonomy over their working life and so are more properly assigned the term 'new middle class' (Callinicos, 1987).

The point of this discussion is not simply to trade possible definitions or categorisation systems, but to point to some connection between the changing nature of late capitalism and the behaviour of different social groups in modern society. This connection is best captured by the concept of class polarisation.

Class polarisation may be deemed to operate at two important levels. In the first place, the changing regime of accumulation that characterises modern capitalism means that elites are now more likely to redistribute resources away from the working population to the owners of capital. In brief, instead of a trickle down effect there is a trickle up. This may be achieved in a variety of ways. There may be efforts to cut social spending in order to promote tax cuts or new subsidies for the wealthy. Marx's traditional categories of how capitalism responds to its economic difficulties are also relevant here (Marx, 1984). He argued that there can be an increase in 'relative surplus value', that is extracting more value from workers during the course of the existing working day. The emphasis on 'flexibility' and removing 'downtime' at work hardly denote neutral and functional categories, but summarise how work is being intensified. There can also be an increase in 'absolute surplus value' by lengthening the number of hours worked. Demands for 'annualised hours', compulsory overtime work or more complex shift patterns are some of the methods used. There can also be a pattern of 'immiseration' of sections of the working class. The current emphasis on new entry grades for young workers are probably linked to a growth in poverty.

Secondly, the term class polarisation implies not just a changed objective relation but a prediction about the actual behaviour of different social classes. Many writers generalised from the experience of the Reagan-Thatcher years to assume that neo-liberal economics were unlikely to provoke any coherent response from a working class that was believed to be close to extinction. Nevertheless, the removal of long-held aspirations that, for example, sons and daughters should expect better economic standards than their parents; that people have a 'right' to be cared for while sick, regardless of income; or that the average worker could aspire to own his or her own home, implicitly carried with it the possibility of greater social conflict. Recent events in a variety of countries would tend to confirm the re-emergence of forms of class conflict, once regarded as a thing of the past. The wave of strikes in the US and Canada, the general strike in France in 1995 and the extensive resistance to downsizing in South Korea all testify to growing resistance by workers. At a more muted level, the return of social democratic governments in many parts of Europe may also be an indicator of a growing awareness of class division.

Contrary to the impression provided in much post-modernist literature then, it would appear that the predicted death of class conflict has indeed been greatly exaggerated.

THE CELTIC TIGER AND INEQUALITY

Let us now return to the Celtic Tiger and offer a different view on how inequality is growing within it. The ideology commonly associated with social partnership acknowledges that there are some inequalities in Irish society. As the numbers below the poverty line have actually increased from 31 per cent of the population to 34 per cent, it can even accept that this inequality may have increased (Callan et al., 1996, p. 81).

However, inequality is still seen as a residual category, in that it affects groups who are marginalised from the labour force. For the rest, social partnership arrangements are supposed to provide a 'positive sum' game where all classes make gains from corporatist bargaining. As Ireland is an example of a 'strong corporatist' society, where the range of issues discussed and the degree of consultation with interest groups is quite high, one could expect significant gains to accrue to workers during an unprecedented boom (Przeworski and Wallerstein, 1982). This, however, is a misreading of the purpose of the social partnership arrangements – they are quite simply not designed to produce gains for 'both sides'. Instead they have become a means by which the corporate elite have won considerable freedom to raise productivity, restrain wages and pursue an agenda that transfers resources to them. This can be illustrated by looking at the issues of pay and productivity, taxation and public spending.

Pay and productivity

A useful way of looking at pay levels in the Celtic Tiger is to apply the criterion used for assessing fair pay norms during the last major boom in Ireland in the 1960s to the situation today. In 1964, the White Paper *Closing the Gap* outlined the Fianna Fáil government's approach to pay policy. It argued that pay rises had to be tied to productivity increases. In order to facilitate this, the National Economic and Social Council was established to produce an objective assessment on how pay might be linked to growth in productivity (Morrissey, 1986).

However, if we apply that same criterion to the situation today, we can see the degree to which the majority of workers have lost out. Productivity in Irish industry has increased dramatically during the decade of social partnership. Table 1 gives some indication of the huge growth in productivity over fifteen years. While the value added per worker increased by 402 per cent between 1980 and 1995, wages only increased by 128 per cent.

Table 1. Productivity in Ireland ($)

	1980	1985	1990	1995
Gross output per worker	70,068	82,191	172,553	253,308
Value added per worker	25,112	32,008	77,266	126,335
Average wage (including supplements)	11,905	11,604	23,770	27,250

Source: United Nations Industrial Development Organisation (Global Report 1997).

The growth in productivity has meant that real unit labour costs have fallen more dramatically than many rival economies. According to Sweeney, real unit labour costs have fallen by 19 per cent in Ireland, 10 per cent in Japan, 2.4 per cent in the UK and 14 per cent in the EU (Sweeney, 1998, p. 61). There are of course many reasons why productivity has risen. A shift from agricultural to non-agricultural employment will tend to be associated with a rise in productivity. So too will a modernisation process which shifts investment from traditional sectors to the new hi-tech industries. Nevertheless, the remarkable feature of Ireland's growth is that the huge rises in productivity have not been associated with a major expansion of investment in machinery and capital stock by the wealthy.

Indeed, Ireland is unique in the EU in showing a decline in capital stock as a proportion of GDP. Capital intensity, defined as net capital stock per employee, is among the lowest in the EU. Fixed capital in the form of machinery and equipment, for example, has fallen in manufacturing from £691 million to £525 million (NESC, 1998). And while this represents an overall average which combines the multinational and indigenous sectors, the situation in the traditional sectors is worse. The low level of investment by the wealthy has led to a significant surplus of savings and an outflow of domestic capital.

All of this would seem to indicate that there have been important increases in labour productivity. One study calculated that labour productivity rose by 10 per cent a year in 1994 and 1995 in the modern sector, compared to 3 per cent a year in the more traditional sectors dominated by Irish industry (OECD, 1997a, p. 17). One of the reasons why productivity has risen is that the unions have supported new forms of work organisation and even forms of atypical employment. Partnership at enterprise level is associated with forms of 'empowerment', where teamworking involves workers imposing a collective discipline on each other in order to raise productivity; flexible work-patterns, where the skilled take on jobs of the unskilled as a means of removing 'downtime'; annualised hours, which help to reduce overtime payments; quality circles, which seek to raise productivity further (Lewchuck and Robertson, 1997). All of this has had an important effect on what Carter Goodrich (1975) called the 'frontier of control' on the shop floor. Instead of strong shop steward organisation undermining managerial prerogatives, as it did during the last boom, the process has gone into reverse. As corporatist forms of bargaining involve greater forms of hierarchy, where as Streeck (1982) argued the leadership are 'sealed off' from the rank and file, local shop stewards have seen their power eroded. Moreover, as pay and conditions are increasingly negotiated on a national basis, the role of the shop steward has atrophied in favour of full-time 'professionals' who see employers as their partners.

While productivity has risen quite dramatically and even though the corporate elite have not significantly increased their investment, the gains are not being shared. Quite the opposite. Despite the ideology of social partnership the increase in labour productivity is associated with a declining share of wages in the national economy, while the share going to profits has risen substantially. Table 2 illustrates the declining share accruing to wages in the economy.

Table 2. Changing factor shares of non-agricultural income (%)

	1987	1992	1997
Profits, interest, dividends, rent	31	36	41
Wages, pensions, social security	69	64	59

Source: CSO, National Income and Expenditure.

Denis O'Hearn puts matters succinctly in describing the overall result of the decade of social partnership: 'during the decade since 1987, which many people refer to as Ireland's economic miracle, the wage share of non-agricultural income fell by about 10% and the profit share grew by the same amount' (O'Hearn, 1998, pp. 124-5).

The shift in the national income towards profits is reflected in many areas. In 1995, for example, US companies earned a post-tax rate of return of 23 per cent on capital employed in Ireland. This was up to five times higher than US companies elsewhere in Europe (OECD, 1997a, p. 16). While the figures were exaggerated by artificial pricing, they reflect the advantages of a highly productive but comparatively low-paid work force. The growing gap is also reflected in how successive national pay agreements have restrained wages, while profits have shown unprecedented increases. Over the three years of the Programme for Competitiveness and Work, the average earnings of workers increased by 11 per cent but total profits grew by 44 per cent. In the first two years of Partnership 2000, average earnings increased by 6.5 per cent while profits grew by 22 per cent.

However, even this growing gap between profits and wages does not fully indicate how a substantial proportion of the working population is losing out. The average figures for wages include, for example, payments to general managers as well as routine clerical employees. Yet wage dispersion has actually widened, despite the belief that social partnership is supposed to benefit the low-paid section of the workforce. The real hourly earnings of the lowest decile have stagnated or even fallen slightly, while those of the top decile have grown by an average rate of 4 per cent annually. As a result the ratio of earnings of the top decile to the bottom for men working full time has increased from 3.5 times to 5 times between the time of the first partnership agreement in 1987 and 1994 (Nolan and Hughes, 1997). The expansion of the Celtic Tiger has quite simply been accompanied by a growth in the number of poorly paid jobs. Despite claims that Ireland has resisted the effects of neo-liberal politics, which are more prevalent in the US, it comes second only to the US in having the highest proportion of its workforce officially categorised as low paid. The share of the labour force earning less than two-thirds of the median earnings is now 23 percent, one of the highest rates in the OECD area (Nolan and Hughes, 1997; see also OECD, 1997a).

This growing gap between the social classes is reflected in some interesting patterns of consumption. As O'Hearn has pointed out, the phenomenal growth in the Celtic Tiger economy has been accompanied by a fall in the share of gross domestic product going to private consumption. So while private consumption accounted for 59.3 per cent of GDP in 1987, it had decreased to 55.4 per cent by 1996 (O'Hearn, 1998, pp. 126-7). However, luxury consumption in some areas has increased quite dramatically. Prestige cars have typically functioned as a symbol of conspicuous consumption for the wealthy. The growth in sales of prestige cars, with average prices ranging from £26,000 to £50,000, provides some indication of the growth in luxury consumption.

Taxation and public spending

The other important area where there has been a sustained strategy to shift resources to the wealthy sections of society has been on the taxation/social spending matrix. One might get the impression from some employer bodies that entrepreneurs are ground down by the tax burden. In fact total taxes are not particularly high in Ireland as a

Table 3. Sales of luxury cars 1987-1998

Year	*Audi*	*BMW*	*Mercedes*	*Other*	*Total*
1987	432	468	490	216	1606
1988	402	609	385	195	1591
1989	678	910	568	251	2407
1990	648	935	799	272	2654
1991	640	814	804	220	2478
1992	863	744	649	267	2523
1993	635	596	606	252	2089
1994	813	808	1126	404	3151
1995	1055	1052	1059	447	3613
1996	1470	1174	1452	478	4574
1997	1563	1780	1869	597	5809

Source: Society of the Irish Motoring Industry (SIMI).

proportion of GDP. They stand at 35 per cent in 1996 compared to 40 per cent in 1987. The average throughout the EU in 1996 was 46 per cent (Sweeney, 1998, p. 179). However, during the decade of social partnership, successful lobbying on a variety of fronts brought major cuts for the wealthy.

The striking feature about Irish taxation is that more than a decade after the huge tax marches little has changed for PAYE workers. Employees are still contributing 90 per cent of all income taxes. Many potential areas, such as family inheritance, are ignored, while campaigns to eliminate wealth tax, residential property tax and to cut the capital gains taxes have been spectacularly successful. In addition, high rates of indirect taxes have a regressive effect on workers, who are more likely to spend most of their earnings.

It should be remembered, however, that official figures on company taxation only tell a fraction of the real story. There is considerable evidence that the Irish rich, like Ivana Trump, believe that taxes are for the little people. Two amnesties have rewarded those who evaded their tax bills. The existence of the Ansbacher account, now reputed to contain over $100 million, shows that not only was a fund established to reward politicians who pursued a business agenda, but it was also used to funnel money to offshore accounts which were extensively used by the Irish wealthy.

Since then, further light has been thrown on the hidden but complex mechanisms of tax evasion by the wealthy. One important mechanism has been the use of Irish registered non-resident companies. Forty thousand of these companies are presently operating and some are used by multinationals to defer payments on US taxes (*Irish Times*, 1998c). According to the IDA they are 'an important but not essential' element in attracting overseas investment (*Irish Times*, 1998b). This form of offshore accounting is, however, also used by the indigenous Irish elite. The tiny Channel Island of Sark has become a popular resort for wealthy Irish clients seeking to avoid tax. According to the chairman of the Sark Association of Corporate Administrators many of his members earn between £20,000 and £40,000 a year as directors of Irish firms, many of whom are connected to the International Financial Services Centre (Irish Times, 1998d). It is estimated that Irish accountancy firms, banks, solicitors and company formation groups are earning £40 million a year servicing this form of tax avoidance (*Irish Times*, 1998a).

However, the scale of tax avoidance is only one aspect of a wider picture whereby the wealthy have managed to reduce their tax obligations. Figures on the cost to the Irish exchequer of tax relief to the corporate sector are based on rough estimates but they give some notion of the scale of subsidies now being provided to the wealthy. At the start of the partnership decade the cost of these subsidies was put at £712 million. The following year the growth in incentives meant it had risen to £1,189 million (Department of Industry and Commerce, 1990, p. 158). While the basis of these estimates seem to have changed, the latest figures from the revenue commissioners put the cost of this form of tax relief much higher. Table 4 shows that even if we focus on the 10 per cent corporation tax relief alone, we find costs have risen to £1,256 million.

Table 4. Some tax relief provision on capital (£m)

	1993-94	*1994-95*
Capital allowances		
Urban rental	19.7	46.0
Rented residential accommodation	17.6	21.5
Other	818.2	819.7
Corporation tax at 10 per cent		
(excluding International Financial Services Centre)	1,078.0	1.256.1
Double taxation relief	90.9	76.1
Investment in films	19.9	38.3
TOTAL	2,045.2	2,257.7

Source: Revenue Commissioners Report 1996.

Even these figures underestimate the full scale of the tax subsidies given to the corporate sector. Figures presented by the revenue commissioners do not include the tax foregone on the Irish Financial Services Centre. As these include measures such as a 'double rental allowance' we can imagine it is quite considerable. Similarly the revenue commissioners believe that a myriad of other tax reliefs are 'unquantifiable'. These include relief for items such as stallion stud fees; income from foreign trusts; commercial woodland; and investment in research and development (Office of the Revenue Commissioners, 1996). The latter provisions ensure that one pharmaceutical company pays a tax bill of less than 1per cent on its earnings.

The culmination of efforts to reduce taxation on the corporate elite can be seen in the new proposals for corporation tax. In 1988, the year after the first partnership programme, the top tax rate on companies stood at 50 per cent. A decade later, that had declined to 32 per cent. This is now set to fall by a further 4 per cent a year until eventually the top rate of taxation on company profits will stand at 12.5 percent. It is a testimony to the strength of the social partnership ideology that this has occurred without major debate; and that it seems to have the support of all major parties and even the leadership of the unions. Yet the ramification of these tax cuts for social spending have barely been discussed.

One of the ways that tax cuts for companies is articulated ideologically is to present the issue in terms of 'Ireland' versus a foreign bureaucracy that seeks to hamper our entrepreneurial spirit. Competitive down-bidding of tax rates by nation states is assumed to be a necessity because of globalisation. Attempts by German finance ministers or European Commissioners, to restrict the scale of tax cuts provided by the Irish state is regarded as an affront to the nation itself. From this perspective, tax cuts provide a positive sum game whereby all sections of Irish society benefit by 'coaxing' investment away from other countries.

However, the working population bear the cost of the accelerated tax cuts that have grown in the decade of social partnership. Not only do they carry a greater share of the tax burden but they also rely more on public spending programmes that are cut back to facilitate tax cuts. Three brief examples may be advanced to indicate how the cutting of corporate taxes can lead to disadvantages for workers.

First: public transport. One of the effects of the Celtic Tiger has been the emergence of major traffic chaos. The possibility of relieving this through the promotion of public transport has, however, been severely undermined by spending cuts. In 1987, the subsidy provided to Dublin Bus amounted to £15 million but today it has declined to less than half that figure. As Table 5 indicates, Dublin has the distinction of providing one of the lowest subsidies to bus users in European cities.

Table 5. Grants/subsidies to bus companies in selected European cities (%)

City	*Grant/Subsidy*
Athens	50.0
Barcelona	39.4
Dublin	4.4
Helsinki	55.3
London	14.5
Paris	57.4
Rome	74.5
Strasbourg	46.0

Source: *Jane's Urban Transport System*, 16th edition, 1997/98.

Second: education. Irish primary schools have now one of the highest pupil teacher ratios in the OECD. Only Turkey, Mexico and Korea are in a worse position. Inside the EU, Ireland has the lowest expenditure per primary student relative to GDP (OECD, 1997b, pp. 101-2). While pupils still attain higher than average reading levels for the 9 to 13 age group, science is still not part of the primary school curriculum. One of the astounding ironies of the Celtic Tiger is that in an economy built on hi-tech industries pupils are still collecting bar codes to get computers for their schools.

Third: hospital beds. Ireland tops the OECD record for cuts in the admission to acute hospital facilities during the decades of partnership. It has cut the number of acute hospital beds per 1,000 of the population by 43 per cent and the average length of stay by 29 per cent between 1980 and 1993. From a situation in 1980 where it had the highest rate of admissions in the OECD, it now has one of the lowest. For public patients, delays for some non-urgent cases have become exceptionally long as nearly 40,000 are now on the waiting list (OECD, 1997a, pp. 134-5).

In the areas of health, education and transport the effects of the policy of cutting taxes on profit are becoming more visible. All of this would suggest that in a social partnership supposedly producing a 'positive sum' gain where all are winners, the losers can be found among a substantial section of the Irish population.

CONCLUSION: THE DISCONTENTED MAJORITY AND ANTI-POVERTY STRATEGIES

Our analysis so far would seem to indicate that the Celtic Tiger is not bringing benefits to all. It is not simply a question of a residual category of the 'socially excluded' losing out. Quite the opposite. A corporate elite has grown richer and more powerful at the expense of major sections of the workforce. In that sense it is more appropriate to discuss how the interests of the poor and the discontented majority coincide.

This raises important questions about the hegemony that the social partnership ideology has achieved. Corporatist structures have ensured that leadership bodies in both the unions and a variety of voluntary agencies have been given a role in bargaining on social policy over the last decade. This has sometimes produced a vague and seemingly radical concern to eliminate poverty. Thus the most recent *Partnership 2000* document notes that 'social exclusion' is the major challenge facing Irish society and claims that a central feature of the programme will be the adoption of a national anti-poverty strategy by the government (chapter 4). Many have taken these claims as evidence that partnership offers the best way of eliminating poverty from Irish society.

However, it is the contention of this chapter that these promises are ideological devices to mask a major transfer of wealth to the already privileged sections of Irish society. It is noticeable, for example, that whereas considerable resources are being employed to interview social welfare recipients to 'encourage' them to take up low-paid, flexible employment, there does not seem to be an equivalent effort put into investigating tax evasion. Ten years after the British Conservative government brought in legislation to impose restrictions on British registered non-resident companies, Irish ministers still insist that these accounts have an important role to play in 'attracting' investment. This begs the question: what is the value of an anti-poverty strategy when discussion on the transfer of wealth from the elite is effectively ruled out?

This question is sometimes not addressed because the interests of the poor and the wider working population are regarded as opposed. It seems that there is a limited cake and either 'the marginalised' or 'sectional' militant trade unionists among public sector employees get hold of the bigger slice. However, this opposition is more artificial than real. Many of the poor come from the low paid, including low-paid public sector employees. Others become 'disposable' workers, temporarily employed in either the black economy or pressurised to take up jobs before returning again to social welfare. They suffer more from the run down of hospital beds or the underfunding of education because they have little access to privatised services. Their exclusion from the Celtic Tiger is an aspect of the wider exclusion of the majority.

Moreover, the poor are not simply objects of state agencies, constituted by either discourses of dependency or 'empowerment' (Mizen, 1998). On a wide variety of fronts there is resistance, resentment, anger and struggle against poverty. As Miliband has pointed out, 'class analysis is largely class struggle analysis' (Miliband, 1989, p.

3). Such a perspective entails that poverty and inequality will only be challenged through critical opposition to those 'social partners' who have shifted resources to the privileged.

A perspective of struggle rather than corporatist participation leads to a search for common interests between the discontented majority and the most impoverished. It means that small victories secured against the corporate elite cannot be dismissed as mere 'sectional greed'. In a society established around the cash nexus, it would be surprising if people did not struggle over pay rises, bonuses, disturbance money and productivity rises. Such struggles, however, contain the germ of self-emancipation that can transform the term empowerment from empty rhetoric to a reality. Rather than seeking to restrain such resistance, lest it destroy social partnership, it should be recognised that a rebirth of confidence by the majority of workers is a precondition for the type of social change that can eliminate poverty.

REFERENCES

Adonis, A. and Pollard, S. J. (1997), *A class act: the myth of Britain's classless society*, London: Hamish Hamilton.

Allen, K. (1997), *Fianna Fáil and Irish labour: 1926 to the present*, London: Pluto Press.

Aronowitz, S. (1973), *False Promises*, New York: Basic Books.

Bell, D. (1976), *The coming of post-industrial society: a venture in social forecasting*, Harmondsworth: Penguin.

Bluestone, B. and Harrisson, B. (1997), 'Why We Can Grow Faster', The American Prospect, no. 34.

Breen, R., Hannon, D., Rottman, D. and Whelan, C. (1990), *Understanding contemporary Ireland: state, class and development in the Republic of Ireland*, Dublin: Gill and Macmillan.

Callan, T., Nolan, B., Whelan, B. and Williams, J. (1996), *Poverty in the 1990s: evidence from the 1994 Living in Ireland Survey*, Dublin: Oak Tree Press, 1996.

Callinicos, A. (1987), 'The New Middle Classes and Socialist Politics', in A. Callinicos and C. Harman, *The changing working class: essays on class structure today,* London: Bookmarks.

Conference of Major Religious Superiors (Ireland), Justice Commission (1993), *Growing exclusion: a review of aspects of the current socio-economic situation with recommendations for the 1993 budget,* Dublin: Justice Commission, Conference of Major Religious Superiors (Ireland).

Danagher, K. (1996), *Corporations are Going to Get Your Mama*, Monroe: Maine.

De Ste Croix, O.E.M. (1981), *The Class Struggle in the Ancient Greek World: from the Archaic Age to the Arab Conquests*, London: Duckworth.

Department of Industry and Commerce (1990), *Review of Industrial Performance,* Dublin: Stationery Office.

Eagleton, T. (1991), *Ideology: an introduction*, London: Verso.

Elliott, L. and Atkinson, D. (1998), *The age of insecurity*, London: Verso.

Financial Times (1998), 26 August.

Galbraith, J. K. (1992), *The culture of contentment,* London: Sinclair-Stevenson.

Gallie, D. (1988), *Employment in Britain*, Oxford: Blackwell.

Goodrich, C. (1975), *The frontier of control: a study in British workshop politics*, London: Pluto Press.

Healy, S. and Reynolds, B. (1990), 'The Future of Work: a Challenge to Society', in B. Reynolds and S. Healy (eds.), *Work, unemployment and job-creation policy*, Dublin: Justice Commission, Conference of Major Religious Superiors (Ireland).

Henwood, D. (1998), *Wall Street: how it works and for whom*, London: Verso.

Hirst, P. Q. and Thompson, G. (1996), *Globalisation in question: the international economy and the possibilities of governance*, Cambridge: Polity Press.

Hobsbawm, E. J. (1995), *Age of extremes: the short twentieth century*, 1914-91, London: Abacus.

Irish Times (1998a), 13 February.

Irish Times (1998b), 27 February.

Irish Times (1998c), 28 February.

Irish Times (1998d), 5 June.

Lewchuck, W. and Robertson, D. (1997), 'Production without empowerment: work re-organisation from the perspective of motor vehicle workers', *Capital and Class,* vol. 63, Autumn.

Marx, K. (1984), *Capital*, vol. 3, ch. 14, Moscow: Progress Publishers.

Miliband, R. (1989), *Divided societies: class struggle in contemporary capitalism*, Oxford: Clarendon Press.

Mizen, P. (1998), 'Work-Welfare and the Regulation of the Poor: The Pessimism of Post-Structuralism', *Capital and Class*, vol. 65.

Morrissey, M. (1986), 'The Politics of Economic Management in Ireland, 1958-1970', *Irish Political Studies*, vol. 1, pp. 79-96.

Murray, C. (1990), *The Emerging British Underclass*, London: IEA Health and Welfare Unit.

National Economic and Social Council (1998), *Private sector investment in Ireland*, Dublin: NESC.

Nolan, B. and Hughes, G. (1997), *Low pay, the earnings distribution and poverty in Ireland*, 1987-1994, Dublin: Economic and Social Research Institute.

Office of the Revenue Commissioners (1996), *Annual Report*, Dublin: Stationery Office.

Ó'Gráda, C. (1997), *A rocky road: the Irish economy since the 1920s*, Manchester: Manchester University Press.

O'Hearn, D. (1998), *Inside the Celtic Tiger: the Irish economy and the Asian model*, London: Pluto Press.

Organisation for Economic Co-operation and Development (1997a), *Economic Survey*: Ireland, Paris: OECD.

Organisation for Economic Co-operation and Development (l997h), *Education at a Glance*, Paris: OECD.

Przeworki, A. and Wallerstein, M. (1982), 'The Structure of Class Conflict in Democratic Capitalist Societies', *American Political Science Review*, vol. 76.

Silver, H. (1995), 'Fighting Social Exclusion', in *Social Exclusion, Social Inclusion*, Democratic Dialogue report no. 2, Belfast: Democratic Dialogue.

Streeck, W. (1982), 'Organisational Consequences of Neo-Corporatism in West German Labour Union', in G. Lehmbruch and P. C. Schmitter (eds.), *Patterns of Corporatist Policymaking*, London: Sage Publications.

Sweeney, P. (1998), *The Celtic Tiger: Ireland's economic miracle explained*, Dublin: Oak Tree Press.

Thurow, L. (1996), 'Almost Everywhere: Surging Inequality and Falling Real Wages', in C. Kaysen (ed.), *The American Corporation Today*, Oxford: Oxford University Press.

United States (1997), *Economic Report of the President*, Washington.

Weber, S. (1997), 'The End of the Business Cycle', *Foreign Affairs,* July/August.

Part Two
Health and the Mixed Economy of Welfare

Administration, vol. 51, nos. 1-2 (Spring/Summer 2003), 143–166

The Irish Hospital An Outline of its Origins and Development*

J.A. ROBINS

Originally published in 1960, vol. 8, no. 2, 145-165.
J.A. Robins was then an executive officer in the Department of Health.

ANCIENT Ireland had her hospitals. In fact the Brehon laws set out in a very specific manner the essential requirements of a hospital. It should be free from dirt, have four doors "that the sick man may be seen from every side" and there should be a stream of water running through the middle of the floor. The patient was to be kept free from dogs and fools and female scolds lest he be worried and if he had to enter hospital as a result of an unjustly inflicted bodily injury the wrongdoer had to pay his hospital expenses. The laws also provided that if a patient's mother were living and available she should be allowed to enter hospital with him.

These hospitals were for the common use of the *tuath* or district and were called "forus tuaithe", i.e. the house of territory. The most famous of them was perhaps that established in 300 B.C. at Emain by Princess Macha. It was known as "*Broin Bearg*" or the "House of Sorrow".

IRISH HOSPITALS FROM EARLY CHRISTIAN TIMES

With the advent of Christianity to Ireland and the development of religious communities the secular "*forus tuaithe*" began to be replaced by the monastery as a place of succour for the sick. That hospitals were to be found in many parts of the country is evidenced by numerous local place names in use to-day. Spiddal and Hospital, for example, are but two instances of districts where it is obvious there was at some distant time a place for the care of the sick.

* A prize winning essay in the 1959 essay competition of the Institute of Public Administration.

Many of the early Christian hospitals were *nosocomia* or places for the care of lepers, for leprosy was one of the scourges of the period, not only in Ireland but throughout Europe. In the 12th century the Benedictines opened a leper hospital in Waterford, another was founded at Kilbixy in Co. Westmeath and the Knights of St John were responsible for a number of institutions, the most important of them being Kilmainham Priory with which Richard Strongbow was associated. Towards the end of the century a general hospital was founded at the Priory of St John the Baptist, Thomas Street, Dublin. In 1361 it was granted a *deodandum* by Edward III for a period of twenty years and this was later renewed in 1378 and 1403.

The famines and pestilences of the Middle Ages gave rise to numerous other institutions such as that at Nenagh (Teach Eoin), Drogheda (St. Mary's) and Cashel (St. Nicholas) but as the epidemics waned their *raison d'etre* ceased to exist and many of them closed down. Those which remained were associated with monasteries and they continued to give not only care to the sick but shelter to the homeless and the traveller. But when the Reformation came they too were forced to close their doors despite the efforts of Lord Deputy Leonard Gray who in 1539 petitioned the King to exempt six of them, of which the best known was Jerpoint, on the grounds that they had been giving shelter not only to the homeless and destitute but also to the King's representatives "in defaute of comen innes".

Edward MacLysaght, writing of Ireland in the 17th century, says:

> "There were no hospitals. The suppression of the monasteries a century earlier had eliminated the only body of men who had made any attempt, however feeble, to supply this need and no step was taken in this direction by the authorities if we except the provision in wartime of some wards for sick and wounded soldiers."

However, the suppression of the monastic institutions did not affect the practice of medicine. From early times all the great Irish families had physicians attached to their households. The office was a hereditary one, the profession passing from father to son in a succession often extending over hundreds of years. Thus the O'Hickeys were physicians to the O'Briens of Thomond and the Cassidys to the Maguires of Fermanagh. In this connection it might be of interest to mention that a descendent of Owen O'Shiel, physician to Owen Roe O'Neill, founded in 1889 the extant Shiel Hospital in Ballyshannon.

THE 18TH CENTURY

In 1703 the necessity for the provision of institutions for the care and shelter of the poor was at last recognised and the Irish Parliament passed legislation providing for the building in James's Street, Dublin, of a workhouse and foundling hospital. This enactment is a landmark so far as the history of social legislation in Ireland is concerned for it marks the first acceptance of the principle that the care of the poor should be met from compulsory taxation. A tax for the purpose was levied on sedan chairs and hackney coaches and, in addition, a rate of threepence in the pound was struck on every house within the city and liberties. In 1735 similar provision was made for the city of Cork. Some idea of the number of paupers at the period may be gauged from the fact that it was estimated that there were almost 35,000 vagrant beggars wandering the roads of Ireland in 1729.

An Act setting up county infirmaries as "receptacles for poor who are infirm and diseased" was passed in 1765. Thus, for the first time, provision was being made for the rural areas. The task of raising the funds for the building and maintenance of these infirmaries was given to the Grand Juries and the Act specified that, in all, twenty-three infirmaries were to be provided. Some years later, on the initiative of Dr Woodward, the Protestant Bishop of Cloyne, further legislation provided for the opening of a "House of Industry" in each county. These institutions conformed partly to the character of hospitals and partly to the character of houses of correction. They were divided into four parts, one for poor helpless men, another for women in similar straits, a third for men fit to work but committed as vagabonds and a fourth for idle, strolling and disorderly women. They were administered by corporate bodies and financed partly from voluntary contributions and partly from grand jury presentments. The Governors of these institutions were empowered to grant licences to approved paupers whose children they took over and committed to the Charter Schools, proselytising agencies granted a Charter by George II on the petition of a number of Protestant nobility and clergymen. Not all counties put this enactment into operation, however, and it is probable that, when one has regard to the ignominies and rigours which the unfortunate inmates of those institutions had to undergo, the paupers lost nothing in consequence.

One was established in Dublin, however, and it was to be the nucleus of what is now one of the City's principal hospitals, namely, St Laurence's Hospital. It had its beginnings when in 1773 a corporation was established to provide a House of Industry. With the help of voluntary contributions and a parliamentary grant of £4,000 this newly formed body opened a number of houses for vagrants from all over the country. They were called Hardwicke, Richmond and Whitworth Hospitals, after the Viceroys who held office at the time of their construction, and they retained the character of a House of Industry until well into the last century. After its foundation it continued to be substantially supported by annual parliamentary grant and it was, in fact, the only institution in the country at that period which derived assistance from central government sources.

John Howard, the British prison and hospital reformer visited Ireland about 1787 and made a tour of inspection of Irish gaols, hospitals and Charter Schools. Later he published a concise and objective report on these institutions which presents us with a picture of appalling misery.

He visited all the existing county infirmaries. In the main they were dirty, overcrowded, ill-ventilated, evil-smelling, without water or sanitary accommodation. In some cases they were failing down or in such a state of disrepair that the shelter they had to offer was little better than that to be found under a hedge. The food was inadequate, unless the patient was in a position to arrange for friends to supplement his meagre rations, and the diet in most cases was comprised exclusively of bread and milk, Howard felt that this diet was the proper one, however, since "the general class of patients admitted into infirmaries in this country ... are subject to scrofulous complaints arising from intemperance and the want of attention to cleanliness". In the Infirmary in Castlebar the patients lay on hay with hardly anything to cover them. In Cavan there was "an upper room full of fowl... a dunghill in the small front court." In Omagh two patients lay in an old bath tub and Howard reported that the prisoners in the local gaol were better provided for and lived in more comfortable surroundings. In the Waterford City Infirmary the only medicament available for the seven patients appeared to be one pot of ointment; and of the institution at Maryborough he reported –

> "In two of the rooms above there were thirteen beds and fifteen patients. In the room called "the tower" two patients and a little dirty hay on the floor on which, they said, the nurse lay. This room was very dirty, the ceiling covered with cobwebs and in several places open to the sky. Here I saw one naked, pale object, who was under the necessity of tearing his shirt for bandages for his fractured thigh. No sheets. . . no vault . . . no water."

When occasionally he found it possible to give some praise it was usually because of the generosity of a local benefactor. The Limerick County Infirmary was in good condition with "a cleanly and notable matron" due mainly, it appears, to the benevolence of Lady Hartstonge, and the Infirmary in Roscommon was in reasonably good condition as a result of the support of a Mrs Walcott, sister of a former Lord Chief Justice.

Howard also visited the Foundling Hospital and Workhouse at James's Street, Dublin, to which reference has already been made and he reported that it was "a noble institution" to which children were admitted without difficulty at all times. This fact prompted him to comment:

> "Foundling Hospitals may be considered in two lights; one as charities for the maintenance and education of poor deserted children who otherwise might fall victims to ill-treatment and neglect. The other, as means to prevent child-murder, by providing a refuge against the shame and disgrace attending the discovery of illegitimate pregnancy. For both these purposes it is requisite that admission into such hospitals should be easy; but particularly for the latter, it is essential that it may be obtained without any form of delay and in perfect secrecy. It is another question whether such institutions may not do more harm than good by encouraging licentiousness; but certainly they cannot prevent the murder of children unless the mothers can get rid of the charge without discovery. These hospitals, therefore, in which admission is made very difficult and only to be obtained by powerful interest and recommendation seem to me absolutely useless and only serve as a provision for the bastards of gentlemen."

ADVENT OF THE VOLUNTARY HOSPITAL

If State provision for the poor and the sick during the 18th century was of relatively insignificant proportions the achievement of voluntary effort in this sphere was noteworthy particularly when one has regard to the fact that the idea of private charity appeared to have had almost vanished with the suppression of the monasteries two hundred years earlier. But the poverty of the great majority of the population was so abject that it fanned into life the long-smouldering embers of Irish philanthropic effort and led to the appearance of the voluntary hospital.

The first one was opened in 1718 when six Dublin surgeons established the Charitable Infirmary at Cook Street. Later they acquired different premises at Inns Quay and in 1786 when that site was required for the building of the Four Courts it was necessary to transfer the Hospital again, this time to Jervis Street, where it remains to this day.

Steeven's Hospital was opened in 1733 although it was provided for as far back as 1710 when, in his will, Dr Richard Stevens, Fellow of the College of Physicians, left all his property in trust to his sister Grizel, and after her death to finance the establishment of a hospital within the city of Dublin. His sister, however, was determined that the project should become a reality during her own lifetime and after twenty years of frustrating delay, occasioned mainly by legal difficulties and shortages of money, the hospital at last opened its doors to the sick poor of Dublin.

In 1724 Miss Mary Mercer built a house in St Stephen's Churchyard as a refuge for poor girls. Some years later she handed the house over to trustees for use as a hospital and in 1734 it was opened as a ten-bed institution. Later it was transferred to larger premises and the present Mercer's Hospital is located in a building which was completed early in the last century. John Howard visited this hospital during his tour of Ireland and he reported:-

> "Mercer's Hospital in the middle of the city, was a few years since very dirty offensive and unhealthy; but now it is one of the cleanest in Dublin."

Not so the Hospital for Incurables, however, which was founded in 1744 by the "Charitable Musical Society". Howard reported:-

> "Both outside and inside dirty; the rooms offensive; no rules; no diet table, the housekeeper in the country."

1745 is a landmark in the history of the Irish voluntary hospital for during that year two important events took place. First it saw the death of Dean Swift who, in his will, left almost £11,000 to provide a Hospital for the Insane. That Ireland needed such a hospital he had no doubt for many a year and as far back as 1731 he had written in a poem relating to his own death "Verse on the Death of Dr Swift –

> "He gave the little wealth he had
> To build a house for fools and mad
> And showed by one satiric touch
> No nation wanted it so much."

A year after his death St Patrick's Hospital for the Insane or, as it was popularly known then, Dean Swift's Hospital, took in its first patients and it was to remain for many years the only hospital of its kind in the country.

The second important event in 1745 was the foundation of the Rotunda Hospital by Bartholomew Mosse, son of the Rector of Maryborough. Mosse qualified as a surgeon in Mercer's Hospital but decided to devote himself to midwifery. His work brought him into constant touch with the poor of the city. He visited their hovels and their tenements, struggling to bring safely into life children whom the world had nothing to offer but dirt and misery and disease. Appalled by the circumstances in which the people were compelled to live he wrote:-

> "Their lodgings are generally in cold garrets open to every wind, or in damp cellars subject to floods from excessive rains; themselves destitute of attendance, medicines and often proper food; by which hundreds perish with their little infants and the community is at once robbed of mother and child."

He decided that he should try in some way to lessen the hardships of these unfortunate people and having formed a Committee of his friends to help him, he acquired a premises in North Great George's Street in 1745. It was named The Hospital for Poor Lying-In Women and was financed chiefly by concerts and other entertainments held for that purpose. Mosse also organised a lottery to raise funds but in 1753 he ran into difficulties with the Lords Justices and was ordered to abandon a lottery on which he had hoped to raise over £13,000.

The demands made on the new hospital were so great that Mosse decided to provide new and larger premises in what is now Parnell Square. Thus came into existence the present Rotunda Hospital on a site which was leased "for three lives, renewable for ever at a fine of a peppercorn on the fall of each life". To help build the new institution ornamental gardens were laid out on the site to which an admission fee was charged. Concerts were held in the gardens and many famous cross-Channel artists visited Dublin in order to perform there. Eventually the new 150-bed hospital opened in 1757 but Mosse, who had laboured so hard to see it become a reality, was to survive its completion by only a little over a year. Worn out by his efforts and maligned by his medical colleagues who accused him of fraud and other forms of malpractice, he died in Donnybrook at the beginning of 1759.

The Meath Hospital was opened by a number of benevolent medical men in 1753 and was originally intended for the use of poor manufacturers living in the Earl of Meath's liberties. At first located in the Coombe it was moved on several occasions and finally occupied its present site in 1822. This site was purchased from the Dean and Chapter of St Patrick's Cathedral and was at one time Dean Swift's garden, or as he named it, "Naboth's Vineyard". In 1774 it was designated the Dublin County Infirmary after its Governors had petitioned the Irish Parliament for such a designation in order that it might secure some State assistance towards its maintenance. It is of interest to note that at this period the Treasurer of the Hospital was Arthur Guinness, James's Gate, the founder of the now world famous brewery.

The Lock Hospital was originally established near Thomas Street in 1755 and was intended as a place of treatment for women and children suffering from venereal diseases. Shortly afterwards it was moved to Townsend Street, and in 1758 when it was found that the husbands of the nurses caring for the patients were in many instances suffering from venereal disease, it was decided to open a special male ward for them in the hospital. With the passage of time other male patients were admitted but the commingling of the sexes in a hospital of this nature was found to be a very unwise arrangement and in 1815 it was found necessary to move the male patients to special wards in Steeven's Hospital. From then, until it closed some years ago, the inmates of the hospital were exclusively female.

Other hospitals were opened in Dublin during this period of which there are no traces today. Some lasted but a few years. Others, such as St Nicholas's, near Meath Street, and the United Hospital of St Mark's and St Anne's in the Westland Row area, were in operation for a considerable time until, for various reasons, they went out of existence.

Cork City too had a number of voluntary institutions opened as a result of the efforts of some of its more benevolent citizens. In the early part of the century the North Charitable Infirmary came into being with the aid of funds collected by the Cork Charitable and Musical Society and some time later the South Charitable Infirmary was established in the suburbs and granted a Charter by the Irish Parliament.

In Limerick St. John's Hospital was opened in 1780 to cater for fever cases, but as far as the rest of the country was concerned no hospital of note was established.

THE 19th CENTURY

Despite the ameliorative measures taken during the 18th century by public and private sources to lessen the plight of the sick and indigent poor, little or nothing was done to eradicate or lessen the root cause of their misery by improving their economic circumstances. "The poor are always with us" was accepted as a God-given axiom, reassuring to members of the landlord class if the thought should cross the minds that something ought to be done about the squalor in which the great majority of the native Irish were living. As a contemporary commentator remarked:

> "Whilst in England it is a principle that every pauper has a right to legal support, in Ireland the principle is rather that the rich owe nothing to the poor".

And after all there was no real demand for any form of social or economic freedom! The echoes from the Paris streets of the cries demanding liberty, equality and fraternity may have reached the workshops and tenements of Liverpool and London, but the Irish peasant, in the gloom of his stone cabin, surrounded by his naked children and his pigs and his hens, heard none of them. There seemed to be no way out for him, no Utopian dream to make the future look brighter, no balm for his miseries except the transient ones which poteen could give. And it seems that many assuaged their hardship in that way, for during the year 1802-1806 almost 14,000 illicit stills were seized by excise men throughout the country.

Gustave de Beaumont, a French traveller in Ireland at the beginning of the 19th century wrote:

> "I have seen the Indian in his forests and the Negro in his chains and thought as I contemplated their miserable condition that I saw the very extreme of human wretchedness; but I did not then know the condition of unfortunate Ireland."

The early part of the century saw little being done by the Government to remedy gross injustices under which the Irish peasant was labouring.

The viewpoint of the *laisser-faire* school of economic thought was generally accepted, and the Government felt it had no right to interfere in the affairs of the landlord class. The best that could be done to ease the prevailing wretchedness was to provide more institutions. A number of fever hospitals were established at the beginning of the century and Grand Juries were authorised to present a sum not exceeding £250 for their support. In 1818 a further Act provided for the establishment of a fever hospital in every county, Grand Juries to present sums towards them not exceeding double the amount raised by voluntary effort.

The erection of lunatic asylums on a national scale was first authorised under an Act of 1817. Hitherto there had been little provision for the mentally afflicted. Special wards for the insane had been set aside in a number of infirmaries or Houses of Industry but, apart from St Patrick's Hospital, the only hospital of any size dealing exclusively up to then with the insane was the Richmond District Asylum opened in Dublin in 1815 as a result of a parliamentary grant made some years previously. Later it was renamed Grangegorman Mental Hospital. The Act of 1817 was radically amended by the Lunacy (Ireland) Act, 1821, which provided for "the establishment of asylums for the lunatic poor and for the custody of insane persons charged with offences". This latter Act has provided the basis for our existing mental hospital system and its present structure it still fundamentally the same as it was then.

As the years went on there was no improvement in the lot of the depressed classes. Successive famines added to their existing plight and brought them to the very nadir of misery. In 1833 the Government of Lord Grey decided that some far-reaching steps were necessary to meet the situation and a Commission was set up to investigate and report on the problem. When they submitted their final report in 1836 they pointed out that there were then, in their estimation, 2.5 million persons in Ireland requiring relief and they expressed the view that any attempt to alleviate their position by introducing the existing English Poor Law system to the country would not only pauperise the landlord class but would fail to bring any sensible improvement in the position of the tenants. They urged that the poor, the hungry and the landless be given an opportunity to earn an honourable livelihood by the provision of suitable schemes of work and that the sick be cared for by voluntary effort supplemented by public contributions.

But the recommendations were not accepted by the British Government. Instead it dispatched to Ireland a Scot, George Nicholls, who after a six-week tour of the country submitted a report which was to form the basis of the Poor Law Bill of 1837. The Bill provided for the formation of Unions through the country and for the erection in each Union area of a workhouse to be administered by a Board of Guardians comprised of ex-officio and elected members. The workhouses were to provide shelter for poor persons who by reason of old age, infirmity or defect might be unable to support themselves and for such other persons as were unable to care for themselves. Both landlords and tenants were to be rated for the support of the poor within the area in which they were living.

The Bill was most unpopular. Meetings of protest were held throughout the country and it was opposed in the House of Commons by Daniel O'Connell and most of his Irish colleagues. But the voices raised against it went unheeded in Westminster and in July 1838 it became law.

Within a few years 130 workhouses had been built. They were primarily places of shelter for the homeless and destitute rather than hospitals for the treatment of the sick but when the Great Famine of 1845 struck they had to open their doors to a great sad stream of starving people many of whom were sick or dying from typhus or cholera or, in most cases, just starvation. They became grim, overcrowded houses of death. Epidemics of various fevers added to the already appalling mortality rates. There was not enough food to sustain the unfortunate inmates, no proper medicines to ease their sufferings, too few physicians to set up any real resistance to the ravages which were wiping out so many. Not only were the inmates themselves swept away but the doctors and attendants who were caring for them very often fell victims.

At the end of 1845 there were 42,000 persons lodged in workhouses At the end of the following year the number had increased to 95,000. During the years 1849 and 1850 a total of almost 1,800,000 persons passed through their doors, accepting gladly the small degree of comfort they had to offer.

In 1862 the necessity to provide specifically for the care of the sick in workhouses was recognised and an Act of that year empowered Guardians to admit poor persons requiring medical and surgical attention and to provide for their maintenance and treatment. Power was also given to charge patients for treatment given where it was felt that they could afford to pay something.

Towards the end of the century it was being recognised that it was desirable that the care of the sick, even though they might also be poor, should be disassociated from the relief of the destitute, and the Local Government Act of 1898, one of the more progressive Acts of the period, gave powers to Guardians to convert workhouse hospitals into district hospitals under separate management. But if Dublin Castle and Whitehall were at last beginning to make some effort to get away from the Poor Law system there was no avant-garde to press forward such progressive ideas amongst the local representatives of Ireland, and consequently only two Boards of Guardians availed of this power; the structure of the Irish local authority hospital system remained practically unchanged for the next quarter of a century.

THE VOLUNTARY SYSTEM IN THE 19TH CENTURY

But the voluntary hospital system was a more progressive one and to the numerous hospitals of this type opened during the previous century private benevolence added others.

In 1801 a meeting of citizens was held in Dublin to form an Association

> "to relieve the destitute poor affected with fever and to check the progress of contagion."

A committee of fifteen persons was appointed and the culmination of their efforts was the opening of Cork Sweet Fever Hospital in 1804. Special carriages hung on springs were made to convey patients to the hospitals and thus avoid the disastrous consequences which had arisen on previous occasions when infected persons had travelled by the then public service vehicles, viz, hackney coaches and sedan chairs. It was a timely project, for no sooner had it opened than Dublin was stricken with a series of cholera epidemics which wiped out many of its citizens. It is recorded that in 1814 there were on one Sunday over 80 funerals and that the coffin-makers of the city had the utmost difficulty in keeping up with demands.

Sir Patrick Dun's Hospital, although not completed until 1816, took in its first patients in 1809. The history of its origins is a long and involved one and it is not proposed to deal with it in detail here.

Sir Patrick Dun, a native of Aberdeen, came to Ireland towards the end of the 17th century as Physician to the Lord Lieutenant, the Earl of Essex. Claims that he took part in the Battle of the Boyne are apocryphal but there is abundant material available to show that he was a successful and highly esteemed physician who became President of the College of Physicians in 1677, a member of Parliament in 1692 and a Knight in 1696. When he died in 1713 he provided a trust in perpetuity to endow a Chair of Physics in the College of Physicians. The Chair was established and the College continued to reap the benefits of the trust for many years. However in 1799 when reports were circulating that the funds were being maladministered the House of Lords felt compelled to set up a Committee to enquire into their application. It found that many of the reports were well-founded and amongst the comments it had to make were: -

> "Your Committee hold themselves bound to notice a present of claret to the President of the College of Physick annually; an immoderate purchase of books, in some instances twice paid for; lawsuits carried on in which the said College were both plaintiffs and defendants and actually paid from said funds the expenses of both; the loans to indigent members of said College which were never repaid in many instances."

In the circumstances it is hardly surprising that the purpose of one of the last Statutes passed by the Irish Parliament before the Act of Union was to sequestrate most of these funds in order to build the new hospital which was to perpetuate the name of Sir Patrick Dun.

The National Eye Hospital was founded at St Mary's Abbey in 1814 by Commander Ryal, Oculist-in-Ordinary to the Viceroy and after many changes of name and place it finally emerged in 1904 as the Royal Victoria Eye and Ear Hospital, Adelaide Road.

The National Children's Hospital in Harcourt Street had its origins in Balfe Street in 1821 when it was known as the Institution for Sick Children.

The Coombe Hospital was opened in 1823 and was originally intended as a general hospital. However, on a cold day in December 1825 two poor women died on their way from the Liberties to the Rotunda Hospital and the next morning their bodies were found frozen in the snow. So great was the feeling to which the incident gave rise that a meeting of some of the wealthier citizens decided to subscribe to the establishment of a Lying-In Hospital in the Liberties. The existing general hospital was converted and re-opened as the Coombe Lying-In Hospital.

As the century proceeded other hospitals were opened. The Adelaide Hospital was established in 1834 to cater exclusively for Protestant patients and after early financial difficulties, which it managed to overcome, it was later to set a headline by its efforts to maintain itself without State aid.

The Royal City of Dublin Hospital was opened about the same time mainly with a view to providing training facilities for the College of Surgeons.

In 1834 the first general hospital under the control of a religious order came into being when Mother Mary Aikenhead, who had founded the Irish Sisters of Charity in 1815, acquired the Earl of Meath's house in Stephen's Green and established St Vincent's Hospital. And almost thirty years later another religious order, the Irish Sisters of Mercy, gave Dublin the Mater Hospital, now the biggest voluntary hospital in the city.

Other notable institutions which came into existence during the century were Temple Street Hospital – 1876, National Maternity Hospital – 1884, Newcastle Sanatorium – 1896, Mercy Hospital (Cork) – 1857, Victoria Hospital, Cork – 1874 and Barringtons's Hospital (Limerick) – 1829.

HOSPITALS IN THE 20TH CENTURY

When, in 1920, it was becoming clear that political freedom was in sight, there were those who turned their thoughts to planning the composition of public authority services in the new nation. In fact they went further.

Acting under Dáil Éireann, the Department of Local Government was set up and, despite the best efforts of the British controlled Local Government Board, it soon secured the allegiance of almost all local authorities in the country. The new Department felt that the existing hospital scheme, established as it was on the British Poor Law system, was neither in accordance with the traditions of the country nor befitting a nation which was now beginning to stand on its own feet. Accordingly, on the initiative and under the guidance of the Department, schemes were drawn up in each county which aimed at a complete break-away from the spirit and associations of the former system. It was not always possible to put those schemes into immediate operation in view of the troubled state of the country and the fact that may local institutions were being used as military establishments. But the blue-print was prepared, nevertheless, so that when the inevitable day of freedom arrived no delay would be incurred in putting it into operation.

After the ratification of the Anglo-Irish Treaty, these schemes were legalised and power to do so was given to the few remaining County Councils which had not already formulated schemes.

In general, the schemes adopted in each case were similar. Boards of Guardians were quashed and workhouses closed as such. Except in a few areas, County Infirmaries and their Committees of Management were abolished. New types of institutions were provided for, which were to be administered by the County Council or County Borough Council acting through Boards of Health, or, in a few cases, through Boards of Public Assistance. These new institutions fell into four main categories. Chief amongst them were the County Hospitals of which one was to be located in each county, usually in the county town, and which was to provide major surgical, medical and limited maternity services. Next came District Hospitals, generally to be located in other large towns in the County, or in areas remote from the County Hospital, and providing medical and minor surgical services. Fever Hospitals were also established in each county and finally there was the euphemistically titled County Home. This latter institution was intended to provide for the aged and infirm and it had, ancillary to it, an infirmary to care for the chronic sick.

But even with the best of intentions, it was not possible for the new broom to sweep absolutely clean. It was a relatively easy matter to alter the nomenclature of the existing hospital system and to introduce an alternative and centralised method of administration. But the new State had not at its disposal the huge sum of money which would be necessary to replace the grey unfriendly stone buildings, the physical manifestation of the old system, by new, up-to-date and less-forbidding constructions. In the circumstances of the time, with so many pressing calls on the limited resources of the Exchequer, there was no choice but to base the re-organised scheme of hospitals on the existing buildings. Thus thirty-three workhouses, or parts of them, were converted into county homes, nine became county hospitals and thirty-two were turned into district hospitals or fever hospitals. The county infirmaries were put to similar use. Reconstruction work was carried out on many of the buildings, new furniture and equipment were installed and every effort was made within the scope of the limited funds available to bring to the highest standard possible the services and comforts they were to offer. Higher qualifications were fixed for medical and nursing personnel seeking hospital posts, and the appointment of doctors and nurses to senior positions in the service became based on the recommendations of the Local Appointments Commissioners and not on the number of votes which could be mustered from amongst county councillors whose choice of candidate was not always determined by his or her professional standing or achievements.

But, despite the great steps forward which took place in the local authority hospital service, it was becoming increasingly apparent that many of the buildings were completely unsuitable for use as modern hospitals and were grievously lacking in elementary requirements such as adequate ventilation and sanitation. The patching and repairing of deficiencies here and there whenever available funds allowed, served merely as temporary improvisation and the position was aggravated by the fact that not only was the existing accommodation unsuitable and lacking in basic amenities but there was also a grievous shortage of it, particularly where provision for tuberculosis was concerned. This shortage of accommodation too had made difficult the transition from the Workhouse, with its motley conglomeration of unfortunate inmates, to the County Home as a place of shelter for the aged and infirm poor. In 1928, the Commission on the Relief of the Sick and Destitute Poor reported:

> "In the County Homes we found the following classes whether the schemes contemplated their admission or not, viz. aged and infirm of both sexes; lunatics, idiots and imbeciles of both sexes; unmarried mothers and their children, in some cases married mothers and their children; and orphan and deserted children. In a number of Homes there were cases of advanced tubercular disease and also cases of cancer".

Early in the 1930s it was accepted that a large scale programme of hospital building would have to be planned and put in hand as soon as possible and the then Department of Local Government and Public Health set about tackling the task.

THE HOSPITALS TRUST FUND

Whilst these radical changes were taking place in the structure of the local authority hospital system, all was not well with the voluntary hospital.

As a system it had ceased to expand before the beginning of the first World War. The last new voluntary hospital opened was the Royal Victoria Eye and Ear Hospital in 1904 and its opening marked the end of an era. For never again were the conditions to exist in which it would be possible for a lay organisation to build a hospital of its scale on voluntary subscriptions and endowments. The war had altered many things and Ireland although somewhat removed from it did not, and could not, remain untouched by the changed, and changing, social patterns and attitudes which came with its aftermath. As in Britain, higher taxation was leaving less money available for charitable subscriptions and the hardest hit were the upper classes on whose benevolence the voluntary hospitals were, in the main, dependent. But there were other changes too which were to seriously affect their future. The growing demands of the working classes, the emergence after many trials of a fairly virile trade union movement, the beginnings of State paternalism and the birth of the new nation with a government of its own bent on removing the vestiges of the former rule; all, to varying extents, tended towards reducing the incentive of many long-standing subscribers to continue to help the voluntary institutions. For many of the more generous patrons of these institutions came from amongst the Ascendancy class and they could hardly view with enthusiasm the political and social changes which were taking place, nor indeed feel much desire to continue to be philanthropic towards a people who, they felt, had determined to look after their own affairs.

The voluntary hospitals, consequently, found that their financial position was rapidly worsening and it was evident that unless some *deus ex machina* arrived on the scene without further delay to snatch them to safety, they were doomed to extinction. It arrived just in time and it took the form of a sweepstake.

In 1929 the representatives of six Dublin voluntary hospitals came together and decided to seek Government authority to the holding of a sweepstake in order to raise funds for their empty coffers. As a means of raising moneys for public services, it was not, of course, new. Nero and other Roman emperors had financed public works in this way, and down through the centuries it had been a frequently used and much abused method of easing the burdens of impecunious rulers and regimes; and although Cavour had described lotteries as a tax upon imbeciles, public authorities in many European countries were still finding them a useful method of helping to pay for services which would otherwise have to be met out of taxation.

Government approval to the proposed Irish scheme came with the passing of the Public Charitable Hospitals (Temporary Provisions) Act, 1930, and the first sweepstake promoted by the newly established Hospitals Trust Limited was held on the Manchester November Handicap of that year. Its success exceeded all expectations and it yielded almost £132,000 for the six participating hospitals. Other hospitals, which had viewed the whole project with extreme caution until then, rushed to join the venture. Twenty-three of than shared profits amounting to £440,000 after the second sweepstake. Thirty-four of them shared £700,000 when the third one was successfully concluded. Here indeed was a cornucopia of plenty with an endless and ever-increasing flow of riches. The days of penury were at last at an end and the future seemed bright and prosperous for the voluntary hospital.

But there was its poor relation, its depressed country cousin, the local authority hospital to be considered. For whilst Dublin, and to a lesser extent Limerick and Cork, were dependent on the voluntary hospital, the rural areas had no hospital services but those provided by the local authority. And as the accommodation, the services and the comforts of the city hospitals were now far outstripping what the available finances of the local authorities could provide, it was not perhaps strange, nor unfair, that the State should decide to seek a portion of the sweepstake pie.

An Act of 1931 provided that one-third of the surpluses of future sweepstakes should be handed over to the Minister for Local Government and Public Health for allocation as he though fit towards the provision of hospital services. The remaining two-thirds would continue to be allocated amongst the voluntary hospitals by a Committee of Reference which would decide the basis on which payments would be made.

The Committee invited the hospitals to state their requirements and within a short time claims for over £8,000,000 were submitted. They included demands to meet the cost of new buildings, of extensions and renovations, of more up-to-date equipment and additional staffing. Some of the schemes were grandiose, many of them had little regard for what the nation would require if its hospital needs were being tackled on a planned basis. The Committee, having reviewed the various proposals, decided to accept claims amounting to £5¼ million, the money to be distributed in proportion to the outstanding balances after each sweepstake.

The sweepstakes continued to be a success. Within a year and a half of their initiation £3,000,000 had been handed over to the voluntary hospitals. In 1933, however, the State again decided to intervene. The effect of the principal provisions of the Public Hospitals Act of 1933 was that in future the Minister for Local Government and Public Health would be responsible for the allocation of the funds which accrued from the sweepstakes and that a newly established body, the Hospitals Commission, would have the task of reporting to and advising the Minister on questions relating to the hospital and nursing services as well as on matters concerning the administration of the funds. The Minister was given absolute discretion in deciding whether a particular request for an allocation of funds should be granted and he was not obliged to maintain any fixed proportion as between local authority and voluntary hospitals in sharing out the money.

Soon the benefits of the sweepstakes began to make themselves felt. With the assistance of grants made available by the Minister, local authorities at last found themselves in a position to start replacing their old hospital buildings by new ones. A new County Hospital of 100 beds was opened in Mullingar in 1936. Within the next five years twelve more new county hospitals made their appearance and over thirty other local authority institutions, including two mental hospitals, were completed. Extensive schemes of reconstruction were carried out in many instances and new and up-to-date equipment was purchased.

Grants made available for the purpose also led to improvements in the voluntary system. The Governors of the National Maternity Hospital built a new institution to replace the old Georgian residences formerly in use. The Sisters of Mercy established St Michael's Hospital in Dun Laoghaire in order to meet a long-felt need in the area.

Many of the other voluntary hospitals added wings or carried out large scale schemes of improvement on buildings which had, in some instances, remained untouched for one hundred years or more. In addition to receiving grants for capital purposes, they were also paid sums to meet deficits in their annual revenues.

But when the war came in 1939, it brought an end to plans for extending the building programme. Many projects then under way were completed with difficulty because of the shortage of essential materials; others which were yet in the planning stage were abandoned or pigeon-holed until the world returned to normality. In the meantime, however, the sweepstakes continued to be held and the available surpluses, considerably diminished because of the loss of overseas markets for the sale of tickets, were allowed to accumulate.

THE POST-WAR HOSPITAL BUILDING PROGRAMME

During the war years the administrative and technical staffs of the Department of Local Government and Public Health kept under constant review the requirements of the country in regard to hospital beds, and planning was put in hand so that no time would be lost in getting the necessary projects under way as soon as possible after the ending of the "Emergency". Surveys were carried out with the assistance and advice of the Hospitals Commission and soon a picture was emerging of the requirements which would have to be met.

The most urgent need was for sanatorium beds. In 1943, there were only 2,200 such beds available although the number of deaths annually from tuberculosis was double that amount. During that year, out of every

100 persons who were dying in this country between the ages of twenty-five and thirty-five 54 were dying from tuberculosis in some form or another. Many were dying in their own homes unable to secure the institutional treatment which might have saved them. Often one member of a family infected another and so tragedy came more than once to many a household. No one could view such a state of affairs with equanimity, or indeed with anything but alarm. It was a situation which demanded to be met immediately and effectively, *pleno jure*, by the Department of State concerned. And having considered the position, the Government decided that the quickest way to tackle the problem was to grant direct powers to the Department of Local Government and Public Health to construct sanatoria and to hand them over when completed to the local authorities which were to administer them. The Tuberculosis (Establishment of Sanatoria) Act, 1945, gave the necessary statutory permission to do so and additional technical staff were immediately engaged to prepare the plans and supervise the building of three large-scale regional sanatoria in Dublin, Cork and Galway.

The setting up of a separate Department of Health in 1947 not only added impetus to the plans for extending accommodation for the tubercular but it also led to the preparation of a programme for hospital building generally; for, although the provision of sanatoria accommodation took priority, there was urgent need for practically all classes of institutional beds. Outstanding proposals, many of them put forward before the war, were reviewed and a list drawn up from amongst them of works which were regarded as of an urgent nature. It was an ambitious and far-reaching programme but it was hoped to complete it by 1955 and to finance it in the main from the Hospitals Trust Fund, although in a number of instances the voluntary or local authorities concerned would themselves have to raise portion of the expenditure involved.

Based on prevailing prices of building materials and current wage rates, the cost and grants which would be involved as estimated in 1948 were:-

Class of Hospital	*Estimated Total Cost*	*Estimated Grant*
General Hospitals	£7,250,000	£5,430,000
Tuberculosis	£4,330,000	£4,330,000
Fever Hospitals	£1,250,000	£1,150,000
Maternity and Children	£1,640,000	£1,100,000
Mental (including mental defectives)	£1,925,000	£1,020,000
Dispensaries and Clinics	£ 750,000	£ 400,000
Smaller works	£ 355,000	£ 70,000
	£17,500,000	£13,500,000

The projects listed included the three regional sanatoria already mentioned, regional general hospitals in Cork, Limerick and Galway, a new St Vincent's and St Laurence's Hospitals and the rehabilitation of St Kevin's Hospital in Dublin, a new Coombe Hospital, children's hospitals at Ballyowen and Crumlin, six county hospitals and many other new institutions as well as extensions and renovations of numerous existing establishments. It was estimated that, when completed, almost 12,500 beds or cots in new or reconstructed accommodation would have been provided. Some of the new buildings would replace obsolete accommodation or premises in temporary use, with the result that the nett gain to the nation's bed accommodation would be in the region of 9,200 beds.

The following is a classification of the beds:

Type of beds	*Gross Number to be provided*	*Net Addition to existing beds*
General, Medical and Surgical	3,790	2,265
Tuberculosis	4,340	3,240
Orthopaedic	520	485
Maternity	770	590
Children	800	750
Fever	340	45
Mental Defectives	1,370	1,370
Mental	500	500
TOTAL	12,430	9,254

For a country of Ireland's size and economic standing, the programme was of courageous proportions. It marked too the advent of a new principle into the Irish hospital system, namely the provision of regional hospitals, catering for patients from more than one county and generally providing services of a more specialised or expensive nature than the existing county institutions.

The planning of the numerous projects immediately went ahead *à pas de géant* and in some instances, as in the case of the regional sanatoria, building quickly started. But soon disturbing omens appeared. The inflationary tendencies of the post-war years were leading to increased costs. Successive wage demands were made and conceded; essential materials started to increase in price. International tensions led to shortages and stockpiling and further increases. And as the spiral of costs went sharply upwards, so too did the estimated cost of the hospital programme. By 1950 it was clear that the available resources of the Hospitals Trust Fund would be unable to finance the proposed undertakings to the extent originally intended. Plans were reviewed; economies were effected; some of the projects were postponed. But most of them were allowed to go ahead. The economic situation worsened, however, and the assets of the Fund reached rock-bottom, with the result that in the financial year 1953/54 the Government found it necessary to provide a grant-in-aid of almost £3,000,000 in order that it could meet current commitments. Grants-in-aid of varying amounts were also required during subsequent years, but after 1956/57 the claims of other and more urgent or more productive capital projects made impossible the provision of further Exchequer assistance to the Hospital Building Programme. Since then, with a few exceptions, no new projects have been allowed to start and the present aim is to allow a sizeable balance to accumulate in the Fund before any further building is undertaken.

If the 1948 programme had been allowed to proceed to completion, it would have cost about £35,000,000, just twice the 1948 estimate.

WHAT HAS BEEN ACHIEVED

But if the difficulties in the way of completing the task had proved insurmountable, the programme had not, nevertheless, been a failure. Approximately two-thirds of the projects included in it have been completed at a cost to the Hospitals Trust Fund of about £24,000,000. Every city and practically every major town in the country has some visible token of its achievement either in the form of a new or renovated hospital, a new clinic or a modern dispensary premises. Three regional sanatoria at Dublin, Cork and Limerick have been completed as well as other major tuberculosis institutions, such as St Mary's Chest Hospital, Dublin, and Ballyowen Sanatorium. Regional general hospitals have been opened in Galway and Limerick, a county hospital at Manorhamilton, a Cancer Hospital at Rathgar, Dublin, an Orthopaedic Hospital at Gurranebraher, Cork, a fever hospital at Clondalkin and a children's hospital at Crumlin. St Kevin's Hospital, Dublin, the largest hospital in Ireland, has been thoroughly renovated and its Poor Law atmosphere brought virtually to an end. Other works completed include numerous new or rebuilt district hospitals, new and extended maternity units and out-patient departments at existing hospitals, and additional mental hospital and mental defective accommodation.

Its results as far as the health of the nation is concerned are, of course, less tangible.

The most striking change in the health pattern of the country since the initiation of the programme has been the decline in deaths from tuberculosis. In 1945 there were 3,694 deaths from this disease. In 1957 there were only 696. It cannot, of course, be claimed that the provision of adequate sanatorium accommodation was the major factor in bringing about this dramatic fall, but it can at least be argued that if the additional beds had not been provided it would not have been possible for many patients to avail, in good time, of the advantages of the new drugs and surgical techniques which were at last effectively conquering the disease The striking change which has taken place with regard to tuberculosis is illustrated by the fact that within the last few years a number of sanatoria have closed as such for lack of patients and have been put to other institutional use. And judging by the steady downward trend of the disease, the closing of others seems inevitable.

Another benefit deriving from the extension of the hospital system is the more easy availability for many communities of institutional services. Some remote districts have, for the first time, their own medical hospitals. Most areas have now had specialist, diagnostic and treatment services brought nearer to them, not only as a result of the building of new regional institutions and county clinics and the improvement of facilities in existing county hospitals, but also because of the appointment of regional specialists for service in them. Whereas formerly it was usually necessary for a person to go to the city when he required any form of specialised treatment, he may now avail of it closer to home with less expense and less delay.

During the past decade it has also been found possible to take effective steps towards ensuring that County Homes will become places exclusively for the care of the aged and chronic sick. A Government White Paper published in October, 1951, announced that local authorities were being asked to transfer to specialised institutions mothers and children, mental defectives, epileptics, etc. hitherto accommodated in the Homes. The Homes themselves were to be brought up to the standards of a modern hospital, their surroundings brightened up and the stigmata of pauperism removed. In view, however, of the over-committed state of the Hospitals Trust Fund, it was not possible to promise capital grants for the work but in order to encourage local authorities to undertake it, they were guaranteed by the Department of Health a State contribution amounting to one-half the annual loan charges on any funds borrowed for the purpose, subject to an overriding maximum of £500 per bed. The work has been slow to get underway, however, due, to a large extent to borrowing difficulties.

THE FUTURE

Generally speaking it may be said that the accommodation now available for medical, surgical, maternity, tuberculosis and most other specialties is ample, although some buildings catering for these categories are obsolescent and others are badly in need of repair. But the position regarding the provision of institutions for the mentally afflicted is far from satisfactory. Most mental hospitals are overcrowded and the number of beds for mental defectives does not nearly meet the demands made upon them. If new buildings were to be provided to relieve the present situation, the capital expenditure involved would probably run to several million pounds, an outlay which available funds would be unable to meet but which, in any event, would have to be considered in the light of an economic situation which demands more productive capital expenditure. On the other hand, however, it may be possible to go a long way towards meeting present mental requirements without opening new institutions. As already mentioned a number of sanatoria have already closed due to the falling incidence of tuberculosis and as it continues to decline more institutions will inevitably have to be put to alternative use. Fevers too have shown a big decline in recent years and if current trends continue, the small local fever hospital will soon become extinct. These emptying sanatoria and fever hospitals may help considerably towards relieving the mental hospital and mental deficiency problem, but not all of them, because of the nature of the buildings, may be suitable for that purpose. Herein lies a lesson for the planner of the hospital of the future. It must be a multi-purpose hospital, built not with just one type of patient in mind but capable of easy conversion to deal with any other category of inmate should the necessity arise.

Current experiments in the treatment of mental patients, if they prove successful, will almost certainly lead to fewer mental hospital beds than heretofore. In the towns of Worthing and Chichester in West Sussex a domiciliary psychiatric service, which is being provided by psychiatrists from the local mental hospitals, is reducing admissions to the hospitals by 60%. The patient is treated in his own home, in his own community, and the role of the hospital itself is fading into the background. If the initial success of this scheme is sustained and confirmed, it must inevitably influence the future approach to mental treatment in this country. The degree to which our current bed problems might be eased if we adopted such a scheme may be gauged from the estimate of the West Sussex experimenters that within ten years the number of mental hospital beds in their area will be reduced front 1,100 to 300.

Finally some reference must be made to current attitudes with regard to the future of the voluntary hospital.

Opponents of the system hold that the title “voluntary” is a misnomer; that it belongs to the days when the hospital was maintained on voluntary contributions and endowments; when its medical staff provided their services free and no charge was made to the patient. Now, it is argued, charitable donations have dwindled to insignificance. The Government, from funds under its control, pays grants to them for capital works and also meets their current deficits. Patients are no longer treated free of charge and, indeed, if they default in payment, legal proceedings are taken against them as a matter of course. Many of the patients are paid for, either partially or *in toto*, by local authorities who are, in turn, recouped 50% of this expenditure by the State. The doctors are now paid and expect to receive what they regard as adequate remuneration for their services.

There those who feel that it would be in the national interest for the State to take over all voluntary hospitals and thus end the present dichotomy in the hospital structure which, it is felt, is to the detriment of the system as a whole. It is held that since the State is paying the piper it should be allowed to call the tune. And calling the tune would put an end to the wasteful expenditure and duplication of services which, it is claimed, have arisen from the rivalries of different hospitals and medical schools. A unified hospital system would, they argue, be a planned one. A particular speciality would be allowed to develop in only one hospital in a region. There would be no overlapping of services; no unnecessary purchasing of expensive equipment. A hospital's accommodation would be directed to the purpose which current exigencies demanded most: institutions not required could be closed down and generally speaking there could be a rational approach towards the organisation of the whole system.

Upholders of the voluntary system argue that its nationalisation would be an unwarranted interference with a field of activity particularly suited for and traditionally associated with private charity and voluntary endeavour. They claim that the present financial situation of the hospitals does not arise from any inherent weakness in the system nor from a change of attitude on the part of the individual towards voluntary charity. If less money is available for charitable purposes, it is, they say, because of the burdens of State taxation. And if the State deprives, albeit indirectly, the voluntary hospital of its traditional means of subsistence there is no reason why it should not help it to meet its consequential debts. It is also pointed out that many of these institutions are run by religious communities who are dedicated to charity and poverty, and that those which are under the control of lay organisations are administered by Boards of Governors comprised of philanthropic individuals, unselfishly devoting much of their time and energy to the work involved without any expectation of material gain. Why, it is asked, in a society where there is an ever-increasing tendency to drift away from private initiative in the field of social service should the State take any action to curb such healthy manifestations? It is argued, too, that the patient in a voluntary institution is assured of a more compassionate, less impersonal and more human atmosphere. Greater flexibility in the organisation of the hospital is claimed, less of a "9 to 5" attitude towards their duties on the part of the staff, no bureaucratic meddling with *minutiae* and greater respect for medical secrecy. Big Brother, it is conceded, may be able to create a more efficient system, a rationally contrived and well-oiled machine, but since the hospital is concerned intimately with day-to-day human suffering he cannot, because of his very nature, imbue it with that desirable and mollifying element – a flesh-and-blood approach.

The arguments on both sides are forceful and at the time of writing (1958) it seems that any effort to change the existing state of affairs will undoubtedly lead to controversy.

Whatever form the hospital system of the future may take, the hospital itself will continue to be an important part of the whole structure of human life. Down through the centuries it has grown in stature as medical science developed its mitigations of human suffering. The temples of ancient Egypt, the nosocomia of the early Christian world, the monastic institutions of medieval times, the squalid infirmaries of later centuries all, in their own time, and in their own way, represented a refuge for afflicted mankind, an alleviation of pain, a place of hope even if these hopes were rarely fulfilled. Yet, now, if we cast our minds back for only two generations we are repelled in horror at the grim institution which then passed for a hospital. But the modern institution stands forth as one of humanity's noblest achievements and to-day it brings great alleviation of suffering.

SOURCES

de Beaumont, Gustave: Ireland; Social, Political and Religious (London 1839).

Browne, O'Donel T.D.: The Rotunda Hospital (Livingstone 1947).

Canavan, Rev. J. E.: Irish Sisters of Charity (Dublin 1941).

Commission on Relief of Poor and Destitute Sick: Report (1928).

Department of Health Reports.

Fleetwood, John: History of Medicine in Ireland (Browne & Nolan 1951).

Freeman, T. W.: Pre-Famine Ireland (Manchester University Press).

Howard, John: An Account of the Principal Lazarettos in Europe (1789).

Joyce: Social History of Ancient Ireland.

Lecky, W. E. H.: History of European Morals.

MacLysaght, Edward: Irish Life in the 17th Century.

Maxwell, Constantia: Country and Town in Ireland under the Georges (Harrap 1947).

Meldon, G. P.: The Lock Hospital (Irish Journal of Medical Science 1914).

O'Brien, George: Economic History of Ireland from the Union to the Famine (Longmans 1921).

O'Brien, R. Barry: Fifty Years of Concessions to Ireland (1831-1881).

O'Sheehan, J. and de Barra, E.: Ireland's Hospitals (Hospitals Trust 1955).

The Irish Builder (1896 and 1897).

The Legacy of Swift (Sign of the Three Candles 1948).

and many minor sources.

Administration, vol. 51, nos. 1-2 (Spring/Summer 2003), 167–172

Against the Tide

RUTH BARRINGTON

Book Review

Noel Browne, Dublin: Gill and Macmillan, 1986.

Originally published in 1987, vol. 35, no. 2, 213-217.
Ruth Barrington is the author of Health Medicine and Politics in Ireland 1900-1970, *Institute of Public Administration, 1987.*

Against the Tide is an unforgiving and unforgettable book. Throughout his life, Noel Browne has aroused strong emotions. His autobiography captures the passions of an extraordinary life. In addition, it is well written, beautifully designed and of great interest to the modern reader who is curious about Ireland's recent past. For this reviewer, what Dr Browne has to say about his period as Minister for Health is of most interest. As with much of his life, his contribution as a minister can be understood fully only in the context of the experiences of his childhood and youth.

That Noel Browne survived his childhood is a miracle in itself. His account of the sufferings and death of his father, mother, sisters and brother from tuberculosis and other disorders is terrifying. The harrowing experiences of his early years left their mark on his personality. He admits that he is 'a solitary serious fellow' who finds it difficult to form close and lasting friendships. Sadly, the tragedy of the Browne family was not unique in the days before a concerted attack on tuberculosis. The Brownes appear to have been particularly unfortunate after the death of Noel's father, when his mother's Ballinrobe family refused to assist the widow and young family and forced her to take the boat to England.

That decision was a fateful one for the young Noel. As if to compensate for the mean portion handed out to the young child, fortune decided to compensate the teenager in other ways. The kindly lady who befriended the family in London organised his admission to a preparatory school in Eastbourne, from which he subsequently won a scholarship to Beaumont, a Jesuit public school. There he acquired a cosmopolitan education of a kind usually reserved for the most privileged boys of his age in Ireland. His intelligence, ability as an athlete and good looks helped compensate for his sense of being an outsider. At school he became friendly with Neville Chance, son of Sir Arthur Chance, who had been one of Dublin's leading physicians. His widow, Lady Eileen Chance (daughter of William Martin Murphy), took an interest in the penniless Browne and financed his education at Trinity medical school. Thanks to this act of generosity, Browne received a university and professional education to which, if his parents had lived, he could hardly have aspired. (There is no reference in this book to the apocryphal story that it was out of a sense of guilt that the Chance family befriended Browne following a shooting accident in which, it is alleged, Sir Arthur Chance injured Browne's father.) Although Browne portrays his attendance at Trinity as the first occasion on which he ignored a dictat of the Archbishop of Dublin, it was not until 1942 – the year in which Browne left Trinity – that Catholics were formally banned from attending the college.

The Chance family came to the rescue again when Browne contracted tuberculosis in 1939. Thanks to their money and connections, Browne was admitted to a leading sanatorium in England where he received the attention of the most skilled surgeons of the day. His experiences of the disease helped direct his medical studies. On qualifying as a doctor, he worked in sanatoria in England and was 'changed irrevocably' by the experience. The contrast between the facilities for treating tuberculosis in England and Ireland during the war years could hardly have been greater. British sanatoria, even under war-time conditions, combined the latest diagnostic and surgical treatment with an egalitarian attitude among staff and patients. Treatment facilities in Ireland remained primitive, compounded by the hierarchical and elitist attitudes of the Irish medical establishment. His period in England convinced Browne of the advantages of a national health service, as advocated by Beveridge and promised by the Labour Party, in which treatment would be provided according to need not income, and doctors paid by salary not fees.

Returning to Ireland after the war, Browne became assistant medical superintendent at Newcastle sanatorium, Co. Wicklow in 1945. Convinced that he could do little to fight the disease as a junior doctor, he decided to campaign publicly for improved facilities. Although he had no republican sympathies, he threw in his lot with the motley assortment of radicals opposed to Fianna Fáil that comprised Clann na Poblachta. Elected in 1948 to fill the third seat in the same constituency as Sean MacEntee and John A. Costello, Browne was made Minister for

Health on his first day in the Dáil. Aged thirty-two he was 'determined to revolutionise the quality of the health services'.

Dr Browne's account of his contribution to improving the health services would be easier to judge if he had given credit to his predecessors for the radical measures they had already set in train. It would also have explained the ferocity of the medical profession's opposition to the mother and child scheme. As his account stands, it is hard to see what all the fuss was about.

By the end of the war, public dissatisfaction with the quality of the medical care available to the poor and those on moderate incomes had convinced people such as Bishop Dignan of Clonfert and Dr John Shanley, president of the Irish Medical Association, of the need for a radical overhaul. Both prepared 'plans' to reform the health services. The Minister, Sean MacEntee, and his Parliamentary Secretary, Dr Con Ward, were open to ideas and responded in 1945 by establishing a departmental committee to assess what needed to be done. Dr James Deeny, the recently appointed Chief Medical Adviser, was appointed chairman. The other members were John Collins, John Garvin and Paddy Keady; Desmond Roche acted as secretary. They produced a report that was little short of revolutionary in its consequences for the health services. Although the report was never published, the Department was moving towards its objectives from 1945 onwards.

The report (a copy of which is on the cabinet files in the State Paper Office) recommended the gradual establishment of a health service free of charge to all. As a priority, it recommended that services for tuberculosis sufferers, mothers and children and those in the public assistance classes be improved and provided without charge. Then the services would be made available to the whole population. General practice and hospital services would be reorganised to provide improved primary care and specialist services. The report envisaged that eventually most doctors in the new service would be employed by salary, and private practice would become a peripheral activity. The capital to pay for the new service would come from the Hospitals Sweepstakes, while its revenue costs would be met from rates and exchequer grants. The report, which was accepted by Dr Ward and Mr MacEntee, formed the basis for the White Paper *Tuberculosis* (1946), the establishment of a separate Department of Health (1946), the White Paper *Outline of Proposals for the Improvement of the Health Services* (1947), the Health (Financial Provisions) Act, 1947, and the Health Act, 1947.

When Dr Browne became Minister for Health in January 1948, he did not arrive in a sleepy backwater but in a new, dynamic department with many ideas for reform. It was his good fortune to become Minister when, much of the preparatory work done, the ship was ready to take to sea. As far as the chief scourge, tuberculosis, was concerned, a great deal had been done to implement the 1946 White Paper. Sites had been acquired for the regional sanatoria and a team of architects and engineers had been recruited to plan and oversee their building. Interim accommodation was being acquired, a mass X-ray and BCG campaign had been initiated and the recruitment of chest surgeons was underway. Critically, the Health Act had extended the free treatment of tuberculosis to the whole population and enabled those undergoing treatment to receive maintenance payments.

So what was Dr Browne's particular contribution to the fight against the disease? By his own account, he was ignorant of the steps that had been taken towards controlling the disease before he arrived in the Custom House. He claimed in the Dáil that it was not until after he became Minister that he discovered that maintenance payments were payable to patients undergoing treatment for the disease. His unique contribution to the campaign was his ability to motivate people to fight the disease and to achieve results quickly. He was the first Minister for Health to use the media extensively to get his message across. No one should underestimate the psychological importance of the urgency he attached to building the new sanatoria or to persuading people to come forward for diagnosis and treatment. For generations, tuberculosis had been a disease to be hidden because of the terrible stigma attached to sufferers and their families. Dr Browne's youthfulness, his own experience of the disease, his medical background and obvious humanity persuaded people to come forward in their thousands for X-rays and treatment. The failure to control bovine tuberculosis in Ireland's cattle herds, despite the enormous financial investment, suggests what might have happened among humans if Dr Browne's campaign had not taken place.

It is often argued that the investment in accommodation and facilities was unnecessary because antibiotics would soon transform the treatment of the disease. This criticism ignores the fact that until the early 1950s, streptomycin was prohibitively expensive to use and often had damaging side effects. It was least effective in treating advanced cases of tuberculosis where the only chance of survival was through surgery. The essential contribution of the sanatoria was to prevent patients with advanced disease from infecting their families, neighbours and workmates and to offer them some chance of survival through surgery. Dr Browne's critics are on firmer ground when they argue that the sanatoria were unnecessarily expensive and elaborate. All became redundant as sanatoria long before the end of their usual lives.

Less groundwork had been done in the Department on expanding the hospital system – apart from the sanatoria – when Dr Browne took office, but it was clear enough what had to be done. It was a case of resuming the building programme begun in the 1930s, with finance from the Hospitals Sweepstakes, but interrupted by the war. When Dr

Browne came into the Department he was presented with proposals for 135 building schemes, at an estimated cost of £27m. He reduced these proposals to a building programme costing £15m. over seven years, an enormous amount in the money values of the day. Some £13m. of the total was to come from the Hospitals Sweepstakes. Not the least attraction of this source of capital to the Minister was that he had discretion over how the monies should be spent. He did not have to seek cabinet or the Minister for Finance's approval for its disbursement. The financial commitment to the programme from the Hospitals Sweepstakes was so great that it effectively consumed much of the funds put in trust to pay the deficits of the voluntary hospitals, and committed all future income solely to the programme. The voluntary hospitals and their consultant establishments were alarmed by the Minister's action, regarding it as an act of piracy. They saw their increasing reliance on state funding as the death knell of their independence. Particularly galling to the Dublin hospitals was the Minister's decision to give priority in the building programme to hospital projects in the provinces. The antagonism aroused among the Dublin medical establishment by the Minister's action played no small part in blocking his plans for a mother and child service.

Much less thought had been given to the third major issue on the agenda for health reform when Dr Browne took up office: improving services for mothers and children. The objective of a free health service for all pregnant and post partum women and children up to sixteen years of age had been set out by the departmental committee on the health services and was facilitated by the Health Act of 1947. But little had been done to develop a consensus about the reorganisation of Irish general practice. Although private practice would remain in theory, the coverage by a free scheme of all mothers and children would make private practice obsolete. What was more, the medical profession saw Dr Browne's scheme as the tip of the iceberg of a universal health service without fees for service; they knew there were plans in the Department, to which the Minister had publicly committed himself on a number of occasions. The doctors were determined to resist his scheme at all costs. Their chief weapon was the influence of the Catholic Hierarchy, who agreed with the doctors' dislike of state medicine and was susceptible to their arguments that the scheme posed a threat to women's moral welfare.

While the Minister found the tide flowing in favour of his campaign to control tuberculosis and to expand hospital accommodation, the current was strongly against his mother and child proposals. A wise sailor, faced with such an unfavourable tide, would have ensured at least that weather conditions were favourable before setting out on his passage. Dr Browne, however, seems not to have appreciated the dangers ahead or if he did, did little to anticipate them.

He did not, for example, secure cabinet agreement for the details of his scheme, but relied on a general discussion two years previously for authority to proceed. By the summer of 1950 when he circulated his proposals, he was no longer regularly attending cabinet meetings. It was clear to his opponents from early on in the controversy that he did not have cabinet support. He had also fallen out with his Chief Medical Adviser, Dr James Deeny (who first proposed the mother and child scheme), over the Minister's refusal to keep lines open to the medical profession – to play one section of medical interest off against another, as Aneurin Bevan did so brilliantly in Britain's post-war Labour government. On the contrary, the Minister seems to have gone out of his way to provoke the profession, most notably with the unsigned document *The Mother and Child Scheme – Is it Needed?* in which he attacked the money-making practices of doctors. Relations between Browne and his party leader, Sean MacBride, were increasingly strained and Browne lacked an independent power base.

Browne does not appear to have appreciated the scope for the profession and the Hierarchy to form an alliance against his scheme. In one of the most extraordinary statements in the book, Dr Browne says that 'while I always believed that a conflict with the medical profession was nearly inevitable ... I had no reason to believe that there would be opposition from the Hierarchy.' The sentence shows a remarkable naiveté about the influence of the Hierarchy in the health services and the tactics of the medical profession. Was the Minister not aware of the Hierarchy's intervention on the 1947 Health Act? The journal of his own profession referred to it, even if he did not see the files. Elsewhere in the book, Dr Browne refers to the Church's power in the health services, through the Catholic hospitals, the Catholic medical schools and their predominantly Catholic staff. Surely he must have been aware that senior figures in the Irish Medical Association were lobbying the Hierarchy over his mother and child scheme, some of which was reported in the *IMA Journal*?

Dr Browne's failure to anticipate and deflect clerical opposition before tackling the profession was, in retrospect, his greatest tactical error. There was room for compromise on the details of his scheme that would have saved face all round – as his successor Jim Ryan found – while still retaining the essence of the service. But that was not Dr Browne's way. He preferred a dramatic shipwreck to careful navigation around the rocks. It will be a matter for continuing debate whether his shipwreck was a necessary catharsis in Ireland's democratic progress, or an avoidable crisis that unnecessarily undermined confidence in the institutions of church and state. *Against the Tide* carries the debate into another generation.

Administration, vol. 51, nos.1-2 (Spring/Summer 2003), 173–190

The Voluntary Sector and the Personal Social Services

M.J. DUFFY

Originally published in 1993, vol. 41, no. 3, 323-344.
M. J. Duffy is a programme manager with the Mid-Western Health Board. *An earlier version of this paper was presented to a seminar of the Federation of Voluntary Bodies Providing Services to Persons with Mental Handicap, Killarney, October 1992.*

INTRODUCTION

The role of voluntary organisations is central to the development of the personal social services. In recent years there have been considerable changes in all sectors involved in this area. The purpose of this paper is to examine some of the key issues and make suggestions about possible options which may be taken. This paper is meant to stimulate discussion rather than be prescriptive. Particular attention will be given to the relationship between the voluntary sector and health boards in relation to the development of child care and family support services.

The role of the voluntary sector in the delivery of the personal social services and its relationship with the statutory sector is a complex and constantly evolving one. Prior to the introduction of the welfare state in Britain the vast majority of personal social services were provided by the voluntary sector. With the onset of the welfare state a number of writers felt that the role of the voluntary sector in relation to the personal social services would eventually fade away. Holman claimed that those who held this view were short-sighted in presuming that 'the post war boom of the welfare state had numbered the days of the voluntary sector' (Holman 1981). The question he posed was 'not whether they [voluntary organisations] would survive but what particular roles they should fulfil within the welfare state'. Interestingly, William Beveridge, who was the chief architect of the British welfare state, speaking in relation to the voluntary sector stated that: 'It involves making and keeping something other than the pursuit of gain as a dominant force in society' (Beveridge 1946). In the context of public policy deliberations which are more and more being driven by budgetary concerns, it is necessary to recognise the different focus which the voluntary sector can offer.

The importance of the voluntary sector in the UK was identified with the publication of the Wolfenden Report (1978). It did not however see a strong voluntary sector as implying a weak state sector. Indeed it was one of the first official publications to specifically address the issue of 'welfare pluralism' or 'the mixed economy of welfare' as it was referred to by Townsend in 1970.

THE MIXED ECONOMY OF WELFARE

At present there are a number of sectors which provide services to people in need. These are the statutory (provided by the state), the voluntary (provided by voluntary organisations), the commercial (provided by private individuals or organisations for profit), and the informal (provided by family, relatives, friends and neighbours) sectors. The combination of these different sectors is what is referred to as 'welfare pluralism' or the 'mixed economy of welfare'.

Jordan (1987) warns that terms such as 'welfare pluralism' or 'the mixed economy of welfare' lack precision. They are open to varying interpretations depending on the perceived role of each sector relative to the others. For the purpose of this paper the focus is primarily on welfare organisations within the voluntary sector. However, it is important to recognise the existence of these two sectors (the commercial and the informal) as they have an influence on the development of the voluntary sector.

The informal sector in Ireland is relatively strong. However, by its very nature it is unstructured. The extent of informal care in Ireland has never been quantified despite recommendations that this be done (e.g. NSSB 1982). Demographic changes, changes in the employment patterns of women and changing public attitudes to the role of women may lead to a substantial change and a diminution in the role of this sector. The reliance of the state sector on unpaid carers is increasingly being challenged. In fact it is a significant issue in the context of pressure on state services for the provision of residential care in particular.

Jordan (1987) points out that the 'evidence that the informal sector provides more care than the statutory, voluntary or commercial sectors is incontrovertible'. However, there are difficulties with trying to quantify the extent of the informal sector and integrating it with the other sectors. Indeed it must he remembered that the informal sector has been shown to be exploitative of women, in particular, and community care has been described as 'care by women' (Finch and Groves 1983).

Recently the state has begun to respond to pressure to recognise the role of carers through, for example, the Carer's Allowance. However, the issue as to what constitutes a carer and the remuneration of carers is one which will continue to attract debate. The Charter for Carers adopted by the Soroptomists is an important contribution to this debate. The setting up of carers' groups is one example of the informal sector moving towards the more structured voluntary sector.

The commercial sector in Ireland is quite limited in the area of personal social services. The greater proportion of this sector is engaged in the operation of private nursing homes. However, there has been a growth in private counselling services, private pre-schools, crèches and child-minding services in recent years. Indeed access to the commercial sector by its nature is limited to those who have money to purchase the services offered. As yet there is not the same political push towards the state providing services through the commercial sector as has been experienced in Britain.

The role of businesses contributing to the voluntary sector either financially or through the provision of skills should not be overlooked.

Ongoing debate and decisions about the potential role of each of these sectors, i.e. the informal and commercial sectors, in the personal social services will be dependent on social, economic and political factors. Favouring one sector at the expense of another will involve making political decisions. Issues such as the emphasis on citizenship rights, equality and equity in services, and the percentage of the state's resources that will be allocated to personal social services are central to this debate.

THE VOLUNTARY SECTOR

Involvement of religious

Ireland has a long history of voluntary involvement in the provision of social services. This involvement in the past has been dominated by religious bodies, for example, in hospitals, schools and orphanages. The situation has changed in recent years with the state taking more responsibility for the provision of services. The nature of religious involvement too has changed over the years. This has been due to the decline in religious vocations; a greater emphasis by religious on the role of the laity in the delivery of services; the move by religious from large institutions to providing community-based services; and the growth in the number of projects initiated by lay organisations and individuals.

Subsidiarity

The personal social services in Ireland have been strongly influenced by the principle of subsidiarity, which is clearly expressed in Catholic social teaching, in particular the Papal Encyclical *Quadragesimo Anno* (1931). Basically the principle of subsidiarity seeks to have decision making and the delivery of services operating at the lowest possible level of organisation in society. The Mother and Child controversy in the 1950s centred around the concern of the Catholic church about the delivery of services for mothers and babies by the state. The Catholic church argued at the time that the appropriate level of competence for child health was the family and not the state. Since the late 1960s there has been a significant change in the Catholic church's position with it placing a greater emphasis on the need for the state to intervene on social policy issues.

The principle of subsidiarity was central to the emergence of social service councils in Ireland in the 1960s and 1970s and is a key principle to an understanding of the voluntary sector. If services are to be developed and delivered at more basic levels of society it is necessary to assess whether they are capable of being so delivered. If they are not, it may be more appropriate to deliver some services at a different level. Clearly a community with high unemployment will have extra difficulties in meeting its own needs and thus will need extra resources if it is to be effective. Increasingly the church has challenged the state to intervene in the family and communities where it feels these units are not capable of functioning effectively without this intervention.

Co-ordination

In the 1960s and 1970s emphasis was placed on the development of social service councils around the country. Examples of these include Kilkenny Social Services, Clare Social Service Council (now Clarecare) and Limerick Social Services Council. In the early years these tended to place an emphasis on the care of the elderly, and as time went on, family support work began to be developed. In the mid-1970s, in particular, the need for co-ordination of services in the non-statutory sector was recognised. The Federation of Social Service Councils was set up in the mid-1970s. This attempt at co-ordination petered out in the late 1970s and the early 1980s. Had this process continued, clearer guidelines for the voluntary/statutory sectors could have developed. Instead, after the hope of the late 1970s little was realised (Butler 1981). There were a number of reasons why this co-ordination did not develop:

- the lack of time among voluntary personnel to give to the overall co-ordination nationally
- the changing nature of the voluntary sector itself (O'Mahony 1985). There appears to be a shift away from middle class benevolent volunteers to more client self-help involvement
- the lack of a co-ordinated response from the statutory sector to the voluntary sector. This was further complicated by the number of state agencies which dealt with voluntary

organisations including health boards, Department of Social Welfare, Department of Labour, local authorities and VECs
- many tasks which in the past were in the domain of the voluntary sector being taken over either wholly or in part by the state sector, e.g. home help service
- the competition among voluntary organisations for limited resources militating against the development of a co-ordinated response within the voluntary sector. This led to particular difficulties for new and emerging groups
- differences in philosophy between voluntary organisations
- the lack of clear long-term strategies by the voluntary sector. O'Mahony points out in her survey of voluntary organisations that they sought piecemeal support from the health boards rather than having a coherent programme
- the perception in the late 1970s by the voluntary sector that the development of community work was one of the key means of enabling it to develop. In most cases this did not occur, with a consequent limiting of the scope and capacity of the voluntary sector.

Centralism

Despite the influence of subsidiarity in Ireland there is the conflicting pull of centralism in relation to the planning and funding of services and a resistance to delegating responsibility down to local units. This centralist approach has been criticised for its stifling effect on local initiative and creativity (Barrington 1979). The failure to develop a clear voluntary/statutory policy framework could be viewed as the result of the predominance of the centralist approach and an ambivalent attitude to working through the complex issues inherent in resourcing services based on the principle of subsidiarity. There is a danger that an unplanned or ill-thought-out move away from this centralist approach could lead to unnecessary fragmentation or greater inequality, with richer communities benefiting from a system of devolved power.

Integrated development and partnership

In recent years subsidiarity has re-emerged as an issue principally at EC level where it has been central to policies under President Delors. This has led to difficulties between the EC and some national governments over the administration of the EC structural funds. The EC has also been to the forefront in pushing the notions of integrated development and partnership between state agencies and others as a means of overcoming the marginalisation of individuals and groups through the model action programmes of the Third Programme to Combat Poverty, programmes such as the PAUL Partnership in Limerick City and FORUM in Connemara.

Partnership is a term which has many meanings and uses. Indeed it can range from mere consultation through to genuine dialogue, power sharing, and citizen control (Arnstein 1971). Inherent in the concept of partnership are notions of power and inequality. Too often the concept has been used to imply an equality of relationship that does not exist. Any honest examination of the role of partnership needs to address the issues of inequality in, for example, access to information resources. It also needs to take into account the importance of public accountability of all organisations to the public at large and to the consumers of services.

Integrated development must focus on relationships between and within statutory and voluntary organisations. It must address overlap and gaps in service. This will involve an investment in training within both the statutory and voluntary sectors.

Citizenship rights

Another emerging concept that needs to be addressed is the whole notion of citizenship rights. The rights of consumers are more clearly defined in relationships with statutory organisations than with the non-statutory sector. There is a need to protect the rights and interests of the more marginalised sectors of our society. This involves giving recognition to the voice of marginalised groups. Included in this would be, for example, victims of Aids, travellers, lone parents and victims of violence in the home. Even within marginalised communities and groups there are those who are more excluded than others. If this concept is taken on board every effort should be made to ensure that these individuals are involved and that their views and needs are taken into account. One small example of this has been the resourcing by the Mid-Western Health Board with the PAUL project of an independent support service for parents whose children are in care. While the voluntary sector has a positive history in highlighting the rights of minorities it is only when these issues are taken on board by state agencies and protected by legislation that minorities can be properly protected.

Funding

The relationship between the voluntary and state sectors has never been fully clarified. This is particularly noticeable in relation to the whole question of funding of the voluntary sector. For over a decade there have been proposals for funding voluntary groups (e.g. National Social Service Council 1977; National Social Service Board 1982; Inbucon 1982; National Economic and Social Council 1987; Commission on Health Funding 1989; and Lavan 1992). Despite this, little clarity has been achieved.

It can be argued that due to the dependence on state bodies for funding by voluntary and community groups, the relationship between them can never be one of equal partnership. A clearer framework for their relationships would provide a better context for this issue to be addressed.

Newly emerging organisations

Newly emerging organisations tend to have particular difficulty in obtaining support for their work. There are a number of reasons for this.

- They have no proven track record and perhaps little or no structure and could be seen as risky investments.
- There is little incentive for state organisations to assist groups to organise if it means that these groups will subsequently be seeking funding from them.
- Many of these new and emerging groups have a self-help focus and are different in nature from the donor-recipient services of the more traditional voluntary organisations.
- Many may provide an advocacy role for 'unpopular' minorities, e.g. travellers.

People involved in these new organisations tend to have little previous experience of working in groups, running meetings, planning or evaluating. This puts them at a disadvantage when competing with the more established organisations. In some cases these new volunteers are less experienced than personnel in the more established organisations. Many of these organisations are grass-root organisations involved with marginalised groups and indeed some of the people involved are themselves marginalised.

It is worth identifying some of the strengths and weaknesses of the voluntary sector that have emerged in the literature and from the experience of the past 20 years.

Strengths

- The voluntary sector provides an innovative role in identifying and responding to new and emerging needs.
- The voluntary sector can provide an advocacy role on behalf of marginalised groups. It also plays an important role in educating public opinion about the needs and rights of these groups. Voluntary organisations and interest groups can and do provide informed expert opinions needed in policy formulation.
- The voluntary sector provides opportunities for involvement of people in their own communities. This involvement of people at a grass-root level can, if effectively developed, lead to the development of more responsive services. The role of the voluntary sector in providing a forum for self-development, group development and community development should not be underestimated.

- The voluntary sector provides services that are not at present being provided by the statutory sector.
- The voluntary sector tends to be less restricted by legislative and administrative limitations. However, increasingly they are taking on legal formats, e.g. as limited companies and trusts which are subject to legal obligations. They are also subject to new legislation such as the data protection and health and safety legislation.
- The voluntary sector has a greater level of organisation than the informal sector. However, in recent years there has been a movement within the informal sector towards a more effective organisational structure.
- The voluntary sector provides a more equitable service for those in need than does the commercial sector.

Weaknesses

- Many groups in the voluntary sector are single-issue focused, in contrast to statutory organisations. This could militate against a more integrated approach among non-statutory groups.
- The emphasis of the non-statutory sector on independence can impede co-operative ventures with others. This is particularly noticeable when organisations are pitted against one another in competing for limited resources.
- Many organisations are run by strong individuals who are their driving force. They decide the policy and direction of the organisations with little or no reference to others. This has been called 'rule by self-elected self-perpetuating minorities'. This can lead to a resistance to accepting the need for change.
- Voluntary organisations can develop a paternalistic approach to their client groups that can often be demeaning. Unlike the statutory sector there exists little or no appeals mechanism for people who feel that they have been wronged by a service provided by the voluntary sector. The Ombudsman's Act does not extend to the non-statutory sector. This militates against the trend towards giving greater recognition of citizens' rights to all.
- The employment status of those employed in the voluntary sector tends to provide less security than the state sector. This could lead to an undesirable turnover of people.
- Lack of resources within the non-statutory sector can lead to inefficiency in administration, volunteer and staff training, planning, evaluation and accountability.
- While the voluntary sector has been to the forefront in taking up the unpopular issues of the day, e.g. lone parenthood,

travellers, victims of domestic violence, drug additions and Aids, it is not in a position to guarantee rights. This can only be done by the introduction of legislation.

- Voluntary organisations operating in the same sphere can lead to unnecessary duplication and act as a block to the development of a cohesive service.

The voluntary sector is made up of a wide variety of groups with varying degrees of structure, size, involvement and philosophy. Some groups employ full-time staff, others have access to professional staff and others have no staff at all. Groups vary in the geographical area they cover and the client groups they serve.

A minimal level of structural organisation is required for voluntary groups to be effective. This includes the ability to run meetings, motivate people, keep accurate accounts, develop and implement plans. This requires training in team building, organisation and evaluation.

As voluntary organisations develop and their administration grows they can become more like statutory bodies. The term 'quasi-statutory' has been used to refer to such groups. Can voluntary organisations hold on to their advantages as they grow?

It is important to recognise that different elements of the voluntary sector have differing needs in their relationship to the statutory sector. Indeed many of the more settled organisations may seek a continuation of the status quo and resist any moves towards the development of a more integrated and equitable service which recognises the rights of consumers.

In view of all these complex factors it is hardly surprising that the state has had difficulty in clarifying, and indeed appears to be hesitant in clarifying, its relationships with the voluntary sector. This has been caused by the centralist approach adopted by the state. It has not been helped by the changing nature of the voluntary sector. This change has been dramatic in the past 20 years. However, with the influence of EC policy new opportunities are emerging which may facilitate more effective dialogue within and between the statutory and voluntary sectors. The proposed White Paper on voluntary activity will hopefully address this issue.

HEALTH BOARDS AND THE VOLUNTARY SECTOR

At regional level the health board is probably the major statutory body interacting with the voluntary sector in relation to the personal social services. With new provisions under the Child Care Act 1991 this level of contact is likely to grow. It is important, nevertheless, to recognise that the health board is only one of the statutory agencies having relationships with the voluntary sector. The multiplicity of funding sources and the separate accountability of the voluntary sector to different state agencies lead to fragmentation. This issue needs to be addressed by the state sector as a whole. State support should be provided by the most relevant and most locally-based state agencies. It will require better liaison between agencies and a clarification of responsibilities, where these are not clear at present. This is not solely a local issue but needs to be addressed at national level.

Relationships between the health boards and the voluntary sector are governed by section 65 of the Health Act 1953 which states:

> A health authority may, with the approval of the Minister, give assistance in any one or more of the following ways to any body which provides or proposes to provide a service similar or ancillary to a service which the health authority may provide.

While section 65 is capable of being interpreted with maximum flexibility, it can be argued that there has been a lack of clarity and consistency in its application. This has been caused in part by differing interpretations of what is meant by a 'similar or ancillary' service (O'Mahony 1985; NESC 1987). It is interesting to note that, despite concerns about the lack of clarity of these terms, they reappear in section 10 of the Child Care Act in relation to funding of voluntary bodies working in the child care area. It can be argued that the difficulties in relation to these sections have a lot to do with the lack of adequate resources and a lack of clarity as to the limits of health boards' responsibilities.

Experience would suggest that there is a bias towards more established groups in the making of grants under section 65 because the limited allocation available has, of necessity, to be allocated so as to ensure the continuation of existing services. This causes difficulties for new and emerging groups. These latter groups have in recent years been seeking funding from other sources such as the Department of Social Welfare. Such groups include women's groups and locally-based neighbourhood development organisations. Such grants tend to be once-off. When funds 'dry up' these groups apply to the health board for a continuation of funding. This can lead to difficulties for these groups and for health boards where funding is not available.

The context in which the health boards themselves operate is also the subject of public debate. Recent publications such as *Promoting Health Through Public Policy* 1987, *Community Care Services: An Overview* 1987, *Health, the Wider Dimension* 1987, *The Report of the Commission on Health Funding* 1989, *The Programme for Economic and Social Progress* 1991, recommended key changes in the way the health hoards operate. These changes include a greater emphasis on the following:

- the involvement of local populations in the development of policy. This is provided for in the Child Care Act of 1991

which recommends the setting up of child care advisory committees to deal with child care and family support
- the management of services by geographical area/units of service rather than by programmes
- inter-disciplinary work and less of an emphasis on professional boundaries
- primary care with emphasis on prevention
- accountability to consumer groups
- the efficiency, effectiveness and the quality of service delivery
- the development of integrated responses between the statutory, voluntary and community groups.

These changes will require a change in the way the health boards relate to groups and communities. They reflect a shift away from an emphasis on an individualised curative model towards one with a community development and preventive approach. Central to this model is the principle of subsidiarity with the model being characterised by partnership. Each element of the partnership, be it statutory, voluntary or community, must be seen as having a role in identifying and responding to needs.

EASTERN HEALTH BOARD REPORT FOR IPA PROGRAMME

A major study has been carried out by a group within the Eastern Health Board (EHB) as part of an Institute of Public Administration (IPA) programme. It has drawn up a report on the operation of section 65 grants and has suggested guidelines for the implementation of these grants.

The Eastern Health Board report points out that:

- There are confused expectations and a lack of clarity with regard to the operation of the grant. Even when expectations were made explicit these tended to be only verbally stated, while due attention was given to ensuring that voluntary agencies accounted for funds received before granting them additional resources. The same stress did not appear to have been laid on planning with the agency and estimating the real cost of service provision.
- The health board staff were adopting different approaches to voluntary agencies. The report expressed concern about what it called 'the individualisation and subjectivity of relationships'. Judgements about standards of performance of voluntary agencies often appeared to be based on anecdotal evidence or subjective impressions.
- Communication tended to focus solely on finances rather than on the purpose and objectives of the service needed. It seemed

to the working group that there was little consistency in the treatment of projects and no evidence was found of an attempt to integrate discussions on finances with the need to develop integrated services.

- Delay in providing funding to voluntary organisations due to cash flow problems within the EHB was leading to an increase in costs for voluntary agencies in respect of their cash flows and interest charges.
- The degree of control which the EHB should have over the operation of the voluntary sector was an area of contention. Was it related to the percentage of funding provided by the board? If this was the case what implications would this have for the independence of the voluntary agencies.
- Difficulties arose in relation to the integration of services when voluntary groups received grants directly from the Department of Health without consultation with the EHB.
- There appeared to be little integration of funding from other government departments.

The major recommendations emerging from the Eastern Health Board working group were that:

- Clear contracts should be drawn up in negotiation with the voluntary sector. This would set out a definite purpose, and expectations would be safeguarded by service objectives, targets, evaluation and review. This would leave less room for confusion and conflict.
- The inclusion of professional staff from a number of disciplines along with administrative staff in making funding decisions would assist in integrating the voluntary sector and health board services.
- Greater emphasis should be placed in broadening the discussions with voluntary agencies beyond finances.
- Funding to voluntary groups should arrive on agreed dates.
- Decisions in relation to funding from the Department of Health should be decentralised to the EHB.
- There should be a greater integration of funding from different government departments.

THE VOLUNTARY SECTOR AND THE MID-WESTERN HEALTH BOARD: A CASE STUDY

As stated earlier, there is a wide spectrum of organisations in the voluntary sector with major differences in accountability, organisation, structure and philosophy. This complexity is reflected in the variety of voluntary organisations operating in the MidWest region, which, in many ways, is typical of other parts of the country:

- local branches of national voluntary organisations, e.g. National Council for the Blind
- local intermediary bodies, e.g. Clarecare, Limerick Social Service Council and Thurles Social Service Council
- self-help groups such as GROW and Gingerbread
- community-based groups with broad remits, e.g. Southill Community Services Board
- single-issue service organisations, e.g. Mount St Vincent Child Care Service, Adapt
- new emerging groups with little organisational structure, e.g. Family Rights Group.

Groups can also be distinguished between those who employ staff and those who do not. Some have a clear philosophy and structure while others are more loosely structured. Groups also vary in the catchment area they cover. Some cover the whole region; some cover a community care area; others overlap between community care areas.

One of the major difficulties in discussing the voluntary sector, as shown above, is that it is not homogeneous. This diversity must be addressed in mapping a way forward. It is essential that a development plan is drawn up. It must take into account the changes in the socio-economic fabric of society and the emergence of new needs requiring new responses. These include the growth in unemployment, the numbers of elderly, marital breakdown, the numbers of single parents, the increase in reported cases of child abuse and family violence, and the onset of Aids.

The challenge to the Mid-Western Health Board is to identify how best to develop a coherent policy with the voluntary sector while at the same time allowing for the differing stages of development, structure, and philosophy of groups within this sector. It also needs to take into account local factors such as tradition, perceived needs, and socio-economic and demographic factors. This must be characterised by openness and by ongoing review of communication processes.

The Child Care Act 1991 clearly places responsibility on the health board for the development of child care and family support services. In addition, the elderly have particular personal social service needs and the voluntary sector has been significantly involved in this area for many years. The focus of the development of a personal social services policy needs to address these two main areas in a special way, as they are the main areas of contact between the health board and the voluntary sector.

The health board has begun taking on board the changes recommended by reports of the late 1980s and has sought to develop an integrated approach to the voluntary sector based on subsidiarity. This is reflected in:

- recent research commissioned by the health board which has emphasised the need for community-based consumer-driven services – *Cherished Equally* (1988), *Speaking Out* (1991), *Seeking a Refuge from Violence* (1992), *Breaking the Silence* (1992)

- the 'Partnership in Practice Conference' hosted by the health board in November 1991 (MWHB 1992)
- the drawing up of a child care policy statement in 1991. This was done through a consultative process involving social workers, child care workers and representatives of the Irish Foster Care Association. Workers from both the voluntary and statutory sectors were involved
- the partnership agreement drawn up between Clarecare and the health board
- involvement of the health board with the PAUL Partnership since 1989. Through this partnership the board has been involved in improving the operation of the 'back to school' clothing and footwear scheme; helping resource a family rights group; setting up a project to deal with the problem of debt; and involvement in an Horizon programme.

If a new model based on partnership between the health board and the voluntary sector is to work, new lines of communication must be developed. It must be recognised that this will not be easy for any of the parties involved. All parties must develop an understanding of others and be aware of their own limitations and needs.

Central to the model must be a recognition that if voluntary community sectors are to become more involved they will require resourcing. This will involve training and organisation, e.g. how to run meetings, draw up plans, evaluate developments, keep accounts. It will also be essential to make more information available to these groups. This extra resourcing is a recognition that at present the balance of power is very much in favour of the statutory sector; this balance must be adjusted. The balance of power within communities needs to be addressed as well in order to ensure the inclusion of the most marginalised elements within communities.

Staff in the statutory sector too will need training to enable them to adopt this new approach. If change is to occur it must permeate all levels of the organisation.

The complexity of the task involved in working this model and its importance require that it be moved into the mainstream and not treated as an optional extra. Responsibility for these developments must be given to people with the skills and experience to make them work. In this context it is worthwhile to explore again the role of professional community workers. It could be argued that the difficulties and confusions which have surrounded the relationship between the statutory and the voluntary sectors is mirrored by the difficulties which have surrounded the development of community work within the health boards.

DEVELOPMENT PLAN

In summary, and taking all the issues raised into account, the following recommendations, if implemented, would help develop a coherent policy between the health board and the voluntary sector.

- The health board needs to set out its own plans and prioritise these.
- Time limited contracts should be developed between the health board and all voluntary groups receiving funding. These contracts would be part of an overall integrated plan for the personal social services and would include issues such as training needs. These contracts would aim to facilitate long-term planning and where possible be for periods of more than one year. The contracts would set out clear goals and would outline service objectives and targets. There would be agreed strategies for review and evaluation.
- Payments from the health board to voluntary groups should be paid on agreed dates.
- Discussions in relation to funding of voluntary groups should involve professional as well as administrative staff. This would facilitate a more integrated approach between those working in the voluntary sector and professionals working in the health board.
- Health boards should examine ways of using their staff in supporting such groups. Failing this the employment of people to provide training whether on a sessional basis or on a full-time basis should be considered by the health board.
- To facilitate the development of local community initiatives there should be a minimum of one community worker per community care sub-area.
- Apart from the need for community workers to work with local organisations there is also a need for community workers to specialise with particular groups. Such groups include the elderly, parents whose children are in care, and lone parents. These community workers could be made available to all community care areas depending on the specialist needs required.
- Special consideration should be given to ensuring the inclusion of the most marginalised in the drawing up of the development plan. Extra resources in training etc. need to be provided to these groups to enable them to get off the ground.
- Special consideration should be given to projects which are consumer driven, community based and have a self-help dimension.
- Special consideration needs to be given to the concept of citizen rights.

- If services are to be driven by the principle of subsidiarity, special resources need to be made available to enable groups meet demands made upon them. Attention has to be given to the needs, other than financial, of the voluntary sector. This would include training in team building, planning and evaluation, keeping of accounts, and generally supporting volunteers on the ground. Subsidiarity should not be used inappropriately. In some cases it would be necessary for the health board to take responsibility for some services. An example of this would be cases of the abuse of the elderly.
- Where voluntary organisations employ full-time professional staff the rates of pay should be commensurate with those in the state sector. This would help avoid the turnover of staff in the voluntary sector.
- Better integration needs to occur between the health boards and these other agencies in developing a strategy in relation to marginalised groups.
- Contact needs to be made between health boards and other state agencies operating or funding in their region in order to integrate the planning and development of services. Areas of overlap and gaps in service need to be addressed.

REFERENCES

Arnstein, S. (1971), 'The Ladder of Citizen Participation', in Cahn, E. and Passet, B. (eds.), *Citizen Participation. Effecting Community Change*, Praeger, London

Barrington, T.J. (1979), *The Irish Administrative System*, Institute of Public Administration, Dublin

Butler, F. (1981), 'Voluntary Inaction', *Community Care*, Feb 19

Beveridge Committee Report (1946), HMSO, London

Child Care Act (1991), Government Publications, Dublin

Clarecare (1991), *Clarecare: A Partnership of Care*, Ennis

Commission on Health Funding, *Report of the Commission on Health Funding* (1989), Stationery Office, Dublin

Eastern Health Board (1991), 'Towards Agreement ... a way forward for voluntary agencies and the Eastern Health Board'

Faughnan, P. (1990), *Voluntary Organisations in the Social Service Field*, Department of Social Welfare, Dublin

Finch, J. and Groves, D. (1980), 'Community Care and the Family: A Case of Equal Opportunity', *Journal of Social Policy*, vol. 9, no. 2

Gladstone, F.J. (1979), *Voluntary Action in a Changing World*, Bedford Square Press, London

Gilligan, R. (1991), *Irish Child Care Services*, Institute of Public Administration, Dublin

Health Act (1953), Government Publications, Dublin

Health Education Bureau (1987), *Promoting Health Through Public Policy,* HEB, Dublin

Health: the Wider Dimension (1987), Department of Health, Dublin

Holman, B. (1981), 'The Place of Voluntary Societies', *Community Care,* Nov 12

Inbucon Management Consultants and the Department of Health (1982), *Community Care Review,* Report, Dublin

Jordon, N. (1987), *The Welfare State in Transition*, Wheatsheaf Books, Brighton

Kennedy, S. (1981), *Who Should Care?* Turoe Press, Dublin

Kramer, R. (1981), *Voluntary Agencies in the Welfare State*, University of California Press, Berkeley

Lavan, A. (1992), 'Is There a Future for Voluntary Welfare?', in Mid-Western Health Board (1992)

Lyons, M., Ruddle, H. and O'Connor, J. (1992), *Seeking a Refuge from Violence: The ADAPT Experience*, MWHB, Limerick

Mid-Western Health Board (1992), 'Partnership in Practice', A Conference on the Personal Social Services held in Limerick, 27-28 Nov 1991

National Council for the Aged (1983), *Community Care Services for the Elderly*, Dublin

National Economic and Social Council (1987), *Community Care Services: An Overview,* Report No. 84, Dublin

National Social Service Council (I 977), *A Chance to Care*, NSSC, Dublin

National Social Service Board (1982), *The Development of Voluntary Social Services in Ireland*, NSSB, Dublin

O'Connor, J., Ruddle, H. and O'Gallagher, M. (1988), *Cherished Equally – Educational and Behavioural Adjustment of Children,* Social Research Centre NIHE, Limerick

O'Connor, J., Ruddle, H. and Craig, S. (1991), *Speaking Out – A Study of Unmet Welfare Needs in the Mid-West Region*, MWHB, Limerick

O'Mahony, A. (1985), *Social Need and the Provision of Services in Rural Ireland*, Socio-Economic Research Series, No. 5

Programme for Economic and Social Progress (1991), Stationery Office, Dublin

Pope Pius XI (1931), *The Social Order,* The Encyclical 'Quadragesimo Anno', Catholic Truth Society, London

Ruddle, H. and O'Connor, J. (1992), *Breaking the Silence*, MWHB, Limerick

Stuart, Sr M. (1987), 'A Rural Response – A Study of Clare Social Service Council', Unpublished Thesis for Masters in Rural Development (NUI)

Townsend, P. et al (1970), *The Fifth Social Service*, Fabian Society, London

Whyte, J.H. (1971), *Church and State in Modern Ireland 1923-1970*, Gill and Macmillan, Dublin

Wolfenden Committee (1978), *The Future of Voluntary Organisations*, HMSO, London

Administration, vol. 51, nos. 1-2 (Spring/Summer 2003), 191–200

Two-speed Public and Private Medical Practice in the Republic of Ireland

W. P. TORMEY

Originally published in 1992, vol. 40, no. 4, 371-81.
W.P. Tormey was then a consultant chemical pathologist at the Department of Chemical Pathology, Beaumont Hospital.

WESTMINSTER'S EARLY ROLE

Since the last century, established medical culture in Ireland has accepted as natural a medical service system where patients are divided into those publicly funded and those paying privately. At the turn of the century, Irish general practitioner fees were 5s or 6s with a reduction to 2s 6d for working class patients, at a time when 20s represented one week's pay for a builder's labourer. Medical relief of the poor had begun in the eighteenth century when the Irish parliament encouraged the building of infirmaries for the relief of the diseased poor. The Irish Poor Law of 1838 required Irish workhouses to include an infirmary for male and female patients, to which a medical officer was appointed. In 1851, the dispensary service was set up where general practitioners received a salary for treating the poor but private patients were seen at the doctor's house. The received wisdom was that 'respectable' people feared the transmission of infections from the poor.

The voluntary hospitals were established by philanthropic individuals or groups of doctors in the eighteenth and nineteenth centuries (e.g. the Charitable Infirmary in 1718, Dr Steevens' in 1720, Mercer's and the Rotunda in 1745, and the Meath in 1753). The doctors were not paid for public work but appointments were greatly valued because they provided an entry to private practice, tuition fees for teaching medical students and the potential for the referral of private patients from former students. In 1839, the Adelaide hospital was opened exclusively for the use of Protestants. Following Catholic Emancipation in 1829, Catholic hospitals were established in Dublin (St Vincent's 1835, Mater 1861), Cork (Mercy 1857) and Belfast by nursing orders of religious nuns. These hospitals set out to provide for the religious as well as the medical needs of their patients. Thus the voluntary hospitals were mainly held in tight Catholic or Protestant sectarian control. They were committed to the treatment of all classes but social and financial pressure led to the introduction of private 'pay' beds. Later private hospitals for the treatment of the well-to-do were built alongside Catholic voluntary hospitals, often with overlapping boards of management. For example, the Mater Private was developed in 1912. Thus a parallel hospital system based on social class slowly evolved in Ireland. There was also a great income disparity between dispensary doctors and those attached to the voluntary hospitals.

The Report of the Royal Commission on the Poor Law in 1909 decided to continue with the dispensary system. However a Minority Report of the Royal Commission on the Poor Law in 1909 argued that 'the function of preventing and treating disease among destitute persons cannot in practice be distinguished from the prevention and treatment of disease in other persons'. It recommended that treatment should be given on the basis of medical necessity, irrespective of the patient's economic condition. This ideal later became conventional wisdom. In 1911, Lloyd George's National Health Insurance Bill as applied to Ireland excluded medical benefit – which entitled the insured to free general practitioner services and to free medicines – against the interests of dispensary doctors but with the support of wealthy general practitioners, hospital consultants and the Catholic Church. The capitation payment system in publicly funded general practice in Ireland was consequently not established until 1989. The 1915 Notification of Births Act as applied to Ireland and the 1919 Public Health (Medical Treatment of Children) (Ireland) Bill were introduced as social class free measures for mothers and children. These were not opposed by the medical profession or by the Catholic Church. The Irish Health Council reported in 1920 that the government had a duty to protect the health of the people, that access should be based on medical need only, and that the state had a duty to assist those who could not contribute to the cost of treatment.

DEVELOPMENTS IN THE NEW STATE

Financial pressures forced the introduction of pay beds in voluntary hospitals and by 1935 only 40 percent of patients were treated free of charge and consultants were also charging private fees. Thus voluntary hospitals had become a mix of public and private beds treating all social classes.[1]

In 1943, the proposals of Dr J. Shanley, President of the Irish Medical Association (IMA), that all persons and their dependants with an income less than £550 per annum should have free medical services were considered too radical by his association, even though a dual system would be continued.[2] In 1945, a government report which remained unpublished recommended the unification of the whole health service with the elimination of private fees.[3] The organised medical profession in alliance with the Catholic Church bitterly opposed a White Paper on Health published in 1947, which proposed in effect a national health service for Ireland. Part of their position was that state medicine would pose a threat to the moral welfare of a Catholic nation. An attempt by the next government in the following three years to introduce a comprehensive free 'Mother and Child' scheme was defeated by the same clerical and professional coalition.

PATIENT CATEGORIES

The 1953 Health Act introduced three categories of eligibility for health services – lower, middle and upper income groups. The medical profession and the Catholic bishops fought its more egalitarian provisions. The IMA used class prejudice in opposing the new health bill warning that the proposal meant 'the birth of your children in public maternity wards. This Bill represented a further and serious stage in the attack upon the middle classes and the pauperisation of large sections of the community'. These comments from Surgeon T.C.J. O'Connell were rightly ridiculed in the Dáil by Capt. Cowan.[4] In 1954, before the Act was implemented, the government fell and a new administration delayed its introduction while producing a voluntary health insurance scheme for the upper income group and for those of middle income who wished to avail of it. The Voluntary Health Insurance Act was passed into law in 1957 and was immediately popular with wealthier patients. By the end of the 1950s, the intention that access to medical services should be based solely on clinical need had been superseded by a system with complex eligibility based on income that varied from service to service.

In 1959, the Labour Party published its proposals for a free health service for all, financed from central taxation and insurance contributions. Fine Gael, the largest opposition party, proposed an insurance scheme to cover 85 per cent of the population but Fianna Fáil, again in government, was now happy with the status quo, although originally it had proposed a comprehensive service in the 1947 White Paper on Health. Despite the evident success of the British National Health Service by this time, the Irish medical profession was happy with the dual public/private system. However, the 1970 Health Act replaced the 120-year-old dispensary system with the introduction of a choice-of-doctor scheme for public patients in the general practice setting, based on a fee-per-item of service, and tried to ensure that no distinction would be made between public and private patients. Two-thirds of the population continued to pay privately for general practitioner services and the fee level for publicly funded patients remained less than the usual private rates. Public patients were often seen in a different setting and at different hours to private patients. Thus for many public patients, there still remained a dual system. However, the rigid social class separation of the dispensary system has been gradually lessened as new GP practices tend to see all their patients under one roof and, particularly in urban areas, dissatisfied patients may easily change their doctor.

In 1989, a new contract based on capitation with other benefits including illness payments, holiday locum cover, salary subsidy for practice staff and pension contributions was introduced for public patients in general practice. For hospital and other services, patients were still formally divided into three categories – full eligibility, limited eligibility and persons with entitlements to certain services. A summary of the development of health legislation and administration in Ireland is contained in a book written by a former Secretary of the Department of Health.[5]

PUBLIC HOSPITAL SERVICES FOR ALL AND PRIVATE BEDS

In 1979, all restrictions on the eligibility for a 'free' public hospital bed were removed and in 1991 'free' consultant services for all were introduced for public hospital beds. However, the latter change was paralleled by the formal separation of some pay beds in public hospitals for consultant private practice, with the introduction of separate waiting lists for this category of accommodation. Although this formal designation of beds was intended in principle to improve equity of access to public hospital beds under the government's Programme for Economic and Social Progress, it has had the actual effect of establishing small private areas within each public institution which are largely funded by the Voluntary Health Insurance Board (VHI). In public hospitals, waiting lists for private patients for computerised tomographic (CT) scanners funded from the public purse are also separate and much shorter. Private medicine continues to be subsidised through tax deductions for health insurance premiums and there is now a formal state-sponsored queue-skipping mechanism for those who can afford to pay. Private hospitals and clinics have flourished, staffed in the main by consultants with public appointments.

Thus there is a well-entrenched dual system. In public hospitals there are separate public and private beds with separate queues for each. Private hospitals are publicly subsidised through a tax allowance on health insurance premiums allowing the middle classes to have a personal escape mechanism to skip public queues for services that are in effect rationed. The more than 30 per cent of the population privately insured with VHI is clear evidence of a widespread belief that to be sure of service on demand, one must be covered.

RELMAN'S PRACTICE GUIDE

In a series of commentaries in the *New England Journal of Medicine,* the recent editor Dr Arnold Relman defined the guiding principle of medical practice: 'doctors, whether salaried or not, must first of all be advocates for their patients'. The economic interest of neither the doctor's employer nor the doctor should be allowed interfere with this imperative.[6] The pressures on doctors will continue to increase because each year medicine can do more and this will cost more. There were virtually no cures on offer in medicine until about forty-five years ago. New drugs and technologies dramatically change the outlook for individual patients and evaluation of these in terms of human welfare and scientific validity is a key role for the profession.[7] However, in Ireland as in the US, much hospital medicine operates in a business climate and Relman has made the following four suggestions for conscientious doctors to preserve their professional integrity. Examples of their relevance to Ireland are also outlined below.

Firstly, he argues that doctors should limit their practice incomes to fees or salaries earned from services personally provided or supervised. Doctors ought not to refer patients to laboratory or diagnostic imaging facilities in which they have a financial interest but over which they exercise no professional supervision. Some surgeons may hold limited partnerships in private clinics to which they refer their patients. Such arrangements may create conflicts of interest that undermine the traditional role of the doctor. In Ireland, the development of pathology subspecialities has been impeded by the practice of histopathologists benefiting from private income from microbiology, haematology or chemical pathology services that have only the most tenuous organisational links with histopathology. Historically, anatomic pathology has dominated laboratory medicine and staffing has been adequate in that area. Because of the low patient volume and high professional input in that subspeciality, there has been a major financial incentive to limit consultant direction of the other laboratory disciplines and to pool and share any private income generated from high-volume activity therein. The effects of this could be seen on laboratory consultant staffing even in teaching hospitals.

Secondly, doctors in practice should avoid any arrangement with a for-profit organisation that rewards them for referring patients to a particular service or that restricts the choices available for patients. In Ireland, private clinics and hospitals actively discourage the use of outside services, for example in pathology and radiology, where these are available on-site.

Thirdly, doctors should try to avoid working directly for commercial hospitals because as employees they would be expected to give their primary allegiance to corporate goals rather than the individual patient's needs. There are many doctors in Ireland who find themselves constrained in this manner. Whether working for commercial or public hospitals, doctors should try to remain self-employed or be part of a self-regulated medical group contracted to the hospital's management board. The doctor must try to preserve freedom of expression on clinical matters. Conflict may arise even in the public sector; for example the chairman of the board of management of Beaumont Hospital has demanded that doctors give their primary allegiance to the hospital, provoking a rebuke from the Irish Hospital Consultants Association. In 1991, the chief executive officer of one health board issued a code of conduct which tried to prevent doctors making any public statements or publications about any health matter without the board's express consent.[8] In the UK, some managers in the NHS have tried to control doctors' access to the media by making press statements a disciplinary offence.[9]

Fourthly, doctors must not accept any arrangement that directly rewards them for withholding services from their patients. In Ireland, doctors are paid £1,944 per annum by the VHI for each renal dialysis patient and £539 for a kidney transplant procedure which could be interpreted as a financial incentive to perform transplant operations on public rather than private patients. That this does not happen reflects well on the profession. In August 1991, the Minister for Health wrote to each GP in the public sector offering development funds for general practice in exchange for limiting drug prescribing to a predetermined target.

HEALTH FUNDING

The Report of the Commission on Health Funding published in 1989 accepted health care as a fundamental right, but then went on to state that the quantity and quality of what the health service could provide would be determined only by what the Exchequer could afford. An extra layer of bureaucracy would be added and administrators would have the primary responsibility for the quantity and quality of services provided. Doctors could be regarded as a means of producing units of health care, all aspects of which would be routinely monitored for efficiency. Clinical research and practice would be centrally controlled by the new administrative structure, which would also have a direct role in professional audit. In the new contract of employment for consultants introduced in 1991, the employing authority has the right, duty and responsibility to determine the range, type and volume of services to be provided by a hospital.

CULTURAL AMBIVALENCE

How can doctors justify two separate, parallel systems? The cultural norms of Irish society allow middle class patients to continue to demand a tax subsidy to effectively bypass the public hospital queues for treatment. While the general public claim to be in favour of an equitable health service for all, those who can afford to do so are more than willing to pay for a queue-skipping mechanism for themselves and the political process reflects this reality. Politicians and their administrative agents continue to operate and fine-tune this system, while often claiming the opposite intent. The political culture in Ireland is by no means unique and the curtailment of health care for the poor is widespread in Western countries; but the Oregon Medicaid Demonstration Project in the US is the first formal explicit rationing system to be introduced.[10]

In an address on medical ethics in Dublin, Sir David Innes-Williams, President of the Royal Society of Medicine, London, stated that he regarded the health budget at national level as a political matter with no special role for the doctor other than in providing information.[11] In addressing the response of the individual doctor to resource rationing, he suggested that the practitioner must confine his loyalty to the individual patient within the boundaries of a collective loyalty to patients at large. He argued that rationing that involved life and death decisions should not be left to the individual doctor, especially not the patient's own physician. He also suggested that at hospital level the medical view should predominate but it must be a corporate voice. This is at variance with Relman's imperatives and there are potential dangers in this response because what doctors may be capable of offering their individual patients may be restricted to various degrees by administrative constraints which may on occasion act through a collective medical executive. Professional jealousy and competition are common features of large hospitals. Thus individual doctors may feel obliged to enter the public arena in their patients' interests.

As in many Western countries, health care in Ireland is increasingly adopting business characteristics with doctors used as ingredients in a business relationship. Disease and patient throughput, resource allocation, clinical budgeting, diagnosis related groups (DRGs), audit and accountability are the new priorities. In this new era of assessment and accountability, the question of how the results of clinical audit and medical outcome assessments are used remains unanswered. The trend towards commercialisation of medicine in Ireland with doctor-owned clinics and private hospital facilities is not unlike the situation in the US and there is the danger of the business ethic undermining traditional medical practice, creating conflicts of interest for the conscientious doctor.[12] Medicine is a social rather than a business contract.

Cost containment in the health services and the philosophical issues raised by a monetary view of human life which depersonalises medicine have been addressed recently in the Irish context[13] but the ambiguities of the present Irish health system have remained unchallenged.

FUTURE CHANGES?

State subsidies have been a driving force in undermining the principle that all patients irrespective of their means should be treated in the same hospital by the same medical and nursing staff.[14] On ethical grounds, it is important that the present financial incentives for doctors to preferentially treat private patients should be removed. Doctors should receive the same fee irrespective of the patient's income, and all hospitals should receive the same fundamental daily capitation fee weighted by speciality and agreed with the Department of Health, which should be monitored by an Oireachtas Committee on Health.

Then the site of hospitalisation would be determined by matching facilities with clinical need and not with money. Consumer choice is an important part of Irish life and the numbers enrolling in the VHI underline this. To ensure equity in access to health services, the best solution for Ireland may be a universal insurance-based health system in which all workers and employers contribute on a sliding-scale means-tested basis and where the premiums for the lowest income groups, including those dependent on social welfare payments, are paid by the state. The whole population would then have equal access to a single system of health care. A model for this system exists in France and Germany.[15] The expense of the bureaucracy needed to collect premiums and make payments is already largely present within the Irish system. The high direct taxes needed for the comprehensive Scandinavian model would more likely run into political difficulties in Ireland. A new consultants common contract and a new general practitioner contract would also have to be negotiated in the light of the new system.

The Canadian provincial insurance model is another possible alterative in which health care funding is public and universal, doctors have retained their professional autonomy and consumers have a free choice of doctor. The Canadian policy sets out to ensure that merely because people can afford to pay, they should not be able to purchase care that is better or more readily available than that available to the less well-off.[16] Private insurers are prohibited by law from paying for care already covered by the provincial plans. Patients may pay privately for medical and hospital care but doctors and hospitals must be either private or remain exclusively in the public provincial system. Extra billing over the statutory insurance rates by doctors in the insurance scheme is prohibited. However implementing the Canadian system in the EC might be difficult due to EC law on competition policy. The Canadian insurance system is tax financed. There is a fee-per-item of service with GP and hospital services covered and the cost is related to family size and not risk. There are no patient payments and the fee relativity scales have been left to the medical profession to determine. The system is not however free of problems because of the cost to government of an open-ended commitment to financing the plans. The rising costs of doctors' services and the demands for new technology have led to conflict between the Medical Association and government. However the system remains popular with the public.

There is no 'correct' solution to health care financing because demands on health services will continue to outstrip supply. Fundamental change bringing real equity in access to services will only come when there is the political will to change the state's well-entrenched policy direction. There is little cause to believe that such change is likely.

NOTES TO ARTICLE

1 R. Barrington, *Health, Medicine and Politics in Ireland, 1900-1970* (Dublin, Institute of Public Administration, 1987), pp. 1-112.

2 J. Shanley, 'The reorganisation of the medical services, *Journal of the Irish Medical Association*, vol. 13, 1943, pp. 74-7.

3 Department of local Government and Public Health, 'Report of the Departmental Committee on Health Services' (Dublin, Stationery Office, 1945), unpublished, 50 copies printed; one on Cabinet file S 13444 C, SPO, pp. 100-1.

4 Capt. Cowan, *Dáil Debates*, 15 April 1953, vol. 138, col. 127.

5 B. Hensey, *The Health Services of Ireland*, 4th edn (Dublin, Institute of Public Administration, 1988).

6 A.S. Relman, 'Salaried physicians and economic incentives', *New England Journal of Medicine*, 319 (1988), p. 784.

7 M. McGregor, 'Technology and the allocation of resources', *New England Journal of Medicine*, 320 (1989), pp. 118-20.

8 'Code of conduct for consultants', *Irish Medical Times*, 25 (1991), pp. 1-2.

9 Malcolm Dean, 'London Perspective. Can the NHS changes be reversed?', *Lancet*, 338 (1991), pp. 499-500.

10 D.S. Greenberg, 'The Oregon plan on Capitol Hill', Lancet, 338 (1991), pp. 808-9; R. Steinbrook, B. Lo., 'The Oregon Medicaid Demonstration Project – will it provide adequate medical care?', *New England Journal of Medicine*, 326 (1992), pp. 340-3.

11 D. Innes-Williams. 'Medical Ethics in paediatric surgery', *Irish Journal of Medical Science*, 159 (1990), pp 237-40.

12 A. Relman, 'Shattuck Lecture – The health care industry: where is it taking us?', *New England Journal of Medicine*, 325 (1991), pp. 854-9.

13 T. O'Sullivan, 'Health service: in the steps of the good samaritan', *Studies*, 79 (1991), pp. 268-77.

14 R. Barrington, *Health, Medicine and Politics in Ireland, 1900-1970*, p. 286.

15 T. Smith, 'NHS: a time to choose – either health insurance or higher taxes', *British Medical Journal*, 298 (1989), pp. 1-2.

16 J. K. Iglehart, 'Canada's health care system faces its problems', *New England Journal of Medicine*, 322 (1990), pp. 562-8.

Administration, vol. 51, nos. 1-2 (Spring/Summer 2003), 201–218

Social Security and Informal Caring – An Irish Perspective

MEL COUSINS

Originally published in 1994, vol. 42, no. 1, 25-46.
Mel Cousins was then engaged in work as an independent research consultant.

INTRODUCTION

This article looks at the policies of social security support for informal carers in the Republic of Ireland. The demographic context and the overall policy context are outlined in parts I and II, including a brief summary of the institutional and community care services available. The development of social security policies is examined in part III, in particular the recent establishment of a means-tested carer's allowance in 1990. Finally, in part IV, some of the issues surrounding social security and informal carers are discussed.

I THE DEMOGRAPHIC CONTEXT

The 1986 census reported 384,400 persons aged 65 years or over (10.9 per cent of the total population) (Central Statistics Office, 1989). There were 143,900 persons aged 75 or over (4.1 per cent of the population), 61 per cent of whom were women. The number of elderly persons is predicted to rise both in total and as a percentage of the total population, but not dramatically. It is estimated that 11.6 per cent of the total population will be 65 or over by 2006 (Central Statistics Office, 1988). The government appointed National Council for the Elderly[1] has estimated that 66,300 elderly persons in the community require care, of whom about 50,000 are cared for by members of the same household (O'Connor *et al.* 1988).

Unfortunately there is relatively little information about the number of non-elderly persons who require care. The 1981 Census of Mental Handicap reported that there was a total of 12,304 persons suffering from medium or more severe mental handicap. However, there is no comprehensive survey of persons suffering from physical disability. In 1991 there were about 74,000 persons in receipt of the long-term invalidity payments (Department of Social Welfare, 1992; Department of Health, 1992).[2] However, it is not possible to say how many of these people require care and attention. There is also no accurate estimate of the number of young persons who require such care.

II THE OVERALL POLICY CONTEXT

Government policy in regard to care of the elderly and of people affected by disabilities has, over the past 25 years, emphasised the importance of community care (Blackwell 1992, p. 8 et seq.). However, there remains a considerable provision of institutional care. The main services available – both institutional and in the community – can be summarised briefly as follows:

Institutional care

Blackwell (1992) reports that in December 1988, there were over 19,000 long-stay beds for elderly persons. Public geriatric hospitals and homes provide 7,000 beds. Seventy per cent of patients are 75 and over and 60 per cent are chronically sick. Public welfare homes provide 1,600 beds for ambulant patients who are not in need of extended nursing care. General hospitals also provide an estimated 1,500 long-stay geriatric beds.

In addition there are over 9,000 beds provided by nursing homes which are run either by charitable and voluntary bodies or on a commercial basis. These figures are in addition to an unknown number of elderly persons occupying acute hospital beds and an estimated 3,600 persons in psychiatric institutions. Blackwell reports that about one-third of those in long-stay geriatric beds have been admitted for social rather than medical reasons.

On the one hand it appears that institutional care is being provided for persons who could be cared for in the community if adequate support was available. On the other hand, there is considerable confusion as to the legal entitlements of those requiring nursing home care, so that many low income persons are either unable to obtain access to institutional care or are forced to rely on financial support from family members, in order to pay the fees (Cousins 1992; 1994).

Community care services

A range of community care services are provided by the eight regional health boards which administer health services, by local authorities and voluntary organisations. However, the information available as to the detailed provision of services is often very limited. These services include public health nursing which combines both preventive health care and domiciliary nursing. Home help services, which provide assistance with everyday living, are also provided by the health boards either directly or through the provision of funding to voluntary organisations. There are currently 12,000 recipients of home help services of whom 9,500 are elderly. There is a considerable degree of regional variation in the provision of this service (see Dramin 1986; NESC 1987).

Some health boards provide day centre care (involving non-medical care) and in 1988 there were six day hospitals providing investigation treatment and rehabilitation services. Again regional variations are considerable with four of the six day hospitals being in Dublin. Sheltered housing is provided by both local authorities and voluntary bodies and in 1989 there were 3,500 such units.

Informal caring

A national survey undertaken by O'Connor *et al.* (1988) estimated that there are over 66,000 elderly persons in Ireland who require some degree of care. It was estimated that 24,000 (36 per cent) require 'a lot of care' with a further 25,000 (38 per cent) requiring some care and 17,000 (26 per cent) needing occasional care. About 50,800 persons receive care from other members of their household. Of these, 92 per cent are cared for by a relative, most often a daughter or daughter-in-law (44 per cent), spouse (24 per cent) or son (16 per cent). Seventy-eight per cent of carers were women and 38 per cent were 55 or over. About 15,500 elderly persons were cared for by persons from outside the household and again the majority of carers (71 per cent) were women.

There have been two in-depth studies of carers (O'Connor and Ruddle 1988 and Blackwell *et al.* 1992). These studies did not focus on the role of social security in supporting informal caring, but the information which they did provide in this regard is outlined in section III below.

Taxation policy

There is one tax allowance which is specifically targeted at persons who require care and attention. This provides an allowance of up to £5,000 towards the employment of a person to provide care and attention.[3] The numbers availing of this allowance are not published but the estimates of the tax expenditure costs of the allowance which are produced by the

Revenue Commissioners (Ireland 1992) would suggest that the numbers claiming the allowance are quite low.[4] In addition, some personal medical expenditure is allowed against tax under the Irish code and the cost of private nursing home care may, in some cases, be allowed under this category. However, the procedures for authorising such expenditure are unclear and persons may find it difficult in practice to have such expenditure allowed by their tax inspector.

There are also general tax allowances in respect of incapacitated children and of dependant adult relatives but these are not specifically linked to caring costs and the levels of the allowance are quite low.[5]

III THE DEVELOPMENT OF SOCIAL SECURITY POLICY

Prescribed relative's allowance

The main social security provision for informal carers dates from 1968 when increases in pensions for the elderly (then over 70 years of age) were introduced for claimants who were so incapacitated as to require full-time care and attention and where a 'prescribed female relative' lived with the claimant to provide such care. The only female relatives initially prescribed by regulation were a daughter and step-daughter.[6] The increase was payable only where the prescribed relative had left insurable employment in order to provide full-time care and attention and where she had paid 156 weeks' employment contributions within the five years before leaving employment. The payment was paid to the pensioner. The weekly rate represented 69 per cent of the then non-contributory old age pension and 62 per cent of the higher contributory pension.

The payment, which became known as the prescribed relative's allowance (PRA), was thus very restrictive. First it was paid only to persons over 70 in receipt of a pension, thus ruling out younger persons who required care, and persons over 70 who were not entitled to a social security pension. Second, the categories of prescribed female relative were extremely restrictive and initially applied only to daughters (or step-daughters) of the claimant who had been regularly employed and who gave up work to care for him or her. The restrictions meant that few persons qualified for PRA and, in the following year, the contribution rule was abolished[7] and the definition of prescribed relative was extended to include a wider range of female relatives.[8] The then Minister for Local Government explained that by this extension of the scheme

> an inducement is being given to people to keep their aged relatives at home rather than have them go into institutions (241 *Dáil Debates* col. 1146).

In 1972 the scheme was extended to the corresponding male relatives [9] and in following years it was extended to a wider range of relatives. A government-appointed Commission on the Status of Women (1972) recommended that credited contributions be granted to a person who gives up employment to provide care and attention and this was implemented in December 1972. The scheme was subsequently extended to persons in receipt of an invalidity pension below retirement age in 1982.

However, PRA remained quite restrictive in that the prescribed relative could not be engaged in employment outside the home of the person for whom full-time care and attention was being provided. In addition if the prescribed relative was in receipt of a social welfare payment, no PRA was payable. Finally, the prescribed relative could not be a married person who was being wholly or mainly maintained by his or her spouse. This effectively disqualified most married women from qualifying as a prescribed relative – a group which made up a large percentage of actual carers. The rationale given for this exclusion was that the scheme was intended to compensate for a situation which does not normally arise; therefore situations in which a wife cared for her husband were excluded.'[10] From 1986, this rule was arguably in breach of the EU directive on equal treatment for men and women (see *Drake v. Chief Adjudication Officer* [1986 ECR 581 and Whyte, 1986, p. 149).

The limited and unsatisfactory nature of PRA led to several proposals for the introduction of a less restrictive payment for carers. The government-appointed Commission on Social Welfare (1986) recommended that prescribed relatives should have entitlement in their own right to a means-tested payment. This recommendation was supported by the National Council for the Elderly which also recommended that this payment should be extended to cover carers who were married and other persons not already covered by the existing scheme (O'Connor and Ruddle 1988). As a first step in this direction, the Social Welfare Act 1989 provided that PRA was to be paid directly to the carer. The following year saw the introduction of a fully fledged carer's allowance.

As might be expected given the very restrictive eligibility conditions, the numbers in receipt of PRA were always quite low. In the 1970s, over 3,000 persons received the allowance (Department of Social Welfare 1982) but this subsequently declined to only 1,850 in December 1989 just before the introduction of the carer's allowance. (Unless otherwise stated, figures are from the annual *Statistical Information on Social Welfare Services* produced by the Department of Social Welfare.) The vast majority of the persons in receipt of care were elderly, although precise figures are not available. Following the introduction of the carer's allowance in November 1990, PRA is no longer payable in respect of any new claims. However, it remains payable to any persons who were in receipt of the allowance at that time and who did not qualify for a carer's allowance. At 31 December 1991, 604 people were still in receipt of PRA.

Over the years the value of PRA relative to other social welfare payments was allowed to decline so that by 1990 it represented only 55 per cent of the non-contributory old age pension or 48 per cent of the contributory pension.

Constant attendance allowance

Under the occupational injuries scheme, introduced in 1967, a constant attendance allowance is payable to a person who, as a result of an occupational accident or disease, is suffering from 100 per cent disablement and who as a result requires 'constant attendance'. This scheme is largely based on the UK industrial injuries code and the payment is derived from the constant attendance allowance under the UK scheme (Ogus and Barendt 1988, p. 307). A weekly payment (currently IR£32.90) is made to a person who 'is to a substantial extent dependent on [constant] attendance for the necessities of life and is likely to remain so dependent for a period of not less than six months' where such attendance is required 'whole-time'. Benefit is paid at a reduced rate where constant attendance is required on a part-time basis, while an increased rate is paid where greater attendance is required because of 'exceptionally severe disablement'. Finally, twice the standard rate is paid where the person is 'so exceptionally severely disabled as to be entirely or almost entirely dependent on such attendance for the necessities of life', where this condition is likely to last for at least six months and where attendance is required whole-time. Figures for the numbers in receipt of this payment have not been published in recent years but given that only 200 or less suffer from 100 per cent disablement, the numbers in receipt of the constant attendance allowance are obviously quite low.

Carer's allowance

The Social Welfare Act, 1990, introduced a means-tested carer's allowance. This is payable to a person who resides with and provides full-time care and attention to a person in receipt of a range of social security payments who is so incapacitated as to require full-time care and attention.[11] The qualifying persons are those in receipt of an Irish pension who are over the age of sixty-six (sixty-five in the case of retirement pension) or those under that age in receipt of a long-term invalidity or blind pension or disabled persons maintenance allowance. The Social Welfare Act, 1991, extended this to apply to corresponding social insurance payments from other EU countries or countries with which Ireland has a reciprocal agreement.

The Minister for Social Welfare, introducing the new legislation, said that despite changes in society such as the greater mobility of young people and the increased participation by married women in the labour force, 'the family continues to be the strongest and most reliable source of care for elderly incapacitated people.' (397 *Dáil Debates* col. 755).

The aims of the legislation, as expressed by the Minister, are to give 'official recognition to the role of carer' and to provide 'a secure and independent source of income' while ensuring that resources are directed at those who need them most (397 *Dáil Debates* cols. 755, 757 and 1042). Accordingly, the allowance is subject to a strict means-test and the disregards for income are minimal (although the Social Welfare Act 1994 introduced a higher disregard in the case of spousal income). In addition the means of the claimant are to include such amount as the person cared for 'could reasonably be expected to contribute'.[12] The carer, who must be 18 years or over, must not 'be engaged in employment or self-employment outside his [or her] home'.[13] A person who is in receipt of another social welfare payment or in respect of whom an adult dependant increase is being paid is not entitled to a carer's allowance.[14] However, all married persons are now eligible to claim the allowance.

It had been estimated by the Department of Social Welfare that over 8,000 persons would be entitled to the carer's allowance (397 *Dáil Debates*, col. 756). However, by December 1991, only 3,355 were in receipt of the payment and by February 1993 this has only increased to 4,400. In 1991, almost 6,000 claims were received but 53 per cent of claims adjudicated on were rejected. This is a very high refusal rate.[15] In addition, 458 cases were appealed to the Social Welfare Appeals Office. Again this is a comparatively high figure which may suggest confusion and dissatisfaction on the part of claimants. Indeed the Chief Appeals Officer (1992) in his annual report commented on the large number of appeals brought by persons who clearly could not satisfy the statutory requirements, in particular because their means, often derived from the means of the spouse, were considerably over the limit or because they were receiving a social welfare payment in their own right (or an increase was being paid in respect of them) and they were therefore disqualified for allowance.

The majority of recipients are women (76 per cent) which broadly corresponds to the general estimates of the sexual division of caring responsibilities. However, the carer's allowance is heavily concentrated on carers in the 40-65 age group (75 per cent). Only 4 per cent of payments go to people of 65 and over, compared to an estimated 25 per cent of carers of the elderly in this age bracket. This suggests that elderly carers are themselves likely to be in receipt of an old age pension (or persons in respect of whom an adult dependant increase is in payment) and therefore ineligible for a carer's allowance. Unfortunately no indication is given of the age of the persons requiring care and attention but it seems likely that, like the PRA scheme, the carer's allowance is largely concentrated on the elderly who require care.

Domiciliary care allowance

In 1973 a scheme of allowances for domiciliary care of severely handicapped children was introduced by the Department of Health.[16] The scheme was aimed at severely mentally or physically handicapped children who were living at home and who required constant care. It was 'designed to alleviate, in some measure, the additional burdens created by the retention of such children in the home'.[17] The scheme was operated under section 61 of the Health Act 1970 which enabled arrangements to assist in the maintenance at home of sick or infirm persons or a person who would otherwise require maintenance other than at home. No statutory instrument was made in relation to the scheme and it is operated on the basis of an unpublished circular.

The scheme applies to children between the ages of 2 (children below the age of 2 are assumed to require constant care and attention in any event) and 16 who 'require from another person constant care or supervision, i.e. continual or continuous care or supervision substantially greater than that which would normally be required by a child of the same age and sex'. The scheme is intended to apply to long-term disabilities only, i.e. disabilities which are likely to continue for at least one year, and is not intended to apply to disabilities which only intermittently or infrequently give rise to a need for 'constant care'.

The care may be provided by the parent(s) or by another person or persons. The allowance is normally to be paid to the mother of the child but may be paid to the father or to the person who is caring for the child. Only the means of the child are taken into account in determining eligibility. In this context means included payments of compensation for injuries or disabilities. The payment was originally set at a rate of £25 per month and is currently payable at £92.50 per month. In 1990 there were 7,453 allowances in payment (Department of Health 1992). This shows a steady increase from 4,044 in 1976 and 6,365 in 1986 (Hensey 1979; 1988).

It appears that the design of the scheme was influenced by the UK attendance allowance, but the Irish payment is significantly different in that, first, it is confined to children and, second, unlike the attendance allowance, the purpose of the payment is explicitly to compensate for the 'additional burden' of caring for a child.

The impact of social security on informal caring

Unfortunately the in-depth studies of carers of elderly persons have not concentrated in much detail on the effect of social security policies and, as we have seen, there is little information available on the situation of carers of children or other adults. However, O'Connor and Ruddle's (1988) study of 200 carers reported that only eight (4 per cent) were in receipt of the prescribed relative's allowance. The lack of coverage was attributed to the limited eligibility requirements, in particular the fact that married women were generally ruled out and, in farm families, the fact that a son or daughter who was working on the farm to even a limited extent was considered not to be providing 'full-time' care and attention.

This study examined the factors which influenced persons to become a carer but the possible social security benefits available were not referred to by respondents in this context. However, 35 per cent of carers did report experiencing financial strain. Only 16 per cent of carers were in paid employment and almost 20 per cent of the elderly persons cared for were not financially independent. Sixty-four households (31 per cent) were totally dependent on social security payments.

A more recent study of 207 households by Blackwell *et al.* (1992) again provides little information about either the financial position of carers or social security support available to them. While it does report that only 22.5 per cent of carers were employed or self-employed, the majority of carers are recorded as being on 'home duties' (i.e. housewives) and it is not possible to estimate the financial circumstances of this group (1992 p. 145). However, the study does report that 37 per cent of carers experienced financial strain and that 77 per cent agreed that direct payment to the carer would help their situation.

Both studies indicated that carers were spending a considerable number of hours per week in caring for the elderly person. O'Connor and Ruddle (1988) found that 50 per cent of carers spent 4-7 hours per day (i.e. 28 to 49 hours per week) on caring, with 35 per cent spending more than this. Blackwell et al. (1992) found that carers spent an average of 47 hours per week in caring activities. However, Blackwell (1992, p. 213) found that less than a quarter of carers would prefer to have the services they provided replaced by outside paid care.

IV POLICY ISSUES

Social security policy for informal carers must be seen in the context of overall policy for providing care. Thus if overall policy concentrates on providing institutional care then the need for social security support is much reduced. Conversely, as has increasingly been the case in many European countries, if the concentration of policy has been on providing care in (or by) the community, then social security policy is of much greater importance (on the increasing emphasis on home care see *European Observatory on Family Policies,* 1991; 1992).

One of the main reasons given for supporting care in the community is that it is significantly cheaper than institutional care. However, this argument normally refers solely to savings in *state expenditure*. Blackwell (1992) costed both institutional care in four hospitals and care in the community. The cost of care in the community included the cost to the carer of the time spent in providing care. The time of the carer was costed at a low value (IR£1.21 per hour) which took account of the age and lack of educational and occupational skills on the part of many carers. At this level of labour cost and at low levels of dependency, informal care in the home was generally about the same level of cost as in three of the four hospitals surveyed. However, this picture changed as the level of dependency increased and at the highest level of dependency hospital care was more expensive in all cases. These findings are very dependent on the cost placed on the labour of the carer. Blackwell used an alternative level of value by costing the carer's time at the level of pay of home helps (IR£2.40 per hour). At this level of cost, care in the home was generally more costly than institutional care and even at the highest level of dependency it was of the same order of cost as three of the four hospitals surveyed.

However, subsequent to the publication of Blackwell's report, an equality officer has decided, in a case involving home helps in one health board area, that the predominantly female home helps are being underpaid, contrary to the Irish legislation implementing EU law on equal pay for men and women.'[18] The equality officer held that the women involved were entitled to be paid at a rate of IR£4.52 per hour. If one uses this rate in costing the care at home then home care is significantly more expensive than institutional care in most cases. Thus care in the home is only less expensive than institutional care if one assumes a low value for the labour of the carer.

While the economic analysis is only one factor to be considered and the research was able to measure only the costs and not the outcomes of the different types of care, this research does suggest that (largely unsupported) informal caring in the community may not be the most effective method of providing care and that further research needs to be undertaken into ways of providing more cost-effective care possibly by providing support for informal carers such as home help services, respite services, hospital day care, etc. Indeed it is hardly surprising that untrained, overworked, often elderly carers (who are frequently in poor health themselves) may not provide the most cost-effective provision of care.

Strategies for social security support

There are a number of different approaches which social security policy can take in providing support for caring and carers. These can be summarised as follows:

- *Caring as an individual risk.* The possibility of needing care can be seen as a risk for an individual. A payment would then be made to the person who required care on the occurrence of the risk. This approach is taken in Germany whereby an insurance based payment is paid to a severely handicapped person in need of domestic care (Bieback 1992). This amounts to about IR£160 per month which would appear to be unlikely to meet actual caring costs. As we have seen, this is also the approach taken under the Irish occupational injuries scheme.
- *Compensation for the carer/family.* Alternatively, having to provide care can be seen as a risk to the family of the person involved or to the individual carer. Having to provide care and attention can impose significant costs on the persons involved through having to forego paid employment, the stress involved in caring, the opportunity costs of lost leisure time, etc. Under this approach a payment would be made to the carer to compensate for these costs. This approach can be seen in the Irish domiciliary care allowance whereby a payment is made to the family of the child who needs care to compensate for the additional costs (in the broad sense) involved. This involves a transfer of resources from households without persons requiring care to households which include such persons.
- *A minimum income for carers.* A further alternative is to provide a means-tested benefit. In this case the principal aim is not to compensate generally for the costs of caring but rather to provide a minimum income so as to prevent poverty or to provide a (small) financial incentive (above the official poverty line) to a potential carer. This type of payment may also compensate (partially) for income loss. It is into this latter category that the Irish carer's allowance falls
- *Caring as paid work.* Under this approach caring would be seen as work and would be remunerated in the same way as 'ordinary' employment. However, whatever the debates about recognising the value of (predominantly) women's work in the home, it does not appear that any EU country has introduced a payment intended to pay a wage to a carer. However, some countries have at least provided social insurance cover for persons with caring responsibilities. For example the French system provides insurance cover for persons (whose means do not exceed a set limit) caring for a handicapped child or adult who are not themselves insured under an occupational social insurance scheme. The insurance

contribution is payable by the social security authorities and gives rise to entitlement to an old age pension (Dupeyroux and Pretot 1989).

The development of the Irish model

The prescribed relative's allowance (PRA) was initially developed as a payment for daughters who gave up work to care for their elderly parents and who would not otherwise be entitled to any benefit. It was structured as an adult dependant addition to the parent's payment although it is not clear why this option, rather than that of a payment direct to the carer, was chosen. Thus is was intended to provide an (indirect) minimum income for the carer rather than to compensate the person requiring care. No means test applied to such dependency additions as adult dependency payments were in the vast majority of cases made in respect of wives who were assumed not to be in work.[19] However, as it became obvious that there were many persons other than daughters who were caring for elderly persons and as PRA was extended to further categories of relatives, the structure of the payment made less and less sense and pressure increased to have it paid directly to the carer. Under the logic of the original payment a married woman, who was dependent on her husband, should not be paid PRA which was also an adult dependency payment. From this point of view, a married woman if she was being supported by her husband had no need for additional support from the person being cared for. In addition, it was assumed that a married woman caring for an elderly or disabled person was a normal eventuality, requiring no financial support. However, pressure increased to have a payment made to married women who made up a large proportion of carers but were excluded from PRA.

Not surprisingly, the Department of Social Welfare accepted that the structure of PRA was no longer sustainable and introduced the carer's allowance. This is a further categorical payment which follows the tradition of the Irish scheme of introducing categorical payments for 'deserving' categories of claimant. However, because of its stringent means test, carer's allowance appears to have benefited few persons except the previously excluded married women.

The primary aim of the carer's allowance was to provide a minimum income for carers but also to do so in a way which provided an independent income for (some) carers. For certain carers the allowance replaced the PRA or the residual supplementary welfare allowance payable to any person whose 'means were insufficient to meet his [or her] needs'. For others it provided a direct income, replacing an adult dependant allowance payable to the carer's spouse. At the same time the rate of allowance was increased from the PRA rate of £28 in 1989 to £45 in 1990. Thus it provides a minimum income and can be seen as compensating in a limited manner for any loss of earnings and providing a (small) financial incentive to carers to provide such services. However, it is obviously quite limited and it is likely that any carers who were in receipt of unemployment or invalidity payments continued to claim these payments since they were paid at a higher rate than the carer's allowance. As from July 1993, the rate of the carer's allowance has been increased to £59.20 which is the same level as most means-tested benefits including the old age pension and unemployment assistance.

A criticism of existing social security support for carers

In many ways the development of the Irish payments has paralleled that of the UK invalid care allowance. The ICA is a non-contributory benefit but subject to income limits. It is payable only to those of working age who provide care for at least 35 hours per week. It is payable at a low rate (60 per cent of standard pension rate). From 1986 to 1990 earnings of only £12 per week were allowed but the income limit has been raised to £20 in 1990 and is currently £50 per week. ICA was also introduced to (partially) compensate caring relatives who gave up work to provide full-time care (Brown 1984, p. 256 *et seq.*). Married women were excluded since they might well be at home in any case. As in the Irish case, officialdom was unable to resist the pressures to extend it to a wider group of carers: first to extended relatives, non-relatives and common-law husbands in 1982 and, after much resistance, to married women in 1986, the latter leading to a six-fold increase in the numbers receiving the benefit. Again it applies to only a small proportion of carers (McLaughlin 1992; Glendenning 1991, 1992).

While highly critical of the *rate* at which ICA is paid, McLaughlin (1992, p. 11) argues that

> The two main ideas behind ICA – that carers, as adults and citizens, have a right to independent income ('money of their own') and that working-age carers providing high levels of care need protection from loss of earnings – are good ones.

She points out that the UK and Southern Ireland (*sic*) are the only countries in the EU to acknowledge these needs and rights. However, it is arguable that the structure of the carer's allowance (and ICA) does not treat carers as 'adults and citizens' at all but rather that it reinforces the existing gender based division of labour within the household with the (female) carer receiving a small financial incentive to go on providing long hours of demanding unpaid work. Both schemes are structured in such a way that the carer is obliged to become a full-time carer and is, at best, able to engage in limited part-time work (which is likely to be low paid). Thus both schemes

- require that the carer provide full-time care and attention (specified as being at least 35 hours in the UK case), and
- prohibit the carer from well paid employment – in the Irish case by

prohibiting employment or self-employment outside the home and strictly means-testing any earnings, and in the UK case by allowing an earnings disregard of only £50 (and remember that the carer must already have worked for 35 hours *as a carer*).

In Ireland there is a total lack of information as to how receipt of the carer's allowance impacts on intra-household resource transfers and, equally importantly, on the distribution of intra-household expenditure responsibilities. We have no clear picture as to whether carers are in fact any better off financially as a result of receipt of the carer's allowance, or whether receipt of the allowance results in the termination or reduction of resource transfers from the persons cared for or from other family members. Thus while carers have a (limited) right to 'money of their own' we do not know how this affects their incomes. This is an issue of some importance which deserves further study.

The carer's allowance can be seen as an attempt to legitimise the state's reliance on women's informal care and as a case study of the way in which a patriarchal state will tend to reproduce patriarchal structures in its welfare system. While even a patriarchal, capitalist state is likely to be more effective than the market in redistributing income, one might question the extent to which reliance is put on the state in intervening within the family/ household. There is perhaps more possibility of flexibility and of change within the (patriarchal) family than within the patriarchal state (Humphries 1977). Thus the maximum flexibility in the provision of payments or services to the individual (or family/household) would be preferable to tightly structured payments such as the carer's allowance.

In contrast to the rigid approach of the carer's allowance, the type of scheme provided by the Irish domiciliary care allowance simply requires that the child needs constant care and attention and that such care is provided by one or both parents or by another person or persons. Any parental earnings are not taken into account. Thus the structure of the benefit allows some freedom for the parent(s) to organise their lives as they wish and to provide care themselves or to get another person or organisation to provide some or all of the care. The family is allowed to decide on resource allocation in relation to the care of family members with minimal interference from the state as to how this is done. In practice, the level of the payment is quite low (at current home help rates it would allow the purchase of 9 hours' assistance per week) but this is a problem which, at least conceptually, is easier to deal with. The National Council for the Elderly have argued that a constant care allowance should be paid in respect of persons who require full-time care (O'Connor and Ruddle 1988). This payment would be made, regardless of the carer's means, subject to medical certification of the person's dependency on constant care. (See Baldwin *et al.* 1988 for a consideration of some issues concerning this approach.)

In terms of administration, the carer's allowance is administered by the Department of Social Welfare in one centralised office. Those administering the benefit have no responsibility for the co-ordination of care services or for providing advice on the other support services which may be available. Thus there is little incentive for the planners or administrators to consider the most effective integration of the allowance with other support services. In contrast domiciliary care allowance is administered by the regional health boards who are responsible for the provision of the other support services and who should, at least in theory, be better placed to provide support and information for carers.[20]

V CONCLUSION

In summary then, we have argued that a policy based on maximising the involvement of informal carers with a social security policy based largely on providing them with a minimum income, while it may be cheap in terms of state expenditure, is not likely to be the most cost-effective method of providing care. Such an approach is only cost-effective if the labour costs are discounted. Informal caring is likely to continue to play a major role in any strategy since this type of care appears to be preferred by both carers and the persons requiring care. If policy is not based on reliance of cheap, (predominantly) female labour, then research is needed as to the most effective ways of supporting informal caring, including social security support which compensates for some of the costs of care.

The carer's allowance, which requires full-time caring by one person (who will in the majority of cases be a woman), has the effect of reinforcing the existing gendered division of caring duties and thus makes any alteration in that division more difficult to achieve. It would be ironic if in arguing for individual payments for carers, one reinforces the gendered division of labour. It would of course be naïve to suggest that the structure of support for carers will in itself have a major impact on the gendered division of labour. However, one could at least hope that social security provision in this area would not reinforce the existing position.

Support through the social security system should compensate the needs of those requiring care and the needs of carers in a more flexible manner than does the current carer's allowance, for example, by a development of (almost) universal payments such as the domiciliary care allowance. Such a payment should be integrated both structurally and administratively with the other support systems available. This approach does not assume that carers will generally require a minimum income support. However, where it is required, it should be provided in a flexible manner rather than in the rigid way in which the carer's allowance operates.

As we have seen, some countries acknowledge the value of the work done by the carer and establish an element of compensation by providing them with social insurance cover. While the Irish system provides limited assistance towards preserving one's social insurance record by granting credited contributions, this is of much less value to carers, both symbolically and practically, than a scheme whereby a contribution is paid for them by the social security authorities.

NOTES TO ARTICLE

1 Formerly the National Council for the Aged. To avoid confusion it is referred to throughout this article by its current name.

2 This figure includes those in receipt of invalidity benefit, the means-tested disabled persons maintenance allowance (most recent figures are for 1990) and those receiving the nominally 'short-term' disability benefit for 5 years or more.

3 Section 3 of the Finance Act 1969.

4 The estimated cost of the allowance in 1989-90 was IR£200,000.

5 Section 141 of the Income Tax Act 1967 as amended by section 3 of the Finance Act 1986 and section 142 of the Income Tax Act 1967 respectively.

6 Sections 9 and 10 of the Social Welfare (Miscellaneous Provisions) Act 1968. The provisions also required that the claimant be living alone (but for the prescribed relative) or with other persons who were unable to provide care and attention.

7 Sections 15 and 16 of the Social Welfare (Miscellaneous Provisions) Act 1969. Parliamentary questions revealed that only a 'few hundred' persons were in receipt of PRA by May 1969, 240 *Dáil Debat*es, col. 411.

8 Sister, half-sister and grand-daughter.

9 Sections 8 and 9 of the Social Welfare Act 1972.

10 See the comments of the then Minister for Finance at 248 *Dáil Debates*, col. 1699.

11 A person is to be regarded as requiring full-time care and attention where s/he is so disabled or invalided as to require (i) continual supervision in order to avoid danger to him/herself, or (ii) continual supervision and frequent assistance throughout the day in connection with normal bodily functions and where the invalidity or disability is such that the person is likely to require full-time care and attention for at least 12 months. Section 163 of the Social Welfare (Consolidation) Act 1993.

[12] Third Schedule to the Social Welfare (Consolidation) Act 1993. However, any sums received by way of social welfare payments are not taken into account in assessing what could reasonably be contributed.

[13] Article 27 of the Social Welfare (Social Assistance) Regulations 1993.

[14] Section 209 of the Social Welfare (Consolidation) Act 1993.

[15] Compared, for example, to a refusal rate of 45 per cent of claims for deserted wife's benefit which has very complicated eligibility criteria and has always had one of the highest refusal rates of all social welfare payments.

[16] While the Department of Social Welfare is responsible for the vast majority of social security payments, the Department of Health retains responsibility for a limited number of health related payments.

[17] Circular No. 24/73 of 25 September 1973.

[18] *The Irish Times* 6 January 1993. The employment of home helps can be seen as an example of the institutionalisation of women's low paid caring work. Under the Irish social welfare system, earnings from 'casual' employment as a home help are generally disregarded in assessing entitlement to means-tested payments. So employment as a home help is seen as a low paid supplement to other household income.

[19] This assumption was reasonably well supported by the facts. In 1966 only 5.3 per cent of married women were active in the labour force (Blackwell 1986).

[20] Unfortunately, we have little information about how this scheme operates in practice.

REFERENCES

Baldwin, S., G. Parker and R. Walker eds. (1988), *Social Security and Community Care*, Aldershot: Avebury

Bieback, K.-J. (1992), 'Family Benefits: The New Legal Structures of Subsidising the Family', *Journal of European Social Policy* 2, 4, 239-54

Blackwell, J. (1986), *Women in the Labour Force*, Dublin: Employment Equality Agency

Blackwell, J., E. O'Shea, G. Moane and P. Murray (1992), *Care Provision and Cost Measurement: Dependent Elderly People at Home and in Geriatric Hospitals*, Dublin: Economic and Social Research Institute

Brown, J. (1984), *The Disability Income Scheme,* London: Policy Studies Institute

Central Statistics Office (1988), *Population and Labour Force Projections 1991-2001*, Dublin: Stationery Office

Central Statistics Office (1989), *Census 1986, vol. i – Ages and Marital Status*, Dublin: Stationery Office

Chief Appeals Officer (1992), *Report 1991*, Dublin: Stationery Office

Commission on Social Welfare (1986), *Report*, Dublin: Stationery Office

Commission on the Status of Women (1972), *Report*, Dublin: Stationery Office

Cousins, M. (1992), 'Nursing Home Care and Grants', *Irish Social Worker* 11, 1, 21-2

Cousins, M. (1994), 'The Health (Nursing Home) Act 1990', *The Gazette* 88, p. 15

Department of Health (1992), *Health Statistics 1991*, Dublin: Stationery Office

Department of Social Welfare (1982), *Annual Report 1979-1980*, Dublin: Stationery Office

Department of Social Welfare (1992), *Statistical Information on Social Welfare Services 1991*, Dublin: Stationery Office

Dramin, A. (1986), 'Home Help Services for the Elderly in the Eastern Health Board Area', *Administration* 34, 4, 527-34

Dupeyroux, J.J. and X. Pretot (1989), *Securité sociale*, editions Sirey, Paris

European Observatory on Family Policies (1992), *Families and Policies; Evolution and Trends 1989-1990*, Brussels: European Commission

European Observatory on Family Policies(1991), *National Family Policies in EC Countries in 1991*, Brussels: European Commission

Glendenning, C. (1992), The Costs of Informal Care: Looking Inside the Household, London: HMSO

Glendenning, C. (1990), 'Dependency and Interdependency: the Incomes of Informal Carers and the Impact of Social Security', *Journal of Social Policy*, 19, 4, 469-97

Hensey, B. (1979, 1988), *The Health Services in Ireland* (Third and fourth editions), Dublin: Institute of Public Administration

Humphries, J. (1977), 'Class Struggle and the Persistence of the Working Class Family', *Cambridge Journal of Economics* 1, 241-58

Ireland (1992), *Statistical Report of the Revenue Commissioners 1991*, Dublin: Stationery Office

McLaughlin, E. (1991), 'Mixed Blessings? The Invalid Care Allowance and Carer's Income Needs', *Benefits* 3, 8-11

National Economic and Social Council (1987), *Community Care Services: An Overview*, Dublin: NESC

O'Connor, J., E. Smyth and B. Whelan (1988), *Caring for the Elderly: Part 1: A Study of Carers at Home and in the Community*, Dublin: National Council for the Aged

O'Connor, J. and H. Ruddle (1988), *Caring for the Elderly: Part 2: A Study of Carers in the Home*, Dublin: National Council for the Aged

Administration, vol. 51, nos. 1-2 (Spring/Summer 2003), 219–230

Consumerism in the Health Services

TIM O'SULLIVAN

Originally published in 1998, vol. 46, no. 1, 14-28.
Tim O'Sullivan worked then as a specialist in the health services unit of the Institute of Public Administration.

INTRODUCTION

In the 1960s, the consumer had a bad press. He or she was sometimes seen as merely a cog – affluent perhaps but still a cog – in the vast, anonymous machine of western capitalist society. Phrases such as the 'consumer society' were often used in a negative sense. In the late 1960s, the student revolutionaries of the time contrasted what they saw as mindless consumerism, on the one hand, and genuine participation in social decision-making on the other. Fashions change and the consumer is generally seen now in a more positive light. He or she is presented as the person who calls the shots and sets the standards in the business world and even in that of social services provision.

The aim of this article is to reflect on the model and language of consumerism, which has grown in importance in recent years, particularly in the health services context. Consumerism in a general sense is here to stay in the health services. Efforts to improve quality or responsiveness to the views and needs of health services users can be seen as one of the most encouraging trends of recent times. 'Consumerism' has grown in a context where there seemed to be little comment by service users on the services they were receiving; still less a sense of participation by them in decision making about their care and treatment.

Consumerism in this wider sense has been very closely linked with 'quality', which is partly about improving responsiveness to the needs of individual service recipients. This article begins therefore with an overview of quality and consumer-orientated trends in the Irish health service.

A stricter or narrower definition of consumerism can also be offered. That definition focuses on the economic origins of the term 'consumer', or customer who is seen as a key player in the health services along with the 'producer' or 'provider'. This article presents a short critique of consumerism understood in this narrower sense, that is to say, a critique of a model of health services which is over-influenced by economics; and looks at the economic origins of consumerist ideas. The final section reflects on the implications of our use in the health services of assumptions which are rooted in economics.

QUALITY AND CONSUMER TRENDS IN IRELAND

User satisfaction, user involvement in the narrower sense and social acceptability in the broader sense are among the major planks on which the health service depends, along with clinical effectiveness and economic efficiency.

In 1994, the Health Strategy, *Shaping a Healthier Future*, stated that the health services in Ireland must be 'consumer-oriented'. It noted that the Charter of Rights for Hospital Patients in 1992 had been an important first step in setting out the reorientation of one major service towards a greater consumer responsiveness.

That charter can he seen as a code of practice, which sets out what patients have a right to expect when they make use of hospital services. It covers areas such as access to services, outpatient services, information about your treatment, complaints etc. Making a complaint can be seen indeed as an active form of consumerism. An earlier document with a strong user orientation was the 1990 Hospital Action Plan of the Minister for Health. This Plan envisaged a patients' charter and called for effective outpatient appointments in all major hospitals, a hospital code of conduct and a patient feedback mechanism in each hospital.

There was also a major user orientation in the reports of the Kennedy Group, which were presented to the minister in 1991.

These reports recommended inter alia that

- out-patients should not be block booked but should be given specific appointment times;
- there should be continuous review and validation of waiting lists with a view to reducing waiting times;
- there should be greater use of day surgery to reduce waiting times for patients.

The Kennedy Group laid emphasis on 'good practice' and saw the development of an effective quality assurance programme as the key to the implementation of its good practice recommendations in relation to out-patient services and the reduction of waiting lists.

In discussing service quality, the 1994 Health Strategy highlighted both the technical quality of service and patient satisfaction. It stated that health authorities from now on will be required to carry out evaluations of patient satisfaction with various aspects of the service and to include such evaluation in their annual reports.

The Strategy noted that legislation to reform the services would include:

- the establishment of advisory groups in each health authority area to give inputs to the health services from users;
- the requirement on all health authorities to put appropriate complaints procedures in place;
- the introduction of a statutory function of the boards of the health authorities to act as a channel to the minister of the views and concerns of their populations.

The emphasis on patient satisfaction continued in 1997 when the Department of Health's *Statement of Strategy*, included (for example) the commitment to put in place effective patient satisfaction measures throughout the acute hospital sector. In December 1997, the department published (as part of the SMI process) its *Customer Service Action Plan 1998-1999*. This document set out how the department proposed 'to examine and improve the services it provides to all its customer groups' (p. 1) and included, for example, a commitment to a Customer Call In Centre in Hawkins House.

In the light of the thinking in recent reports and policy documents, the case for greater user input in the health services can be summarised as follows:

1. It contributes to improved quality of care.
2. It helps professionals and patients – or those delivering and using the service – to come closer together.
3. User influence is a counter-balance to the strength of powerful interest groups, such as the state (seen as an interest group) and the professions.
4. It heightens awareness of patients' individual and collective needs.

In relation to point 1, the link between consumerism and quality was stressed by Blennerhassett (1993), who linked quality improvement and the adoption of a consumer-oriented philosophy of management.

A similar connection may be found in the influential work of Peters and Waterman, *In Search of Excellence* (1982), which stressed the notion of excellence. According to Peters and Waterman, the most successful ('excellent') companies were those that were 'close to the customer'.

A more customer-orientated approach was also linked to greater efficiency. Blennerhassett argued that in the cost-cutting climate of the

1980s, it seemed an attractive prospect that a more customer-orientated approach would produce financial savings as well as higher quality.

ECONOMIC INFLUENCES ON CONSUMERIST IDEAS

The link referred to at the end of the last section between consumerism, quality and cost control is significant. To the question, 'where does consumerism in the health services come from?', part of the answer at any rate is 'free-market' thinking about the health services and its associated objective of expenditure control. Consumerist developments in Ireland have been influenced by the growth of market thinking in Britain, which sought both to deal with what were perceived as rigid and inflexible state services and to cut back on the state sector. An important part of the market agenda in the British health services in the 1980s was the 'general management' reforms inspired by Sir Roy Griffiths, which sought among other objectives to increase responsiveness to the consumer. Sir Roy's approach was strongly criticised by Fedelma Winker (1987), who described it as 'the supermarket model of consumerism'. Her view was that this model was about customer relations, not patients' rights and that it required 'little serious change but much public visibility'. Nevertheless, the Griffiths reforms had a major impact during the 1980s. The 1989 White Paper in Britain was also strongly influenced by a market-based understanding of the health services.

While free-market economic ideas have influenced health services consumerism, an even more basic influence is economic thinking as such. By economic thinking here is meant key economic principles such as the basic principle that what happens in the health services, and particularly the relationship between doctor and patient, is essentially an economic relationship. It is within the context of this basic framework that the descriptions of 'consumer' and 'provider' come to be applied to health services professionals and patients. This growth of influence of economics in the health services recalls Schumacher's comment twenty years ago that economics had moved to the very centre of public debate in modern societies. In economies which have been more geared in recent decades to consumption than to the manufacture of products, the role of the consumer has been greatly emphasised. Economic thinking also tends to stress the primacy and independence of the individual consumer more than the bonds which link one person to another in society – that is, much economic thinking tends towards an individualistic view of the world.

THE CONTRACTOR MODEL OF THE DOCTOR-PATIENT RELATIONSHIP

Robin Downie (1988) has summarised some of the main characteristics of the *market relationship* between two parties as follows:

1. The trading parties each attempt to maximise their own self-interest.
2. They have information to guide them on maximising their self-interest.
3. They are free to choose whether they will trade or not.
4. The relationship is a competitive one in a double sense: producers are competing with consumers to maximise their profits and producers are competing with other producers to attract consumers.
5. There must be a legal framework to ensure fair competition.

The market-based consumer model is one of *contract* trading relationships. In contracts, as indicated above,

- each party should be able to protect his or her self-interest;
- parties to a contract each enter freely into the relationship;
- neither is at an undue disadvantage in terms of dependency on the other or in terms of inability to secure full knowledge of the situation.

Contracts also imply strict limits. In other words you must fulfil what is in the contract but not any more than is in it. The reciprocal obligations set out in a contract also cease to be binding when its conditions are not fulfilled.

The possible advantages of what he has called the contractor model of the doctor-patient relationship have been outlined by May, an American writer on medical ethics (1983). These include its break with 'more authoritarian models', its emphasis on informed consent rather than blind trust and its specification of rights, duties, conditions and qualifications. In effect, says May, it establishes 'some symmetry and mutuality in the relationship between doctor and patient as they exchange information and reach an agreement, tacitly or explicitly to exchange goods (money for services)' (p. 117).

The difficulties of this model in the health services context, however, should be noted. One difficulty is that it tends to encourage an individualistic view of the needs of patients rather than a broader vision of the needs of the whole community. Another issue is that while health care products or services can be measured and therefore contracted for, the desired outcome ('good health') is much more difficult to attain or even define. The impact of health services on health is also very difficult to predict or measure. May notes that the helping professions serve unpredictable needs and that no contract can exhaustively specify in advance what is to be done for each patient or client.

Politt (1990) succinctly presented the implications for dependent groups of a narrow economic framework. The consumer of some of the official documents, he argued, sounded rather like the abstract figure of elementary economic texts. In the real world, he continued, many health care consumers were already disadvantaged by reasons of race, gender, disability or some combination of these. In his view, there was a grave danger that in the excitement of managing the new internal market, considerations of equity and equality would slip down the agenda.

The question therefore arises as to whether the market-based contractor model is an adequate framework for vulnerable people. By definition, patients are often at a disadvantage, vulnerable and dependent. They are unable to look after their own interests in the way that a consumer can. They frequently do not have access to all the relevant information and they cannot act in a wholly independent manner.

May argues that contractualism builds few constraints upon professional action other than those that prudent self-interest and explicit legislation impose. Contractualism, he argues, 'tempts the doctor simultaneously to do too little and too much for the patient – too little in that one extends oneself only to the limits the contract specifies, and too much in that one orders procedures that are useful in pampering the patient and protecting oneself, even though the patient's condition does not demand them' (p. 122). He thus links contractualism to defensive medicine, which seeks to ward off the threat of litigation.

In considering the applicability of the consumer or contractual model to the health services, it is useful to dwell on some of the specific characteristics of medical care. These include:

- its distinctively personal nature
- unusual features, views from an economics perspective, such as the uncertainty of demand for medical care and the 'agency relationship' between doctors and patients
- structural characteristics, such as the technological and organisational complexity of medical care (these characteristics are clearly not exclusive to medical care).

The personal nature of medical care – to focus on this characteristic – makes such care different in kind to other types of transactions, which are outlined for example in economics or consumer theory. Being a 'heart operation consumer' is a qualitatively different experience from being a shopping centre consumer. In the first place, his or her health is central to each person. In health, too, as well as being the 'consumer', one is also the object of the care being carried out – in effect, it is being carried out on one's own body.

THE COVENANTAL MODEL OF THE DOCTOR-PATIENT RELATIONSHIP

Because of these distinctive characteristics of medical care, the consumer language and model do not seem fully adequate in the health services context. An alternative model, which is more favoured by May

(1983), is what he has called the 'covenantal' model of the doctor-patient relationship. The covenantal model has roots in the biblical concept of the covenant, which encompasses ideas such as mutual indebtedness (for example, between marriage partners) and responsiveness for gifts received (in particular, the 'gift' of the training which the doctor has received from his or her teachers).

May's argument is that the doctor-patient relationship is not simply a business relationship but a deeper covenant-type relationship; in other words, a relationship in which the doctor has a deeper responsibility for the patient than that of being simply the provider of a commercial service; and one in which there is deeper interaction between doctor and patient than there is between a supplier and a customer.

He argues that the doctor-patient relationship can only function well if there is *trust* between both partners. He also argues that the doctor is not just a giver or provider of services. He is also someone who has received – from his teachers, from the community which has subsidised his training and from patients on whose trust the doctor depends. The significance of patient trust is especially evident when the doctor is inexperienced, but such trust is important at all stages of the doctor's career.

In May's model, the professional relationship is nourished by 'a reciprocity of giving and receiving' (p. 115) and obliges the more powerful to 'accept some responsibility for the more vulnerable and powerless of the two partners. It does not permit a free rein to self-interest, subject only to the capacity of the weaker partner to protect himself or herself through knowledge, shrewdness and purchasing power' (p. 124). The covenantal model envisages a much more open-ended commitment than the contractual model, what May calls 'the steadfast commitment to protect, nourish and heal the needy' (p. 126).

In the absence of such an open-ended commitment doctors may not feel obliged to provide services to certain inconvenient categories of patients.

On the other hand, the 'steadfast commitment to the needy' envisaged in May's framework cannot mean that there are no financial limits in healthcare or that the cost control issues with which managers are grappling can be ignored by doctors. What the covenantal model does usefully emphasise, however, is the need in the health services for some form of open-ended commitment to the vulnerable person, a commitment which is not guaranteed by the consumerist framework. The covenantal model suggests that the needs of the patient must be centre-stage in any framework which is adopted for the management of medicine and that priority must be given to these needs. In other words, the needs of the patient must take priority over the rights of professional groups and even over the preferences of the articulate, well-informed consumer.

Where the consumer model stresses the independence of the consumer, the covenantal model emphasises the *inter-dependence* of professional and patient. In other words, the patient depends on the skills and commitment of the professional but the professional also generally needs the trust and commitment to a particular course of action of the patient if treatment or intervention is to be successful. The espousal of a covenantal model does not imply that contracts are unimportant; but it does suggest that the commitment of the doctor to the patient must go beyond the minimum standards laid down in a contract.

It is clearly important to avoid confusion here. May's models are not two alternative ways of organising medical practice, one of which can be found in one country and one in another. They are simply two ways of looking at, or thinking about, the doctor-patient relationship. Both ways of thinking probably have some influence in every country but the argument in this article is that with the growth of consumerism, the contractor model or way of thinking about the doctor-patient relationship has become more influential than the covenantal model, which is closer in some respects to traditional medical ethics; and that the contractor model is therefore becoming more influential in day-to-day medical practice. The growth of litigation involving doctors in Ireland and elsewhere would seem to bear this out: where the possibility of litigation becomes stronger, both doctor and patient become more focused on the letter rather than the spirit of the doctor-patient contract.

I suggested earlier that the consumerist/contractual model is open to criticism for its narrow, individualistic view of the doctor-patient relationship, which tends to take for granted the presence of an articulate, well-informed consumer. Might not the same criticism, however, be levelled at the covenantal model – that it elevates the relationship between the doctor and the individual patient and ignores the needs of the patients or of society as a whole?

May argues that this need not be the case. He maintains that society has a basic responsibility for the comprehensive delivery of professional services and that the obligation to distributive justice falls primarily but not exclusively on the state (the professionals also have a responsibility here). Moral purposes, he says, must be built into the very purpose of the healthcare institution. It cannot, he argues, depend on the fitful efforts of individual persons alone to keep the covenant. However, if structures which support distributive justice are the responsibility of the state, May argues that these structures will not work if professionals lack strong moral commitments.

Proponents of consumerism might argue that the covenantal model is advocating a return to an old-fashioned world of paternalistic doctors and passive patients. May rejects this view. The paternalistic approach, he argues, is a one-way approach, that of the doctor giving to the patient. However, the covenantal approach sees the doctor as a receiver as well as a giver; he receives from his teachers, from the community which subsidised his training and from his patients. The covenantal approach also stresses commitment to the patient; this means acknowledging the fact that the patient is a person with rights which must be respected and taking account of the views and needs of the patients.

TRENDS IN IRELAND

In Ireland, the influence of both a contractor and a covenantal model can be perceived in the doctor-patient relationship, with the contractor model perhaps more dominant in recent years. In 1997, as on a number of earlier occasions, difficult negotiations accompanied the agreement of a consultants' contract. In reporting the negotiations, the *Irish Medical News* emphasised in October 1997 the key sticking-points of 'money and monitoring'.

Agreement on a new Consultants' Contract was eventually reached and the Memorandum of Agreement in the Consultants' Contract Documents (1997) sets out agreed statements on three key areas:

(i) the unique nature of the consultant's work;
(ii) the nature of the consultant's role and responsibilities;
(iii) the nature of the employing authority's role and responsibilities (par 6.2).

The memorandum also states that the exercise of his rights by a consultant 'carries a corresponding responsibility on the consultant, recognising the finite nature of resources, to operate and manage his practice in a manner which makes best use of available resources by scheduling his work and coordinating it with that of his colleagues' (par 6.4.5). The memorandum adds, in the following paragraph:

> By recognising the finite nature of the resources available to his practice, a consultant does not relinquish his role as advocate on behalf of his patients or patients waiting for consultation or treatment. In this contract, the process of negotiation and re-negotiation of resource and activity levels between the consultant and the employing authority will provide a forum, in the first instance, for the consultant's advocacy role. Neither does it preclude the profession as a body advocating more or better services for patients (par 6.4.6).

Clearly, contract negotiations must give detailed attention to pay rates and to related issues such as hours worked or consultant availability at specific times. Nevertheless, it is worthy of note (the above references to advocacy notwithstanding) that public discussion in Ireland about (for example) hospital consultants and their relations with public authorities focuses much more on their pay and conditions than on doctor-patient interaction per se or on the consultant's possible role as an advocate for the patient.

On the other hand, discussion of legal or ethical issues, of ethical conduct among doctors or of specific issues such as confidentiality, would appear to be based in Ireland on an implicit covenantal model. In his introduction to the *Ethical Guide* of the Irish Medical Council (1994) Browne emphasises both the importance of trust between doctor and patient and the special responsibilities of a doctor faced with someone who is vulnerable or less knowledgeable:

> Just as the lawyer knows more about the law than does his client, doctors know more about medicine than do their patients.

He notes that patients' attitudes are divided. On the one hand they trust the learning and skill of the doctor; on the other hand they find themselves in a state of anxiety and uncertainty. In such an ambivalent situation, Browne concludes, 'it is the function of medical ethics to ensure that ... the doctor does not abuse his/her professional superiority' (p. 7).

In an article on the specific issue of medical confidentiality, Kieran Doran, an Irish writer on medical law, notes that the doctor's duty of confidentiality is based on a duty in contract, equity and morality. He states that the ethical obligation placed on the doctor to respect confidentiality becomes a legal duty. In relation to what he calls the 'equitable duty', Doran writes: 'Even if a specific contractual term is not expressly agreed by the parties, an equitable duty is imposed on the medical practitioner to respect medical confidentiality by reason of the relationship of trust' (1997, p. 21).

In terminology similar to that of May, Doran argues that the concept of trust has been the key element of a new legal interpretation of the doctor-patient relationship, that is, the fiduciary relationship. He adds:

> In the case of *Mclnerney v. McDonald*, the Supreme Court of Canada characterised the doctor-patient relationship as being 'fiduciary' in nature i.e., one based on mutual trust and a duty of confidence. The patient entrusted personal medical details to the doctor on the understanding that they would be treated in the strictest confidence (p. 22).

In Ireland as elsewhere, the contractor and covenantal models would seem to co-exist, perhaps in an uneasy way. Clearly, the type of model adopted for the doctor-patient relationship will have an important influence on how medicine is managed. The adoption of a model with a contractor emphasis leads to a more direct emphasis on the measurement and management of clinical work and on issues of management control. The adoption of a model with a covenantal emphasis, on the other hand, leads to more emphasis on the primary importance of the doctor-patient relationship and on the professional responsibility of the clinician. It is worth noting that both the contractor and covenantal models emphasise patient or consumer rights but in a different way. The contractual model strongly emphasises the rights of patients under their contracts and stresses the mutual independence of patients and providers; the covenantal model suggests that the needs of the patients must be centre-stage but views the patient-doctor relationship in a more inter-dependent way.

CONCLUSION

Responsiveness to the views and needs of health services users, who are sometimes described as consumers, is one of the encouraging trends of recent times. Nevertheless, serious questions can be raised about the appropriateness of the consumer model and language (as defined at the beginning of the article) in the health services.

I have argued here that the consumerist model is grounded in at least two questionable assumptions: first, that health is a consumer good that can be bought and sold; and second, (the primary focus of this article) that the doctor-patient relationship is primarily an economic relationship rather than one based on trust and commitment.

There is obviously much to be learnt from consumerist ideas and approaches. The development of the consumer movement in the health services points to a hunger for a more equal relationship between service provider and user and for greater participation by the user. Nevertheless, the argument of this article has been that a model based on trust and commitment between professional and patient is more likely than the consumerist model to offer adequate protection to the health services patient and particularly to dependent inarticulate groups.

REFERENCES

Blennerhassett, Evelyn (1993). *Quality Improvement in the Irish Civil Service*, Dublin: Institute of Public Administration

Department of Health (1994). *Shaping a Healthier Future. A Strategy for Effective Healthcare in the 1990s*, Dublin: Stationery Office

Department of Health (1997). *Consultants' Contract Documents*, Dublin: Department of Health

Department of Health (1997). *Customer Service Action Plan 1998-1999*, Dublin: Department of Health

Department of Health (1997). *Statement of Strategy*, Dublin: Department of Health

Doran, Kieran (1997). 'Medical Confidentiality: The Role of the Doctrine of Confidentiality in the Doctor-Patient Relationship', *Medico-Legal Journal of Ireland,* 3, (1), 21-26

Downie, R.S. (1988). 'Traditional Medical Ethics and Economics in Health Care' in G. Mooney, A. McGuire (editors), *Medical Ethics and Economics in Health Care*, Oxford: Oxford University Press

May, W.F. (1983). *The Physician's Covenant, Images of the Healer in Medical Ethics*, Philadelphia: Westminster Press

Medical Council (Ireland) (1994). *Guide to Ethical Conduct and Behaviour and to Fitness to Practise*, Dublin: Medical Council (4th edition)

Peters, Thomas J. and Robert H. Waterman (1982). *In Search of Excellence*, Lessons from America's Best Run Companies, London: Harper and Row

Pollitt, Christopher (1990). 'Consumers, Markets and the NHS', *K F News,* vol. 13, no. 2, June 1990

Reports of the Dublin Hospital Initiative Group (Kennedy Reports) (1991), Dublin: Department of Health

Secretaries of State for Health, Wales, Northern Ireland and Scotland (1989). *Working for Patients* (CM 555), London: HMSO

Winkler, Fedelma (1987). 'Consumerism in Health Care: Beyond the Supermarket Model', *Policy and Politics*, vol. 15, no. 1-8, 1987

Part Three
Social Change and Social Citizenship

Administration, vol. 51, nos. 1-2 (Spring/Summer 2003), 233–239

Women in the Civil Service

NEANS DE PAOR

Originally published in 1955, vol. 3, no. 2, 141-147.
This article was based on a paper read in January 1955 to a discussion group of the Association of Higher Civil Servants. Neans De Paor was then a higher civil servant.

WOMEN entered the British civil service in the year 1870 – entry being effected by a back door, when the telegraph service was nationalised and the staffs of the old Telegraph Company absorbed into the State service. The back-door entrants apparently proved satisfactory, a few years later a small number of women clerks were appointed by nomination to the Post Office Savings Bank. With the introduction of typewriting machines in the nineties the employment of typists to operate the machines became necessary and this resulted in the appearance of women in Departments other than the Post Office where they worked in segregation. These early pioneering civil servants appear to have been regarded with considerable mistrust and suspicion. It is on record that the one woman in the Board of Agriculture was secluded in a room in the basement and that the Chief Clerk issued an imperative order that no member of the staff over the age of 15 was to enter her room. Of another Department it has been written that "women typists worked in a locked room in the upper part of the building and their work and meals were served to them through a hatch in the wall. They left a quarter of an hour before the men and no man was allowed to take work to them without a special permit-only obtained with great difficulty. The only time when they were let loose in the office was when they went to draw pay and even then, in the early days, they are said to have been marshalled in a crocodile by the Superintendent. All this, of course, made them intensely interesting to the men, who used to hide behind the pillars in the corridors to watch them pass.

The first world war, following as it did on a period during which the higher education of women had become a commonplace, brought about a change in the official view as to the employment of women civil servants and when the Irish Free State was established many of the government departments taken over from the British included a proportion of women officers. To-day there are 9,000 women in the Irish civil service.

In the light of these hastily sketched developments a discussion of women's place in the civil service may seem pointless. Women are an integral part of the service to which we all belong – if they were to be excluded from it the entire structure would collapse; all positions in the general service grades are open to them, in theory at least. I cannot imagine a meeting of women being called together to discuss in public, "Men in the Civil Service" – although many women could in private discourse entertainingly on the subject. I can only conclude that the now unavoidable presence of women in the service may be thought to constitute in some way a problem. What can that problem be? I can only suggest that reflection and careful examination of conscience may yield the conclusion that while the presence of very large numbers of women and girls in the lower ranks is readily accepted there is a feeling that in general those lower ranks are their proper place.

That this was the view of those in control of the service in the early days of the State can be readily demonstrated by citing two cases. When the servants of the first and second Dáil Éireann were being absorbed into the Free State service a case arose of a woman engaged on work outside the country at a salary of about £350. Considerable delay arose in connection with her establishment and when she made confidential enquiries she learned unofficially that she constituted a problem as the employment of women in a grade corresponding to her salary had not been contemplated.

Some time afterwards two vacancies to be filled by competitive examination were announced in the junior administrative grade. When the result of the examination became known it was discovered that the first two places had been obtained by two women. The shock in official quarters was so great that preparations were set on foot to exclude women from future examinations of the same kind. These preparations came to nothing as it was brought to the notice of the government that such a procedure would be unconstitutional. The proposed method of exclusion was then dropped, but the basis of competitive examination was also jettisoned and a new system introduced in which the determining factor is the mark secured at an interview.

When women first entered the civil service in Britain they worked in groups in particular departments, particularly the Post Office. In those departments they worked in segregation under female supervisors and in general their prospects of promotion were confined to their own class. They were recruited on a different basis from men and were not in competition with the latter. This was the position obtaining in 1923 as it was only in 1928 that women were admitted in Great Britain to the open competitions for the clerical and executive grades. Since then the principle of segregation – relic of the nineties – has tended to disappear. It was, however, a very live issue at the time when the Brennan Commission was holding its sittings to take evidence on which to base its report on the organisation of the civil service. I gave some evidence before that Commission on behalf of a committee representing women of all grades and was urging that the continuance of the system limited the women's prospects of promotion. Greatly to my surprise a member of the Commission asked if I did not realise that if men and women were working side by side a great deal of time would be lost in flirtation. Knowing the manners and customs of what I may describe as the aboriginal civil servant I could only reply that in my view it was unlikely that any male servant would waste his time in such a manner. Since those days the practice of segregating the sexes has tended to disappear. It survives chiefly in the Department of Posts and Telegraphs, largely no doubt by reason of the very large numbers of writing and sorting assistants employed there and not as a conscious policy.

With the mention of writing assistants I come to the chief difficulty which affects women civil servants, so many of whom belong to that grade. In theory the educational qualification on which the examinations for writing assistants are based is a full primary school course; in fact the majority of successful candidates in recent years have completed a secondary school course and possess the Leaving Certificate, frequently with honours. The competition is restricted to girl candidates and, in consequence of their unnecessarily high educational qualifications, they are commonly engaged not on work of the completely routine type contemplated when the grade was established but on duties indistinguishable from those of the clerical grade. For the vast majority of writing assistants, no promotion is possible.

I see no reason why boys as well as girls should not be allowed to compete for places as writing assistants and I am sure that if the grade consisted of males as well as females the opportunity for promotion would be more favourable. During the British régime examinations were held for boy clerks – who correspond roughly to writing assistants – and many gentlemen who now occupy senior posts entered the service originally in that grade. Women do not wish to reserve this low grade for themselves, any more than they wished the junior administrative to be reserved for men. The fact that large numbers of women are recruited annually for the lowest grade of the service to which men are not admitted – presumably as being beneath male dignity – puts women in an inferior position straightaway.

The question may be put "why do girls with unnecessarily high qualifications enter for these posts?" In reply I can only say that it is due to the short-sightedness of parents and teachers and their ignorance of conditions. A teacher may think on these lines: "M.B. is a very clever girl and is sure to get a high place in the writing assistants' examination. If however, she enters for the clerical officers' examination she will not do quite so well-possibly some boys will do better on the mathematics papers. It would be safer to go forward as a writing assistant and she is so intelligent that she is sure to secure promotion after her appointment".

The fallacy, of course, is in the conclusion, for it is more than likely that M.B. will remain a writing assistant until she dies or retires, unless she turns her intelligence to securing a husband.

In the higher ranks, the promotion of women is proceeding slowly although there has been some improvement in recent years. Still, the very small number eligible for membership of the Association of Higher Civil Servants would suggest that promotion to the highest ranks is more difficult in the case of women. The position appears to be that any woman who is promoted must be greatly superior to her male competitors. It is not enough for her to be as good as them – or even a little better – she must be so outstandingly good that her claim cannot be ignored. Perhaps this is not altogether a bad thing as it results at least in placing beyond all question the efficiency of the female promotee. One can only look forward to a time when the male prejudice which now undoubtedly exists will gradually disappear. This prejudice emerges only when there is a question of a woman occupying a higher post-men have no objection to their being employed on the lowest rungs of the ladder.

As an example of the existence of this prejudice the Report of the Brennan Commission may be cited. Paragraph 180 of the Report contains the following remarkable statement: "In those cases in the Civil Service where men and women may be employed indifferently we find special reason for supposing that on the whole when all relevant aspects are taken into account the woman does not give as good a return of work as the man". One would expect that the signatories would have thought it essential to substantiate such a categorical statement by some reference to the evidence on which it was based, but the only justification put forward by them was the "general expressions of opinion which we have heard". Evidence bearing on the point in so far as higher officers were concerned was indeed given by an assistant secretary of the Department of Finance but as his statements were contrary to the "general expressions of opinion which we have heard" they were disregarded. The following replies were made by the assistant secretary to questions put to him by members of the Commission: "So far as my experience goes no woman, to the best of my knowledge, has been rejected on probation as unfit for her work. We have not heard from any department that any woman has been rejected". "Any reports we have had from the departments are favourable to the work of women employed in these departments. They are all reported as efficient and we have never had any difficulty at all in regard to the work of women". "We have no reason to think that they (i.e., women) may not be just as good" (as men).

And, despite these very clear statements by the person in the best position to judge, the Commission, with three dissentients, of whom two were the only women members, committed themselves to the sweeping statement quoted above. Two of the gentlemen concerned had formerly been Secretaries of Departments, a sufficient indication, to my mind, of the existence of the prejudice which undoubtedly existed in the Commission period and which still survives although happily to a diminished degree.

In this connection I may perhaps be allowed to describe an experience of my own. It happened that I was discussing with a principal officer the subsidiary qualifications necessary for a post under a local authority, the post being one for which the essential qualification was based on a particular course of university training. Our discussion related to a minor additional qualification which had been required for some years previously but which the principal officer in question desired to have dropped. When I pressed for his reason he said: "Because of this condition we have been getting inferior people". When I queried the inferiority aspect, seeing that all candidates must be fully qualified, he replied: "But we are getting women", and to his mind he was merely stating an axiom, something which no one, not even the woman to whom he was talking, would venture to refute.

Whenever questions relating to women in the service are discussed, such questions as equal pay for equal work or promotion, two hoary arguments are invariably brought forward. We are told that the average of women's sick leave is higher than that of men and that the retirement of women on marriage makes it wasteful to train them for higher posts.

As regards the first of these points it must be emphasised again that the mass of women civil servants are employed in the lowest grades with smallest rates of pay and the least allowance of annual leave. They are in the main young girls who have left home for the first time and are faced, inexperienced as they are, with the problem of stretching their salaries to cover the high cost of Dublin lodgings, bus fares which can amount to a considerable sum and all the incidental expenses of city life. It is not to be wondered at if in these circumstances they are inclined to economise on food with the inevitable results to their health. Further, they have been accustomed to long school holidays and must adjust themselves to working throughout the year except for a period of 15 days. There is no class of male civil servants with which writing assistants and the typing grades can be compared so there is really no sincerity in the contention that women are more often absent through illness than are men. It would be interesting to obtain figures of the sickness ratios in the executive and higher grades; I am satisfied that if the figures were available the women's record would not suffer.

To anyone who knows civil service methods the argument that time would be lost on training women for higher posts is particularly specious. One of the flaws in the existing system is the complete absence of training for either men or women and the new entrant gains his knowledge and experience by empirical methods, possibly with the assistance of a neighbour. It has been known to happen that a woman has not been preferred for promotion because of the possibility that she might marry; if she does marry she is compelled to resign, so she suffers either way as far as her service career is concerned, no matter what she does.

The much-debated question of "equal pay for equal work" would require a paper to itself.* Theoretically, the existing differentiated scales have a certain logic on the assumption that a married man has dependants for whom he must provide while a single man or woman has none. In fact, of course, the married man may have a rich wife and no children while the single man or the woman may be supporting parents or contributing to the maintenance and education of younger brothers and sisters. Still, the differentiated scales do not discriminate excessively against women but they are resented very much by unmarried men who have been heard to complain of the indignity to which they are subjected in being compelled to work for women's rates, and if logic is to be invoked what logic is discernible in the case of re-instated widows who are treated as single, even though they are working to support their children. Beyond the limits of the general service grades the 'logical' basis of the differentiated scales has come to be completely disregarded. It is common to read advertisements announcing vacancies for professional appointments in the Government service in which two scales of salary are set out, one for women and another (higher naturally) for men. To qualify as a solicitor, doctor or architect requires the same amount of intelligence, industry, time and money in the case of a woman as of a man. If a woman is appointed she will be engaged on the same duties as her male colleagues and the same output of work will be required of her. The fact that she will be paid less for her work is definitely degrading, not alone to the woman but to the profession to which she belongs. The women who apply for these positions are not to be blamed. In most cases their training has cost their parents a large amount of money and they feel the necessity of securing posts at all costs but it is difficult to understand why the professional associations concerned condone the continuance of this system.

In thus setting out the grievances felt by many women civil servants because of the discrimination against them under the various heads indicated I should not like it to be thought that they are seething

* The principle has been conceded recently in the British civil service.

under a load of bitterness and frustration. Far from that being the case they are happy in their work and glad to be engaged in their country's service. They rejoice to see that male prejudice is diminishing gradually as indicated by the slow infiltration of women into the higher grades. They know too that the public service could not continue to exist without their aid, which is a most satisfying reflection.

Administration, vol. 51, nos. 1-2 (Spring/Summer 2003), 240–256

Commission on the Status of Women: Progress Report

THEKLA BEERE

Originally published in 1975, vol. 23, no. 1, 31-46.
Dr. Beere was chairman of the Commission on the Status of Women. A former secretary of the Department of Transport and Power (1959 to 1966) she served as a member of the Public Service Organisation Review Group (1966 to 1969) popularly known as the Devlin Committee. The paper gives the situation as it stood in April 1975.

For the benefit of those who are not familiar with the background of our discussions, I should perhaps begin at March 1970 when the Commission on the Status of Women was established with the following terms of reference.

> "To examine and report on the status of women in Irish Society, to make recommendations on the steps necessary to ensure the participation of women on equal terms and conditions with men in the political, social, cultural and economic life of the country and to indicate the implications generally including the estimated cost of such recommendations".

The Commission comprised six men and seven women, including myself as Chairman.

Shortly after our appointment the then Minister for Finance requested the Commission to prepare, as a matter of urgency, an interim report dealing with the question of equal pay, with particular reference to the public sector. This interim report was submitted in August, 1971, and was published that October. In addition to dealing with equal pay, we included recommendations on the marriage bar and on women's employment. This material was incorporated in our final report – an agreed report I am glad to say, which was presented in December 1972.

A beginning was made at an early stage by the Employer/Labour Conference towards implementing equal pay and the Minister for Finance stated in his 1972 Budget Statement that the general arrangements adopted by the Employer/Labour Conference would be applied in the Public Service. He also dealt with the question of the early removal of the marriage bar. The next land-mark was the statement in the 14-point plan announced by the Coalition in February 1973 that legislation would be introduced to end all forms of existing discrimination against women.

In his Budget speech of May 1973 the Minister for Finance welcomed the report and announced new provisions to give effect to a number of the Recommendations.

In July 1973, Senator Mary Robinson moved a Motion on the Report in the Senate. The debate was attended by the Taoiseach – an unusual, and very welcome honour. The Taoiseach welcomed the Report and re-affirmed the commitment of the Government to end all forms of discrimination against women. The Minister for Labour has already made his views and intentions clear when he announced details of the Government's plans for International Women's Year and in earlier statements.

This then is the background and my purpose is to give you an account of what has already been done, what is in process of being done, and what still is not being done to implement the Report. I have tried to give you as full and accurate an account as possible, but there may well be mistakes or omissions as it was a very wide field to cover. I have been greatly assisted by staff in the various Government Departments concerned whom I would like to thank publicly. I found them very well-briefed and co-operative and I am satisfied that an enormous amount of work has been done and is being done and that there has been a vast change in the realm of women's affairs over the last few years. Two final points – some of the recommendations in the Report could only be carried into effect by individuals or groups in the community and here much of my information is incomplete. Secondly, we are dealing with discriminations against women rather than with all the social and economic problems common to both sexes.

WOMEN AND EQUAL PAY

In its Interim Report of August, 1971, the Commission recommended that women should receive the same pay as men for jobs which are the same, or similar, or of equal value and that a phased implementation should be completed by 31st December, 1977. Legislation to ensure effective implementation was also proposed.

The Employer-Labour Conference, 1972, accepted in principle the recommendations made by the Commission and made provision for a first phase – 17½% elimination of differentials from 1st June, 1973. The Employer-Labour Conference National Agreement, 1974, provided for a further 33.33% of the remaining differentials, or a different adjustment if agreed between the negotiating parties. The present position is broadly that if the terms of the agreements are availed of, approximately 45% of the differentials should have been removed which leaves substantially more than half still to be eliminated. In the case of the Civil Service and the teachers more than half of the differentials have been removed.

The Anti-Discrimination (Pay) Act, 1974, promoted by the Minister for Labour became law on 1st July, 1974. It provides for full equal pay by 31st December, 1975, which is the target date set for all EEC countries. The Commission in suggesting 31st December, 1977, as the final date had anticipated that all but the most extreme differentials would have been closed by the phasing arrangements well before that date: they had noted the slow progress towards equal pay made over many years by the 'Six' and had been concerned to avoid inflation, a backlash and loss of jobs for women. No doubt the climate of opinion has altered since 1972 and we must hope that under the new legislation many women will enjoy equal pay sooner than the Commission had anticipated that this would have been possible. The other Sections of the Act follow closely the recommendations in the Report – including (the circumstances in which equal pay should apply: the appointment by the Labour Court of Equal Pay Officers to investigate and make reports on disputes arising out of the application of equal pay. There is also a right of appeal to the Labour Court, and, on a point of law to the High Court. The Minister for Labour has added two useful provisions in the Act which will come into effect at the end of this year. He has taken power to refer cases himself to Equal Pay Officers where it appears to him that an employer has failed to comply with the provisions of the Act and where it is not reasonable to expect the employee concerned to refer the case to an Equal Pay Officer. Secondly, there is a provision which makes it an offence for an employer to dismiss a woman for the sole reason that she sought equal pay.

An Equal Pay Commissioner was appointed over two years ago. Some thirty cases from about 15 different employments have been referred to him and are in various stages of progress. So far it has been necessary for him to issue only two formal reports, but he has been very active in advising managements and trade unions and in helping them to reach fair settlements. The first formal report related to women employed in the Confectionery Industry and was at "industry" level. The Commissioner found that the jobs for men and women employed in the industry were not the same or similar or of equal value taking the industry as a whole. The report suggests that the parties might well examine the adequacy of the existing job structure in the Confectionery Industry and accept job evaluation techniques as an aid to agreeing on job values. The Report recognised that there were women confectioners in some firms performing jobs that in comparison with jobs being performed by male confectioners in the same or other firms would probably satisfy the criteria necessary to qualify for an equal pay award. The Report is a valuable one and merits careful study by all those interested in securing equal pay awards.

The Second Report issued by the Commissioner relates to employment in the Agricultural Institute in the production of mushrooms and glass house crops. In this case the Commissioner found that the overall scale or range of the work performed by the men and women in this area of operations was similar enough to justify treating the jobs for pay purposes as of equal value.

The Minister for Labour has announced his intention to set up an Equal Pay Review Committee composed of representatives of employers and Trade Unions to monitor the progress towards equal pay and to recommend on any deficiencies which become apparent in the Anti-Discrimination (Pay) legislation.

It has not been possible to obtain statistics of the number of women who have achieved equal pay for work of equal value or who are well on the way to reaching equality. In the Public Service, State companies, Banks, teaching and the Tobacco Industry, arrangements have been made to implement equal pay by the end of 1975. Negotiations are on-going in Sugar Confectionery, Distributive Trades, Bacon Curing and Textiles. Claims are under discussion in Insurance Cos., Footwear industry and the clerical end of Bakeries. Many private companies have made arrangements and some are talking with the trade unions. There still remains, however, much work to be done by the women themselves and their Trade Unions as there is no doubt but that some industries are dragging their feet.

The small number of cases which have been referred to the Equal Pay Commissioner is rather disappointing and very strong pressure will be required if equality is to be achieved by the end of the year.

In the Civil Service, in those grades in which both men and women are employed, the pay scales have been differentiated on a sex basis or a marriage basis. Where scales have been differentiated on the basis of sex (mainly applicable in professional and technical grades), the pay of women is now being brought up towards that of men. Where the scales are differentiated on the basis of marriage, the pay of women and single men is being brought towards that of married men and full equal pay should be achieved by the end of the year. Certain differentials which applied to the pay of clerical officers in the local authority and health services are also to be phased out.

A review is also being carried out in the Service to ascertain what posts at present restricted to either sex could be opened to both sexes.

The Commission felt that job evaluation could be of considerable assistance in identifying areas in which equal pay is applicable, that managements and unions should be acquainted with its techniques, and that women should be represented when a job evaluation exercise is being set up. I understand that Congress has had a seminar on job evaluation and that the officers of the FUE have also been trained. Courses have been provided by the IPA and IMI. It is also noted that under the Employer-Labour Agreements of 1972 and 1974 the Trade Unions have undertaken to co-operate fully in the use of job evaluation and other techniques for the purpose of establishing the validity of a claim to equal pay.

The Irish Government has now ratified the ILO Convention (No. 100) on equal pay.

WOMEN IN EMPLOYMENT

Under this heading the Commission made a number of recommendations concerning a wide range of subjects. I will deal firstly with the recommendations which have broadly been accepted.

Sex Discrimination

The Commission was concerned that permanent machinery should be set up for action against sex-discrimination in employment and suggested that the Labour Court might be given responsibility for investigating complaints of discrimination on the basis of sex in relation to access to employment or in training or promotion in employment, and that the Court should indicate the legal or other powers which it considered necessary for enforcement. It is most gratifying that the Minister for Labour announced in his Estimates speech of May 1973 that it was his intention to introduce legislation on discrimination on grounds of sex in the selection of workers for industry and their advancement. He indicated also that the proposed legislation would cover matters such as access to employment, opportunities for advancement and continued employment after marriage, maternity leave, return to employment after absence due to family responsibilities etc.

Though I do not know the details of the proposed Bill I am aware that staff are busily engaged in its preparation. This is a most complex field of legislation and we must wish the Minister well in this venture and assure him of the co-operation of women and of their Associations.

Marriage Bar

The next recommendation to be accepted is the removal of the marriage bar. The marriage bar, which was a legal bar to the recruitment of married women to the Civil Service, or their retention after marriage, has been removed as from 31st July, 1973. The marriage bar has been removed also in the Local Authorities and Health Boards. In so far as a marriage bar may still exist, by custom or as a part of employment contracts, we can expect that it will be removed in the legislation to which I have just referred.

Maternity Leave

The Commission also made a number of recommendations on the subject of maternity leave. This is another matter, which the Minister has undertaken to include in the proposed legislation. Since our Report was prepared the means limit on insurability has been abolished with the result the most women employees are covered for maternity benefit. Agreement has been reached with the civil service staff interests for maternity leave of 12 weeks at full pay. I understand that maternity leave for teachers is under consideration.

Apprenticeship

Another recommendation was that the Department of Labour and AnCO, the Industrial Training Authority, should initiate discussions with employer and Trade Union interests with a view to formulating proposals under which restrictions (imposed either by trade unions, or employers and trade unions) on the entry of women to skilled occupations which are predominantly male at present, would be removed over a number of years. At the request of the Minister, AnCO set up a working party in July, 1974, to advise on the establishment of a pilot scheme for the recruitment and training of girl apprentices. The Working Party is representative of the Trade Unions and Employers as well as of Department of Labour and AnCO. I understand that their Report is in an advanced stage. An enormous amount of work remains to be done in this important field, particularly in securing a change in attitudes.

Employment of married women and re-entry of women to employment

The Commission was concerned that national employment policy should be enlarged to ensure that every category of willing and available workers can be employed; that facilities should be provided to advise women on all aspects of re-entry to the labour force and that consideration should be given to part-time or flexible working hours. The Expansion Programme of AnCO for 1974-78 quotes extensively from the Commission's Report and refers specifically to the relative scarcity of women for jobs and to the need for a sharp rise in the labour participation of women including married women. AnCO has expanded the range and location of Training Courses for women and continues to examine areas where further courses for women may be introduced in the future. Courses have been run at various centres throughout the country in sewing machine operating, electronic assembly, office procedure training and hairdressing. In certain cases special efforts were made to interest mature women. A series of "Introduction to Industry" courses have been introduced in many centres. These courses are designed for people who have never worked in industry or who have not been in industrial employment for a number of years. The purpose of these courses is to give people some indication of what is involved in working in industry and how training can prepare them for a job in industry. Courses are run in mobile AnCO Centres and in Vocational Schools during the summer. They are open to both men and women of all ages. Research work is also being undertaken on various problems associated with the re-entry of women to the labour force.

The National Manpower Service assists people to obtain employment, which is suitable to their ages and capacities. It gives advice on job opportunities, opportunities for training or retraining and is in a position to help women who wish to return to work. An Occupational Guidance Service is being developed within the Manpower Service and this will provide guidance and advice to women (as well as men of course) who may have special problems in obtaining or keeping suitable employment.

It is part of the function of the Manpower Service to advise employers who may have difficulty in attracting or holding workers, as to the measures they should take to remedy the situation. In the case of women workers these recommendations can involve the introduction of flexible hours of work (to facilitate women with families), the provision of crèches or restructuring the work generally to enable women to be employed.

Other recommendations on the employment of women related principally to night work by women, confinement of job openings in newspaper advertisements to one sex, occupational pension schemes, day care of children and training of home helps.

From insurance sources I understand that advances have been made with occupational pension schemes: that where a woman is ineligible to enter a pension scheme before a certain age or period of service, and where such a condition does not apply to a male employee, it is now a matter of practice to include in her pensionable service the years during which she was precluded from joining the pension scheme.

From a recent statement of the Minister it seems that we may expect something in the new Bill on bias in newspaper advertisements.

There seems to have been little development in day care facilities for children. The policy of the Minister for Local Government, however, is to improve progressively the provision of facilities for children, including crèches in Local Authority schemes and where the cost is not too great to allow a fair proportion against the scheme.

I am informed that there has been some training of home helps by a few of the Health Boards.

WOMEN AND SOCIAL WELFARE

The Commission made many recommendations on Social Welfare Services designed to remove certain discriminations, and substantial improvements have been secured which generally follow closely the lines of our recommendations.

Unemployment and disability benefit – the case of widows.

Widows in receipt of contributory pensions had to pay the full contribution but were entitled to only half the rate of unemployment and disability benefit. The Social Welfare Act, 1973, provides that women receiving widows pension, deserted wife's benefit or allowance or an allowance as an unmarried mother and who take up employment are no longer liable for any deductions from earnings in respect of social insurance. They will continue to be eligible for half rate unemployment and disability benefit, if they become ill or unemployed, in addition to their pension or allowance.

Disqualification of married women for certain benefits

The Commission recommended that a woman should retain any accumulated title of Social Insurance Benefit after marriage, but that the small marriage grant (£10) should at the same time be abolished. Effect was given to these recommendations in the 1973 Act. The Commission also recommended that married women (including widows) should become eligible for the same rate of benefits as single persons. This has not yet been achieved.

Payment of Unemployment benefit to Women employed in Agriculture or Private domestic services

The Commission recommended the abolition of the 10 year contribution condition which applied to these employees. This has now been effected as from July, 1973, and women employed in private domestic service or in agriculture are now eligible for unemployment benefit on the same conditions as apply to other female insured workers.

Female applicants for unemployment assistance

The Commission recommended that the condition that a female applicant for unemployment assistance must have at least one dependant or must have at least 52 ordinary rate employment contributions over the four preceding years should be abolished and that as an immediate measure, women employees in agriculture and private domestic service should be eligible to receive unemployment assistance when they have made 52 contributions at any rate. The latter part of the recommendation has been implemented since October, 1973.

Children's Allowances

The child's mother has now title to the allowance in her own right, but she may nominate the father to receive the allowance.

"Housekeeper" Allowance

The "housekeeper" allowance payable to single men and widowers with dependant children during periods when they are in receipt of unemployment or disability benefit or unemployment assistance has not yet been extended to single women and widows in similar circumstances, but the recommendation is being considered.

"Credited" Contributions

The Commission's recommendation that credited contributions should be granted to an insured woman who leaves her employment for the purpose of caring for an aged relative who is incapacitated and in receipt of a prescribed relative allowance has been implemented since December, 1972.

Non-Contributory Widows pensions for all widows

The Commission was concerned that contributory pensions should be available to all widows and recommended that consideration should be given to the introduction of a compulsory insurance scheme for those who were not at present insurable, and that pending a compulsory scheme, a voluntary scheme should be introduced. The Social Welfare Act 1973 has provided for the abolition by Ministerial Order of the insurability limit for non-manual workers. This order became effective from 1st April, 1974. The abolition of this limit (£1,600) per annum brings in an estimated 70,000 additional employees into insurance. This is a major break through. The question of a compulsory scheme of Social Insurance for the self employed is under consideration in the Department of Social Welfare.

I have not been able to find that there has been progress with new and improved schemes of survivors benefits in collective agreements and in contracts of employment as suggested in the Commission's Report, though I am informed by insurance sources that there is some movement in this direction.

Special assistance for Widows or Widowhood

The Commission recommended special assistance for widows in the first six months of widowhood. The Department of Social Welfare has met this in part by providing that the Social Welfare benefit payable to an insured man who dies is continued for six weeks beyond the date of death and is payable to the widow.

Deserted Wives

Previously there was only an assistance Scheme for deserted wives.

Substantial improvements have now been made and a specific benefit is provided for deserted wives on broadly the same basis as the widow's contributory pension. The qualifying period has also been reduced from 6 to 3 months. The position as regards what constitutes desertion has also been eased. The former practice of regarding a deserted wife as being ineligible to receive the Social Welfare allowances if she was divorced abroad has been abandoned. An agreement for the reciprocal Enforcement of Maintenance Orders between Ireland and Britain was signed in December, 1974, and the Maintenance Orders Act, 1974, will enable effect to be given in this country to the agreement. This Act and the corresponding British legislation came into operation on 1st April, 1975, and the Agreement came into force on the same date.

Prisoners' Wives

A new scheme of social assistance for the wives of prisoners was introduced with effect from 4 July, 1974. An allowance is payable to a woman whose husband has been committed to custody for a period of not less than six months, who is under pensionable age and who, if she is less than forty years of age, has at least one qualified child residing with her. A means test applies and the amount of the allowance is the same as the widows (non-contributory) pension.

Unmarried Mothers

The Commission recommended that an unmarried mother who keeps her child should be entitled to a Social Welfare allowance at the same rate and on the same conditions that apply to a deserted wife, for a period of not less than one year after the birth of her child. The 1973 Act provides for such an allowance which will in effect be payable until the child ceases to be a dependant of the unmarried mother – age 18 or if the child remains at school, age 21 years. This is an improvement on our recommendation.

Women required to retire under contract of service before 65 years of age.

The Commission drew attention to the fact that a break in continuity of insurance as a result of early retirement can adversely affect the rate of retirement pension payable at age 65. With the abolition of the £1,600 remuneration limit affecting insurability under the Social Welfare Acts, all persons who are required to retire before age 65 can preserve their title to full retirement pension by qualifying for credited employment contributions through furnishing medical evidence of incapacity to the Department or through furnishing evidence of unemployment as appropriate.

A new provision has also been introduced to give an allowance to single women between the age of 58 and pensionable age who are in poor circumstances.

Adjustments in Social Welfare allowances on the Introduction of equal pay

The Commission proposed that there should be an adjustment in Social Welfare allowances on the introduction of equal pay and suggested that a special allowance at the rate of £125 p.a. should be made to families where there is at least one child under 5 years, or where if there are two children or more, the youngest child is under 7 years. So far, no action has been taken on this recommendation.

While much progress has been made in the last few years, the only fully satisfactory solution to problems of equitable imposition of contribution rates at various income levels would seem to lie ultimately in a universal wage-related contribution and benefit scheme.

The present pay related benefit scheme is calculated by reference to the amount by which a person's earnings exceed a certain sum. As women predominate in the lower paid employment – they are relatively less likely to reach the minimum earnings at which they would stand to benefit.

WOMEN AND TAXATION

A survey carried out by the ESRI had shown that over one-third of the working married women (non farm) felt that the most helpful policy to assist married women who were interested in working would be a change in the existing tax law. We, therefore, gave very careful attention to this matter. The position in 1972 was that if the husband was availing of the full earned income relief of £500, his wife, if her earnings were £99 or over, could not earn more than £74 tax free in any year. We recommended that a standard rate personal allowance should be introduced which would apply equally to all persons whatever their marital status (except for widowed persons who enjoy a preferential rate), and that the allowance should be available to a spouse for use against his or her own income or in whole or part against the other spouse's income. A married woman should in future be allowed earned income relief at the rate of one-fourth of the earned income subject to a maximum of £500 or such ceiling as might be in force.

What has happened since?

In his Budget Speech of 1973 the Minister for Finance announced that the allowance for a wife's earned income was being increased from £74 to £104. While this was welcomed as a token improvement it did not alter the position that the wife's earned income did not attract any earned income relief in its own right unless the husband was entitled to less than the full earned income relief of £500.

Under the reformed tax structure announced in the 1974 Budget, the concept of earned income relief was abolished and revised personal allowances were introduced, £800 for a married person (increased to £920 in the recent Budget), £50 for a single person (now increased to £575) and a "working wife's allowance" of £200 (now increased to £230). Under the revised structure a basic rate of 26% applies to the first £1,550 of taxable income, 35% to the next £2,800 and so on on a sliding scale. Obviously under this system the fact that the husband's and wife's incomes are aggregated must work to their disadvantage as compared with two single persons and this is particularly significant in the higher income brackets. While there has been some improvement more still remains to be done on the taxation of working wives. I cannot help wondering whether a difference in the tax burden is compatible with the EEC concept of equal pay. On Estate Duty, the Commission was concerned that families, particularly of farmers, should be protected from undue hardship caused by the liability of duty on the husband's death and proposed certain alleviations. In 1973 the abatement for widows and dependants was substantially increased, so that, for example, a widow with 3 dependant children would be exempt from estate duty on an estate of about £42,000 (Previously £30,000). The White Paper on capital taxation proposed the replacement of estate duty, legacy duty and succession duty by a new package of capital taxes. The present three death duties are abolished in respect of death after 1st April, 1975. These proposals should greatly improve the position of widows and children and appears to meet the case very satisfactorily

Another recommendation was that the rates reduction of £17 a year allowed to the rated occupier of land in respect of male agricultural workers should be extended to include the daughters and female employees on the same conditions, except that "agricultural work" should be defined to include work in the farmhouse. There has been no action on this proposal but I understand that it will be considered when amending legislation is being prepared during 1975.

WOMEN AND THE LAW

The Commission recommended that the legal obligation to support the family should rest on both husband and wife according to their means and capacity and that in the event of any dispute it would be for the Courts to decide whether reasonable arrangement had been made for the disposal of the family income; that neither spouse should have power to dispose of the matrimonial home without prior consultation with the other spouse; that the system of co-ownership of the matrimonial home should be investigated and that in the event of a separation the wife should have a claim to the value of a moiety of the matrimonial home.

In 1973 the Minister for Justice extended the terms of reference of the Committee on Court Practice and Procedure to enable the

Committee to examine and make recommendations upon matters relating to such aspects of family law as the maintenance of spouses and children, affiliation, attachment of wages, desertion of wives and children and guardianship and custody. The Committee has already issued a Report on "Desertion and Maintenance" and has made a number of important recommendations and the Minister for Justice has stated that very urgent and comprehensive study of the recommendations had been made by his Department. He has recently announced that preparation for legislation is at a very advanced stage and that he hopes to be able to bring a Bill before the Dáil in a matter of weeks rather than months. Whilst one cannot anticipate fully the exact terms of the legislation, it would be reasonable to infer from the Minister's remarks that the substance of the Committee's recommendations has been adopted, although it is likely that in respect of certain individual recommendations made, there may be difference in detail.

I am hopeful that the legislation will cover most, if not all of the Commission's recommendations on the "Partners in Marriage". I have already dealt with "Deserted Wives" under Social Welfare.

We also recommended that a System of Community of property to be realised at the end of the marriage should be further investigated. I understand that this investigation is proceeding although it would be unwise to anticipate what conclusions will be reached since there are strong arguments both for and against general introduction of a Community System. The English Law Commission, for example, has recently come out against such a fundamental change in favour of the far more modest recommendation that there should be a legal presumption of joint ownership between the spouses. We also recommended that in the absence of any agreement to the contrary, savings from the house-keeping allowance should be treated as belonging to husband and wife in equal shares. Let's hope this matter will also be covered in the forthcoming Bill.

The Commission recommended that women should be qualified and liable for jury service on the same terms as men with exemption in the case of a person in primary charge of young children or elderly incapacitated persons. No change has since taken place, but I understand that the Department of Justice is investigating this matter. With regard to the present legal provision it may be relevant to this country to note that there has recently been a great increase in Britain in the proportion of owner occupiers who own the home jointly (74% in 1970/71). If there is a similar development in Ireland, we should have an increasing number of women who would have the minimum rating qualification for jury service. In some cases the Rating Authority may not include the wife's name as "rated occupier" and in such cases no notice of the wife's ownership would be available when the jury lists are prepared. It should be a simple matter to contact the local rating authority to ensure that the wife's name is included and then to inform the Summoning Authority of her wish to exercise the right to jury service. The Commission had suggested that married couples should be encouraged to place the matrimonial home in joint ownership. This suggestion is being considered by the Department of Justice. One of the difficulties to be resolved is the matter of cost which can at present arise as legal costs, stamp duties and registration fees payable to the Land Registry or the Registry of Deeds.

The Commission recommended that the investigation of complaints of discrimination on the basis of sex in relation to the granting of bank loans and mortgages and hire purchase finance should be a function of the Restrictive Practices Commission. I am advised that the powers of the Commission are strictly limited under existing legislation and I would suggest that the Women's Representative Committee or other interested bodies might make further enquiries as to the kind of complaints which could he submitted to the Examiner of Restrictive Practices and the procedure which should be adopted.

WOMEN IN POLITICS AND PUBLIC LIFE

The Commission was concerned at the small number of women on the boards of statutory companies and other bodies. The Women's organisations have since been trying to identify qualified women, able and willing to undertake public service and have established a 'Talent Bank'. In 1972 only one woman was serving on the Boards of ten of the major State Boards and Companies, with a total membership of 69 (including chairmen). Women, have now got 3 seats on these Boards. On a further 18 public bodies for which I was able to obtain figures, women total 48 out of 469. The women are chiefly represented on the Health Boards (18 out of 240), the Advisory Committee for the Metric System (6 out of 20), the National Consumers Advisory Council (6 out of 15) and the Women's Representative Committee (9 out of 13). The latter two bodies are chaired by women. I understand that women have at present no seats on State Sponsored Companies, 3.8% of the seats on Statutory Boards and 10.4% of the seats on other State Sponsored Boards.

It is regrettable that there is still no woman on the Labour Court. I am glad to say that a second woman has been appointed a District Justice. Of the 60 members of the Senate, 11 are nominated by the Taoiseach. In each Senate between 1957 and 1969, one or two women (3 in 1965) were included in this number. No woman was appointed to the present Senate. An elected member – a woman – is, however, the present Leas Ceann Comhairle of the Senate. We continue to have a very small representation in the Dáil and we have no Minister or Parliamentary Secretary. The Commission was convinced that the best course for anyone who aspired to politics on a national level was to commence at the local level. If this view is correct, the results of the 1974 local elections are most encouraging. Compared to 1967 the number of women elected in 1974 increased from 20 to 25 on County Councils, decreased from 6 to 5 in County Borough Councils, increased from 20 to 44 on Borough and Urban District Councils and from 8 to 14 on Town Commissioners. Though the proportion of seats held is small, the increase from 54 to 88 seats (about 63%) is remarkable. There were some spectacular successes. One woman at her first ever election topped the poll in a Dublin area without benefit of a party machine. Another newcomer also topped the poll in a Co. Limerick area. A well known Labour Deputy also did well in a Co. Cork area and she is now the Chairwoman of the recently appointed Women's Representative Committee. These are only a few examples of the successes. The Commission hoped that some of the Women's organisations would concentrate on some specific problems and work at them to a conclusion. There seems to be a trend in this direction and there have been some good results already. The Commission had suggested that some financial assistance should be made available to a body recognised by the Government as being representative of women's interests to assist them with secretarial services, seminars etc. We had envisaged this body as the liaison body between Departments and individual organisations on legislative proposals and matters arising out of the Commission's Report. The Minister for Labour has taken a rather different line in setting up the Women's Representative Committee. I hope, however, that it will develop in such a way as to serve a similar purpose and I wish it all success. My regret is that some such body was not appointed two years ago.

EDUCATION

In regard to Primary Schools we were anxious that co-education should be extended and that there should be joint training of male and female teachers. I am advised by the Department of Education that there is a growing demand for mixed schools, which they are prepared to meet in so far as practicable, and that most of the teacher training is now mixed. We also suggested that instruction should be given in subjects which go beyond the traditionally accepted range of interests of one sex. I understand that this is developing and that in some schools boys and girls are sharing subjects such as cookery and sewing. Recent proposals for setting up Committees of Management for both Primary and Vocational Schools provide, inter alia, for two elected representatives of parents one of whom must be a woman. This will be a new development. We were anxious also that girls should not always be depicted in school text books in the "traditional" female roles but that they should be seen in active occupations and pursuits. The Department of Education is conscious that a bias did exist and in revised text books the illustrations showing girls in traditional pursuits are being eliminated. We also suggested that measures should be taken to increase the small number of girls taking mathematics and science subjects to Leaving Certificate level. I understand that the number of girls taking these subjects is gradually increasing, probably due to greater availability of teachers of these subjects, and to a gradual erosion of prejudice.

We also recommended effective career guidance and the identification of areas of technical and skilled employment in which job opportunities for girls are likely to expand and that girls should be encouraged to pursue the course options relevant to such employment. There has since been a marked expansion of career guidance. The School Authorities are in constant touch with factories, and courses are given in local Vocational Schools in advance of demand. The teaching of Civics as a subject is now available in all Schools and Training Colleges.

WOMEN AT HOME

Under the title "Women at Home" the Commission dealt mainly with marriage counselling, family planning, advice bureaux and education for household management.

We felt that measures should be taken to strengthen and expand the operation of marriage counselling services and recommended that financial assistance should be made available to recognised counselling services to enable them to provide training for their counsellors and to improve their central administration.

Action is being taken by the Department of Health on this recommendation.

On Family Planning it was recommended that information and expert advice should be available through medical and other appropriate channels to families – this advice to respect the moral and personal attitudes of each married couple. Medical requirements should then be made available under control and through channels determined by the Department of Health. We are all no doubt aware that the Government's Bill was defeated and that Senator Mary Robinson is proceeding with her Second Bill in the subject.

We recommended the formation of a National Advice Bureaux Organisation which would embrace the existing information centres, would be responsible for general development, would include representatives of the Women's Organisations, and should operate from easily accessible places, the Government to make some financial assistance available. It has recently been announced that the National Social Service Council is being reconstituted by the Minister for Health and that one of the Council's new functions is to promote the establishment of community information centres and to provide a back-up service to existing centres.

We recognised the need for education for household management so that women could cope efficiently with paid employment, home management and motherhood responsibilities, on the basis also of a spirit of equality and mutual assistance between husband and wife. I do not know of any action by Government Departments along these lines but this work is probably more appropriate to voluntary organisations.

CONCLUSION

There will be no lack of work for the Women's Representative Committee to do. It is, however, a matter of great satisfaction to know that Government Policy on the participation of Women in the life of the country is largely based on the Commission's report. So far as I know there is no voice in opposition – only in support. On a rough estimate I find that 50% of our recommendations have been implemented or are in process of implementation, 30% have been accepted in principle, and work is proceeding towards their implementation. On 20% I can find no action.

It has not been possible to measure changes in attitudes and indeed the period of two years would scarcely be long enough for this purpose. On my recent visits to Government Departments I have, however, been greatly encouraged by the change of attitudes and considerable enthusiasm displayed.

Administration, vol. 51, nos. 1-2 (Spring/Summer 2003), 257–283

Protecting Irish Children in Time: Child Abuse as a Social Problem and the Development of the Child Protection System in the Republic of Ireland

HARRY FERGUSON

Originally published in 1996, vol. 44, no. 2, 5-36.
Harry Ferguson was then a senior lecturer in the Department of Applied Social Studies in University College Cork.

There have been dramatically increased levels of public disclosure of serious cases of child abuse involving sexual violence and physical abuse and neglect in recent years in the Republic of Ireland (McGuinness 1993; Moore 1995; Keenan 1996). These disclosures have focused unprecedented public and political attention on child protection policies and practices. While the Irish Society for the Prevention of Cruelty to Children (ISPCC) carried administrative responsibility for child protection for many decades, it has only been since the late 1970s that we have seen the actual emergence of distinct child protection policies in the Irish state. The implementation of a new Child Care Act, and new church and state child protection guidelines in the 1990s, exemplify how over the last decade or so there have been more developments in child care law, policy and practice than occurred in the previous eighty years (Ferguson and Kenny 1995; Irish Catholic Bishops' Advisory Committee 1996; Department of Health 1987, 1995).

My aim in this article is to examine the process of the construction of child abuse as a social problem and the emergence and development of the Irish child protection system. The social construction of child abuse, and childhood adversity more generally, as technical problems about which something can and should be done is a twentieth century western phenomenon (Scheper-Hughes 1987, p. 2; Cooter 1992). This paper explores this construction as it emerged in child protection discourse in Ireland, by charting the changing meanings of 'child abuse' and how Irish policies which constituted the 'child protection' system developed across the twentieth century.

EXPERT SYSTEMS, KNOWLEDGE AND CHILD ABUSE AS A SOCIAL PROBLEM

The social problem of 'child abuse' is in large measure a product of modern societies. This does not mean that prior to the birth of the 'modern' era at around the turn of this century, citizens were indifferent to the well-being of children who were the victims of violence (Ferguson 1990). The point is rather, that the rise of organisations like the Societies for the Prevention of Cruelty to Children and the codification of laws and modern forms of social administration introduced a new institutional framework of social regulation, which had the effect of 'inventing' and classifying social deviation in parent-child relations to produce new kinds of knowledge of social problems like child abuse (Cooter 1992; Giddens 1991, p. 160).

Modern nation-states and their expert systems – medicine, social work, penology – began to construct the universe of events that became known in modern idioms as 'child abuse' and actively constitute the parameters of trust and risk in child protection. As Giddens argues

> The reliance placed by lay actors upon expert systems is not just a matter – as was normally the case in the pre-modern world – of generating a sense of security about an independently given universe of events. It is a matter of the calculation of benefit and risk in circumstances where expert knowledge does not just provide that calculus but actually creates (or reproduces) the universe of events, as a result of the continual reflexive implementation of that very knowledge (Giddens 1990, p. 84).

As a modern social problem, child abuse must be analysed as a social construction which has relied historically on a process of recognition, identification and labelling by expert systems (Gelles 1975; Dingwall *et al* 1983). The changing constructions of the problem in Ireland, and responses to it across the twentieth century, must be explored through an analysis of the role of institutions and the management of trust and risk. Against this background, three main formative phases in the construction of the social problem and the child protection system can be identified: the periods 1889-1914; 1970-1989; and 1990 to the present. While the conditions for the possibility of full recognition of child abuse as a social problem were laid in Ireland as long ago as the turn of the century, it was in the 1970s that the issue began to be defined as such and child protection institutionalised in Irish social policy. The 1990s, meanwhile, have seen a new kind of public disclosure through high-profile child abuse inquiries (McGuinness 1993; Keenan 1996) and an 'opening-out' of the routines of the expert system and science of child protection. At the heart of the new public politics of child abuse is a new 'risk profile' of child protection and a transformation in the relationship between expertise, knowledge and lay people.

'CRUELTY' COMES TO IRELAND: 1889-1914

The beginnings of modern child protection in Ireland are to be found in the formation of a Dublin branch of the National Society for the Prevention of Cruelty to Children (NSPCC) in 1889, whose headquarters were in London. The Dublin NSPCC Branch was quickly followed by the founding of branches in Cork, Waterford and Belfast. Irish branches would remain under the administrative control of the NSPCC's central office in London until 1956 and the founding of a self-governing Irish Society (Allen and Morton 1961, p. 26). The NSPCC had two broad aims: to press for the reform of the criminal law surrounding the social regulation of parent-child relations, and to develop an inspectorate that could investigate cases of suspected cruelty to children. The 1889 Cruelty to Children Act criminalised child cruelty and gave Inspectors new powers to remove cruelly treated children from parental custody (Behlmer 1982).

In 1889 the first NSPCC inspector arrived in Ireland, servicing the Dublin branch. It was some years before the whole of the thirty-two counties of Ireland were covered by NSPCC committees and an inspectorate active in child protection work. Twenty inspectors were at work in Ireland by 1908, servicing committees covering 100 centres across the country. By the late 1930s there were twenty-six inspectors who were 'covering with their supporting District Committees the whole of the Free State and Northern Ireland, and maintaining in full measure the Society's aims and objectives' (NSPCC 1934, p. 15).

The provisions of the Cruelty to Children Acts of 1889, 1894 and 1904 were extended into the Children Act of 1908 which provided the statutory basis for child protection in Ireland until as recently as 1995. The 1908 Punishment of Incest Act criminalised incest for the first time in Irish society. As the legislative base and work of the Society expanded in Ireland, the number of child 'cruelty' cases reported correspondingly grew. The Dublin and Districts Branch annual figures, for example, increased from 771 cases investigated in 1899, to 1,507 cases in 1901. Thereafter, the annual casework rate levelled out at around 1,400 (Dublin and Districts Branch NSPCC 1914). Correspondingly, the numbers of children involved in casework increased in both absolute and relative terms; from 953 children investigated in 1894, the Dublin and Districts annual figure had risen to 4,027 in 1901. Similar trends were evident outside of urban districts. Waterford was a good example of an area where a particularly well organised and active NSPCC branch developed. Between 1894 and 1908 the branch investigated 2,712 cases involving 7,278 children (Waterford and District Branch NSPCC 1908, p. 3). The more limited scale of casework outside of the cities was a product of areas having different numbers of inspectors reporting with varying levels of zeal, differences in population density and the accessibility of cases.

'Neglect' predominated in the early classifications of child 'cruelty' cases, accounting for 87 per cent of casework in the Dublin Districts between 1889 and 1914. 'Ill treatment and assault' accounted for 4.6 per cent of cases, while 'abandonment' was 2.2 per cent and 'begging/exposure' 1.8 per cent of cases. 'Criminal assault/immoral surroundings', the category which contained sexual offences against children, was the classification in less than half of one per cent of cases reported.

Significant changes in casework approaches to 'cruel' parents and child victims occurred between 1889 and 1914. In the Dublin and Waterford districts in 1895 the prosecution rate was 19.2 per cent and 22 per cent respectively. By 1914, the rate of prosecutions brought under the 1908 Children Act in each district had dropped to 4.7 and 6 per cent, respectively, of a much higher number of cases handled. This shift in penal practices reflected a major transformation that occurred in the casework ideology of 'child protection'. From the outset, preventing cruelty to children had fallen heavily on parents, and mothers in particular (*see* Gordon 1989). The primary objective of the NSPCC was not to relieve parents of the care of their children, but rather to enforce their responsibilities as conceived for them by the state. In the early years, prosecution was a key strategy towards this objective, the incarceration of parents in prisons being the main reformative resource utilised. After 1908, the 'pre-modern' punishment-centred ideology was replaced by a casework ideology and practice which was based on the supervision of parent-child relations in their homes. A new optimistic professional ideology lay at the foundation of the 'rehabilitative ideals' of modern welfare states (Garland 1985) which, in child protection, primarily extolled the moral reformation of deviant parents. Professionals, in what after 1904 were officially termed 'emergency cases' (NSPCC Inspector's Directory 1904; 1910), gained enhanced powers of discretion and autonomy to judge and carry out the newly conceived therapeutic tasks of child protection (for further discussion of this shift, *see* Ferguson 1990; 1992, pp. 163-5).

The great paradox of Irish *child* protection during much of the twentieth century has been its family-centred ideology, focused firmly on parents. This orientation was further consolidated with the establishment of the Irish Free State through the profound influence on social policy of Catholic social teaching and the 1937 Constitution.[1] Article 41 'recognises the family as the primary and fundamental unit group of society, and as a moral institution possessing inalienable and impresciptable rights, antecedent and superior to all positive laws' (Bunreacht na hÉireann 1937). The NSPCC argued that this principle constituted 'Perhaps the greatest of rights of the child which we are continually fighting to maintain [which] is the right to a secure and happy home with its family'. Tensions came to pervade the reconciliation of the use of discretionary powers to protect children with the principle of minimum intervention into the family prescribed by the Constitution. The Society regularly sought to correct the 'mistaken impression in the minds of many people that we regard the committal of children to industrial schools as a sovereign remedy for unhappiness or unsuitable conditions in the home', and that 'committal is only sought or advised where there is no other way out' (NSPCC 1954, p. 7). The numbers of children actually removed from parental custody appears to have been low, amounting to less than 2 per cent of all children coming to the attention of the Society.[2] Those children taken into care were 'committed' to the large industrial and reformatory schools where, for some, the experience was one of further institutional abuse (Doyle 1988; Touher 1991; Buckley 1996).

The more casework developed, ironically, the more childhood adversity was revealed in child protection. From 1909, a year when 'eighteen children died while their cases were under inquiry' (Dublin and District Branch NSPCC 1909, p. 13), the Dublin NSPCC Branch systematically provided information on the numbers of children who died annually in child protection cases. Between 1884 and 1914, some 13,613 children were classified as having died in NSPCC cases in England, Wales and Ireland. (For more detailed analysis of Irish figures, *see* Ferguson 1993.) These children had by no means all been directly killed by their parents. NSPCC work intersected with broader and very serious social problems of poverty and infant mortality. Thus, in many SPCC cases children were probably *dying anyway* from a variety of causes and became caught up in the new powers and classifications of child protection.

Rather than being hidden and a source of shame and embarrassment to child care agencies (as it is today), the structure of meaning in which early child protection work was constituted meant that statistics on child deaths were used to assert the *value* of NSPCC work. A key dynamic of the early phase of the child protection movement was an emphasis on growth and development and gaining access to children across geographical boundaries.

The more children were reached – dead or alive – the more successful the child protection movement viewed itself. High death rates were viewed with dismay, but were a vital resource to demonstrate 'that it is certain that the Society is telling on the life of children' (NSPCC 1897, p. 38). The 'pre-modern' concept of risk which held prior to the 1900s was such that childhood adversity was not constituted as preventable through social intervention. Child deaths were placed in a context of explanation in which they were associated with concepts like sin, natural wastage and seasonal rhythm, and assimilated into natural processes of decay (Wright 1987, p. 108). But as children became child cruelty 'cases' and the science of child protection developed in the twentieth century, the expert system began to constitute a new conception of risk, which held that child life could be promoted and reformation of deviant parenting effected through social intervention. This was heavily influenced by developments in medical science and technology which were transforming cultural practices generally. The invention of the telephone and the bicycle, for instance, transformed people's experiences of time and space (Kern 1983). It became possible for cases to be reached more quickly, making it thinkable that children 'at risk' could now be protected in time.

Public disclosure of deaths continued through to the 1930s. At Wexford, for example, in 1922, ten children died while their cases were under enquiry (Wexford NSPCC 1922). By now, however, fewer child protection cases were ending in death (NSPCC 1936, pp. 34-5). This was not only due to effective child protection interventions, but crucially because children were generally healthier due to better diet, public health reforms and child welfare services. Child protection had come to surround children who were, by and large, *living anyway*. By the late 1930s information about the deaths in child protection cases ceased to be made public and had gone out of sight. This key shift in the discourse of child protection did not arise because the problem of 'cases ending in death' had been 'solved', but rather from a process of sequestration which involves the 'institutional repression' of troublesome information concerning death and other signs of organisational 'failure' (Giddens 1991; Ferguson 1996). At the heart of this were heightened sensitivities toward public disclosure and visibility of existential crises in society, and a new premium on the trustworthiness of welfare agencies to be effectively seen to manage risk. The sequestration of child protection also reflected how a new concept of risk had entered social policy and practice, one which was no longer derived externally from nature and concepts of sin but from the internal codes of expertise and science. A form of 'manufactured risk' (Giddens 1994), it is based on the use of reflexively organised knowledge and the competence and decision-making skills of expert systems (Beck 1992). The conditions of possibility had been laid for science and expertise to expand the concept of 'child abuse' and for exhaustive inquiries into apparent system failures in child protection.

In 1956 the Irish Society for the Prevention of Cruelty to Children (ISPCC), covering the twenty-six counties of the Republic of Ireland, finally split from the NSPCC, the Ulster branches remaining under the latter's control. The trends in casework and the classification of cases identified here were consolidated in such a manner as to constitute the normative foundations of child protection in Ireland through to the 1970s. By the 1930s, it was actually stated that 'cruelty is little known in Ireland' (Mayo and District Branch NSPCC 1938), by which was meant that physical abuse as opposed to child neglect was comparatively rare. The first reports of the ISPCC were 'able to record a low number of cases of assault or ill-treatment, i.e. of actual physical cruelty', while at the same time feeling 'compelled to record an astounding number of cases of neglect' (ISPCC 1957, p. 11). Recognition of incest cases remained, on the other hand, virtually non-existent at well under one per cent of cases. By 1958 the ISPCC recorded 'with pleasure' that the number of prosecutions initiated by the Society had dropped to an all time low figure of nine out of a total of 2,266 cases investigated that year (ISPCC 1958, p. 13). During the years (1889-1955) that it was managed by the UK Society 'no fewer than 478,865 children were helped by the NSPCC in the Republic of Ireland' (Mayo and District Branch NSPCC 1955, p. 2). While this is suggestive of the significant impact of child protection in Ireland under the management of the UK Society, it was at this point in history, when the ISPCC became self-governing, that a truly distinctive Irish child protection system began to develop.

ORGANISATIONAL INTERESTS AND THE EMERGENCE OF THE IRISH CHILD PROTECTION SYSTEM, 1970-1989

In most parts of the Republic of Ireland, SPCC inspectors were the sole welfare agents doing casework on behalf of children during the first sixty years of the twentieth century. This changed following the 1970 Health Act and the establishment of the eight health boards (Curry, 1980) and the community care teams through which the state took over primary responsibility for child care and protection (McGinley 1995). In addition to the on-going pressure group activity of the ISPCC, policy recommendations were shaped by the work of government sponsored committees, in particular the Kennedy Report (1970) and the Final Report of the Task Force on Child Care Services (1980). The first half of the twentieth century saw the institutionalisation of key *system principles* in child protection in terms of a minimalist, pro-family ideology on state intervention, and the sequestration of child protection work. From the 1970s, the professionalisation of welfare services and a series of national and international developments provided the organisational context in which the problem of child 'cruelty' underwent a process of (re)definition and 'diagnostic inflation' into child 'abuse' (Dingwall 1989) and which resulted in the actual *emergence* of child care and protection policies in the Republic of Ireland.

The creation of health boards greatly expanded the expert system to include such pivotal child welfare positions in community care teams as social workers, public health nurses, area medical officers and the senior management position of directors of community care/medical officers of health (Kelly 1995). By 1974, some ISPCC social workers were 'now participating as ISPCC members of the new community care teams' which were 'only beginning to get under way' (ISPCC 1974, p. 18). The 'emphasis during the past year has been on co-operation and co-ordination with other social work agencies'. Two years later ISPCC social workers nationally were attending some 160 case conferences a year (ISPCC 1976, p. 11).

Thus, a more sophisticated child protection system began to develop in Ireland before formal policies aimed at co-ordination were made by central government. This reflected the first impact of the conceptualisation of what became known as the 'battered baby syndrome' as requiring a multi-disciplinary approach (Hughes 1967). Developments in Ireland to some extent mirrored those in the USA and the UK, where more sophisticated models of programme co-ordination between various agencies began to be established from the early 1970s (Hallett and Stevenson 1980).

In a section headed *Guidance and assistance received on the battered baby syndrome*, the 1974 ISPCC annual report observed:

> Upon receiving reports of the tragic death of Maria Colwell in England, the Society felt that as a Child Protective Agency we had a duty to develop our knowledge and understanding of the 'Battered Baby Syndrome'. Ray Castle, Executive Head of the National Advisory Centre on the Battered Child, came to Dublin in October for a very busy and intensive three day visit. (ISPCC 1974, p. 18)

In his role as an NSPCC expert on the battered child syndrome, Ray Castle was a key actor in the shaping of the UK child protection system (Castle, 1977). While in Ireland he had talks with the Department of Health and the Dublin Chief County Medical Officer 'on the advisability of setting up a Register of all cases of suspected Child Abuse. There was general agreement that one should be set up' (ISPCC 1974, p. 19). It was proposed that further discussions between the ISPCC and the Department of Health would take place during 1975 'to decide what is the best way to get this Register "off the ground", whether the ISPCC or the Department should be responsible for this undertaking, and whether it should be kept on a national or regional level' (ISPPC 1974, p. 19). Castle also addressed The Irish Association of Social Workers, members of the medical profession, the press, and council members of the ISPCC (ISPCC 1974, p. 19).

If a major concern of the child protection movement during the first half of the century was to grow and develop in order to cover national boundaries and become institutionalised into governmental strategies within the welfare state, from the 1970s Irish system development entered a new phase in which influences were global as well as local. Institutional developments were shaped by a key shift in conceptions of child cruelty/abuse and the management of the problem; this arose out of the influence of the work of an American paediatrician Henry Kempe and his medical colleagues, and their construction of the 'battered child syndrome' (Kempe *et al* 1962). This development is often referred to as the 'discovery' of child abuse, a characterisation that is misleading as it belittles the child protection work that preceded it (Ferguson 1990; Behlmer 1982, pp. 224-5). There is no doubt, however, that Kempe's work helped to reorient conceptions of child cruelty/abuse in professional and popular consciousness throughout the western world (Nelson, 1984). By the 1980s it would no longer be so easy to claim that 'actual physical cruelty' was little known in Ireland.

Henry Kempe and his associates had been researching the problem of child abuse with the support of the American Humane Association since the late 1950s. In 1962 they coined the phrase 'the battered child syndrome' to describe their findings and they published an article of that name in the prestigious medical journal *The Journal of the American Medical Association*. The article claimed that the 'syndrome' characterised a clinical condition in young children, usually under three years of age, who had received serious physical abuse, usually from a parent, and that it was a significant form of childhood disability and death. It argued that the syndrome was often misdiagnosed and that it should be considered in any child showing evidence of possible trauma or neglect, or where there was a marked discrepancy between the clinical findings and the story presented by the parents. The use of X-rays to aid diagnosis was stressed and it was argued that the prime concern of the physician was to make the correct diagnosis and to ensure that a similar event did not occur again. The article recommended that doctors report all incidents to law enforcement or child protective agencies (Nelson 1984, pp. 12-13; Parton 1985, p. 51; Zigler and Hall 1989).

Kempe's paper stimulated a new awareness of the problem in the professional and lay media in the USA. The emotive title 'battered child syndrome' was deliberately used to provoke public interest. In a matter of a few years – by the late 1960s – mandatory reporting laws were passed in most American States, whereby when child abuse was suspected by professionals they were legally required to report it to designated child protection agencies. In Britain, sections of the medical profession were central to taking up the issue in the late 1960s, the impetus coming from forensic pathologists and paediatricians. The NSPCC Battered Child Research Unit was established in 1968, under Ray Castle's stewardship. It was named 'Denver House' in deference to the origins of Kempe' s work in Denver Colorado, and became a key agency in defining how the problem of 'child abuse' was conceptualised and managed in the UK.

It was only in the mid-1970s, however, that the problem of 'non-accidental injury', as it was now being defined, began to gain formal recognition in policy and practice on this side of the Atlantic. An important international event in these developments (as the above quoted comments of the ISPCC indicate), was the Maria Colwell case. Maria died on 7 January 1973 at the age of seven, at her home in East Sussex, England. She was one of nine children that her mother had borne at that time. She spent over five years in the foster care of her aunt, but was returned to her mother and stepfather (Mr Kepple) at the age of six years and eight months, being placed on a supervision order to the local authority from that date. However, Maria was beaten to death by her stepfather on the night of 6 January 1973, and was found to weigh only about three-quarters of what could be expected for her age and height. Kepple was convicted of manslaughter and sentenced to eight years imprisonment (Colwell Report 1974).

An inquiry into the role of the social services led to the case gaining national attention in the media, and from the British government. The DHSS inquiry report argued that failures in the inter-agency system were largely accountable for Maria's (avoidable) death from abuse: 'Maria fell through the welfare net primarily because of communication failures (Colwell Report 1974). In Britain, DHSS guidelines for working with 'non-accidental injury' (NAI) to children quickly followed, in which a primary emphasis was placed on the process and procedures of inter-agency work: 'The outcome of any case will depend on the communicating skills of the professionals involved as much as their expertise' (DHSS Circular 1974). A new emphasis was placed on the child protection system as being the crucial variable in the effective management of NAI cases.

The precise influence that events outside of Ireland had on the development of the Irish system requires careful judgement. Articles and debate on the battered child had been available in international medical journals since Kempe's precursory article in 1962, of which at least some Irish medics were no doubt aware. It is not being argued here that Irish professionals simply passively followed the example of their UK and American counterparts in absorbing the apparent lessons of Kempe's work and the Maria Colwell case. In (post) modern social conditions, policies and practices of particular nation-states are always a product of hugely complex processes which surround the dialectic between globalisation and localisation (Lash and Urry 1994). Notions of the 'battered child syndrome' reached Australia, for example, by 1965 (Thorpe 1994, p. 14).

A radicalised consciousness of risk to children is facilitated by information flows in advanced modernity and knowledge being truly global. In late modernity place becomes 'phantasmagoric' (Giddens 1990), in that the structures by means of which it is constituted are no longer locally organised as the local and global become inextricably intertwined. The emergence of globalised media alters the 'situational geography' of social life. Although feelings of close attachment to or identification with places still persist, these are themselves disembedded: 'The local community is not a saturated environment of familiar, taken-for-granted meanings, but in some large part a locally-situated expression of distanciated relations' (Giddens 1990, pp. 108-9). 'We could say', observes Beck, that 'people meet every evening around the world at the *village green of television* and consume the news' (Beck 1992, p. 133, original emphasis).

However, global influences were at all times mediated by the system principles which dictated the 'master pattern' (Cohen 1985) of Irish policies and practices. The localised influences that were critical in shaping the form and direction of Irish policy lay in professional and organisational interests, the implications of the changing role of the ISPCC and the newly emergent health boards. Although ISPCC social workers worked closely with the new health board community care teams from their beginnings, in reality the latter were usurping the ISPCC's traditional role in child protection. The newly created health boards were in the ascendancy and by the late 1970s the ISPCC's influence in the field of child protection was much diminished. It was in this context that the ISPCC took the opportunity that arose from the 'discovery' of child abuse, to try to develop a specialist role in child protection again; and this influenced how the agency used global knowledge and took up the issues of the battered child syndrome and the Maria Colwell case. Henry Kempe himself addressed a conference in Dublin on Non-Accidental Injury organised by the ISPCC in May 1976 (Kempe 1976).

In the mid-1970s, the ISPCC sought to inaugurate a 'National Advisory Centre on the Battered Child', which would 'provide advice on the management of NAI cases to professionals throughout the country, and as well as researching the Irish scene, would also operate a small treatment unit linking with a Children's Hospital' (ISPCC 1977). However, local conditions and organisational interests also influenced how the ISPCC's efforts were received. The idea for the centre was shelved in 1977, 'because the Department of Health now has decided that it is better to refrain from isolating violence to children, and the programme managers of the health boards feel they can contain any problems of NAI which may arise in their areas' (ISPCC 1977, p. 3). The health board's – and, more broadly, the Irish state's – apparent professional interests to control child care policy and contain the child abuse problem won the day.

The significance of the outcome of these struggles cannot be over-estimated. The ISPCC ceased to do child protection investigations and social casework, developing instead projects such as Family Centres (Nic Giolla Choille 1983) and, since 1988, its successful flagship service, the telephone helpline for children at risk, *Childline* (ISPCC 1991, pp. 16-19). The way in which the ISPCC made knowledge about the battered child syndrome and the Colwell case more available contributed to a momentum for recognition of NAI in Ireland. The agency played a key role in generating interest in new concepts of child abuse outside of the medical profession in Ireland, and perhaps even within it. This, in turn, influenced how the issue was conceptualised and the direction of the child care and protection system and policy in Ireland. But the State having won ownership of the problem, the management of child abuse and the culture of Irish child protection became inseparable from the culture of the health boards, the Irish State and the system principles on which policy traditionally developed.

POLICY DEVELOPMENT: THE EVOLUTION OF THE CHILD ABUSE GUIDELINES

It was against this background of the dialectic between global influences and local struggles around organisational interests and conceptions of child cruelty/abuse that Irish child care and protection policy emerged and developed. The first initiative that was taken to update Irish policies occurred in May 1975 when the Department of Health invited interested parties to a meeting to discuss the problem of non-accidental injury to children. It was agreed at this meeting that (i) there was a significant problem of non-accidental injury to children in Ireland; (ii) the position should be examined and procedures should be suggested to deal with such cases to ensure co-operation of parties dealing with such cases; and (iii) a central register of such cases should be established (DOH 1976). A 'Committee on Non-Accidental Injury to Children' was formed, which had a very high representation of senior medical personnel.[3]

A medical model of non-accidental injury to children predominated in the *Report of the Committee on Non-Accidental Injury to Children* published in March 1976. Emphasis was placed on the need for early identification of battered children which should be assisted by the wider distribution of knowledge and education for all members of the helping professions to help them recognise it. The establishment of a central register of cases of suspected abuse was recommended as an important aspect in the multi-disciplinary approach and management of the problem. It was envisaged that a central register of suspected NAI cases would involve *all* cases of injury to children presenting at hospitals being registered, and enquiries being made to substantiate their 'accidental' nature. Physicians were to have no hesitation in having children admitted to hospital where suspicion persisted and to report their concerns to the health boards (DOH 1976).

In March 1977, the Department of *Health Memorandum on Non-Accidental Injury to Children* was issued in response to the Committee's recommendations, constituting the first formal guidelines on the abuse of children issued to professionals by the Irish government (DOH 1977). This was followed in 1980 by the publication by the Department of Health of *Guidelines on the Identification and Management of Non-Accidental Injury to Children* (DOH 1980), which were based largely on the recommendations of the 1976 *Report* and 1977 *Memorandum*. Responsibility for monitoring and co-ordinating the management of non-accidental injury was vested in the health boards as part of the child care services provided within the community care programme. The Director of Community Care/Medical Officer of Health (DCC) was the person with overall responsibility for monitoring and co-ordination of cases in their areas (DOH 1980, p. 3). It was, however, expected that 'all the agencies involved (with protecting children) will continue to accept the need for co-operation and co-ordination and that health board staff will facilitate the staff of other agencies and general medical practitioners in every way possible in discharging their functions in this particular matter' (DOH 1980, p. 4). A checklist was provided to help professionals in the identification of non-accidental injury, investigation and initial action. Sections were included on 'index of suspicion', 'suggestive features on clinical examination', and 'examination and investigation in hospital' (1980, pp. 13-15). The legal position was laid out (pp. 9-10) and the role of the Gardaí cautiously stated. Their involvement was to be 'considered, having regard to the circumstances of the individual case' (p. 17). No mention at all was made of the rights and involvement of parents in NAI cases at this time.

With respect to 'Management of Cases', the emphasis was on co-ordination through 'team effort' and case conferences which, it was claimed, were 'widely accepted as a valuable method in dealing with this type of problem' (DOH 1980, p. 6). To further facilitate co-ordination and exchange of information it was recommended that each DCC should 'under his (sic) personal supervision or that of an officer designated by him, maintain a list of suspected and actual cases of non-accidental injury. The information contained in the list will be available from the cases referred to him as co-ordinator'. It was stressed that the 'list should be reviewed regularly and where initial suspicion has proved to be unfounded, details should be expunged from the list' (DOH 1980, pp. 7-8). In effect, earlier proposals for a central registry of cases to include all cases of accidental injury to children had become an 'NAI list' which would cover only those cases that were suspected or confirmed following notification and investigation by the health board. This marked a key shift from the abstract 'strict liability' position, typical of the medical profession, where all injuries to children are treated as suspicious based solely on *clinical* evidence, to a policy position which integrates child protection into the political realities of the need for social evidence to support operational definitions of children at risk, and legitimate intervention into the family (Dingwall 1991). Remarkably, however, at no time did any of the Irish guidelines published in the 1970s and 1980s actually provide definitions of the phenomenon of NAI/child abuse.[4]

In February 1983 a revised edition of the guidelines was issued under the title *Guidelines on Procedures For The Identification, Investigation and Management of Non-Accidental Injury to Children* (DOH 1983). The format established in 1980 remained, with an emphasis on identification and management through co-ordination, NAI lists, and case conferences. New sections were added clarifying the role of 'Investigation by a General Practitioner', and 'Investigation at Hospitals' (DOH 1983, p. 9). Emphasis on the importance of inter-agency and inter-professional co-ordination was greatly increased. The 'Need for Co-operation' was specifically addressed in terms of a re-emphasis of the importance of the DCC's co-ordinating role and the support of other child care agencies and professionals (DOH 1983, p. 8). The section on 'Case Conferences' was greatly expanded; it provided guidance for community care teams reviewing and standardising case conference procedures to take account of the need for 'the maintenance of lists of suspected and of confirmed cases' of children at risk, the development of criteria for listing children, and the need for regular case reviews. It was now stressed that it 'is important to have the case conference called as quickly as possible' (DOH 1983, pp. 11-13). A separate section was now devoted to 'Exchange of Information on Non-Accidental Injury Cases', which stressed that it was 'important that full and accurate information on all non-accidental injury cases is maintained at local community care area level' (DOH 1983, p. 14). It was now recommended that 'Parents should be kept informed of decisions being made with regard to the child' (DOH 1983, p. 25).

The emphases of the 1983 Guidelines were shaped by a small-scale examination in 1982 by the Minister for Health, Dr Michael Woods, of the circumstances surrounding children who died from the effects of abuse while under the protective supervision of Eastern Health Board professionals (*see* Ferguson 1994). In a statement that ran to a mere four pages the minister concluded that the professionals involved 'acted, as individuals, in a concerned and conscientious manner. Nevertheless it would appear to him that they did not initially work cohesively as a team with full communication of facts and co-ordination of efforts'. The minister stressed that 'those working in the field of child care have a difficult job to do, resources are scarce, and the special bond between children and their parents is, in itself, a particular inhibition where the question of intervention arises.' He referred to the 'strong tradition of family life in this country and of keeping families together' and the fact that this tradition is underlined by the provisions of our Constitution and is reflected in social policy (Government Information Service 1982).

Such a low key analysis reflected the Irish system principle of minimalist state intervention into the family. However, while the professionals involved were divested of *individual* responsibility for the children's deaths, some *collective* responsibility for the better protection of children by the expert system was assumed. It was now implicitly accepted that child abuse was a technical problem about which something could, and should, be done and that better co-ordination of the work of the expert system was the key to this, reflecting 'the ascendancy of the idea that social and economic life can be *humanly controlled*' (Giddens 1994, p. 137, original emphasis).

The focus of the 1983 Guidelines was still on identification and management of cases of physical abuse and neglect. However, for the first time in official guidelines brief mention was made of 'injury resulting from sexual abuse.' Because child sexual abuse was located here within the definition of non-accidental injury to children, no specific guidance was given as to how identification and management of child sexual abuse might differ from physical abuse and neglect. This changed dramatically in the 1987 edition, re-issued as *Guidelines on Procedures for the Investigation and Management of Child Abuse* (DOH 1987). The term 'child abuse' had become common currency and included a broad range of abusive behaviours: NAI, neglect, emotional abuse and sexual abuse. The 1987 guidelines emphasised identification, management and co-ordination, but with a clearer definition being given to the role and responsibilities of community care social workers, public health nurses, general practitioners, hospital paediatricians and child psychiatrists. A broad category of 'others' included teachers, day care staff, residential staff and Gardaí. Systematic recognition of child sexual abuse was now made on the basis that it 'has particular features which require special attention' (DOH 1987, p. 23). Repeated interviews with and examinations of the child should be avoided if at all possible (DOH 1987, p. 24). It was recommended that multi-disciplinary teams should be designated for the examination of children and 'the validation of alleged child sexual abuse'. Policy and such intervention strategies to deal with child sexual abuse were here again at all times formed against the backdrop of major global events, such as the lessons of the 'Cleveland affair' (Butler-Sloss 1987; Law Reform Commission 1990). One consequence of this has been the development of specialist child sexual abuse assessment units around the country which constitute one of the few distinct institutional services to protect Irish children that emerged out of these policies.

OUTCOMES AND TRENDS IN CHILD ABUSE

The impact of policy developments and changing definitions of child cruelty/NAI/abuse is clear in the number and nature of cases coming to the attention of health boards. Coincident with the development of NAI/Child Abuse Guidelines and the Department of Health's review of its response to children at risk in the 1970s was codification of 'the number of such cases coming to attention in this country' (Task Force on Child Care Services 1981, p. 54). In a period of twenty-one months up to December 1978, 243 cases were reported to health boards and ninety-eight confirmed. For the year 1979, 136 cases were reported, seventy-five of which were confirmed (Task Force on Child Care Services 1981, p.105). Since the early 1980s the Department of Health has produced annual statistics on cases coming to the attention of health boards. The total number of cases reported to health boards increased almost ten-fold during the 1980s, from 406 cases in 1982 to 3,856 cases in 1991.

It should be noted that this rate of increase is calculated from a relatively low baseline of reports to health boards, rather than viewed across a longer time-scale to take account of the 2,500 or so cases that were being reported per annum to the ISPCC up to the early 1970s. Yet it is crucial to also note that the phenomenon of child abuse being reported from the late 1970s was substantially different. In line with changing definitions, recognition of different forms of child abuse has changed dramatically. This is most obvious with respect to child sexual abuse. In 1989 the proportion of confirmed child sexual abuse cases stood at 34 per cent. Emotional abuse was 8 per cent, physical abuse was 11 per cent, while neglect was the highest category at 47 per cent. Such trends reveal the absorption of expanding definitions and extra categories of abuse as government guidance has developed (*see*, also, Birchall 1989). They tell us as much about the investigative and administrative workloads and changing perceptions of child welfare and protection agencies as they do about the real incidence of abuse in Irish society.

The translation of child protection policy into practice is invariably a complex one. Considerable regional variation is apparent in how health boards came to operationally define child abuse and respond to the problem (Kenny 1995). Evaluations of the system in the 1980s found 'a degree of procedural informality, or even laxity' in relation to the (non)use of aspects of the child abuse guidelines in some areas which gave 'rise to concern' (Law Reform Commission 1990, p. 15). One revealing illustration of this is what became (or rather did not become) of NAI/child abuse lists. Figures were gathered by the Department of Health on the numbers of cases on health board NAI/child abuse lists for the years 1982-86. Thereafter, the Department of Health ceased gathering statistics on listed children, and enormous uncertainty has always surrounded how such lists are supposed to have been used in practice. This is hardly surprising given that the Department of Health appears never to have bothered to put in place a consultative or training programme which would promote a deeper understanding of such policy mechanisms and attempt to ensure uniformity of standards.

On the other hand, some very significant general trends are in evidence concerning the impact of policy development in the Irish system. Referral patterns are a good indicator of the impact of the guidelines on professional identification of the expanding category of child abuse. Some 60 per cent of all reported cases between 1982-7[5] were recorded as coming from professional sources (Ferguson 1995a, p. 24). The increasing numbers of cases reported involving complex phenomena such as alleged sexual abuse were investigated by a more or less static pool of health board professionals. This resulted in the institutional development of the Irish system being heavily weighted in the allocation of (scarce) resources to child sexual abuse, to the neglect of preventative services (Ferguson 1995a; Murphy 1996, this volume). In the process, the Irish child *care* system has essentially become a child *protection* system, and a highly controversial one at that.

CHILD ABUSE, INQUIRIES AND RADICALISATION OF THE IRISH CHILD PROTECTION SYSTEM IN THE 1990s

During the 1980s, the emergence and development of child care and protection policy was largely contained *within* the expert system. Although changing, levels of sequestration remained quite high as knowledge about child deaths and other organisational 'failures' continued to be institutionally repressed. Low levels of public visibility and accountability reflected traditional system principles and preferences. Ownership of the problem having been won by the health boards and the state in the 1970s; ultimately, the management of child abuse came to reflect the culture of the health boards and, more generally, the relatively unregulated form of public administration in Ireland.

As I have shown, from the 1960s the medical profession was central to processes of recognition and definition of the changing forms of child abuse. Yet work with child abuse was firmly conceived as a multi-disciplinary task, and increases in the numbers of cases coming to the attention of professionals reflects changing definitions and a broadening in policy and practice of the category of child abuse. As definitions and knowledge of the problem have become more complex, so too has the child protection system become more sophisticated. Indeed the very term 'child protection' is of relatively recent coinage in the *official* language of social policy and practice (Parton 1991). The changing emphasis in government guidelines since the mid-1970s reflects developments in the recognition of different forms of child abuse and of the concept of child protection. From the 1970s to mid-1980s, procedures sought to develop co-ordinated programmes of child abuse work by encouraging the *identification* of child abuse, and the development of inter-agency *structures* and *co-operation* to deal with it. Guidelines were primarily concerned with sensitising professionals to the 'first signs of abuse' and the 'index of suspicion', and with co-ordination through teamwork, and case conferences. Little or no formal concern with involving parents or children in decision-making, or even informing them of decisions was evident during this time.

Since the late-1980s, Irish guidelines and the law have become much more concerned to influence what practitioners actually *do* in suspected cases. The most recent edition of the Department of Health Guidelines (1995) are highly prescriptive about the handling by health boards and Gardaí of suspected cases of child abuse, with an increased emphasis on accountability, narrowing discretion as to whether professionals follow procedures or not. This is occurring in a context where, during the 1990s, the politics of child welfare and protection in Ireland and the policy process have entered a new phase. More accurately, child protection has *become* politicised. Relations between professionals, families and the state have ceased to be private affairs and have become matters of intense public concern. Even the Irish State has not been able to stem the tide of globalisation and de-traditionalisation that has been characteristic of the recent history of western nation-states. This situation of 'reflexive modernity' (Beck 1992; Giddens 1994) is on one level the culmination of social processes established earlier this century. But on another level it reflects deep-seated changes in social regulation and the radicalisation of the relationship between trust and risk, knowledge, lay people and expertise.

The environment of trust and risk in Irish child protection is being reconstituted around two main axes. Firstly, the role of the state in child welfare and protection has been clearly specified through the implementation of the Child Care Act (1991). For the first time since its foundation, the Irish state – through the health boards – has been given powers and responsibilities to be proactive in promoting the welfare of children at risk, and not just reactive in terms of possible criminal offences. The second axis, most dramatically, is the impact of a series of scandals and child abuse inquiries which have come to surround every aspect of the child care and protection system – from failures to identify and manage all forms of child abuse within the family (McGuinness 1993; Keenan 1996), by Catholic priests (Moore 1995), to the abuse of children in care, and public knowledge of the fact that the safety of children cannot even be guaranteed by removing them from high risk home situations.[6]

This process began with what became known as the Kilkenny Incest Investigation – the first major child abuse inquiry of its kind in

Ireland – which examined why action was not taken sooner by the health services to halt the serious physical and sexual abuse by her father of a girl/woman over a sixteen year period from 1976-1992. Virtually every theme addressed in policy and encoded in the *Child Abuse Guidelines* – most particularly inter-agency and inter-professional co-ordination and the operation of the child protection *system* – became the subject of critical analysis and recommendations for change in *Report of the Kilkenny Incest Investigation* (McGuinness 1993; Buckley 1993). The fact that it was not until the Kilkenny case that Ireland had a major high-profile inquiry does not mean that there have not been any such cases available within the system on which to focus public attention. It would be misleading to see the Kilkenny inquiry and other scandals in the 1990s simply as a humane response to public disclosures of the hidden reality of child abuse.

Nor should the onset of inquiries be seen as reflecting declining professional standards. Research and the inquiry reports undoubtedly show that problems persist not just in child protection systems and some front-line practice, but at every level of the system. This includes the apparent ideologies and technical problems which prevent children from being viewed as credible witnesses in court, and the adult-centred nature of the judicial system which result in relatively low rates of prosecution in criminal cases of child sexual abuse (McKeown and Gilligan 1991). But viewed in historical perspective, probably more Irish children are being effectively protected in time today than ever before. The numbers of cases reported to health boards has continued to rise, amounting to 4,110 in 1993, the most recent year for which figures are available (Department of Health, *Child Abuse Statistics*). In addition, increasing numbers of survivors of abuse from the 1950s, 1960s and 1970s have disclosed abuse and appear to be finding support and some opportunities for healing. The release by the government of some £35 million to implement the Child Care Act following the publication of the Kilkenny Report has led to unprecedented levels of system development in terms of more staff, training and so on. While it may be far from enough, the key point and paradox of child protection in the 1990s is that in a context in which public perceptions of the effectiveness of the expert system's work with child abuse have never been lower, standards of service have never been higher. Similarly, at a time when the expert system has never been more skilled and equipped to do effective work, individual professionals and entire systems appear to have never been more fearful and prone to defensive practice to avoid the possible risk of blame should intervention turn out to fail (Ferguson 1995c).

The starting point for an explanation of this paradox is the degree of transparency in welfare organisations and accountability of the state and professionals, that is demanded by a new public interest. Scandals and inquiries push knowledge about child protection and risk, that has been available to the expert system for decades, into the public domain. The result is a 'return of the repressed' (Giddens 1991) and raising of existentially troublesome questions about the technical competence of experts to regulate the domains of sexuality and intimate relations and promote life. Thus, it is not the risk of professional failure that is new. It is our greater awareness of the risk of failure and an increased knowledge of these risks as risks that is different today. How such knowledge is managed will be crucial. An awareness of risk as risk involves knowing that knowledge gaps exist in terms of risks which cannot be converted into certainties by religious or magical knowledge (Giddens 1990, p. 125). This goes hand in hand with awareness of the limitations of expertise, knowledge that 'no expert system can be wholly expert in terms of the consequences of the adoption of expert principles' (Giddens 1990, p. 125).

Awareness of such knowledge gaps is not confined to expert systems. The child abuse inquiry is a classic example of how increased awareness of the limits of expertise leaks out into the public domain and becomes part of lay knowledge. In a context where in the 1990s media coverage of child abuse issues in Ireland has reached quite extraordinary levels, the lay public's knowledge has been radicalised and they too have become experts of sorts. The resulting new discursive space politicises lay people whose demand for accountability and explanations for apparent system failures increases dramatically. The role of adult survivors of abuse in this radicalisation process is particularly noteworthy in Ireland where a survivor's movement which appears unprecedented in scale and significance across the western world has taken shape.[7] Public disclosure of the testimony of survivors and their criticisms of failures of the system to stop their abuse has been crucial as a dramatic event, sensitising the public and politicians to the issue of extreme child abuse and the need for accountability and, above all, justice (Wood 1993; Moore 1995; Buckley 1996). The justice-seeking of survivors is a compelling example of the genuine possibilities that the reflexive nature of advanced modern social relations create for the re-appropriation of power by individuals and groups who were abused and marginalised by traditional society (Giddens 1991).

The opening out of the science of the expert system of child protection to lay people has also resulted in a radicalisation of doubt about the ability of professionals to protect children in terms of a structural crisis in trust relations. These processes are leading to a re-structuring of the church-state hegemony and to a critical debate on the legitimacy of the system principles which constitute the master pattern of Irish policy and practice. Disclosures of clerical child sexual abuse have shattered the sacred trust of lay people in the Catholic Church and resulted in priests and religious being tarnished with the label of paedophilia and viewed with suspicion (Ferguson 1995b). Publication of new child protection guidelines by the Church constitutes the first real attempt to restore the trustworthiness of that institution (Irish Catholic Bishops' Advisory Committee 1996). Similarly, the new Health Board/Gardaí child abuse guidelines (DOH 1995) are at least a beginning in restoring public confidence and meeting the growing demand for a more proactive stance by the state in child protection. This includes a growing consensus about the need to introduce mandatory reporting of child abuse (DOH 1996), and for constitutional reform to institutionalise children's rights in a much more rigorous way (McGuinness 1993).

These developments reflect how in many respects the social problem of child abuse has taken on a profound sociological significance in the de-traditionalisation and liberalisation of Irish society. However, as this paper has shown, these extraordinary social changes have also contributed to a trajectory where, within the expert system, child care and protection is being pushed more and more in the direction of a bureaucratic, investigative approach to working with children and families. A major challenge lies ahead in terms of the development of an Irish child care system which, while it cherishes the gains that have been made in recognition of traditionally repressed problems such as domestic violence, sexual and institutional abuse, moves beyond a relatively limited focus on children 'in abuse' to include a broader conception of children 'in need' and integrates child protection and preventative welfare services (Ferguson and Kenny 1995). As we approach the end of the twentieth century, the outlook for child protection in Ireland is a dynamic and contradictory one, containing a radicalised sense of opportunity and danger, security and risk. Viewed within the wider panorama of history and social change, how well we manage the tensions that constitute the new environment of trust and risk in identifying and dealing with child abuse, and child care problems more generally, will ultimately determine how effectively we go on to protect Irish children in new times.

NOTES TO ARTICLE

1 The enmeshed relationship between Church and State in modern Ireland was exemplified by the controversy over the celebrated Mother and Child Scheme in 1951. A proposal by the then Minister for Health, Dr Noel Browne, to introduce a scheme of national insurance to support mothers was stopped following the intervention of the Catholic bishops on the 'natural' role of mothers in the home and the autonomy of the family as the primary institution for the socialisation of children (Whyte 1980).

2 This estimate is based on my reading of archival NSPCC/ISPCC records. The idea that systematic 'rescue' of children from 'cruel' parents and the placing of them in care was the experience of most children who came to the attention of child protection agencies during the twentieth century is a myth (*see* Ferguson 1992).

3 Not only was the Committee dominated by medical experts, it also took advice from British experts on child abuse who had been instrumental in shaping the UK system, such as Ray Castle and the well known paediatrician Christine Cooper (see Castle 1977; Skinner and Castle 1969; Cooper 1985).

4 The 1995 Department of Health Guidelines do offer some definitions of child abuse, but adopt an extremely minimalist approach.

5 1982-87 were the only years for which the Department of Health included a category, and gathered data on, the source of referral in cases reported to health boards.

6 Although a number of inquiries into the institutional abuse of children are known to have taken place in Ireland in the 1990s, at the time of writing no actual inquiry reports have been published. For media coverage of the Madonna House case, see *Sunday Tribune* July 3, 1994.

7 Of particular significance is the work of Christine Buckley, a survivor of alleged institutional abuse in the Goldenbridge children's home in Dublin in the 1950s, who was the subject of a documentary on RTE television about her life (Buckley 1996). Ms Buckley has helped to mobilise survivors' groups, including organising a 'Happy Day' event at a Dublin hotel in April 1996 to which 500 survivors of institutional care in Ireland turned up, many of whom related stories of institutional abuse.

BIBLIOGRAPHY

Allen, A. and A. Morton, (1961), *This is Your Child: the story of the National Society for the Prevention of Cruelty to Children*, London, Routledge

Beck, U. (1992), *The Risk Society*, London, Sage

Behlmer, G.K. (1982), *Child Abuse and Moral Reform in England 1870-1908*, Stanford, Stanford University Press

Birchall, E. (1989), 'The frequency of child abuse – what do we really know?', in O. Stevenson (ed), *Child Abuse: Public Policy and Professional Practice*, London, Harvester Wheatsheaf

Buckley, C. (1996), *Dear Daughter*, RTE Documentary, 22 February 1996

Buckley, H. (1993), 'The Kilkenny Incest Investigation: Some practice implications', *Irish Social Worker,* vol. 11, no. 4, pp. 6-7

Bunreacht na hÈireann (1937), *Constitution of Ireland*, Stationery Office

Butler-Sloss, Lord Justice E. (1988), *Report of the Inquiry into Child Abuse in Cleveland in 1987*, London, HMSO

Castle, R.L. (1977), *Case Conferences: A Cause for Concern?* London, NSPCC

Cohen, S. (1985), *Visions of Social Control*, Cambridge, Polity

Colwell Report (1974), *Report of the Committee of Inquiry into the Care and Supervision Provided in Relation to Maria Colwell*, London, HMSO

Cooper, C. (1985), 'Good-enough, border-line, and bad-enough parenting', in *Good-enough Parenting,* London, BAAF, pp. 58-80

Cooter, R. (1992), 'Introduction', in *In the Name of the Child: Health and Welfare, 1880-1940*, London, Routledge

Curry, J. (1980), *Irish Social Services*, Dublin, IPA

Department of Health (1976), *Report of the Committee on Non-Accidental Injury to Children*, Dublin, Stationery Office

Department of Health (1977), *Memorandum on Non-Accidental Injury to Children*, Dublin

Department of Health (1980), *Guidelines on the Identification and Management of Non-Accidental Injury to Children*, Dublin

Department of Health (1983), *Guidelines for the Identification, Investigation and Management of Non-Accidental Injury To Children*, Dublin

Department of Health (1987), *Child Abuse Guidelines: Guidelines on Procedures for the Identification, Investigation and Management of Child Abuse*, Dublin

Department of Health (1995), *Notification and Reporting of Suspected Cases of Child Abuse*, Dublin, Stationery Office

Department of Health (1996), *Putting Children First: Discussion Document on Mandatory Reporting*, Dublin, Department of Health

Department of Health and Social Security (1974), *Non Accidental Injury to Children*, LASSL (74) 13, London, DHSS

Dingwall, R. (1989), 'Some problems about predicting child abuse and neglect', in O. Stevenson (ed), *Child Abuse: Public Policy and Professional Practice*, Brighton, Wheatsheaf

Dingwall, R. (1991), 'Labelling Children as Abused or Neglected', in Wendy Stainton Rogers, Denise Hevey and Elizabeth Ash (eds), *Child Abuse and Neglect: Facing the Challenge*, London, Batsford

Dingwall, R., J. Eekelaar, T. Murray (1983), *The Protection of Children: State Intervention and Family Life*, Oxford, Blackwell

Doyle, P. (1988), *God Squad*, London, Corgi

Dublin and District Branch NSPCC (1909; 1914), *Annual Report*, London, NSPCC Archives

Ferguson, H. (1990), 'Rethinking Child Protection Practices: A case for history', in *The Violence Against Children Study Group, Taking Child Abuse Seriously*: Contemporary issues in child protection theory and practice, London, Routledge

Ferguson, H. (1992), 'Cleveland in History: The Abused Child and Child Protection, 1880-1914', in R. Cooter (ed), *In The Name of The Child: Health and Welfare*, 1880-1940, London, Routledge

Ferguson, H. (1993), 'Surviving Irish Childhoods: Child Protection and the Deaths of Children in Child Abuse Cases in Ireland since 1884', in H. Ferguson, R. Gilligan and R. Torode (eds), *Surviving Childhood Adversity: Issues for Policy and Practice*, Dublin, Social Studies Press

Ferguson, H. (1994), 'Child abuse inquiries and the Report of the Kilkenny Incest Investigation: A Critical Analysis', *Administration*, vol. 41, no. 4

Ferguson, H. (1995a), 'Child Welfare, Child protection and the Child Care Act 1991: Key Issues for Policy and Practice', in H. Ferguson and P. Kenny (eds), *On Behalf of the Child: Child Welfare, Child protection and the Child Care Act 1991*, Dublin, A. and A. Farmar

Ferguson, H. (1995b), 'The Paedophile Priest: A Deconstruction', *Studies*, vol. 84, no. 335, pp. 247-56

Ferguson, H. (1995c), '"Sitting on a Time-Bomb": Child Protection, Inquiries and the Risk Society', *Irish Social Worker*, vol. 13, no. 1

Ferguson, H. (1996), 'The Protection of Children in Time: Child Protection and the Lives and Deaths of Children in Child Abuse Cases in Socio-Historical Perspective', *Child and Family Social Work*, vol. 1, no. 4

Ferguson, H. and P. Kenny (1995), 'Towards an Integrated System of Child Care Services', in H. Ferguson and P. Kenny (eds), *On Behalf of the Child: Child Welfare, Child protection and the Child Care Act 1991*, Dublin, A. and A. Farmar

Garland, D. (1985), *Punishment and Welfare: A History of Penal Strategies*, Aldershot, Gower

Gelles, R.J. (1975), 'The social construction of child abuse', *American Journal of Orthopsychiatry*, 45, pp. 363-71

Giddens, A. (1990), *The Consequences of Modernity*, Cambridge, Polity

Giddens, A. (1991), *Modernity and Self Identity*, Cambridge, Polity Press

Giddens, A. (1994), *Beyond Left and Right: The future of Radical Politics*, Cambridge, Polity Press

Gordon, L. (1989), *Heroes of Their Own Lives: The History and Politics of Family Violence 1880-1960*, London, Virago

Government Information Services (1982), *Press Release Issued on Behalf of Department of Health*, 26 July 1982

Hallett, C. and O. Stevenson (1980), *Child Abuse: Aspects of Interprofessional Co-operation, London*, Allen and Unwin

Hughes, A. (1967), 'The Battered Baby Syndrome – A Multi-Disciplinary Problem', *Case Conference*, vol. 14, no. 8, pp. 304-8

Irish Catholic Bishops' Advisory Committee (1996), *Child Sexual Abuse: Framework for a Church Response*, Dublin, Veritas

Irish Society for the Prevention of Cruelty to Children [ISPCC] (1956), *First Annual Report*, Dublin, ISPCC

ISPCC (1957), *Annual Report*, Dublin, ISPCC

ISPCC (1958), *Annual Report*, Dublin, ISPCC

ISPCC (1974), *Annual Report*, Dublin, ISPCC

ISPCC (1976), *Annual Report*, Dublin, ISPCC

ISPCC (1977), *Annual Report*, Dublin, ISPCC

ISPCC (1991), *Annual Report*, Dublin, ISPCC

Keenan, O. (1996), Kelly: *A Child is Dead, Interim Report of the Joint Committee on the Family*, Dublin, Government Publications Office

Kelly, A. (1995), 'A Public Health Nursing Perspective', in H. Ferguson and P. Kenny (eds), *On Behalf of the Child: Child Welfare, Child protection and the Child Care Act 1991*, Dublin, A. and A. Farmar

Kenny, P. (1995), 'The Child Care Act, 1991 and the Social Context of Child Protection', in H. Ferguson and P. Kenny (eds), *On Behalf of the Child: Child Welfare, Child protection and the Child Care Act 1991*, Dublin, A. and A. Farmar

Kempe, C.H., F.N. Silverman, B.F. Steele, W. Droegmuller, H.K. Silver (1962), 'The battered child syndrome', *Journal of the American Medical Association* 181, pp. 17-22

Kempe, C. H. (1976), 'Keynote Address', *National Symposium on Child Abuse*, Dublin, 5 May 1976, Dublin, ISPCC Archives

Kennedy Report (1970), Committee on Reformatory and Industrial Schools, *Report on the Reformatory and Industrial Schools System*, Dublin, Stationery Office

Kern (1983), *The Culture of Time and Space*, 1880-1914, Cambridge, Cambridge University Press

Lash, S. and J. Urry (1994), *Economies of Signs and Spaces*, London, Sage

Law Reform Commission (1990), *Report on Child Sexual Abuse*, Dublin, Law Reform Commission

Mayo and District Branch NSPCC (1938), *Annual Report*, London, NSPCC Archives

Moore, C. (1995), *Betrayal of Trust: The Father Brendan Smyth Affair and the Catholic Church,* Dublin, Marino

McGinley, M. (1995), 'A Programme Manager Perspective', in H. Ferguson and P. Kenny (eds), *On Behalf of the Child: Child*

Welfare, Child protection and the Child Care Act 1991, Dublin, A. and A. Farmar

McGuinness, C. (1993), *Report of the Kilkenny Incest Investigation,* Dublin, Stationery Office

McKeown and Gilligan (1991), 'Child Sexual Abuse in the Eastern Health Board Region of Ireland in 1988: An Analysis of 512 Confirmed Cases', *The Economic and Social Review*, vol. 22, no 2, pp. 101-34

National Society for the Prevention of Cruelty to Children (1897), *Annual Report*, London, NSPCC Archives

National Society for the Prevention of Cruelty to Children (1934), *Annual Report*, London, NSPCC Archives

National Society for the Prevention of Cruelty to Children (1936), *Annual Report*, London, NSPCC Archives

National Society for the Prevention of Cruelty to Children (1954), *Annual Report*, London, NSPCC Archives

National Society for the Prevention of Cruelty to Children (1904; 1910), *Inspector's Directory*, London, NSPCC Archives

Nelson, B. (1984), *Making an Issue of Child Abuse: Political Agenda Setting for Social Problems*, Chicago, University of Chicago Press

Nic Giolla Choille, T. (1983), *ISPCC Wexford Family Centre*, Dublin, ISPCC

Parton, N. (1985), *The Politics of Child Abuse*, London, Macmillan

Parton, N. (1991), *Governing The Family: Child Care, Child Protection and The State*, London, Macmillan

Scheper-Hughes, N. (ed) (1987), *Child Survival: Anthropological Perspectives on the Treatment and Maltreatment of Children, Dordrecht*, Holland, Reidel

Skinner, A.K. and A.L. Castle (1969), *78 Battered Children: a Retrospective Study*, London, NSPCC

Task Force on Child Care Services (1981), *Final Report*, Dublin, Stationery Office

Thorpe, D. (1994), *Evaluating Child Protection*, Milton Keynes, Open University Press

Touher, P. (1991), *Fear of the Collar: Artane Industrial School*, Dublin, O'Brien Press

Waterford and District Branch NSPCC (1908), *Annual Report*, London, NSPCC Archives

Wexford and District Branch NSPCC (1922), *Annual Report*, London, NSPCC Archives

Whyte, J. H. (1980), *Church and State in Modern Ireland, 1923-1979*, 2nd edn, Dublin, Gill and Macmillan

Wood, K. (1993), *The Kilkenny Incest Case*, Dublin, Poolbeg

Wright, P. (1987), 'The social construction of babyhood: the definition of infant care as a medical problem', in A. Bryman, B. Blytheway, P. Allat and T. Keil (eds), *Rethinking the Life Cycle*, London, Macmillan

Zigler, F. and Hall, N. (1989), 'Physical child abuse in America: past, present, and future', in D. Cicchetti and V. Carlson, *Child Maltreatment: Theory and research on the causes and consequences of child abuse and neglect*, Cambridge, Cambridge University Press

Part Four
Conflicts and Debates

Administration, vol. 51, nos. 1-2 (Spring/Summer 2003), 287–299

Social Policy in Modern Ireland

JAMES KAVANAGH

Originally published in 1978, vol. 26, no. 3, 318-330. It is the text of the fourth Sean Lemass Memorial Lecture delivered at Exeter University on 3 February 1978. Dr Kavanagh was then Auxiliary Bishop of Dublin. He was formerly Professor of Social Science in University College, Dublin.

A first question one must ask is, 'What is meant by "modern. Ireland"?' I would suggest there are three distinct phases – first, the period from the 1880s to 1921; secondly, the period of the Constitution of the new Irish Free State from 1922 to 1937; and thirdly, the period from 1937 (when Eamon de Valera brought in the new Constitution) to the present time.

The first period differs from the other two in that one could then write of Ireland unambiguously as the whole country of thirty-two counties. The legislative body for Ireland at that time was Westminster to which the Irish sent representatives. State policy, including social policy depended on the parliament of Westminster. Irish MPs tried to influence that policy, but most of their concern was with the attainment of home rule. Social matters were, of course, not forgotten as we shall see.

What was the Church concerned with in that early period? Most ecclesiastics were anxious to stem the flow of population from Ireland. But they regarded 'industrialisation' as inimical to the Irish tradition. Bishop Hoare of Ardagh said in 1902: 'People thought if they had big factories like Belfast and Birmingham they would have plenty of employment and no need for emigration. Well, there were some drawbacks to that system too. It was a well known fact that the taking of people from the rural districts into the large towns and cities had led to physical decadence. If they could get honest work and an honest wage for the poor people in their cottage homes it would, in his opinion, be much better than those hives of industry, as they were usually called, but he would call them huge destroyers of the morals of the people.[1]

It is perhaps salutary (at least for Irishmen) to reflect on what Fredrich Engels had to say away back in 1845 about the Irish and their agricultural pursuits:

> With the Irish, feeling and passion predominate; reason must bow before them. Their sensuous, excitable nature prevents reflection and quiet, persevering activity from reaching development – such a nation is utterly unfit for manufacture as now conducted. Hence they held fast to agriculture, and remained upon the lowest plane even of that. With the small sub-divisions of land, which were not here artificially created, as in France and on the Rhine, by the division of great estates, but have existed from time immemorial, an improvement of the soil by the investment of capital was not to be thought of; and it would, according to Alison, require 120 million pounds sterling to bring the soil up to the not very high state of fertility already attained in England. The English immigration, which might have raised the standard of Irish civilisation, has contented itself with the most brutal plundering of the Irish people; and while the Irish, by their immigration into England, have furnished England a leaven which will produce its own results in the future, they have little for which to be thankful to the English immigration.
>
> The attempts of the Irish to save themselves from their present ruin, on the one hand, take the form of crime. These are the order of the day in the agricultural districts, and are nearly always directed against the most immediate enemies, the landlords' agents, or their obedient servants, the Protestant intruders, whose large farms are made up of the potato patches of hundreds of ejected families. Such crimes are especially frequent in the South and West. On the other hand, the Irish hope for relief by means of the agitation for the repeal of the Legislative Union with England. From all the foregoing, it is clear that the uneducated Irish must see in the English their worst enemies; and their first hope of improvement in the conquest of national independence. But quite as clear is it, too, that Irish distress cannot be removed by any Act of Repeal. Such an act would, however, at once lay bare the fact that the cause of Irish misery, which now seems to come from abroad, is really to be found at home.[2]

Pace Engels and his view that the Irish nation is utterly unfit for manufacture and indeed for any sort of industrial activity; most ecclesiastics seemed to favour agricultural pursuits with ancillary rural cottage industries as the means of keeping the population at home in salubrious moral surroundings. (Those of you who watch the TV programme 'The Good Life' will appreciate the excellence of the ideal and its profound economic limitations!)

In the principal address to the Maynooth Union in 1903 the Reverend Thomas Macken said 'No lover of, Ireland – no genuine Irishman – can contemplate without feelings akin to horror, an Industrial Ireland with centres of manufacture such as are to be found in Germany, in England and in America.'[3]

To further this ideal, Wyndham in 1902 brought in his famous piece of legislation whereby the Irish tenant could purchase his holding from the landlord. This was, I believe, one of the best things the English parliament had done for Ireland. The bishops at their June meeting in 1902 welcomed the Bill in principle, but added that the neglected grazing lands of the country should be made available on fair terms to the agricultural population. I think Miller is somewhat unfair when he says the bishops forgot about land redistribution when Wyndham's Bill was passed in 1903, because they were anxious that government money be given to Catholic university education. The fact of the matter was that the Bill did so much to assuage agrarian discontent that to look for more radical land distribution at that time would have been futile and unrealistic. 'Between 1903 and 1920 nearly nine million acres had changed hands and two million acres more were in the process of being sold.'[4]

The 1898 Local Government Act had revolutionised the composition of the local councils – now the farmers and the shopkeeper's were in control and not the landowners and 'the gentry'. Horace Plunkett had started his Irish Agricultural Organization Society – that great co-operative movement which was to do so much, particularly for the dairy industry. At the same time many 'nationalists' were not so keen on continued co-operation with the landlord class; lest the push for home rule would be weakened. Many churchmen were ambivalent regarding the new rapprochement with 'the gentry' taking place not only in the Co-Operative movement, but in various *ad hoc* committees which sought betterment of social conditions. Individuals like the great Jesuit Father Tom Finlay, Professor at the Catholic University, supported co-operation, but Plunkett rather tactlessly attacked Catholicism as being too authoritarian and too little concerned with economic realities. Most of the bishops were home rulers and also they would find it difficult to separate themselves from the more vocal and more numerous nationalist politicians who felt that home rule must be the first objective and that further economic and social progress could wait till that objective was achieved. (The parallel with the present situation in Northern Ireland is not too fanciful.)

In the early years of the twentieth century, James Connolly and James Larkin were to attempt to organise the labourers in the cities. Trade unions up to this time had mainly catered for craft trades and were eminently respectable. Connolly with his syndicalist socialist views and Larkin with his flamboyant oratory were regarded by 'trade unions' as rather strange additions to the trade union scene. Irish employers were terrified of them and it is true to say that churchmen – with a few exceptions – were anything but sympathetic to these two new Labour leaders. The Marxist language of Connolly was enough to make him suspect and the Churchmen felt that Larkin's use of the strike weapon, which culminated in the lock-out by the employers in 1913, caused much hardship and suffering, though ultimately Connolly and Larkin were to bring about a new sort of trade unionism in Ireland which was to cater for the unskilled labourers of the cities.

When the Home Rule Bill was put into cold storage through the Orange revolt in Ulster and the intransigence of the House of Lords, the impatience of many with parliament and the Irish Parliamentary Party led to the rebellion of 1916. The execution of the leaders by the British government canonised the rebellion for the Irish people – what had been seen by most people as a courageous but ill-conceived rebellion, now became a glorious revolution. 'Sinn Féin' began to sweep across the country and when in April 1918 a Conscription Bill was passed to include Ireland, the whole country, with the exception of the Orangemen in the north-east, was in a conflagration of fury and protest. The bishops denounced the conscription of Ireland and thus became recognised as supporters of Sinn Féin (with one or two cautious exceptions). The elections of 1918 resulted in a massive victory for Sinn Féin who were pledged to abstain from Westminster. On 21 January 1919 the first session of Dáil Éireann took place with half of its elected members still held in prison in English jails. A Declaration of Independence was approved and ministries were set up. A Democratic Programme was adopted, a Programme which has particular relevance for the subject of this lecture. Some of its provisions were that 'all right to private property must be subordinated to the public right and welfare'; 'each citizen has a right to an adequate share of the produce of the Nation's Labour'; 'the odious, degrading and foreign Poor Law System' was to be abolished, and a rather grandiloquent paragraph said:

> It shall be the first duty of the Government of the Republic to make provision for the physical, mental and spiritual well being of the children, to secure that no child shall suffer hunger or cold from lack of food, clothing or shelter, but that all shall be provided with the means and facilities requisite for their proper education and training as Citizens of a Free and Gaelic Ireland.[5]

The Democratic Programme, it may be said, was accepted generally by the Hierarchy. Theological debates took place in the *Irish Theological Quarterly* about the rights and limitations of private property and the semantics of socialism. But no hackles were raised by the Democratic Programme as passed. (A Labour man, Thomas Johnson, had prepared the first draft and certain of his expressions had been toned down by Seán T. O'Kelly, who was later to become President of Ireland.)

It would have been difficult in the circumstances of the time for the bishops not to be favourably inclined, because almost all of the Sinn Féin clubs across the country had clergymen on their executives, clergymen who included not only the 'young bloods' but many of the grey-haired 'respectable' parish priests. Of course nothing much could be done by this first Dáil about its Democratic Programme, because soon they became involved in what is called the War of Independence which lasted till the truce of July 1921 and the Treaty which was signed in London on 6 December 1921. This Treaty set up the 26 Counties as 'the Irish Free State'.

The Treaty was ratified by the Dáil by 64 votes to 57 on 7 January 1922. Mr de Valera refused to accept the Treaty and the way was open for civil war. The bishops backed the Provisional Free State government set up after the Treaty. The civil war ended with the capitulation of the anti-Treaty forces on 24 May 1923. (Griffith had died on 12 August 1922 and Collins was shot dead in an ambush on 22 August 1922.)

This rather long look at the period up to 1922 is helpful in the appreciation of later developments in both Church and State. A great deal of the time had been spent on the seeking of home rule; the changes in land tenure and the agitation leading up to it were also significant. In these areas bishops had vied with the politicians in holding the centre of the political and social stage. Very few days went by without some Episcopal effusion in the daily papers and it was not unusual for bishops to differ in public with each other on some point of policy or procedure. Bishops regarded it as their right to speak and write on most topics. (Archbishop Walsh in the busy metropolis of Dublin found time to write a treatise on Bimetallism.)

John Whyte in his admirable *Church and State in Modern Ireland* has suggested that there is an authoritarian strain in the Irish character which accounts for the bishops' paternalist concern on so many issues. Perhaps the answer lies in the small-farmer background of so many Irish people. The farmer is by nature conservative and tended to be patriarchal towards his children up to fairly recent times. A son of forty or even fifty was still the 'boy' around the house and was not given a great deal of initiative. Irish bishops in the main in this first period were from a rural small-farming background and with their education were naturally inclined to lead and be looked up to.

It is commonplace among writers, especially Irish writers, to assert that even up to the present day Church leaders still adopt an authoritarian attitude. My belief is that after the founding of the Irish Free State, bishops in general have become less and less authoritarian and that particularly in the social sphere they have tended to suggest rather than impose possible lines of approach, and the rare occasions when they did appear to impose only highlight the change from the previous decades. I shall return to this point later on.

Given the predominance of ecclesiastics on the political scene, it is somewhat strange to note that the Constitution of the Irish Free State of 1922 enshrined the separation of Church and State. Article 8 declared: 'Freedom of conscience and the free profession and practice of religion are, subject to public order and morality, guaranteed to every citizen, and no law may be made directly or indirectly to endow any religion . . .' When one reflects that Leo XIII in his encyclical *Immortale Dei* in 1885 had argued against the separation of Church and State, the acquiescence of the Irish bishops to the new Constitution is quite remarkable. Cynics may argue that since the Church pretty effectively controlled primary and secondary education the bishops had nothing to fear. Nevertheless one might not have expected so ready an acceptance of the principle of separation in the Constitution.

What about the Democratic Programme of the First Dáil of 1919? Very little of it was incorporated in the new Constitution. My friend Professor Patrick Lynch has called it 'the social revolution that never was'. But considering the manifold difficulties of the new State, few will deny that the Free State government in those early days did a remarkable job in consolidating the new structure. One does not have to subscribe fully to the views of Michael Oakeshott to accept that at that particular time the enterprise of keeping the ship of state afloat was paramount. His words in his inaugural address on 'Political Education' are worth quoting and although not in my opinion universally valid are apposite for the beginnings of the new State:

> In political activity men sail a boundless and bottomless sea, there is neither harbour for shelter nor floor for anchorage, neither starting place nor appointed destination. The enterprise is to keep afloat on an even keel; the sea is both friend and enemy; and the seamanship consists in using the resources of a traditional manner of behaviour in order to make a friend of every hostile occasion.[6]

The notion of founding a society upon a Declaration of Rights was a creature of the rationalist brain according to Oakeshott. It is interesting to note in a fairly long list the sort of rationalisms he despised – the Beveridge Report, votes for women, the Education Act of 1944 and the revival of Gaelic as the official language of Éire. In short, a self-consciously planned society was an object of scorn to him.

Be that as it may (and I have simply introduced here the ideas of Oakeshott to show that there is at least a debatable alternative approach to political endeavour from that to which most people today adhere) the new State succeeded in accomplishing many good things. By a system of tariff-protection, by 1931 over 18,000 new jobs were created in industry. Professor George O'Brien, writing in 1932, said 'Protection is the obvious method of State assistance and will no doubt be extended . . . Undue reliance on State assistance for industrial development, is, however, to he deprecated. The true function of the State is to provide the conditions in which healthy and well-directed enterprise can thrive.'[7] This was no ideological approach, but hard commonsense and it is easy to see how the bishops could agree to this sort of social and economic policy.

A great success of the new government was the construction of the Shannon Power Scheme (begun in 1925 and completed in 1929), run by a Board nominated by the government. The Board manages the electricity supply as a business concern free from political interference. In spite of the Church's general fear of the extension of State activity (the encyclical *Quadragesimo Anno* of 1931 had stressed the principle of subsidiarity), there has developed in Ireland a network of State enterprises, some of which are highly successful (with a few geese among the swans!). The fact is that this big extension of State enterprise was welcomed by the Church in Ireland, with only an occasional expression of fear about State encroachment.

Mr de Valera introduced a new Constitution (after a referendum) in 1937. Several articles in it contain 'Directive principles of Social Policy'. In Article 41 the State guarantees to look on the family as the basis of the social order and no divorce legislation will be allowed. It also will 'endeavour to ensure that mothers will not be obliged by economic necessity to engage in labour to the neglect of their duties in the home'. Article 42 declares that the family is 'the primary and natural educator of the child'. Article 43 recognises the right to private property, but entitles the State to reconcile the exercise of this right with the requirements of the common good. Then follows the rather famous (or infamous) Article 44 which 'recognises the special position of the Holy Catholic Apostolic and Roman Church as the guardian of the Faith professed by the great majority of the citizens', but all other denominations are recognised as well.

There is undoubtedly a certain Catholic quality in these directive principles. Article 44 has caused the greatest controversy in the past, though it is likely that Article 41 in its denial of divorce legislation will be the subject of increasing debate in the future. Regarding Article 44, Mr de Valera indicated in his speech to the Dáil in June 1937 that this Article was stating a statistical fact and that the value system of the vast majority of citizens would have to be taken seriously into account. Some people were unhappy with article 44, presumably because it did not state explicitly that the Roman Catholic Church was the true Church of Christ.

Mr de Valera was, without doubt, a fervent Catholic. But he always managed to keep a firm independence of episcopal or clerical control. He was always his own man. In his last days I was privileged to visit him several times and was struck by the calm prayerful way he faced death. There was a certain grandeur about it – death kept knocking on the door for several days and one felt that Mr de Valera only answered the knocking when he himself had decided. During his days in government he had complete control of his cabinet. I think the tragic episode of the 'Mother-and-Child' in 1951 would not have been allowed to develop in the way it did, if Fianna Fáil, with Mr de Valera, had been in power. Also, Mr de Valera would not have given the appearance of yielding to episcopal pressure. He managed very astutely to quell the fears of the bishops on the 1953 Health Act. (Some might use the expression 'to pull the teeth' rather than 'to quell the fears'.) But then he never had to deal, as Mr Costello had, with a Minister of Health, not from his own party, who was young, energetic, filled with concern for the underprivileged but politically naive.

Mr John Whyte in his *Church and State in Modem Ireland*,[8] already referred to, discusses in a fair and scholarly way the issues wherein Catholic elements of one sort or another and bishops tried to intervene in the affairs of the State. Perhaps one may be permitted to add a little comment on some of these issues in the social sphere. The organisation *Maria Duce* which operated in the fifties and which attacked Article 44 for not being Catholic enough, was regarded by clerics generally as a lunatic fringe group. Newspaper reports and comments are not always the best guide to popular feeling – I do not accuse Dr Whyte of relying on such alone (he is too good a scholar for that), but a great deal modern 'history' relies far too much on newspaper reports and comments made at the time by people often more interested in literary expression than the pursuit of the facts.

Again, Cardinal D'Alton's suggestion in 1948 that Irish trade unions should affiliate to the international Federation of Christian Trade Unions – this at a time when there were two rival Congresses of Irish Trade Unions – was I believe the Cardinal's own idea and not an Episcopal one. I know that Dr McQuaid, Archbishop of Dublin, did not think so well of the suggestion believing that it might only split Irish trade unionism into so-called Christian and non-Christian camps.

Earlier Dr Michael Browne, Bishop of Galway, and an admitted supporter of Fianna Fáil, had been appointed Chairman of a Government Commission on Vocational Organisation. This Commission reported in 1943. The government reaction was hostile. Mr Seán Lemass, then Minister for Industry and Commerce, described it as 'a slovenly document'. Whether he threw it there, personally or not, the Report ended up in the government waste paper basket. Bishop Browne, let me repeat, had been an acknowledged supporter of Fianna Fáil.

In 1944 Dr Dignan, Bishop of Clonfert, who was Chairman of the National Health Insurance Society (a body set up by the Minister for Local Government and Public Health, Mr Sean McEntee) issued what came to be known as the Dignan plan for social insurance. The Minister was enraged that anybody should try to interfere with the Minister and his Department. The scheme was dismissed out of hand, not apparently on its merits or demerits, but because of the presumption to initiate such a plan without the Minister's approval. In 1945 when Dr Dignan's term of office expired, his position was given to a more amenable civil servant.

Here I would like to add a footnote to Dr Whyte's account of this incident. Kaim-Caudle, who worked at the Economic Research Institute and produced his book in 1964 on *Social Security in Ireland and Western Europe*, has declared that when he came to recommend a system of social insurance in the light of modem developments, he found that what he chose had already been put forward by Dr Dignan some twenty years before. Dr Dignan's recompense was dismissal from office. One heard little of this incident in the intervening years – indeed Kaim-Caudle says he only heard about it by chance. The Health controversy of 1951 to which I have referred is like Agatha Christie's 'Mousetrap', likely to hold the stage for ever.

I would suggest then that if in the fifties the Church is charged with being conservative and over-occupied with fears of increasing State control, the attitude is at least understandable in the light of some of these issues. If some bishops held their croziers at the ready, Ministers and their civil servants gave the impression that their fastnesses were unassailable.

The 'accepted' view of the early fifties, however, seems to have been that Irish Catholic social theorists were opposed to State intervention, and this in spite of the fact that the system of state bodies and state-sponsored bodies had developed to quite a remarkable degree without any opposition from the Church. Professor Patrick Lynch wrote in Studies: 'If, however, the then prevailing attitudes of formal Irish sociology towards government intervention had decisively influenced public policy in the 1960s the economic revival that followed Mr Whitaker's publication might not have taken place.'[9] My distinct impression was that Dr Whitaker's Economic Development published in 1958 was greeted by formal and informal sociologists with enthusiasm. They did not have to wait for the improvement in economic conditions to change their attitude.

The production of *Economic Development*[10] and the First Economic Plan which followed were to bring an unprecedented upsurge in economic growth. Mr Lemass, then Minister for Industry and Commerce and Deputy Prime Minister (he became Prime Minister in 1959), threw his full weight behind the new approach. Whitaker was Secretary of the Department of Finance. Here was a remarkable combination of two people with drive, enterprise, expertise and common sense. Not only was the country given economic development (the growth rate per annum over 1959-63 was 4%) but the psychological uplift generated in the whole community was equally significant. Things would never be the same again. Bishop Philbin, then at Clonfert (1954-62), before being transferred to Belfast, was inculcating in his speeches and papers,[11] a patriotism in which religion would influence a spirit of hard work and enterprise. He said little about State power, but emphasised the duties of all Irishmen to build up the economy.

Since that time the tensions between Church and State in social and economic matters have practically disappeared. The publication of Pope John's *Mater et Magistra* in 1961 with its approving words on socialisation and the necessary role of the State and his encyclical *Pacem in Terris* in 1963 with its *apertura a sinistra* (opening to the left) – he said we could learn from the social and economic developments in Marxist countries even though we could not accept their basic philosophy – greatly aided the better relationship between Church and State.

The Vatican Council (1962-65) called by Pope John, was another great influence in this relaxation of tensions. In its document 'The Church in the Modern World' the Council states: 'In their proper spheres the political community and the Church are mutually independent and self-governing. Yet, by a different title, each serves the personal and social vocation of the same human beings. This service can be more effectively rendered for the good of all, if, each works better for wholesome mutual co-operation, depending on the circumstances of time and place.'[12]

The entry into the European Economic Community was, of course, another important factor. In 1961 Seán Lemass had announced that Ireland would apply for EEC membership. Difficulties with De Gaulle and Great Britain's entry slowed the process and it was not until May 1972 that in a referendum, the Republic of Ireland by a huge vote (just over 2 million against 212,000) decided to enter the EEC. It would need a separate paper to discuss the influence of the EEC on Irish affairs, but suffice it to say in our present context, that social questions (particularly with Dr Patrick Hillery as Vice-President of the Commission of the European Communities) were certain to loom large in Irish affairs. Also, the dimension of international relationships was bound to diminish a certain parochialism in both Church and State.

There is, too, a far greater emphasis on social research. The Economic and Social Research Institute, the Universities, the National Economic and Social Council, the Agricultural Institute, the Institute of Public Administration and the Bishops' Council for Social Welfare have by their studies focused attention on poverty, social insurance, social assistance and unemployment and have helped in the better understanding of how well these schemes do help those they are intended for.

The last government and now Mr Lynch's government have accepted the principle that welfare benefits will not at least fall below the increase in the cost of living. In fact, there has been a major increase in income maintenance over the past eight years – in the Third Programme for Economic and Social Development, initiated in 1969, the targets for housing and income maintenance were 5.1 and 4.9 per cent respectively; in the early years housing only reached 0.9 while income maintenance reached 11.6. This sort of emphasis has been maintained. It is true that too large an expenditure on social policy may hinder economic growth, but one has to balance this with equitability and general morale. I would recommend strongly Finola Kennedy's *Public Social Expenditure in Ireland* (Dublin 1975) for discussion of this and related topics.

The Bishops' Council for Social Welfare (and if I single this out, it is because I am more closely acquainted with it) sponsored a national conference on poverty in Kilkenny in November 1971.[13] Out of this came two working parties – one on social policy and the other on social administration. They produced a 'Statement on Social Poliey'[14] which was greeted as a worthwhile contribution to the general debate. The Council also commissioned a research study on the meaning of poverty.[15] Other documents included a Statement on Family Law Reform[16] and 'Planning for Social Development'[17] in November 1976.

The tone of these contributions is by no means minatory or authoritarian. In the introductions one reads sentences such as: 'Our plea is for dialogue and consultation with the policy decision makers' and 'we would like to think that the document will at least provide a basis for worthwhile discussion.'

The Irish Hierarchy after its June meeting in 1975 issued two important statements on 'The Economic Situation' and 'Public Morality'.[18] In the first statement they urged 'a renewed sense of national purpose and co-operation … Economic recovery can be delayed, perhaps disastrously, if various sectors are too greedy or too selfish to accept the sacrifices which the situation demands.' And they pointed out that politicians had a special responsibility for leadership and guidance of the people, a leadership which would he constant and firm. In the second statement, it was felt necessary to point out that it is not the view of the Catholic hierarchy, that, in the law of the State, 'the principles peculiar to our faith should be made binding on people who do not adhere to that faith.' Legislators in discussing changes in the law have to consider the impact on society – would it tend to change the character of the society for the worse? This leaves the prudential judgement up to the political rulers of the country. In many ways, it makes their task more difficult, but in the long run it is better that way for a democratic institution.

At the present time, then, Church and State in the area of social policy are pretty much in harmony. A feature of Irish life is the vast upsurge of voluntary community care, which is helped greatly by the various statutory health boards (some being better than others). Local committees are really becoming interested in and concerned, in effective ways, about the old, the lonely and the handicapped. But for the nation generally at the present time the great problem is still unemployment. This year our growth rate will he in the region of 7-8 per cent (so my economist friends tell me). How to diffuse the benefits achieved to the weaker sections of the people, especially in the provision of jobs, is the great and pressing concern.

Basil Chubb in his *The Government and Politics of Ireland,*[19] published in 1970, discusses the influence of the Church in his section on 'Interest Groups'. In a rather restrained comment on Church interference, he makes the point that 'the Bishops have not been notable in the past for taking positive positions on social questions, at least in public.' Since that time the publications of the Bishops' Council for Social Welfare and the Hierarchy's recent Pastoral on Justice indicate a positive change, especially in the suasory tone of these documents.

If I were to conclude with a personal wish regarding the function of the Hierarchy I would like to see an extension of trust in the laity on more and more fronts. I would also like to see this extension, not only in the social welfare field but to all other aspects of our community relations. Following Christ who was 'meek and humble of heart', bishops have to err even on the side of openness and frankness in discussion. As the pastoral (which I commend strongly to you) declares: 'We who preach and serve the gospel must be willing to be tested by it and judged by its standards in our own lives.'[20]

As a bishop I may be expected to round off my talk with some sort of pious reflection. I cannot do better than quote from that very English Englishman so revered in Ireland for all he did for university education, John Henry Newman. He was speaking about the England of his day but his words are valid for Irishmen and Englishmen at the present time:

> I do not know anything more dreadful than a state of mind which is, perhaps, the characteristic of this country, and which the prosperity of this country so miserably fosters. I mean that … low ambition which sets everyone on the look-out to succeed and to rise in life, to amass money, to gain power, and intense, sleepless, restless, never-wearied, never satisfied, pursuit of mammon in one shape or other, to the exclusion of all deep, all holy, all calm, all reverent thoughts.[21]

REFERENCES

1 David W. Miller, *Church and State in Ireland 1898-1921*, (Dublin 1973), p. 72.

2 'Marx and Engels on Ireland', (Moscow and London 1971), p. 42.

3 David Miller, op. cit., p. 73.

4 F. S. L. Lyons, *Ireland Since the Famine*, (London 1973), p. 219.

5 Ibid., p. 402.

6 Michael Oakeshott, *Rationalism in Politics*, (London 1962), p. 127.

7 *Saorstát Éireann Official Handbook*, (Dublin 1932), p. 148.

8 J. H. Whyte, *Church and State in Modern Ireland 1923-1970*, (Dublin 1971).

9 Patrick Lynch, 'Escape from Stagnation', *Studies* Vol. LII, Dublin, pp. 136 etc.

10 T. K. Whitaker, *Economic Development*, (Dublin 1958).

11 e.g. 'Patriotism and the faith: Landmarks and horizons', *Christus Rex,* Oct. 1959 and pamphlets: *Patriotism* (1958); *The Irish and the New Europe* (1962).

12 *Documents of Vatican II*, (Abbot, London-Dublin 1966), p. 288.

13 *Social Studies,* (Maynooth August 1972) for lectures at this Conference.

14 *Statement on Social Policy*, Council for Social Welfare, 169 Booterstown Avenue, Co. Dublin (November 1972).

15 *The Meaning of Poverty*, Council for Social Welfare, 169 Booterstown Avenue, Co. Dublin (1974).

16 *Statement on Family Law Reform*, Council for Social Welfare, 169 Booterstown Avenue, Co. Dublin (1974).

17 *Planning for Social Development*, Council for Social Welfare, 169 Booterstown Avenue, Co. Dublin (1976).

18 *The Furrow*, (Maynooth July 1976).

19 Basil Chubb, *The Government and Politics of Ireland* (London 1970), pp. 102-108.

20 *The Work of Justice*, (Irish Bishops' Pastoral 1977), p. 69.

21 John Henry Newman, *Parochial and Plain Sermons VIII*, (London 1890).

The Reports of the National Economic and Social Council, Stationery Office Dublin, – especially 'An Approach to Social Policy' 1975; 'Towards a Social Report' 1976; 'Some Major issues in Health Policy' 1977 – are invaluable for any discussion on social policy in Ireland.

Administration, vol. 51, nos. 1-2 (Spring/Summer 2002), 300–303

Ireland in Crisis: A Study in Capitalist Colonial Development

TOM GARVIN

Book Review

Ireland in Crisis: A Study in Capitalist Colonial Development, by Raymond Crotty, Dingle: Brandon, 1986. 296 pp., £12.50.

Originally published in 1986, vol. 34, no. 4, 553-555.
Tom Garvin was then a lecturer in politics in University College Dublin.

Raymond Crotty has written an interesting and maddening book. He sets out to explain why it is that, for over a century, so many of the Irish have, as he puts it, 'been denied a livelihood' in Ireland. He points to the starvation that was the fate of perhaps millions in the mid-nineteenth century, and to the fact that a huge proportion of the population of the island have emigrated from it in the century and a quarter or so since 1850.

Crotty believes that the mechanism of traditional emigration has permitted those left in the island to enjoy a better standard of living than otherwise would have occurred, and that emigration has also permitted the Irish to avoid facing up to the inefficient and unfair way in which Irish economic life is organised and has been organised since the Cromwellian period. Essentially, Ireland was, like much of the under developed world, colonised by the English who superimposed a politico-economic system which he labels individualistic capitalism. This system involves cultural emphasis on the individual's interests and achievements at the expense, if necessary, of the community's. It also involves the rule of law, which enforces impersonal rules on people and protects the institution of private productive property. This very dynamic and creative system of social organisation, which originated in early mediaeval western Europe, has dominated the world for centuries. It has, however, had disastrous effects on societies to which it was carried by European conquerors. These societies, organised in communal, non-individualistic ways, found an alien system imposed upon them which conflicted profoundly with their traditional ways of doing things. The result has been corruption, cultural confusion, and the chaos which has engulfed much of what is labelled the Third World.

Crotty argues that only two kinds of society have either escaped the baleful effects of this system or have actually benefited from it. The 'settler colonies' of North America, Australia and New Zealand, where the indigenous inhabitants were either insignificant in numbers or were exterminated by the settlers, prospered under the individualistic capitalistic system. On the other hand, the east Asian cultures of China, Japan and the other nations of that area by and large escaped colonisation and have borrowed eclectically from the West, thereby keeping their own cultures intact while taking from the West only what suits them. Crotty informs us that the half of the earth's population which lives in societies which underwent colonisation by the West 'undevelops' and is in a cultural and structural trap; a small, privileged and westernised elite maintains the system imported from the West, while the rest of the population is disorganised and exploited under it.

We are told that the ease of Ireland differs from those of the third World only in the peculiar fact that Ireland is not, like most of the other colonised countries, a jail; one can get out of it. However, Crotty feels that this option is now disappearing, and if the population increases, Ireland will share the apocalyptic fate of many underdeveloped countries; overpopulation, falling living standards, revolutionary politics and a garrison state. He suggests that there are ways out of this situation, but these solutions will be opposed by the privileged in Irish society. The privileged are first of all the farmers, whose interest is in high food prices, and all those who work for the public sector, broadly defined, in permanent, pensionable and often unproductive jobs, usually defended by aggressive trade union action. This system has historically been financed by an exploitative fiscal policy toward business and labour: labour is taxed heavily, while property, particularly farmland, is scarcely taxed at all. The result is a low growth rate. In recent years, the system has become disequilibrated and a desperate resort has been made to foreign borrowing to avoid taxing the powerful privileged groups. The Republic now enjoys the highest per capita foreign debt in the world

Crotty's solution centres around the idea of correct factor pricing. Ireland's colonial history resulted in the farmers inheriting the privileged position in the economy of the old landlord class. Irish agriculture is inefficient, and Irish land is underutilised because incompetent land use by landowners is never penalised; it is, in fact, subsidised. He suggests a tax on land to penalise those who refuse to use it to the enrichment of the community. A side-effect of the situation is that labour is costly in Ireland, because of the narrow tax base and the high cost of food. Because of this, investment in Ireland tends to be capital rather than labour-intensive, and the surplus labour force is squeezed out of Ireland. Crotty also proposes the shrinking of the civil service and the abolition of security of tenure. He further suggests the repudiation of the national debt.

The book also contains a series of appendixes, one of which amounts almost to a book itself, being a remarkable, wide discussion of the evolution of western society from the pastoralist stage to that of modern capitalism. His awareness of the relationships between human beings and the biological environment is strong and yields many fascinating insights. In some ways, this is, in Ireland at least, bound to be an academically unfashionable book, as it is really a work in a now unfashionable subject, political economy as distinct from economics.

It is a very original work. It is, however, maddening. Crotty's vivid vision involves certain assumptions which I find arguable. I suspect that these assumptions are ethical rather than scientific, which is unobjectionable, but they are not quite clearly articulated. A basic premise of the book, for example, is that Ireland has denied large numbers of its children a livelihood. Surely it could be argued that most of the jobs that were available here fifty years ago in the form of ill-paid positions as menial servants and agricultural labourers are still here, but none would be willing to take them? The fact that Irish people feel able to refuse such work is itself a cultural change of great magnitude and not a despicable achievement. It is not Ireland's fault that it has been placed between two of the greatest economies the world has even seen and has internalised the expectations of English and American society. Furthermore, Crotty, although he is convincing about the disorganising effects of colonialism in many cases, is a little too glib about the successes of other types of society; Communist China, for example, although never colonised, has yet to make an economic breakthrough, and, on the other hand, the thoroughly colonised Indian sub-continent has made much impressive progress. The 'settler colonies' of Argentina, Chile and Uruguay, which should have enjoyed high rates of economic growth, have in fact slid into economic stagnation and political chaos. The Irish growth rate, although unimpressive, is as good as that of the Soviet Union, a country that, according to Crotty, was never colonised, and far better than that of Poland, a country which has arguably been ruined by state hostility to the peasantry.

A great merit of Crotty's argument is that, whatever its theoretical and empirical weaknesses, it points directly to one major obstacle to reform: the existence of a series of powerful and irresponsible veto-groups in the Irish polity. The Irish political system is so arranged as to give the power of prohibition to groups which do not have to live with the consequences of prohibiting change. The Catholic Church encourages large families, but demands that others provide employment for the resulting young people: trade unions drive up wage rates and demand higher taxes, thus squeezing worker's out of the system, but since these workers are not there anymore, the unions escape the political consequences of their own hostility to workers who are not unionised; farmers refuse to be taxed, but vote against any party which attempts to bring their subsidies down to a level appropriate to their meagre contribution to the society. The system as a whole exports surplus labour and has indeed tried to shore up its incompetent and inefficient political economy by a mixture of clientelist politics and foreign borrowing. My own suspicion is, however, that the resumption of emigration means that the Irish have got away with it again, and will be allowed to shuffle forward for another while in the slovenly fashion to which they have become habituated. This is a book whose parts are superior to the whole. The parts, however, are sometimes very good indeed.

Administration, vol. 51, nos. 1-2 (Spring/Summer 2003), 304–308

Understanding Contemporary Ireland

ANN LAVAN

Book Review

Understanding Contemporary Ireland: State, Class and Development in the Republic of Ireland, by Richard Breen, Damian F. Hannan, David B. Rottman and Christoper Whelan, Dublin: Gill and Macmillan, 1990. 248 pp., £9.99.

Originally published in 1990, vol. 38, no.1, 92-95.
Ann Lavan was then a lecturer in Social Administration and Social Work, University College Dublin.

Ten years of sociological research on Irish society form the basis for this important book. The authors argue that despite general prosperity, the benefits of Ireland's belated economic development have been very unevenly distributed, leading to a growing polarisation between social classes. The book is divided into a preface and ten chapters covering: the social/class structure since independence; the patterns of change in the Irish class structure; the role of the state in distribution/redistribution of income via taxes and transfers; state policy in the area of the family; education and the promise of reform; employment, unemployment and industrial policy; industrial relations and the state; and agricultural policy and politics.

Ireland is depicted as a country which industrialised late and rapidly, consequently sharing with other countries on the European periphery an uneasy intermingling of tradition and modernity. Unlike other European countries, however, Ireland has a long history of political and economic domination by a colonial power. This makes it a unique testing ground for ideas concerning the development process and its consequences. The authors examine and highlight elements in the social structure, but the main emphasis is on social process: 'the sequence of development that has shaped modern Ireland and the dynamics for future change implicit in the structure of contemporary Irish society'.

In chapter 2 the changing autonomy and capacity of the Irish state is assessed. Autonomy refers to the ability of a state to formulate and pursue its own goals while capacity indicates the state's ability to implement the policies suggested by its goals. Four structural features are identified which affected the autonomy of the Irish state. In addition five factors that largely restricted the capacity of the Irish state are identified: (i) a role of financier rather than provider of services, (ii) the extent of the voluntary sector, (iii) the yield from taxation, (iv) allocation of responsibility for implementation to state-sponsored or state-owned enterprises and (v) a heavy reliance on expert advisers and official commissions. The combination of an auxiliary state, church and state partnerships, and state autonomy was, by the 1940s, ineffective for achieving the goal of economic viability and the mechanisms for a new strategy and a restructured and revitalised state evolved. It is in this context that 1958 has a claim to be one of the significant milestones in the evolution of Irish society and Irish nationalism. During the 1950s and 1960s Irish society was cast in its modern mould: problems of the 1980s are traceable to decisions about industrial policy or taxation policy. Expansion was funded not by increased taxation or reduction of expenditure but by borrowing. A modernising elite within the civil service provided the momentum for developments which were conceptualised in national rather than in class terms. Successive governments sought to negate distributional conflict through growth. Hence, the significance of the 1960s catchphrase, 'the rising tide that lifts all boats'. From 1958 onwards, say the authors of this work, 'state and class structure evolved in tandem'.

Economic expansion, when it was finally achieved, created a new range of opportunities, primarily for wage employment, and by the 1970s the class structure had been transformed to one based on skills and educational qualifications. By the 1980s, the new class structure was fully in place. Ireland had clearly ceased to be characterised as *petit bourgeois*: the predominant categories of large scale employers and well-qualified employees was established. The changes in the class composition of the Irish work-force emerged from an industrial development that was more state inspired than in most West societies. 'Even in 1983, a substantial share of the work-force was in residual classes stranded in the course of industrial development, especially farmers on marginal holdings and labourers without skills. The only European parallels for such a presence are in the south: Greece, Portugal and Spain. People in these marginal categories have little opportunity to transfer to the more favourably-placed categories: their children's chances are little better, perpetuating marginality within families'.

Chapter 4 scrutinises the various forms of income available in Ireland over the 1970s and the 1980s, focusing on the role of the state in channelling that distribution throughout the class structure. The state's most direct role was through creation of numerous places in the more advantaged employee categories within the public sector itself. Rapid expansion of state social services ensured the viability, although at a low standard of living, of small farmers and low skilled manual workers. Providers of services experienced substantial rises in their incomes. A distinctive feature of this Irish welfare state is the state's extensive commitment to finance services, and its lack of control over how the taxpayer's money is spent. Education and health remain under the firm control of those subsidiary groups which provide the services. As the state sought to play a mediating role through establishing and ultimately participating in corporatist structures, its commitments and thus its expenditure rose. Public expectations for enhanced social services comparable to the neighbouring British welfare state increased despite disparities in resources.

The rising tide of economic prosperity and the increased activism of the Irish state ended Ireland's demographic uniqueness. Irish people now marry at much the same age as in other European countries. (On the other hand while Irish fertility may be declining rapidly, present rates are significantly higher than all other member states of the EC.) New family forms emerged with the introduction of social welfare payments to deserted wives and unmarried mothers. The increased participation of married women in the labour force is one of the clearest indicators of the extent and suddenness of the change in the Irish family. Today the State possesses rather more autonomy in determining its policies relating to the family, though the decisive rejection by the electorate of a referendum permitting divorce provides dramatic evidence of limits to state action in Ireland in contrast to the rest of Catholic Europe.

In chapters 6-9, the argument is further elaborated: the Irish state has not (a) sustained economic growth, or (b) moderated inegalitarian tendencies in the class system. The logic of industrial and agricultural development led to an increasing bifurcation of the class structure between, on the one hand, the urban middle and upper working class and, on the other, the better-off farmers. The welfare state, it is argued, emerged in the 1960s largely because of the intensification of competition for political office which led to a remarkable expansion in public expenditure accompanied by active maintenance of political ideologies which deny the importance of class conflict. New advisory fora did not develop into genuinely neo-corporatist structures serving the function of interest intermediation. State action in Ireland altered the distribution of occupational opportunities but without exercising a great deal of influence over access to such opportunities. Those in the marginal categories had little opportunity to transfer to the expanding categories. The restrictions on the mobility opportunity of their children ensured that in today's class structure one quarter of the gainfully occupied are in positions which depend for their viability on state social welfare schemes. The major factor dictating policy is political expediency.

What is striking in the Irish case, it is argued, is the very direct nature of the link between public expenditure and the viability of class positions: (1) those who rely directly on the state for their income: the unemployed, the disabled, the aged, deserted wives, unmarried mothers and marginalised farmers, who are wholly or partially dependent upon social welfare payments; (2) direct employees of the state: public servants defined to include workers in central and local government, state-sponsored bodies, health board employees, teachers and so on; (3) those contracted by the state to provide services: General Medical Service and consultants employed by government departments; (4) those who rely on industry and agriculture subsidies, tax expenditures and favourable taxation schedules; (5) those who own or hold all forms of property dependent on the state's lenient taxation policy.

The authors conclude that recent trends indicate that addressing the unemployment problem will have to await the solution to the debt problem. The question which remains is whether genuine neo-corporatist fora can be developed which will advance the inevitably increased visibility of the interests served by the role of the state.

This book will be a particularly valuable textbook for teaching with a rich source of data, analysis and theoretical perspective. The central argument and discussion on specific policy areas will undoubtedly form the basis for on-going debate. The declared intention of this book is to contribute to a growing body of work which seeks to improve understanding of the circumstances which encourage the pursuit of autonomous goals by the state and the conditions which affect its capacity to pursue such goals effectively. The failure, therefore, to include a number of seminal references is surprising, e.g. P. Clancy, S. Drudy, K. Lynch, L. O'Dowd, (eds) *Ireland, a Social Profile,* Dublin, Institute of Public Administration, 1986, with the Sociological Association of Ireland; R. Crotty, *Ireland in Crisis, A Study in Capitalist Colonial Undevelopment*, Brandon Books, 1986; Peillon, *Contemporary Irish Society, An Introduction*, Dublin: Gill and Macmillan, 1982. The complexity of the picture with regard to social mobility is underlined by Michael Hout in *Following in Father's Footsteps*, Cambridge Mass: Harvard University Press, 1989. The increasing appearance of local and regional studies and indigenous work both on and by marginal groups is undermining premature and sometimes misleading national generalisations and forging new awareness of the richness, complexity and varieties of Irish society. A particularly disconcerting perspective in this work is the casual use of the term 'underclass'. Though used repeatedly in the text (p 11, p 17, p 49), it is not included in the index and is not subjected to rigorous analysis. Given the central argument of the authors this is puzzling. The publication of Charles Murray, *Losing Ground*, New York: Basic Books, 1984, rekindled a very specific currency for the term 'underclass'. Its introduction into the discourse on contemporary Irish society must be challenged vigorously. If the role of *critical social science* is about raising discussion on crisis tendencies (C. Offe and J. Keane, *Contradictions of the Welfare State*, London: Hutchinson, 1984), a proposition about an *Irish underclass* has yet to be formulated. This work is a powerful critique of the differences in *life chances* evident in the Irish social structure.

Administration, vol. 51, nos.1-2 (Spring/Summer 2003), 309–325

The Politics of Conviviality: Voluntary Workfare and the Right to Useful Unemployment

GEORGE TAYLOR

Originally published in 1995, vol. 43, no. 3, 36-56.
George Taylor was at the time Director of the Centre for Public Policy, University College, Galway.

INTRODUCTION

I choose the term 'conviviality' to designate the opposite of industrial productivity. I intend it to mean autonomous and creative intercourse among persons, and the intercourse of persons with their environment; and this is in contrast with the conditioned response of persons to the demands made upon them by others, and by a man-made environment. I consider conviviality to be individual freedom realised in personal interdependence and, as such, an intrinsic ethical value (Illich, 1973, p. 11).

As the most recent budget in Ireland testifies, political discourse has become increasingly concerned with the cost, impact and function of the welfare state. Once viewed as a component crucial to the completion of any democracy, the institutions of the welfare state are now the subject of intense scrutiny. Indeed, irrespective of political persuasion it has become increasingly evident that the final curtain-call on the Keynesian Welfare State (KWS)'[1] has been made; charged with being a monolithic institutional apparatus ill-suited to the prevailing conditions of contemporary capitalism, it has been fatally wounded by persistent unemployment and increasing poverty. Appraisals from a wide variety of political commentators have argued that capitalism has moved into a new, dynamic phase in which flexibility of productive systems, personnel and organisational strategy are paramount. Business, it is argued, can no longer sustain the level of economic growth upon which both the welfare state and trade union influence upon public policy were predicated.[2] Put simply, the KWS is now viewed as an increasingly anachronistic structure within an era of flexible specialisation.[3] Debate is concerned no longer with equity, redistribution, and efficiency, but with the complicated process of organising consent around new definitions of poverty.

Clearly, one of the more important influences stimulating the search for alternatives to the KWS has been the emergence of a new underclass, a socially excluded layer that has been ostracised progressively from labour, housing and educational markets. As Hoggett observes, the dominant paradigm of the 1960s and 1970s revolved essentially around attempts to incorporate the socially disadvantaged (Hoggett 1994). By the 1990s, this process had been largely reversed as a succession of west European governments sought to abandon the level of commitments embodied within the political and institutional apparatus of the KWS. In stark contrast, the emergent themes within public policy appear now to hinge upon political and spatial exclusion (Hoggett 1994). This is highlighted in the case of Germany, where, as Offe remarks, the austerity measures of the 1980s were designed to effect peripheral groups in society, reducing the possibility of becoming a focal point of collective action. Such measures were 'largely imperceptible to the wider public' (Offe 1991, p. 138). This strategy, Offe argues, was rationally 'inclined to grant relative protection to active labour market participants' (Offe 1991, p. 140).

The persistence of a combination of high levels of structural unemployment and increasing levels of poverty has made the search for alternatives to the KWS of paramount importance Moreover, the changing structure of households and labour markets would appear to offer little respite from such a bleak picture. It is in this context, then, that the work of Healy and Reynolds should be welcomed as part of an initiative to extend the debate on the future of the Irish welfare state (Healy and Reynolds 1993). In essence, their work is motivated by an attempt to reassert the social dimension to citizenship and question the assumptions about public policy and efficiency which lie at the heart of both the KWS and its neo-liberal critique. Thus, Healy and Reynolds argue vigorously that successive decades of state intervention have ignominiously failed either to reduce the level of poverty or to ensure adequate levels of employment. Their conclusion remains both forceful and unequivocal: that the dominant paradigm of the post-war period has been a 'spectacular failure' (Healy and Reynolds 1993, p. 54).

The work of Healy and Reynolds forms part of a burgeoning body of literature which attempts to provide the basis for a new form of citizenship (see Purdy 1995). This body of research argues that a reconstructed view of citizenship needs to be capable of embracing both the ecological and feminist agendas within an individualist framework. It proposes the rejection of the traditional dichotomies of modern society: feminism and patriarchy; capital and labour and economic growth and ecological degradation. However, although the work of Healy and Reynolds can be placed firmly within this emerging field of research, their position differs from the consensus in one important respect: they explicitly acknowledge the importance of work to the dignity of the human being.

This paper argues, however, that while controversial proposals such as voluntary workfare and a basic guaranteed income raise important issues for debate, they do not offer the basis for a new paradigm towards full citizenship. More specifically, this paper challenges Healy and Reynolds on four key areas.

First, it suggests that their work lacks a consistent understanding of the relationship between the state and the economy. All too often, they assume that policy emerges simply from within the institutional apparatus of the state and pays scant regard to the complex constraints imposed by the dynamics of national/international capital.

Second, it criticises their conception of work and, in particular, the failure to address the importance of issues such as power, discipline, order and control which pervade day-to-day working relations. Nowhere is the omission more glaring than in their perception of the public sector which is presented as little more than a cosy idyll, immune from the more onerous inequities imposed by market forces.

Third, it questions their perception of the relationship between citizenship and the nation state. The growing internationalisation of employment, the problem of immigration and/or a return of emigrants all pose serious questions to a purely 'national' response to the development of full citizenship.

Finally, there is a discernible tendency to conflate those sectors of the 'potential workforce' that are acutely vulnerable to unemployment within the all-encompassing group of unemployed. I am more than willing to concede, for example, that voluntary workfare may well appeal to a particular group of unemployed people who have little prospect of future employment because they are nearing retirement. However, that is a far cry from providing a policy initiative to which the youth or long-term unemployed of this country will respond. In sum, their analysis is underpinned by a convivial view of the world, one which ignores the dynamics and conflicts endemic to capitalist relations of production. As such, this paper maintains that the idea of voluntary workfare forms less of a basis for a new paradigm toward full citizenship and more a manifesto for a right to useful unemployment.

Consequently, this paper is divided into three sections. The *first* section offers an introduction to both the social democratic consensus which underpinned the post-war welfare state and its neo-liberal critique. The *second* section details the two core themes of the framework which Healy and Reynolds propose as an alternative:

voluntary workfare and the right to a basic guaranteed income. The *third* and final section offers a number of substantive criticisms of their position.

SOCIAL CITIZENSHIP AND THE WELFARE STATE

> The plan for social security is put forward as part of a general programme of social policy. It is one part of an attack upon the five giant evils: upon the physical *Want* with which we are directly concerned, upon *Disease* which often causes Want and brings many troubles in its train, upon *Ignorance* which no democracy can afford among its citizens, upon *Squalor* which arises mainly through the haphazard distribution of industry and population, and upon *Idleness* which destroys wealth and corrupts men ... the purpose of victory is to live in a better world than the old world.... (Beveridge 1942, p. 171).

To many political observers the institutionalisation of the welfare state represented a decisive victory for the political forces of the labour movement, a vindication of the positive sum reformism of social democracy (Pierson 1991, p. 1). Within this historic compromise between the forces of capital and labour there are two key elements: a series of concessions made to the working class and a shared status that everyone then enjoyed as full citizens of the nation state.

There are few who would find difficulty in accepting the view that what sustained the appeal of Keynes' vision of managed capitalism was its ability to reconcile the conflicting interests of both capital and labour through a political promise to deliver full employment. For a succession of post-war European governments it provided the tantalising prospect of both an electoral mandate and a succession of economic tools for an interventionist government (Pierson 1991, p. 27).

An explicit theme within the emerging social democratic consensus of the immediate post-war period was that an extension of the welfare state was predicated not upon establishing a minimum level of welfare, but upon an extension of social as well as civil and political rights. As a consequence, the welfare state extended beyond the realm of education, health and income maintenance to encompass full employment policies, environmental regulation, work safety, low wage councils and retraining programmes (see Pfaller and Gough 1991, p. 2 and Hills *et al* 1994).

However, it is important to recognise that such an evolutionary conception of citizenship fell short of endorsing the need to establish formal equality. Certainly, those such as Marshall anticipated that an expansion in social rights would lead to a 'general enrichment of the concrete substance of civilised life', a reduction in risk and insecurity, and an 'equalisation between the more or less fortunate at all levels' (Bottomore 1992, p. 33). However, while the alleviation of poverty was certainly a crucial consideration for any progressive democratic polity, formal equality remained an aspiration and not an explicit policy objective. As Marshall noted:

> The more you look on wealth as conclusive proof of merit, the more you incline to regard poverty as evidence of failure – but the penalty of failure may seem to be greater than the offence warrants ... as the social conscience stirs to life, class abatement … becomes a desirable aim to be pursued *as far as is compatible with the continued efficiency of the social machine* (Bottomore 1992, p. 20) (my emphasis).

Klausen, in a recent critical review of Marshall's work on citizenship has argued that it is erroneous to regard social citizenship as the equivalent of civil and political rights and instead it is important to distinguish between rights and redistribution (Klausen 1995). In his opinion, civil and political rights are indivisible and non-transferable rights belonging to the individual. In contrast, social rights are redistributive and are therefore premised upon the fiscal capacities of the state (Klausen 1995, p. 245). As he observes, a closer scrutiny of the welfare programmes throughout western Europe suggests that the assumption that social citizenship implies the granting of social rights with no strings attached, to certain groups, is misleading. Ideas such as universalism, citizenship and solidarity may have pervaded the rhetorical themes of social democracy, but few programmes ever lived up to their expectations. As Klausen points out, entitlement policing, based on the willingness to work or market availability, was an integral feature of most welfare programmes throughout the post-war period (Klausen 1995, p. 248).

The central thrust of many developments in the welfare state during the 1980s was to tighten the grip on entitlement policing. Social rights, as an attribute of citizenship, have been gradually eroded as governments sought to reduce public expenditure, privatise public industry and to reassert the primacy of individual self-help. However, Klausen's contention that civil and political rights are fundamentally different to social rights ignores the fact that civil and political rights have also been the subject of struggle and change. As Bottomore maintains, for those citizens who have been increasingly marginalised, the prospect of seeking redress in the courts to affronts on their civil rights, has significantly diminished (Bottomore 1992).

The debate over the social dimension to citizenship has been pivotal to the New Right's critique of the welfare state. The power of this critique rests upon its assertion that the welfare state represents a constraint upon individual freedom and an exercise in economic mismanagement. For authors such as Hayek, there is a crucial distinction to be drawn between two competing conceptions of security which underpin debates about the welfare state:

> A limited security which can be achieved for all and which is, therefore, no privilege, and an absolute security, which in a free society cannot be achieved for all ... the latter is closely related to the third main ambition that inspires the welfare state: the desire to use the powers of government to ensure a more even or more just distribution of goods (Hayek 1960, p. 259).

Hayek's view of citizenship implicitly acknowledges a radical departure from that which has prevailed in the post-war period. Citizens are no longer entitled to expect an expanding set of social and political rights. Rather, individuals have a set of necessary obligations and duties that they must perform before they can be considered citizens. For Hayek, liberty and responsibility are inseparable and a free society will not function unless its citizens regard it as right that 'each individual occupy the position that results from his action and accept it as due to his own action' (1960, p. 72). Here, Hayek, among others, argues that there is an irreconcilable conflict between the aspiration toward equality embodied within the welfare state and the liberal view of freedom. Liberals such as Hayek argue that individuals are endowed with different levels of ability and motivation. Policies designed to promote equality thus represent a forlorn attempt on the part of the state to impose uniformity upon what is extreme social diversity. As a consequence the state is engaged in a paternalistic exercise designed to impose a politically-defined form of equity that ultimately impinges upon the freedom of individuals.

For the New Right, then, the welfare state's role should be a residual one, acting only to ensure a safety net for those who are unable to secure employment because of either ill-health, disability, or lack of initiative. In a 'truly free' society entitlements to health care, education or pensions are goods that should be provided by the free market. There is no substantive difference, then, between the purchase of cigarettes or private health insurance. Within such a social policy configuration, welfare benefits are targeted only according to needs and not to some spurious commitment to redistribution or equality (Green 1988).

Within the New Right's case against state intervention, it is possible to discern at least two other themes that have an important bearing on Irish public policy. First, there is the immediate call for the withdrawal of the state from public sector industry. Not surprisingly, *Team Aer Lingus* and *Irish Steel* are cited as cases symptomatic of the sclerosis which has become endemic to Irish public sector industry. It is not just that these industries suffer twin poor management/union relations, although it is rare for this not to be cited as the major factor, rather the state imposes a series of institutional rigidities which are a burden upon any industry operating within an internationally competitive environment.[4] The second theme, one integral to this overall neo-liberal position, is the issue of macro-political bargaining. Here, opponents to such agreements argue that macro-political forms of bargaining impose rigidities on labour markets which undermine the ability of management to exploit local labour market conditions (Taylor 1994).

It has always been a common assumption of neo-classical economists that efficiency in the use of labour can he provided through the minimisation of recruitment costs and the ease with which people can be dismissed. In this context neo-classical economists argue that the wave of corporatist bargaining of the 1970s and 1980s increased the level of employment protection legislation, diminishing the prospect for labour markets to be 'cleared' (workers to be fired with ease) (Dore 1988, p. 400). From such a perspective, macro-political bargaining simply exacerbates this problem by allowing unions to secure wage increases above the market level in periods of high unemployment. In the Irish context, the balance between tax and its alleged burden on private sector enterprise has become an increasingly politicised issue. It is not simply a question of the level of welfare entitlements, although this in itself tends to raise the hackles of any committed neo-liberal economist; rather it is a debate about what are the limits to governmental activity.

VOLUNTARY WORKFARE: THE RIGHT TO USEFUL UNEMPLOYMENT

A cursory glance at the Irish economy would suggest that despite recessionary times in most of Europe, Ireland's current position contains encouraging signs. Government debt may still be ominously large but present budgetary constraints have eased. Moreover, forecasts suggest that the picture of relatively high levels of economic growth and low inflation is likely to continue for the next two or three years. And yet, even the most optimistic observers appear resigned to the fact that growth rates in excess of 5 per cent per annum will be insufficient to reduce significantly the current levels of unemployment. It seems quite clear that, along with most of its west European counterparts, high levels of unemployment will remain a semi-permanent feature of the Irish economy.

It is from this painful observation that Healy and Reynolds' position stems. They argue that Irish socio-economic policy continues to be formulated around the misplaced conviction that:

> full-time jobs should be available for everyone seeking them, that these jobs should provide adequate income for people holding them and that ... good social insurance should be available for people who were sick or unemployed (Healy and Reynolds 1993, p. 40).

For Healy and Reynolds the link between unemployment and poverty has been well established. Further, they believe that the previous paradigm, organised as it was around the right to work, patently failed to remove poverty within contemporary Ireland. This failure has been compounded by the insistence on the part of the Irish welfare state that people make themselves available for non-existent jobs. They maintain that if we are to construct a new paradigm we must question the assumptions which underpin the relationship between work and income. From the outset, we need to confront the unchallenged assumption that 'working' and doing a job are identical. Echoing calls from feminist groups, Healy and Reynolds suggest that traditional interpretations of the relationship between useful work and jobs ignore key features of work undertaken by women in society. Those whose work is carried out primarily in either the household or a voluntary organisation are not recognised as being 'in work'.

Consequently, one of the essential changes required in this new paradigm is that the promise of 'wealth, power, control and economic growth' associated with full-time employment needs to be complemented with the 'dynamics of belonging, nurturing, caring, receptivity and self-giving' (Healy and Reynolds 1993, p. 69). It is an issue upon which Klausen concurs. He notes, for example, that while motherhood and nurturing belong to the private domain, and as such are not commodified, it is nevertheless socially desirable work that the state should provide (Klausen 1995, p. 260)

Under the consensus established within the post-war period, the issue of income distribution was intrinsically linked to full-time employment. In the aftermath of the fiscal crisis of the 1970s and the persistent levels of unemployment in the 1980s, this consensus has become increasingly challenged. Such a prolonged period of unemployment has meant that almost a third of the Irish population now depends on social welfare payments of one form or another (Healy and Reynolds 1993).

It is a position which has been complicated further by changes which are currently taking place in household structures and labour markets. In this context it is hardly surprising that there are few observers who do not believe that the relationship between work and citizenship will become an increasingly politicised issue. In the light of such difficulties, Healy and Reynolds suggest that a radical departure from the Keynesian welfare paradigm is required, one which recognises that meaningful work is dependent upon:

> the introduction of some system of income distribution which provides a guaranteed basic income to every person in society… an income paid unconditionally to all on an individual basis without means test or any requirement to work (Healy and Reynolds 1993, p. 73).

A guaranteed basic income represents the first step towards a new paradigm for citizenship. In the variant proposed by Healy and Reynolds, this is to be complemented by a programme of voluntary workfare. Such moves explicitly anticipate the removal of entitlement policing. As Healy and Reynolds observe, the very presence of such a policy denies a large body of the population access to meaningful work because they have to be available for non-existent jobs (Healy and Reynolds 1993, pp. 74-5). The removal of this regulation could reap immediate and tangible benefits. In the British case, for example, it has been estimated that the costs associated with the administration, policing and litigation far exceed the delivery of routine transfers which could be easily automated (Purdy 1995). Although Healy and Reynolds would find little difficulty in accepting such arguments it is the link between work and dignity, in an environment of high unemployment, which remains important. In this context they argue that:

> We are not advocating compulsory workfare programmes where unemployed people are forced to do specific work under threat of forfeiting their dole payments if they refuse. Such an approach would only create greater division in Irish society. But we believe strongly that the vast majority of unemployed people wish to contribute to development and should be enabled to do so voluntarily. Such an approach would go a long way towards reducing the current exclusion experienced by unemployed people (Healy and Reynolds 1993, p. 75).

This programme of voluntary workfare, largely organised through public sector bodies, would not only re-establish the link between work and dignity but would also tackle the current culture of enforced dependency among unemployed people. The remaining sections of this paper provide a number of substantive criticisms of the ideas contained in this programme of voluntary workfare.

WELFARE UNDER CAPITALISM

> Capitalism cannot coexist with, neither can it exist without, the welfare state (Offe 1984, p. 153).

It seems almost inconceivable that any discussion of changes in the nature of the welfare state could be undertaken without an analysis of the changing nature of the relationship between the state and the capitalist economy. The welfare state is a phenomenon peculiar to capitalism, precisely because it is engaged in the reproduction of the social relations of production. However, this need not ignore the fact that the relationship between the welfare state and the economy involves tensions and contradictions (Jessop 1991). Thus, as Jessop amply demonstrates, the relationship between the market and the state is conflictual, problematic and unstable. Nevertheless, while welfare policies are linked to the particular political conjuncture in which they developed, they also impact on its function in social reproduction (Jessop 1991, p. 83). In this sense, the state may be deemed capitalist only in the extent to which it maintains the conditions for capital accumulation. However, as the vast welfare programmes of the post-war period show, welfare policies are largely concerned not with the nature of capitalist production but with maintaining the social conditions of production and alleviating its excesses.

Since the fiscal crisis of the state during the 1970s and early 1980s, a vast body of literature has highlighted the tensions in the relationship between the welfare state and the economy. Tax revenues declined sharply while welfare commitments rose as governments in western Europe experienced sustained periods of structural unemployment. These problems were exacerbated by features endemic to the KWS; centralisation, bureaucracy and clientelism (Jessop 1991, p. 92).

Within the work of Healy and Reynolds the changing nature of the relationship between the state and the economy is almost totally ignored. Little or no attention is paid to the role of the welfare state in reproducing the conditions for capital accumulation. Issues such as low pay, poverty and entitlement policing are addressed in isolation, with little understanding of how they relate to the problems of capital accumulation with which west-European governments are currently grappling. The real issue that remains is the extent to which the welfare state can be restructured or reduced without seriously undermining the capitalist economy. Had Healy and Reynolds addressed this question from the outset they would no doubt have examined the relationship between the role of voluntary workfare programmes and the nature of work, the function of entitlement policing and the changes which have taken place in the public sector during the 1980s. All of these issues are linked to the changing role of the state and its relationship with the economy.

VOLUNTARY WORKFARE: A WOLF IN SHEEP'S CLOTHING?

One of the more commonplace objections to proposals for a voluntary workfare programme is the possibility that it could act as a precursor to a fully-fledged programme of compulsory workfare. In their defence, Healy and Reynolds have been particularly keen to distance themselves from such an avenue. However, while they may wish to reject such a policy this paper argues that they have paid insufficient attention to this dilemma. Indeed, if we were to agree with their central proposition that voluntary workfare would provide meaningful work, this automatically poses a very serious question: why should anyone not want to do meaningful work? Here, there is the very real prospect that a new division among the disenfranchised will emerge – the deserving unemployed and the undeserving unemployed. Envisage a scenario, for example, in which the programme became either an outstanding success or the economy lurched into a prolonged period of economic retrenchment. In such instances it is all too easy to see a situation in which the 'voluntary' dimension would be quickly jettisoned. A further source of ambiguity lies in their failure to identify the nature of the tasks that will form the basis of 'meaningful work'. Within the framework devised by Healy and Reynolds, voluntary workfare programmes are intended to take place almost exclusively inside the public sector. And yet, what they patently fail to address is the nature of the voluntary jobs to be found in local authorities, health boards or libraries. Are we to take seriously, for example, the claim that voluntary recruits can simply be placed in hospitals or local authorities where a host of meaningful opportunities exist or, should we be more sceptical and suggest that it is more likely that voluntary recruits will perform the menial tasks deemed expendable in the rush toward cuts in public expenditure?

This decision to locate voluntary workfare programmes inside the 'public sector' reveals further flaws in Healy and Reynolds' position. Of particular interest is the question of why meaningful work (voluntary workfare) cannot take place in the private sector. Is it simply the fact that voluntary workfare is incompatible with the managerial imperative to assert control and power within the workplace? There are two further flaws to be found in this position. First, all too often Healy and Reynolds perceive the public sector as some form of politically constructed sanctuary, removed from the excesses of competitive capitalism. Second, they neglect consideration of the dramatic changes which have taken place in the public sector during the 1980s. Both points reinforce the 'convivial view of the world' which permeates the framework endorsed by Healy and Reynolds.

'MEANINGFUL WORK' IN A CAPITALIST SOCIETY

> The degradation of work brings with it the de-colonisation of knowledge; employers do not like the educated, above all the intelligent worker ... Still absence of mind won't do either: inattention and forgetfulness could occasion as many disasters as lucid thought; it is necessary to be there, a vigilance without content, a captive consciousness kept awake only the better to suppress itself (Sartre, J.P., *The Communists and the Peace*).

At the very heart of Healy and Reynolds' position is the belief that the dignity of the human being is intrinsically related to the inherent features of work. It is through voluntary work, Healy and Reynolds argue, that those who have been socially excluded can once again begin to reconstruct their identities and re-establish their position within the community. In this view, voluntary workfare represents an avenue through which people can remove themselves from the culture of dependency. This perception of unemployment, however, tends to support the view that such experiences follow a familiar pattern: shock – optimism – pessimism – fatalism. However, whether shock or outrage at the initial experience of unemployment is followed by other stages depends on a wide variety of factors: age, health, local labour market conditions and any severance conditions granted by the employer (Sinfield 1980). Presumably, a voluntary workfare programme, in whatever guise, would be required to consider the different experiences entailed in being unemployed if it was to have any sustained appeal to the large majority of unemployed people.

Perhaps one of the more glaring omissions within Healy and Reynolds' position is the fact that they appear not to recognise that work under capitalism is not simply about 'meaning', about jobs: it has a single purpose, profit. Dignity for most workers is expressed in not co-operating with management, in resisting new forms of work practices and the introduction of new forms of technology (Nichols and Beynon 1977). The social relations of production under capitalism must necessarily produce workers who are controlled and exploited. Work relations inevitably involve a struggle between workers and management within the context of changing market opportunities and technological innovations. It is not that the organisation of work should be perceived as the result of a particular managerial strategy, rather that it should be perceived as the complex interaction between new technology, trade unions, management and state activity. The issues of control, power, exploitation and struggle appear to be irreconcilable with Healy and Reynolds' conception of voluntary workfare (Wood 1982; Hyman 1987, 1989). As if to compound this problem they ignore the fact that relations of power and exploitation are an endemic feature of the public sector.

COSY IDYLLS AND POLITICAL SANCTUARIES: VOLUNTARY WORKFARE IN THE PUBLIC SECTOR

A vast body of literature has emerged over the last decade which details the assault that has taken place on the public sector as governments sought to reduce public expenditure. Although the programme of privatisation pursued in Britain was perhaps the most visible expression of this process, it was by no means an isolated case. Strategies aimed at reducing the public sector deficit ensured that commercialism moved to the fore in dictating managerial practices in the public sector (see A. Ferner 1988; C. Pollitt 1993; L. Metcalfe and S. Richards 1987).

The tendency within Healy and Reynolds' work is to ignore the presence and impact of such changes. And yet, as Pollitt notes, within the contemporary public sector context it is possible to substitute the phrase 'market forces' with 'cash limits, performance indicators and staff cuts' (C. Pollitt 1993, p. 302). Moreover, as a number of studies have highlighted, the challenge for public sector management during the 1980s was to develop a new culture around which learning, adaptability and flexibility could flourish. Salaman, for example, argues that the preoccupation within Taylorism for 'the stick and carrot' has been replaced with a concern to create the 'right climate' in which to encourage identification with corporate goals, high motivation and the internalisation of constructive attitudes (Salaman 1981). Ireland has not been isolated from such changes. It is becoming increasingly likely that the provision of services in the health sector will no longer be administered but managed. This process involves a new strategy of control, a shift from the bureaucratic paradigm of controlling professionals through managers to one that converts professionals into managers. The responsibility for achieving predetermined objectives on information, performance and evaluation will be an inherent feature of the managerial task in the public sector (Joyce and Ham 1990; Hoggett 1994).

The issue of control and its function in managerial strategy also raises important concerns about the relationship between paid, full-time staff and voluntary recruits. Here it is important to caution against the superficial view that because voluntary recruits are not paid in the conventional sense, there will he no antagonism between the respective forms of employment. Certainly, research into these relationships in the voluntary sector suggests that differences over performance, commitment, status and professionalism represent key areas of tension. Faughnan, for example, points out that 'there are sharp differences ... in the role they [volunteers] play, the level of commitment expected and the extent to which time and resources are allocated at organisational level in providing support and training' (Faughnan and Kelleher 1990, p. 20).

Similarly, Bulmer's contribution in this field claims that 'professional roles and the roles of informal care-givers are different, and there exist considerable problems in attempting to integrate the two. It cannot be assumed that the two will happily co-exist side by side' (Bulmer 1986, p. 214). A significant obstacle to integrating the work of professionals and volunteers is the difference in status. In many of the neighbourhood caring schemes studied, for instance, Bulmer notes that the professionals, who were generally from a higher social class than the volunteers, were accorded a higher status. Other sources of tension to integrating the work of professionals and volunteers discussed by Bulmer include the differences in roles, the gap between the often emotional involvement of volunteers and the detachment of professionals, and the difficulties posed by integrating volunteers into formal channels of accountability (Bulmer 1986).

In the case of the US, Schindler-Rainmann (1988) identifies a number of problems that develop between professionals and volunteers in voluntary agencies. She claims that the use of volunteers to extend the work of professionals can give rise to concern about professional standards and that the 'idea that volunteers with relatively brief training can be expected to do some of the things the professionals spent years getting trained for is a threat and a source of genuine professional concern' (Schindler-Rainmann 1988, 17.9). This is compounded by the fact that professionals tend to lack any specific training in relation to recruiting, training, supervising and supporting volunteers. The research undertaken by Schindler-Rainmann also suggests that many professionals would prefer working with paid para-professionals rather than volunteers, as they 'feel that volunteers are much more difficult to deal with in defined role relationships, and much less predictable in terms of commitment and responsiveness to supervision' (Schindler-Rainmann 1988, 17.9). Although much of this research has been undertaken in the voluntary sector, it nevertheless highlights the potential difficulties which could emerge in a large-scale programme designed to introduce voluntary sector recruits into the public sector (Varley and O'Donovan 1995).

CITIZENSHIP AND IMMIGRATION

One of the more difficult problems encountered in post-war attempts to enhance the social dimension to citizenship was the large-scale immigration of foreign workers into particular countries. It is an issue that has returned to the political agenda as the growing internationalisation of employment, especially in the European Union, casts doubt on whether the nation state can still be regarded as the principal locus of citizenship (Bottomore 1992, p. 72). In such instances, the changing nature of the global economy, the problem of immigration and/or a return of emigrants all pose serious questions to a purely 'national' response to the development of full citizenship.

There are few observers in Ireland who would not concur with the view that emigration during periods of high unemployment has acted as a safety valve through which to dissipate potential social division. However, a paradigm for citizenship which entails high levels of public policy commitments poses obstacles to the ease with which immigrants can be welcomed. Indeed, it would not be implausible to suggest that, should citizenship entitlements in Ireland exceed those in the UK, then a return of past emigrants could be a likely scenario.

CONCLUSION

Few observers of the Irish polity would deny that current levels of unemployment represent a formidable political obstacle to government policy. As the most recent budget testifies, shifts in public policy have been made not as a response to the pressures emanating from the disenfranchised, but from those active in the labour market. Within the paradox of high levels of structural unemployment and high economic growth, the Irish state is now presented with the daunting task of organising consent around the need to reformulate a new paradigm for citizenship. It is in this context that Healy and Reynolds' work should be welcomed as part of an attempt to raise important issues in this debate. However, their work remains inhibited by the fact that it is underpinned by a convivial view of the world. As a consequence, their attempt to present a reconstructed view of citizenship represents less a paradigm for full citizenship and more a manifesto for the right to useful unemployment.

NOTES TO ARTICLE

1 For many political commentators the emergence of the welfare state in the post-war period entailed an expansion in *social* rights. Such rights, according to Marshall, involved a set of rights to a basic standard of living, health and education (see Bottomore 1992). While such developments were welcomed by social democrats, it still left the thorny issue of reconciling the problems of increased public expenditure and the need to ensure economic growth. Here, Keynes' advocacy of state intervention in order to curb the 'excesses' of unbridled capitalism and ensure stable economic growth established a modicum of political control over economic life. For more detail on competing interpretations of the welfare state see Pierson 1991.

2 For a discussion on whether the welfare state impinges upon economic growth see A. Pfaller *et al.* 1991.

3 For a critical discussion of this concept see A. Pollert (1988), N. Gilbert, R. Burrows and A. Pollert (1992), R. Hyman (1988), S. Clarke (1992).

4 Although reports such as those of the National Economic and Social Council (1979, 1982) and the Industrial Policy Review Group (1992) (Culliton) fell short of arguing for full-scale privatisation, they nevertheless reflect a decade of disenchantment with the operation of public sector industry in Ireland.

REFERENCES

Beveridge, J. (1942), *Social Insurance and Allied Services*, Cmd. 6404, London, HMSO

Bottomore, T. (ed) (1992), *Citizenship and Social Class*, London, Pluto Press

Bulmer, M. (1986), *Neighbours: The Work of Philip Abrahams*, Cambridge University Press

Clarke, S. (1992), 'What in the F***d's Name is Fordism?' in Gilbert *et al.*

Dore, R. (1988), 'Rigidities in the Labour Market', *Government and Opposition*, pp. 393-412

Ferner, A. (1988), *Government Managers and Industrial Relations: Public Enterprises and their Political Environment*, Oxford, Blackwell

Faughnan, P. and Kelleher, P. (1993), *The Voluntary Sector and the State*, Dublin, Conference of Major Religious Superiors

Gilbert, N., Burrows, R. and Pollert, A. (1992), *Fordism and Flexibility: Division and Change*, London, Macmillan

Green, D.G. (1988), 'Everyone a Patient: An Analysis of the Structural Flaws in the NHS and How they Could Be Remedied', Hobart paperback 27, London, Institute for Economic Affairs

Hayek, F. (1960), *The Constitution of Liberty*, London, Routledge

Healy, S. and Reynolds, B. (1993), 'Work Jobs and Income: Towards a New Paradigm', in Healy, S. and Reynolds, B., *New Frontiers for Full Citizenship*, Dublin, Conference of Major Religious Superiors

Hills, J., Ditch, J. and Glennerster, H. (1994), *Beveridge and Social Security: An International Retrospective*, Oxford, Clarendon Press

Hoggett, P. (1994), 'The Politics of Modernisation of the UK Welfare State', in Burrows, R. and Loader, B., *Towards a Post-Fordist Welfare State*, London, Routledge

Hyman, R. (1987), 'Strategy or Structure: Capital, Labour and Control', *Work Employment and Society*

Hyman, R. (1988), 'Flexible Specialisation: Miracle or Myth?' in Hyman, R. and Streeck, W, *Industrial Relations and New Technology*, Oxford, Blackwell

Hyman, R. (1989), *The Political Economy of Industrial Relations* Basingstoke, Macmillan

Illich, I. (1973), *Tools for Conviviality*, London, Calder and Boyars

Illich, I. (1978), *The Right to Useful Unemployment,* London, Boyars

Jessop, B. (1991), 'The Welfare State in the transition from Fordism to post-Fordism', in Jessop, B. *et al*, *The Politics of Flexibility*, Aldershot, Edward Elgar

Joyce, L. and Ham, C. (1990), 'Enabling Managers to Manage: Health Care Reform in Ireland', *Administration*, 38.3, pp. 215-37

Klausen, J. (1995), 'Social Rights and State Building: T.H. Marshall in the Hands of the Social Reformer', *World Politics*, 47, pp. 244-67

Metcalfe, L. and Richards, S. (1987), 'Evolving Public management Cultures', in J. Kooiman and K.A. Eliasman (eds), *Managing Public Organisations: Lessons from Contemporary European Experience*, London, Sage

Nichols, T. and Beynon, H. (1977), *Living with Capitalism: Class Relations in the Modern Factory*, London, Routledge

Offe, C. (1984), *Contradictions of the Welfare State*, London, Hutchinson

Offe, C. (1991), 'Smooth Consolidation in the West German Welfare State: Structural Change, Fiscal Policies, and Populist Politics', in Priven, F.F., *Labour Parties in Post-Industrial Societies*, Cambridge, Polity Press

Pierson, C. (1991), *Beyond the Welfare State?*, Cambridge, Polity Press

Pfaller, A., Gough, I. and Therborn, G. (1991), *Can the Welfare State Compete?*, London, Macmillan

Pollert, A. (1988), 'The Flexible Firm: Fixation or Fact?', *Work, Employment and Society*, 2, pp. 281-316

Pollitt, C. (1993), 'The Development of Management Thought', in Hill, M., *The Policy Process: A Reader*, pp. 299-313, Hemel Hempstead, Harvester Wheatsheaf

Purdy, D. (1995), 'Citizenship, Basic Income and the State', *New Left Review*

Salaman, G. (1981), *Class and Corporatism*, London, Fontana

Schindler-Rainmann, E. (1988), 'Motivating People to Volunteer Their Services', in Connors, T.D., (ed), *The Non Profit Organisation Handbook*, New York, McGraw-Hill

Sinfield, A. (1980), 'Being out of Work', in Littler, C. (ed), *The Experience of Work*, Oxford University Press, pp. 190-206.

Taylor, G. (1994), 'Rigidity and Flexibility in Macro-Political Bargaining: Some Comments on the Recent Experience in Ireland', *Centre for Public Policy working papers*, University College Galway

Varley, T. and O'Donovan, O. (1995), 'Paid Employment in the Voluntary Sector: A Literature Review', *Centre for Public Policy working paper series*

Wood, S. (ed) (1 982), *The Degradation of Work: Skill, Deskilling and the Labour Process*, Hutchison

Administration, vol. 51, nos. 1-2 (Spring/Summer 2003), 326–340

Democracy and the Constitution*

SÉAMUS Ó CINNÉIDE

Originally published in 1998-99, vol. 46, no. 4, 41-58.
Séamus Ó Cinnéide is Jean Monnet Professor of European Social Policy in the National University of Ireland, Maynooth.

The most central principle in *Bunreacht na hÉireann* is that of democracy. Article 5 describes the state as being, among other things, a 'democratic state', and Article 6 introduces the classic formula of separation of powers. According to which, the system of government is taken to have different functions, which must be conducted by different branches or different bodies, thus providing checks and balances against the abuse of power. Article 6.1 states:

> All powers of government, legislative, executive and judicial, derive under God, from the people, whose right it is to designate the rulers of the State and, in final appeal, to decide all questions of national policy, according to the requirements of the common good.

The principle of democracy informs the whole constitution, not just the articles dealing with the machinery of government, but also the articles dealing with personal rights. In deciding on the personal rights that the state must defend (Article 40.3) the courts have often referred to the democratic nature of the state, and have linked democracy to the equality of citizens.

Despite the importance of democracy in principle, the idea is not much discussed in Ireland. It should be, for democracy has been under threat in recent years in a number of ways. The major political scandals, including those about beef exports, Hepatitis B and payments to

* This article is based on a paper given at the Patrick MacGill Summer School in Glenties, Co Donegal in August 1997. It was not possible to take account of the most recent developments before publication. The assistance of the editor of *Administration* is gratefully acknowledged.

politicians, show that there has been an over-concentration of power in some hands. The checks and balances which should have worked did not work. Abuses and malpractice, which compromised both politicians and officials, had continued over years, and had come to public attention only haphazardly or through the doggedness of individuals. To make matters worse, there is such a smothering consensualism in politics that many public issues are not properly discussed at the political level. Therefore, elected representatives cannot or do not represent the broad range of citizens' views. This has happened recently on major issues, such as divorce and the abolition of the right to bail, and in relation to European monetary union.

There are three main things wrong with the system. Firstly, the executive, that is the government and the civil service, has gradually become more and more powerful, while the Dáil and the Seanad have become less important. Secondly, political consensualism is made worse by the creeping corporatism of the last twenty years, which ties in major interest groupings – including voluntary bodies – with the government system. This shifts the real debate from Leinster House to closed committee rooms where there are no elected representatives. Thirdly, the bureaucracies have become more powerful and, notwithstanding information booklets and better telephone etiquette, have become less accountable and at the same time less independent of the politicians. We will discuss these three developments in turn.

THE WITHERED BRANCH OF GOVERNMENT

Over the years the state as a whole has acquired more power and functions, and that power has become more and more centralised. As a result a lot of people now feel more excluded from the political process and are cynical about the whole system. Divisions between the haves and the have-nots, between city and country, between believers and unbelievers, between those who are 'in' and those who are 'out', are probably widening. Political representation, the bedrock of democracy, is perceived as being biased, corrupt or irrelevant.

We have not tackled these fundamental problems in any systematic way. We may have tried to deal with some specific issues in referenda and tribunals and fora, but we have dealt with them in isolation. There is a general malaise, which has to do with democracy and the lack of it, and which has not been diagnosed, much less tackled. Not even by the Constitution Review Group.

In 1996 the Constitution Review Group published its very impressive report: 700 pages of working papers, analysis and prescription, by far the most comprehensive review of its kind ever (CRG, 1996). It was produced, incredibly, in twelve months, by fifteen distinguished lawyers, scholars and public servants – under the chairmanship of Dr T. K. Whitaker – with the assistance of expert technical staff. But look up 'democracy' in the index and you will find only one entry, under 'democratic deficit', and that refers to EU legislation. As if there was no democratic deficit in Ireland!

The review group's methodology was to deal with the articles of the constitution seriatim, but this meant that some of the biggest issues, which transcend the divisions between the articles, were not discussed at all. Dr Gerry Whyte of Trinity College, Dublin, has highlighted a remarkable and unfortunate consequence of this approach, his example is that of religion. The review group makes a number of separate recommendations about references in the constitution to religion, in particular Christianity, which cumulatively would have the effect of 'purging the Constitution of its religious flavour' and '[shifting] the philosophical template of our constitutional order from a religious base to an altogether more secular setting' (Whyte, 1996). The point is that, regardless of the merits of the specific recommendations in relation to specific articles, the overall issue of the place of religion in the constitution is not, as such, faced up to and debated at all, much less the effect of the recommendations in their totality. Similarly with democracy: there are many specific references (elections to the Dáil and Seanad and to the Presidency; referenda; local government), but no overall discussion of what is wrong and what should be done, indeed no acknowledgement at all that there is something seriously wrong.

If such a discussion had taken place, the key issue addressed would have been the role of the Dáil, with its democratically elected TDs, vis-à-vis the government, or to put it technically, the division of power between the legislature and the government. This has implications for the Seanad, but let us concentrate here on the directly-elected house to keep the argument simple.

Discussions about the separation of powers are nearly always about the relationship between the courts (the judicial branch) and the government (the executive branch), and about their respective functions; the Houses of the Oireachtas (the legislative branch) hardly ever come into the reckoning. The *Report of the Constitution Review Group* provides several examples of discussion of the separation of powers in this limited sense. For example, it devotes a lot of attention to the role of the courts in identifying and proclaiming new personal rights of the citizen. Before the Ryan case in 1965 (about the compulsory fluoridation of the water supply to prevent dental caries) it was taken for granted that the only personal rights of the citizen that the state had to respect, defend and vindicate were those specifically listed in the constitution (Article 40.3). In the Ryan case the right to 'bodily integrity' was recognised as a constitutional right, even though it is not referred to in the constitution (IR, 1965). From then on further rights have been identified by the higher courts, taking a progressive and constructionist approach to constitutional jurisprudence.

In all the review group lists eighteen rights discovered in this way, including the right to have access to the courts, the right to privacy and the right to travel. This shows that in important areas of policy the courts have been way ahead of the government and the Oireachtas, and a good thing too. But the review group does not like it. Why? Because the present position 'allows the courts too much latitude in the identification of personal rights, is *undemocratic*, infringes the principle of the separation of powers and leads to uncertainty' and because 'the identification of personal rights ... *should be made by the 'people themselves*' (CRG, 1996; emphasis added). So in making proposals about the power of the courts, the review group relied in part on a concern about the principle of 'democracy'.

One might expect that this concern would have led the review group to pay particular attention to the role and functions of the Dáil, the branch of government that is most directly representative of the people, vis-à-vis those of the government, the executive branch. In an articulate and well-argued submission to the review group, the Institute of Public Administration referred to the tension between the two branches and concluded that in Ireland '[w]e have, in practice, an executive dominated system, and that executive [the government and the civil service] dominates both central and local government' (Litton, McNamara and O'Connor, 1995). Indeed it could be said that in this case the notion of separation of powers is a fiction: the Dáil (even less the Seanad) can offer no effective checks and balances to the power of the government, being totally controlled by the government through the political parties, except in very rare circumstances. The review group contemplated this domination by the executive, and the relative impotence of the Dáil, with equanimity. Indeed the overall effect of the recommendations it makes in this area would be to increase the powers of government and diminish those of the Dáil.

This is dealt with in great detail by Alan Ward, an American professor of government, in a very well-informed article (Ward, 1996-97). This outside observer offers a trenchant critique of the review group's neglect of how the democratic machinery of government works, or does not work. The group, he says, 'makes no recommendations to improve the performance of the Dáil in legislation, estimates or scrutiny of the executive, the three core functions of any legislative body. Indeed the report finds, in the facts of modern life, new justifications for the dominant role of the government', while paying only lip service to the need for 'full democratic checks'. He contrasts this approach with the conclusions of royal commissions in New Zealand and Australia 'that the expansion of the executive state in a complex modern world makes it more necessary than ever before to create effective instruments of democratic accountability in parliamentary systems'. It is not as if we in Ireland have not had evidence of the failures in accountability; proof, if proof were needed, of the axiom that power corrupts. To deal with these failures we need to go beyond ad hoc enquiries and tribunals. We should have recourse to the constitutional structures and enhance the role of the Dáil to ensure that it really can provide a democratic check on a powerful government. Otherwise the Houses of the Oireachtas will become more and more the withered branch of government.

Ward highlights one 'very troubling recommendation' that for him demonstrates the review group's indifference to the Oireachtas. This relates to its endorsement of the corporatist institutions that can be seen as robbing the Oireachtas of power.

PARTNERSHIPS WITH EVERYTHING

If the Dáil and Seanad together are a withered branch of government, then the invasive creeper that has done them no good at all is of the genus corporatism, and is now commonly called 'partnership'.

At one time a partnership meant simply a legal or functional entity consisting of two or more parties bound by contract or agreement. Now, because of its 'feel-good appeal, the term is widely and imprecisely used in Ireland for a wide range of 'participation' and 'consultation' arrangements in public affairs. These arrangements are in fact a version of corporatism, the political system by which policy is made not by elected representatives meeting openly in parliament but by organised interests making agreements among themselves and/or with the government. These agreements, which bind the rest of us, are made around committee tables behind closed doors.

Given present day secular enthusiasms it is ironic that in the past corporatism has usually been identified with the Catholic social teaching of the 1930s, and sometimes with fascism (Lee, 1979b). Modern corporatism in Ireland dates from the early 1960s, but the promotion of the idea is most closely associated with the Commission on Vocational Organisation, chaired by Bishop Michael Browne of Galway, which published its report in 1943. The report was highly critical of the Irish bureaucracy, which may partly explain why it was unceremoniously rejected by the Fianna Fáil government.

Twenty years later, in the years of the First Programme for Economic Expansion, Seán Lemass saw the need for new structures, representative of business and the trade unions as well as the public service, to spearhead economic development. And so, with organisations like the Committee on Industrial Organisation and the

National Industrial Economic Council (the precursor of today's NESC), Ireland, as Joe Lee puts it, 'began to shuffle towards a version of the corporate state' (Lee, 1979a).

Subsequently, the government became involved in centralised wage negotiations, first simply as an employer, but later by linking commitments about taxation policy with the national wage agreements. The National Understanding for Economic and Social Development in 1979 was the first of a new kind of tripartite agreement between the government, the employers and the Irish Congress of Trade Unions (the farmers' organisations also had a role) in which industrial peace was bought by the promise of tax concessions and better social services. Similar national understandings and programmes have followed, up to and including the present programme: *Partnership 2000*.

How does partnership come into all this? By European usage the representatives of the two sides of industry – the employers and the workers – are designated 'social partners', hence the 'social partnership' involved in the national programmes. However, the term partnership is now also used for formal structures at a local level involving a variety of interests. For example, since 1992 'Area Development Partnerships' have been set up in areas of high unemployment to promote job-creation and training. These partnerships have involved the social partners (in the above sense), representatives of state agencies and representatives of what are referred to as voluntary and community organisations – but no elected local representatives.

The national understandings and national programmes agreed by the social partners and the government, in conjunction with the national wage agreements are generally thought to have been a good thing, and are credited by many with contributing to our present economic boom. Each of the three sides – government, trade unions and employers – had bargaining power and a formal mandate (which more recent 'partners', like voluntary bodies for instance, do not have) and all three had something to gain from the process. In addition, the trade unions went beyond representing their members and on each occasion, with the admirable commitment of their leaders, insisted on improvements in social welfare being part of the bargain, against the European trends. At the same time these agreements represented a major shift in power from elected representatives to full-time officials in the civil service and in the organisations of the major interests. They were signed, sealed and delivered as a *fait accompli* to the nominal legislators of the country. Professor Joe Lee, one of the few public commentators to address the issue, points out that even Lemass's new corporatism, which was only a paltry version of today's full-blown profusion, diminished the authority of the Dáil, because the essential planning decisions were taken elsewhere; but, he suggests, 'Lemass himself had little confidence in the capacity of the average Dáil member to contribute intelligently to economic decision-making' (Lee, 1979a). Dáil members today undoubtedly have a greater capacity to take responsibility for policy and legislation but being still deprived of power are probably more frustrated than their predecessors.

The major puzzle is this: corporatism, despite its challenge to representative democracy, seems to be expanding, in some cases with the collusion of elected representatives, and with the active support of spokespersons of the so-called 'voluntary and community sector', who are ostensibly committed to democratic principles. There are three areas in which this game plan is pursued: the National Economic and Social Forum (NESF), the system for arriving at national programmes, and the reform of local government.

The NESF produces half a dozen reports a year but it is not as well known as it should be. It has forty-five members, one-third of them members of the Dáil and Seanad, one-third from the social partners (employers' organisations, ICTU and the farmers' organisations), and 'the third strand' is an arbitrary collection of representatives of non-governmental organisations. It has no legislative basis, and some of its functions until now seemed to replicate those of the NESC. Uniquely, however, it incorporates 'representatives', of women, people with disabilities, Travellers and so on, into an ongoing discussion on issues of public policy. But why couldn't the Dáil itself do this, through committees and hearings, so that elected representatives retained the democratic initiative? Are voluntary organisations more influential working within a body like the NESF, or lobbying from outside? And after all the discussions and reports, how much are they taken into account? These are some of the important questions that have to be asked about this flagship of 'partnership'.

Flushed with their participation in the local area partnerships and the NESF, representatives of voluntary bodies sought to have greater power as national partners. Through the NESF they demanded a role in negotiating the next national agreement. After much toing and froing the 'voluntary and community sector', a sector that nobody is able to define, was given a role in the discussions/negotiations leading to *Partnership 2000*. This meant that in December 1996, in the lead up to *Partnership 2000*, a committee system of Byzantine complexity was operated in Dublin Castle: officials met four different groups separately in four rooms, each group presumably pushing its own agenda, with the officials mediating. Instead of challenging corporatism, the voluntary representatives had decided to opt into it and so help to strengthen it.

Local government is the latest area of corporatist innovation. Strategic policy committees are being set up, bringing in 'representatives' of 'the voluntary and community sector' to join elected representatives in planning local services. How this will affect the balance of power between central government and local government, and between local authority management and the elected representatives, remains to be seen. What is striking is how such important changes in the workings of local democracy could be introduced on a top-down basis and with so little discussion.

This extension of 'partnership' is misconceived in a number of ways. Firstly, many of its proponents base their case on an elitist criticism of the capabilities in policy-making of today's elected representatives, for whom they have little or no regard. There is an insidious circularity in this argument. The more parliament, and parliamentary committees, are circumvented in the policymaking process, the more ineffective they will be, and be seen to be. This means that the quality and challenge of the work that elected representatives are expected to do, and the rewards they get for it, will be further diminished and prospective candidates with good qualifications will be discouraged from running for election. Secondly, the fact that politicians have been tarred with the brush of corruption seems to cast others in a better light. But there is no evidence that representatives of national 'partners', including voluntary bodies, are any less personally ambitious, less authoritarian or less venal than politicians. Thirdly, councillors and TDs are implicitly accused of not representing all their constituents and, in a curious misuse of language, the partnership process is justified as being an example of 'participative democracy', in contra-distinction to the longer-established old-fashioned 'representative democracy'. It is, of course, neither participative (except for a small group of activists) nor democratic in any ordinary sense of that word. Representatives of voluntary bodies will admit that they have their own political (though non-party) agenda, which they pursue single-mindedly when they get the chance, and yet they are virtually accountable to no-one. More often than not 'the disadvantaged' are represented by full-time administrators, community workers and lobbyists. In some cases they are committed to 'consulting' and 'reporting back' to constituents, but given the general difficulties involved, the process is nugatory in my experience.

But the most fundamental criticism of the preoccupation with 'partnership' is that it is unconstitutional, or even subversive of the constitution. It is for this reason that the treatment by the Constitution Review Group of the articles of the constitution on the Oireachtas, in effect their treatment of the democratic control of the state, is profoundly inadequate. As Professor Alan Ward points out, 'what political parties do in Ireland, and particularly what they do in the Oireachtas as deputies and senators, is of less significance to public policy than the contributions of extra-parliamentary organisations with no democratic mandate' (Ward, 1996-97). The review group diagnosed a problem, 'the fact that so many new participatory structures have been established is itself an indication of the weaknesses of the existing systems of representation', but instead of recommending how these weaknesses could be dealt with, how the Oireachtas could be strengthened, it simply goes along with reinforcing existing trends. There are things that could be done: Ward points to interesting innovations in New Zealand and in Israel.

There is a view that Ireland's present prosperity is due, in part at least, to our success in developing consensual economic and social policies, by means of our extra-constitutional 'partnership' structures and processes. The NESC and the national agreements are undoubtedly valuable national institutions, but they should be linked back into the legislature. For there is a downside to creeping corporatism, which we would have to live with through good times and bad. Who knows what 'partners' will come to the fore when the Oireachtas has become a cypher? Political power at the national level is a zero-sum game: the more power the 'partners' have, the less TDs and senators have; the less power TDs and senators have, the more power there is in the hands of the government; and the fewer checks and balances will lead to results of which we have only become too aware through scandals and tribunals.

This is the malaise in Irish politics: over-concentration of power, distrust of elected representatives, lack of accountability. All the time discussion and decision-making are moving from public fora to meeting rooms behind the scenes. These are the most serious issues that we have to deal with as a democracy, not the PR system or whether we should continue to have a Seanad. They need to be on the agenda of the All-Party Oireachtas Committee on the Constitution, which is sitting at the moment.

In addition to the unelected partnership representatives, the other actors behind the scenes – who are being asked to take on more and more responsibility – are the public officials, the civil servants. Is it fair to them that we should expect so much of them? Is it fair to ourselves as citizens?

MASTERS OR SERVANTS?

On Friday 2 April 1982, Argentina invaded the Falkland Islands/Islas Malvinas, completely unexpectedly. The following Monday, Lord Carrington, the British Foreign Secretary, resigned from office. He was accepting responsibility for the fact that the British government had been caught unawares. Nobody would have expected that Lord Carrington himself should have been haunting the dockside bars of Buenos Aires, monitoring the movements of Argentinean naval vessels; but somewhere in the foreign service someone was at fault and the responsible government minister had to take the rap. This was in line with the doctrine of ministerial responsibility, and based on the legal principle of 'corporation sole'. Corporation sole means that a government minister and all the officials and employees of his or her department, together comprise one legal entity, one legal person: everything that an official does is in law done by the minister. As the landmark Devlin Report of 1969 put it: '...normally all the Department's acts are the acts of the Minister. He is responsible to Parliament for these acts and cannot devolve that responsibility on any member of his staff' (PSORG, 1969).

In other words, at that time, if an official failed or blundered the minister took responsibility. The advantage of that system was that someone was held responsible if things went wrong, and the notion that there were things for which no-one could be held responsible was untenable. And when things were not going wrong there was a clear and shared understanding of the role-relationships of civil servants and politicians.

In effect, within the executive branch of government there was a further division of functions, as between the administrative system and the political system: civil servants presented options and gave advice; politicians made choices and arrived at decisions. Good government depended on a certain distance and balance between the two sides. Civil servants ensured continuity of responsibility, objectivity and professionalism of analysis, bureaucratic fairness in the state's dealing with citizens and an adherence to the rules. Politicians made sure that public opinion was heard, that red tape was unravelled, that hard cases got special attention and that when risks had to be taken the people were brought along. Too much power with the bureaucrats could mean over-cautiousness, conservatism or rigidity on policy issues, or too much attention to detail to the detriment of policy planning. Too much power with the politicians could mean nepotism, the feathering of nests, or populist initiatives to buy votes reckless of the long-term common good.

The main point is that both sides had power; no-one would have gainsaid that the higher echelons of the civil service had power. The late John Healy referred to 'the permanent government' (as distinct from the transient ministers), and the television series *Yes Minister*! made an elaborate joke out of it.

Whatever the merits and demerits, whether in theory or in practice, of the old system, it no longer exists: both sides still have power, but otherwise the position has completely changed in regard to both ministers and civil servants. These changes represent an unspoken revolution in our system of governance, all involving greater power with the executive and less accountability. The role of ministers, as exposed in tribunal reports, has been well documented. What we have learned about the role of civil servants is important too. The problem is that we do not know what exactly has replaced the old system. This very uncertainty is yet another challenge to democratic values.

It appears that the doctrine of ministerial responsibility is no longer taken seriously at all. The issue was addressed most explicitly in November 1996, when, through oversight or negligence, a judge who had been removed from the Special Criminal Court panel was not informed, and so continued to serve as a member of the court, with the risk of mistrial in serious cases. The Minister for Justice at the time in defending herself and her department distinguished between 'accountability' and 'culpability'. Even though there was an investigation, it was impossible to find anyone to blame. There were to be no resignations. At the same time, in the Hepatitis B affair, the Minister for Health was denying all responsibility for The Blood Transfusion Service Board (BTSB), and in particular for its legal defence of the case taken by Mrs Bridget McCole for negligence.

There are other relevant examples. At the Beef Tribunal a former Minister for Agriculture, who as minister had given responsibility for the reboxing of beef by a Goodman company, defended himself as follows: 'It could well be at some point, some day, someone came to my office and said "Minister, would you sign that?" And it could well be that I did, but, subject to that, I don't have the facility for total recall of all events' (quoted in O'Toole, 1995). And a former Minister for Industry and Commerce explained to the Dáil that when he was introducing legislation to increase credit cover for Goodmans he was merely reading a speech prepared by his civil servants (O'Toole, 1995).

Not only is ministerial responsibility now at issue; the role of civil servants is not the same as it used to be either. Civil servants, individually and collectively within departments, still have power; indeed for a number of reasons they probably have more power now than ever. The business of government gets steadily more complex and ministers find it increasingly difficult to keep on top of important developments. It is mainly civil servants who represent the state in the plethora of partnership arrangements. On major issues, the civil servants are very often the ones with the experience, the expertise and the contacts: they commission research (or deem it unnecessary), they hire consultants from academia or business, they decide on contracts. Heads of departments now retire after seven years and in many cases can look forward to directorships and consultancies in the private sector. Two things have changed: the distance and balance between senior civil servants and ministers has been blurred; and, worse than that, in the welter of investigations about wrongdoing in government, the civil service itself has not come out unscathed.

The Beef Tribunal disclosed, among other things, the closeness of relations between the civil service and politicians. This also comes through in Sean Duignan's account of his period as Government Press Secretary (see Duignan, 1996). In the term of office of the next government, when the Minister for Justice came in for criticism over the Special Criminal Court appointment, the Association of Higher Civil Servants came to her defence, describing her as 'one of the most able, hard-working, and personable Ministers we have ever had the privilege to work with'.

There was a time when there was no such closeness. But nowadays civil servants and ministers are thrown together more, in marathon sessions in Brussels, and in flying to and fro; their backgrounds and new conventions of informality have abolished caste distinctions; and few go home for their dinner in the middle of the day. And yet the old notion of distinction and balance is still seen to be useful. When the second GSM mobile phone licence was awarded to Esat Digifone in November 1996 by the Minister for Transport, Energy and Communication there were rumours of political favouritism. These were so persistent that the following April the secretary of the department organised a press briefing in which he and five of his senior staff reassured the public that 'the Minister had no hand, act or part in the process ... (of awarding the licence) ... this is as squeaky clean a competition as you can imagine being run by any public sector in the European Union'. It was a good thing that such reassurances could carry weight, but they could only do so to the extent that the civil service could be seen to operate above reproach. That is why evidence against the civil service is so serious: if we could not trust the civil service, then who could we trust?

The evidence given in the Beef Tribunal showed some politicians in a very poor light, but it may have done more damage to the reputation of the civil service because more was expected of civil servants. A number of officials in the Department of Agriculture were shown to have gone too far in what might have been seen as protecting departmental interests. The extreme example was the matter of Emerald Beef Ltd and the licence to import GATT beef: the High Court (upheld by the Supreme Court) indicted the department of being in breach of EC regulations and being at fault in furnishing wrong information to the European Commission.* This is not the only case of administrative irregularity that has come to light. The Department of Health was found to have been at fault on a number of counts in their handling of the blood transfusion scandal (Tribunal, 1997). Apart from these specific episodes there is a more general unspoken and unanswered question in the air. When the financial affairs and business relations, over many years, of holders of political office are the cause

* *Emerald Meats Ltd v Minister for Agriculture, Ireland, Attorney General, Goldstar Meats Ltd and Rangeland Meats Ltd*: Supreme Court, 1991 Nos. 262/272, 1992 nos. 237/241, *Irish Law Reports Monthly*, 1997, vol. 2 pp. 275-296.

of concern, who should have known what was going on, and who could have blown the whistle?

There are important lessons to be drawn from all this. From the foundation of the state, the civil service was a force for stability. It could take credit for major national innovations, for example in economic planning and in educational reform, and for all its failings (for it was regularly accused of being out-of-date and inefficient) it could be trusted. We can still depend on officials of exceptional ability to analyse, negotiate on, and respond to, the most intricate and intractable problems of state. But in moving from the old system, described earlier, we may end up with the worst of both worlds: public officials with a great deal of power, which in many cases is not subject to effective democratic scrutiny, and yet not enough power to prevent abuses of power by others. And it is not at all clear what is done if, or when, things go wrong within their own ranks.

Where do we go from here? Is there a need, for instance, for a mechanism whereby officials who become aware of abuses can ensure that those responsible are challenged? The Ombudsman has suggested that there are difficult issues involved in this; but he has also raised the question of whether we need a formal code of practice to regulate movement from the senior public service to the private sector (Murphy, 1998). The fact that these issues are not much discussed in public is not to the credit of, or in the interest of, the public service.

Some observers will be comforted by the changes that are at present afoot in the civil service. In 1996 the Strategic Management Initiative (SMI) was launched, and 1997 saw the coming into force of the Public Service Management Act. In both cases the emphasis is on improving effectiveness and efficiency in the civil service. The new legislation provides a basis in law for practices that were already in operation, but introduces some new rules too. Henceforth, for example, the heads of government departments will have to produce 'strategy statements' and may be called on to discuss them with committees of the Oireachtas; and they will be able to hire and fire staff below the rank of principal officer. Some of the innovations were first mooted thirty years ago. But, they say, the principles of ministerial responsibility and corporation sole are not affected. The Freedom of Information Act, 1997, which came into operation on 21 April 1998, promises to be more radical still: subject to certain restrictions, to be monitored by the Ombudsman, acting as Information Commissioner, citizens will have a right to official information based on a presumption of openness and transparency.

The implications of all this remain to be seen, but it is worth reiterating that from the point of view of democratic principles the main challenges to public service reform are not efficiency and effectiveness (which only raise the question of who is to decide on the criteria for measuring efficiency and effectiveness) but accountability and probity. The Ombudsman has said that 'there is a need for more research and enquiry into how the two great institutions of state, the Oireachtas and the courts, can be made more effective in ensuring the greater accountability to citizens of government and public administration', in other words the executive branch of government (Murphy, 1998). Recently a senior civil servant acknowledged that 'adequate and effective arrangements for governance and accountability within the civil service and between the civil service, the political level and citizens generally are fundamental elements of a democratic system of government' (Tutty, 1997). If these elements are to be guaranteed then all the problems have to be confronted, not just the management ones, but the constitutional-political ones too.

REFERENCES

[CRG] Constitution Review Group (1996), *Report of the Constitution Review Group,* Dublin: The Stationery Office.

Duignan, S. (1996), *One Spin on the Merry-go-Round*, Dublin: Blackwater Press.

Gwynn Morgan, D. (1996), 'Hard to Replace Ministerial Responsibility', *Irish Times*, 15 November.

Lalor, S. (1982), 'Corporatism in Ireland', *Administration*, vol. 30, no. 4, Dublin: Institute of Public Administration.

Lee, J. J. (1979a), *Ireland 1945-70*, Dublin: Gill and Macmillan.

Lee, J. J. (1979b), 'Aspects of Corporatist Thought in Ireland: The Commission on Vocational Organisation, 1939-43', in A. Cosgrove and D. McCartney (eds.), *Studies in Irish History*, presented to R. Dudley Edwards, Dublin: University College Dublin.

Litton, F., McNamara, T. and O'Connor, T. (1996), 'A New Constitutional Balance?', *Administration*, vol. 44, no. 1, Dublin: Institute of Public Administration.

Murphy, K. (1998), 'Accountability to the Citizen', in R. Boyle and T. McNamara (eds.), *Governance and Accountability: Power and Responsibility in the Public Service*, Dublin: Institute of Public Administration.

O'Toole, F. (1995), *Meanwhile Back at the Ranch*, London: Vintage.

[PSORG] Public Services Organisation Review Group (1969), *Report*, Dublin: The Stationery Office.

[Tribunal] (1997), *Report of the Tribunal of Inquiry into the Blood Transfusion Service*, Dublin: The Stationery Office.

Tutty, M. (1998), 'Implications of New Organisational Structures', in R. Boyle and T. McNamara (eds.), *Governance and Accountability:*

Power and Responsibility in the Public Service, Dublin: Institute of Public Administration.

Ward, A. (1996/97), 'The Constitution Review Group and the Executive State', *Administration*, vol. 44, no. 4, Dublin: Institute of Public Administration.

Whyte, G. (1996), 'Discerning the Philosophical Premises of the Report of the Constitution Review Group: an Analysis of the Recommendations on Fundamental Rights', a paper to a seminar at Trinity College, Dublin, 25 September.

Name Index